TO YOUR
GOOD
HEALTH

CONSULTANTS

Harriett B. Randall, M.D., Former Director of Health Services, Los Angeles Unified School District

Ruth Rich, Ed.D., Instructional Specialist, Health Education, Los Angeles Unified School District

Milton Lesser, Former Chairman, Department of Biological Sciences, Abraham Lincoln High School, New York City

GENERAL EDITOR

Saul L. Geffner, Former Chairman, Department of Physical Sciences, Forest Hills High School, New York City

AUTHORS

Charlotte A. Resnick, R.N., M.S., Teacher of Health Science, Pasteur Junior High School, Los Angeles Unified School District

Gloria R. Resnick, R.N., M.S., Teacher of Health Science, Audubon Junior High School, Los Angeles Unified School District

TO YOUR GOOD HEALTH

Charlotte A. Resnick
and
Gloria R. Resnick

When ordering this book, please specify
either **R 211 P** *or* TO YOUR GOOD HEALTH

Dedicated to serving

AMSCO

our nation's youth

AMSCO SCHOOL PUBLICATIONS, INC.
315 Hudson Street   New York, N.Y. 10013

ISBN 0-87720-163-3

To the Student

To Your Good Health addresses you on a subject of utmost importance: how to promote and maintain your physical, emotional, and social well-being. More than that, it examines your lifetime role in contributing to a more healthful environment for everybody.

The text supplies ample material to stimulate your interests and challenge your abilities as you pursue a course of health investigations. The health science information contained in *To Your Good Health* is both up to date and comprehensive. Major topics that you will investigate include the following:

- Health problems and practices, past and present
- Your body's parts and systems, how they work, and why they sometimes don't work well
- Proper nutrition and activity for your lasting personal health
- Accident prevention and first aid
- Problems and satisfactions of growing up
- Smoking, drinking, and drug use—matters for serious decisions
- Diseases and the continuing fight against them
- Kinds of pollution and what can be done about them
- Careers in health

As you proceed through the 27 chapters of *To Your Good Health*, your learning will be enriched by the following features:

1. *Liberal use of headings* makes your step-by-step learning easy. This is especially important if you are encountering for the first time some of the complex concepts of health science. The text headings will also serve you as ready tools for review.

2. *"Your Parts"* abound throughout the text. They are ready-made opportunities for you—both alone and as a team member—to conduct experiments and investigate health issues. Some "Your Parts" are activities you will perform under teacher supervision; others are on-your-own assignments within the classroom; still others are independent studies for you to pursue at home or in the community. All are aimed at developing your abilities for sound thinking and informed decision making.

3. *Looking Back* and *Looking Ahead* are chapter-by-chapter summaries and previews. They highlight the key points just covered and prime you for new work ahead. In addition, your learning pace within the longer chapters is regulated by *Let's Pause for Review* sections.
4. *End-of-chapter questions* provide a thorough test of your recall and comprehension of subject matter. The question groups are of five types: Modified True-False, Matching, Completion, Multiple Choice, and Thought.

For the most part, you will find the language of *To Your Good Health* straightforward and easy to read. But you will also be introduced to the less familiar vocabulary of health science. To help you identify and master these important technical words, they are printed at first occurrence in boldface type and clearly defined for you. Pronunciation guides are also given, whenever necessary. In addition, all such terms are brought together in an extensive alphabetical glossary at the back of the book.

The authors wish to express their grateful appreciation and special thanks to A. C. Brocki and Berti Brocki for their contributions in the preparation of the manuscript. The authors also warmly thank their family, friends, and colleagues for encouragement and support during the entire preparation of this textbook.

Acknowledgments

Grateful acknowledgment is made to the following sources for permission to use copyrighted and other materials, which appear in this book on the pages indicated in italics:

American Heart Association: *310*, questions adapted from the American Heart Association *Cigarette Quiz*, © 1967, reprinted with permission; *417*, graph adapted from The Framingham, Mass. Heart Study, © American Heart Association, reprinted with permission.

American Medical Association: *466*, excerpt from AMA Directory, reprinted with permission.

Connecticut State Board of Education: *245–246*, 37 student questions adapted from *Teach Us What We Want to Know*, reprinted with permission.

Consumers Union: *459*, "False Claims Laid to Natural Salt Marketer," *Consumer Reports*, February, 1974, page 162, reprinted with permission.

Prentice-Hall: *183*, brain wave tracings adapted from *Night Life*, by Rosalind D. Cartwright, page 12, copyright © 1977 by Prentice-Hall, Inc., Englewood Cliffs, New Jersey, reprinted with permission.

Public Affairs Committee: *146*, graph adapted from Public Affairs Pamphlet No. 251B, *Water Fluoridation: Facts, Not Myths*, copyright © 1957, reprinted with permission.

Random House: *3*, excerpt from *Mad Ducks and Bears*, by George Plimpton, copyright © 1973 by George Plimpton, reprinted with permission.

The photographs in this book were supplied through the courtesy of:

Alcoa: *441* (both). American Cancer Society: *322*. Copyright by the American Dental Association, reprinted with permission: *138, 143* (both), *144, 147, 149*. American Heart Association: *414*. American Optical Corp.: *95*. Lester V. Bergman & Associates: *398*. Black Star: J. Bruce Baumann, *15* (left); Bob Fitch, *27*; John Launois, *445*; Ivan Massar, *72*; Franklynn Peterson, *438*. Brown Brothers: *11, 185* (both), *272–273, 310* (both), *311* (left, top right). Carolina Biological Supply: *376* (both). University of Cincinnati: *15* (right). Culver Pictures: *311* (bottom right), *463*.

Fitzpatrick, Reeder, Mastroianni, *Maternity Nursing*, 12th edition (Philadelphia: Lippincott, 1971): *407*. P. M. Hahn, Laboratory of Environmental Neurobiology, UCLA: *182.* Grant Heilman Photography: Runk/Schoenberger, *355.* International News: *81* (right). Kemper Insurance Companies: *340.* Jonathan Lang: cover. Los Angeles County, Community Health Services: *405, 406* (both). Los Angeles County Sanitation Districts: *442.* Los Angeles County Sheriff's Office: *125* (all). Magnum Photos: Shalmon Bernstein, *364;* Serge Bramly, *349;* Leonard Freed, *471;* Roger Malloch, *478* (left); Wayne Miller, *358.* City of Milwaukee Health Department: *479* (right). Monkmeyer Press Photo: *262* (top left and right); Mimi Forsyth, *6, 315* (right), *467;* Mahon, *314–315;* Hugh Rogers, *2* (right), *477;* George Zimbel, *5* (right), *261.*

National Institute of Mental Health: *362.* National Institutes of Health, Bethesda, Maryland: *483.* National League for Nursing Inc., 10 Columbus Circle, New York, NY 10019: *474.* National Library of Medicine, Bethesda, Maryland 20014: *19* (left), *351, 363, 378* (both). New York Public Library: *377* (left). The New York Times Company: *264* (both). New York University College of Dentistry: Orthodontic treatment by student in the Department of Orthodontics, *150* (both). New York University Medical Center: *403* (both). Parke, Davis & Company: *380.* Pfizer Inc.: *384.* Scholl, Inc.: *129.* Stock, Boston: Jeff Albertson, *105;* Frank Siteman, *439;* Harry Wilks, *476.* The Stockmarket, L.A.: Greg Brull, *3;* David Cherkis, *475;* Jean-Claude Le Jeune, *377* (right), *381, 450;* Marshall Licht, *28, 109, 122, 123* (left), *126, 319, 338, 482;* Karen Simmons, *418* (both).

Taurus Photos: Beth Irwin, *388;* L. L. T. Rhodes, *473.* Taylor Instrument, Health Care Products, Sybron Corp.: *391.* Todd Shipyards Corp.: *332.* Total Environmental Action, Inc., Harrisville, New Hampshire: *446.* United Press International: *81* (left), *461.* U.S. Bureau of Reclamation: *449.* U.S. Department of Agriculture: *131, 166* (both), *167* (both), *375* (right). U.S. Department of Housing and Urban Development: *23* (both). U.S. Fish and Wildlife Service: *448.* U.S. Food and Drug Administration: *464.*

Visiting Nurse Service of New York: *479* (left). © Carroll H. Weiss, RBP, 1973: *123* (right). © Carroll H. Weiss, RBP, 1977: *422.* Welch Allyn, Inc.: *390.* Wide World Photos: *460.* Doug Wilson: *2* (left), *189, 314.* WNBC TV 4: *221.* World Health Organization: *9, 19* (right), *421, 478* (right), *484, 485.* Copyright © Donald Yeager, 1973: *258.*

Contents

Unit One: YOU AND YOUR HEALTH

Health is not valued till sickness comes.

No one knows who first put this idea into words or exactly when it was written down. It first appeared in a collection of proverbs almost 250 years ago. No doubt it was true of people then, and it is true of many of us now. That's too bad, because each of us can do much to achieve good health and to maintain it for a lifetime at the highest possible level. This book is designed to help you improve and maintain your health so that you will be able to do your best in the years ahead—at work, at play, as a family member, and as a member of society.

What do you need to maintain good health? You need some knowledge of scientific findings in the field of health. You need good habits of daily health care. And you need attitudes (states of mind) that promote health. For example, if you have a positive (accepting, approving) attitude toward yourself and your body, you are likely to give this amazing machine the care it deserves.

When you have good health, you are both physically and emotionally well. As you probably know already, your feelings and beliefs affect your physical well-being just as your physical well-being affects the way you think and feel. The two chapters of Unit One explore these and other views of health.

Unit One also introduces you to the work of some of the scientists in the fields of health. These scientists constantly add to our knowledge of the mind, the body, and the emotions. Almost daily, new discoveries are made about the way the changing environment affects our health. Knowledge of such discoveries can help you to form the habits and attitudes you need to stay healthy.

1

Chapter 1: What Is Health?

John Gordy, one-time offensive guard for the Detroit Lions, gives us some idea of how a professional football player looks at health:

> . . . And in the off-season many of us should be in the training room lifting weights. That sounds like a dumb thing for a man to be doing on a winter morning, but I'm worried about . . . my shoulder problem, and the *tendinitis* in my arm, and the operation on my knee, and the twisted Achilles tendon—all that *junk*. I have to do it. If I can build up a certain muscle tone . . . by lifting weights . . . I'm likely to have a better year as a result.

Health means different things to different people. To John Gordy health might mean freedom from injury. To others health might mean freedom from illness. To you it might also mean fitness, vitality, strength (see Figure 1.1).

Figure 1.1. Whatever your age and condition, maintaining health at its highest possible level is a desirable goal.

1. In a sentence or two, write out your own definition of health.
2. Compare your definition with those of other students.
3. As a class or in small groups, combine the various definitions into one complete definition.

Now compare your definition with one from a dictionary: **"Health:** physical and mental well-being; freedom from disease, pain, or defect; normality of physical and mental functions; soundness."

In 1948, the United Nations set up the first World Health Assembly, where delegates from 54 nations agreed on a broader definition of health, which may be more like yours: "Health is a state of complete physical, mental, and social well-being and not merely the absence of disease or infirmity." This definition of health is widely used today.

Health Is Dynamic

The term *dynamic*, as used here, means "constantly changing." As you know, the way you feel changes from hour to hour and from day to day. Imagine that you can weigh your health on a scale like the one in Figure 1.2. One end of the scale represents perfect health, the other end zero health, or death. Throughout your life, your health rating moves back and forth on this scale, never touching either end. Perfect health remains something no one can achieve; yet you, as well as everybody else, keep striving for it.

What Affects Your Health?

Many factors affect, or influence, your health. Health scientists divide the influences into four categories: heredity, environment, behavior, and scientific knowledge.

HEREDITY   **Genetics** (juh-NET-iks), one of the most active research fields in health today, is the study of hereditary traits and how they are passed from parents to children. The traits you are born with are major factors in determining your health. Some genetics scientists have even suggested that all diseases are influenced to some degree by heredity.

At one extreme are diseases that are always inherited. Two examples are *Tay-Sachs* (TAY SACKS) *disease*, which affects the eyesight and brains of infants, and *sickle-cell anemia*, a blood disease. At the other extreme are illnesses like *influenza*, or flu, and the common cold, which are hardly affected by heredity at all. But even so, you probably know some families

Figure 1.2. On the scale
of health, health is
dynamic (always
changing).

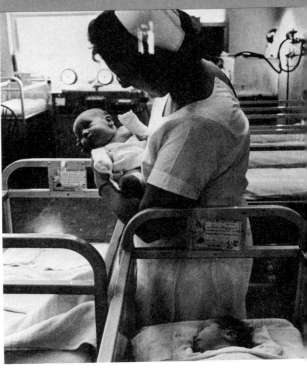

Figure 1.3. A baby's feelings affect the
baby's health.

who catch everything that's going around and others who never get sick.

In the middle are diseases like *diabetes* (dy-uh-BEE-teez), which interferes with the body's use of sugar, and some kinds of heart disease. The tendency to develop these diseases may be inherited. If a close relative has one of these diseases, your doctor may suggest that you take certain precautions—follow a special diet, keep your weight down, and have regular tests for the presence of the disease. By taking the first two precautions, you stand a good chance of avoiding the disease. And should a test show the disease in an early stage, prompt treatment may keep the disease from becoming disabling.

ENVIRONMENT   **Environment** means "surroundings," both physical and social. Everything from polluted air, which is part of your physical environment, to trouble with friends, which is part of your social environment, can affect your health. An affectionate family helps encourage you to take good care of your health. In fact, affection early in life is so vital to health that nurses nowadays cuddle the babies in their care (see Figure 1.3).

What Is Health?   5

BEHAVIOR   Your behavior, the things you do or fail to do, affects your health. For example, if you eat, rest, and exercise wisely, you should have the energy you need for school and recreation. On the other hand, if you eat the wrong foods, keep late hours, and fail to keep in good physical shape, you'll probably feel lazy, short-tempered, and unable to cope with a full day's activity. Your behavior, which is influenced by the way you feel and think, affects your physical health, just as your physical health affects your behavior.

SCIENTIFIC KNOWLEDGE   Before much was known about science, people believed that sickness was caused by supernatural forces such as gods, demons, and witches casting magic spells. Such *superstitions* held back investigation into the real causes of disease. Today, however, science has helped us learn both the causes and cures of many diseases. And we are convinced that health scientists will find the causes and cures of others.

The Health Scientist

The health scientist is a professionally trained person who works in a field related to health. He or she may be a physician in a hospital, a dentist in a clinic, or a staff member in a laboratory. Like the scientist in Figure 1.4, he or she may be a medical technician whose work helps a physician treat patients. Many physicians and dentists seek additional training so that they may practice a specialty. Thus, a physician may become a **cardiologist** (kahr-dee-AHL-oh-jist), a medical specialist who treats diseases of the heart. Or a dentist may choose to become an **orthodontist** (awr-thuh-DAHN-tist), a dental specialist who treats poorly positioned teeth, usually in young people.

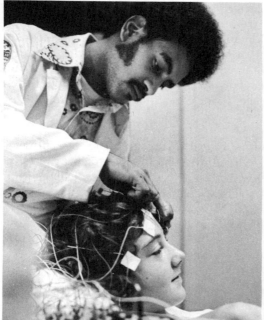

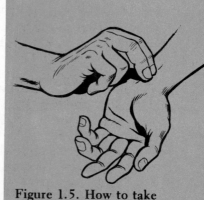

Figure 1.4. A medical technician helps to treat a patient.

Figure 1.5. How to take your own pulse.

Considerable progress has been made in the detection, treatment, and prevention of diseases. Much of this improvement is the result of experimentation, or research, carried on by highly trained health specialists who form a research team. Members of such a team may include:

- **Biologists,** who study the activities of living things.
- **Chemists,** who study nonliving matter and the changes that affect it.
- **Nutritionists** (nyoo-TRISH-un-ists), who study the kinds and amounts of food in a balanced diet.
- **Statisticians** (stat-uh-STISH-unz), who collect, assort, and report important numerical health information of various kinds.
- **Computer programmers,** who plan operating instructions for electronic machines that store and report health information.

THE SCIENTIFIC METHOD Health scientists work on many different projects, but, like other scientists, they all follow the scientific method of planned investigation:

1. They set up experiments to test specific theories.
2. They observe results carefully and record them accurately.
3. They compare their findings with those of other scientists.

If other scientists get different results, the theory is not proved, and more work needs to be done. In doing the following experiment, you will have a chance to observe and record results as health scientists do and to arrive at your own conclusions. Note that we have limited this experiment to the study of one particular problem. However, other problems can also be investigated in the same way.

YOUR PART

PROBLEM
How does activity affect the pulse rate?

STRATEGY
Your pulse rate is the speed at which your heart beats, pumping blood through the **arteries,** or blood vessels leading from the heart. The throbbing you can feel in an artery is caused by the blood pushing against the flexible wall of the artery. This rhythmic throbbing is in time with your heartbeat. The pulse can be felt at any point where an artery can be pressed against a bone. In this experiment, you will use the artery on the inner side of your wrist at the base of your thumb. Figure 1.5 shows how to hold the wrist when taking a pulse.

MATERIALS
- Clock or watch with sweep hand to measure seconds.
- Recording sheet like the one that follows:

One-Minute Pulse Rate Recording Sheet

	(1) You	(2) Classmate of Opposite Sex (Optional)	(3) Adult (Teacher)
Sitting quietly (normal)			
After exercise			
After 2-minute rest			
After 4-minute rest			
After 6-minute rest			

PROCEDURE

1. On a separate piece of paper, make a pulse rate recording sheet like the one shown. _Do not write in this book._
2. Find your pulse on the inside of your wrist near the base of the thumb (see Figure 1.5). Use the index and middle fingers of the opposite hand and press gently. _Do not use your thumb,_ because the thumb has its own pulse, which may be confused with the pulse in the wrist.
3. After finding your pulse, use the clock or watch and practice counting the beat for exactly 1 minute.
4. When you know how to take your pulse, count your pulse beat for 1 minute while sitting quietly. Record the result in column 1 on your chart.
5. Run in place or do sit-ups for 2 minutes. Then sit down and count your pulse rate again for 1 minute. Record this result in column 1. How much does it differ from the first count?
6. Rest for 2 minutes, and once again count your pulse. Record the result in column 1. How does this count compare to the rate before exercise? How does it compare to the rate immediately after exercise?
7. Continue counting and recording your pulse rate at 2-minute intervals twice more. What happens to the pulse rate?
8. Exchange your pulse rate figures with those of a classmate of the opposite sex, if possible, and enter your classmate's figures in column 2 of your recording sheet.
9. Enter your teacher's (or another adult's) figures in column 3 of your recording sheet.

QUESTIONS AND CONCLUSIONS

1. Why is it important to press gently against an artery when counting the pulse?
2. Why should you avoid using your thumb to take a pulse?

You and Your Health

3. What accounts for the difference in the pulse rate before and after exercising?
4. How long did it take for your pulse rate to return to normal?
5. Compare your results with those of a member of the opposite sex. Are there differences? If there are differences, what may account for them? What sex-related differences in pulse rate did others in your class find?
6. Compare your results with those of your teacher or another adult. Are there differences? If there are differences, what may account for them?
7. What conclusions can you draw from this experiment?

No doubt you concluded that pulse rate varies from person to person, and that the variations are related to activity, age, and sex. Suppose you took your pulse only after exercise. How might this pulse rate differ from your pulse rate at rest?

To give meaning to the results of an experiment, scientists compare the results with a standard. The standard of comparison is called a **control**. In the experiment you just did, you compared the pulse rate during exercise with the pulse rate during rest, which was your control.

THE CONTROL GROUP IN HEALTH EXPERIMENTS   In experiments like the one you have just done, health scientists usually make sure that their findings are reliable by comparing findings from the experimental group with those from a control group. The groups are closely matched, but the experiment is tried on the experimental group only.

Anthrax Experiment   In 1877, Louis Pasteur, a French chemist (see Figure 1.6), used a control group to test his idea that the *anthrax* organism was responsible for a disease that killed many sheep in France. Pasteur selected 100 healthy sheep of similar breeding and environment

Figure 1.6. Louis Pasteur, preparer of a vaccine against anthrax.

9

and divided them into two groups. He injected the 50 sheep in the experimental group with anthrax organisms. To the 50 sheep in the control group, he did nothing. Soon all 50 sheep in the experimental group were either sick or dead. The sheep in the control group remained in good health.

Since the only difference in treatment between the two groups was the injection of anthrax, Pasteur had proved that these organisms were the cause of illness and death in the experimental group. Later research made it possible to *immunize* (IM-yuh-nyz), or protect, sheep against anthrax, so that today this disease is rare.

YOUR PART

1. As a class or in small groups, decide how you would match two groups of students for an experiment on the effect of exercise on weight reduction.
2. List the characteristics you decide are important for closely matching the two groups for this experiment.
3. Can you divide your class into two groups suitable for this purpose?

Even without deciding what kind of exercise should be used and how much of it would be necessary in the experiment, you probably realized that your class isn't large enough to provide two well-matched groups. The important point is that you have followed some of the steps a scientist takes in setting up control and experimental groups.

Two Kinds of Science

The four main branches of science are *mathematics, biological* (life) *science, behavioral* (social) *science,* and *physical science* (physics, chemistry, and geology). All of these fields can be divided into two categories: basic, or pure, science and applied science.

Basic science provides fundamental information. For example, biology provides facts and principles about living things; physics, chemistry, and geology relate to nonliving things and deal with matter and energy.

Applied science puts that knowledge to work. For example, in 1928, Dr. Alexander Fleming, a British biologist (see Figure 1.7), discovered *penicillin* (pen-uh-SIL-in) while doing basic scientific research. Later, in 1940, Dr. Howard Florey, a British pathologist, and Dr. Ernst Chain, a British biochemist, prepared enough penicillin in pure form to treat infections in animals and in humans. Thus, Dr. Florey and Dr. Chain applied in a practical situation the basic information provided by Dr. Fleming.

Figure 1.7. Alexander Fleming, discoverer of penicillin.

Health science is an applied science. The practice of medicine is an applied science, too. Doctors and other health scientists apply knowledge from all the basic sciences to accomplish their goal of helping promote, develop, and maintain the best possible health for everybody.

Looking Back

Health means not only the absence of disease, but also a sense of physical, mental, and social well-being. Health is affected by heredity, environment, and behavior. Health scientists and specialists working in many fields use the scientific method of planned investigation. They promote health and solve health problems by applying the information provided by others who do research in the pure sciences.

MODIFIED TRUE-FALSE QUESTIONS

If the statement is correct, write the word *true*. If the statement is incorrect, substitute a word or phrase for the italicized term to make the statement true. (**Note:** When you are answering the questions in this book, do your work on a separate sheet of paper. *Do not write in the book.*)

1. Superstitious beliefs _helped_ the investigation of the causes of diseases.
2. Positive attitudes contribute to _good_ health.
3. Your health always _remains the same_ at a given age.

4. Heredity is responsible for _all_ diseases.
5. A disease involving the body's use of sugar is _sickle-cell anemia_.
6. Scientific discoveries _decrease_ the chances of good health.
7. A scientist who specializes in diseases of the _throat_ is a cardiologist.
8. The scientific method involves _planned_ investigation.
9. Your pulse rate _increases_ with exercise.
10. Health science is _a basic_ science.

MATCHING QUESTIONS

Match the items in column A with those in column B. One item in column B will be left over.

Column A		_Column B_
1. tendinitis	_a._	a sheep disease
2. genetics	_b._	a blood disease
3. diabetes	_c._	a common disease of athletes
4. orthodontist	_d._	the study of heredity
5. anthrax	_e._	a disease that interferes with the body's use of sugar
	_f._	a dental specialist

COMPLETION QUESTIONS

Write the word or expression that correctly completes each statement.

1. When you have good health, you are physically and _____ well.
2. A blood disease that is always inherited is _____.
3. When you measure your pulse rate, you are really measuring your _____.
4. An experimental group and a (an) _____ group are needed for a scientific investigation.
5. Unlike biology, the sciences of physics and chemistry deal with_____ matter.

MULTIPLE-CHOICE QUESTIONS

Write the letter preceding the word or expression that best completes the statement.

1. Health is
   a. dynamic and changes from day to day
   b. the result of many things
   c. more than the absence of disease
   d. all of these

You and Your Health

2. Your health is influenced by
a. heredity   b. environment   c. behavior   d. all of these
3. A scientist who deals with the body's food requirements is the
a. cardiologist   b. orthodontist   c. nutritionist   d. programmer
4. Of the following, which practice is *not* commonly followed by the health scientist?
a.   comparing results with those of other scientists
b.   publicizing a hunch
c.   relying on observation
d.   developing a planned experiment
5. Which of the following is a basic science?
a. medical practice   b. health   c. dentistry   d. biology

THOUGHT QUESTIONS

1. Discuss the statement "You don't appreciate health until you become sick."
2. Write a brief report on each of the following diseases, telling who might get the disease, what are some of its symptoms, and how it is treated: (a) Tay-Sachs; (b) sickle-cell anemia; (c) diabetes.
3. Take a typical day in your life and indicate the ways in which your environment influences your health.
4. Look up the definition of (a) psychology and (b) psychiatry. Tell whether each is a basic or an applied science. Explain the reasons for your choice.
5. The names of several pioneers in health follow. Choose one name from the list and complete a library report on that person:

Marie Curie   Joseph Lister
Alexander Fleming   Florence Nightingale
Edward Jenner   Elizabeth Kenny

6. Why must a control be part of a scientific experiment?
7. Certain people have to be more concerned about their health than others do. Write a short paragraph telling why you agree or disagree with this idea.
8. Why is health a world, rather than just a national or local, concern?
9. People are more concerned about the environment today than ever before. Why?
10. How does behavior affect your health?

Looking Ahead

Now that you know what health is, you are ready to study health practices of the past and present. Chapter 2 also explores some problems that are likely to need solving in the future.

Chapter 2: How Health Practices Are Changing

Canton Closes Places To Children

City Acts Quickly to Combat Infantile Paralysis

Special to *The Chicago Telegram-Sentinel*

CANTON, Ill., July 8, 1941 — City officials today closed all public gathering places and conveyances here to persons under 21 years of age in a quick step to combat a feared outbreak of infantile paralysis. All public parks and playgrounds have been shut, and the homes of eighty-six girls and boys who were swimming at Tyson Lake where the first case was reported have been quarantined until further notice.

Such news reports about the closing of public places were common in towns and cities across the country back in 1941. Since doctors couldn't halt *infantile paralysis* (IN-fun-tyl puh-RAL-uh-sis), or polio, they advised that young people avoid crowds. Swimming pools closed in the heat of summer. Dances were canceled. Young people had to stay away from movie houses.

The success of the Salk *vaccine* (vak-SEEN) in 1955 and the Sabin vaccine a little later changed all that, at least for infantile paralysis (see Figure 2.1). But other ancient threats to health remain unconquered, and

14

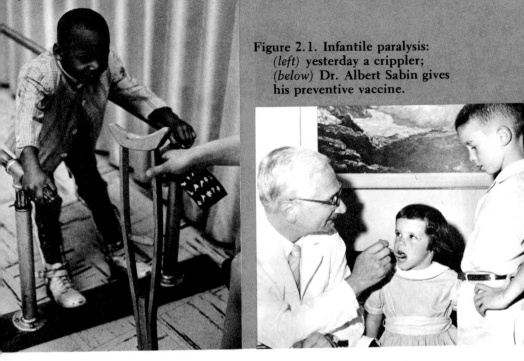

Figure 2.1. Infantile paralysis:
(left) yesterday a crippler;
(below) Dr. Albert Sabin gives
his preventive vaccine.

new ones, like pollution, have developed. We will discuss these threats in some of the following chapters, along with ways of dealing with them.

Health Problems in the Past

Motion pictures and television sometimes have a way of making the past seem colorful, safe, and inviting. In one sense, there's nothing wrong with that. People enjoy sharing the lives of others on a motion picture or television screen. But we should not let entertainment confuse our picture of the past. In terms of health, the past has frequently been unsafe and unhealthful.

TWENTIETH-CENTURY EPIDEMICS   An **epidemic** is an outbreak of disease that affects many members of a community at the same time. In its section "Disasters/Catastrophes," the *New York Times Almanac* lists, among other disasters, a number of serious epidemics occurring between 1906 and 1948 (see Table 2.1, page 16).

The word **pandemic** means a disease that is spread over a wide area and kills an unusually large number of people. As you can see in Table 2.1, the influenza pandemic at the end of World War I (1917–1919) was world-wide. The question marks in column 4 of Table 2.1 show that it was not possible to determine accurately the number of people killed in many past epidemics. Even so, the overall picture is clear: conditions of life in the past have posed many serious threats to human safety and health.

Table 2.1: Some Epidemics of the Past

Year	Place	Disease	Number of People Killed
1907	India	Bubonic plague	1.3 million
1909–1918	China, India	Bubonic plague	1.5 million (?)
1910	Manchuria	Pneumonic plague	60,000 (?)
1915 (Summer)	Serbia	Typhus	150,000 (?)
1917–1919	(Worldwide)	Influenza	20–30 million
1917–1921	Russia	Typhus	2.5–3 million
1920	India	Bubonic plague	2 million (?)
1921	India	Cholera	500,000 (?)
1924	India	Cholera	300,000 (?)
1926–1930	India	Smallpox	423,000 (?)
1935	Uganda	Bubonic plague	2,000 (?)
1947 (Sept.–Dec.)	Egypt	Cholera	10,000

LIVING IN 1900   It is, of course, hard for us to know how people in 1900 felt about their day-to-day lives. But we do know—from old books, letters, photographs, and even some silent motion pictures—that in outward ways they lived differently from us.

YOUR PART

1. Write down at least five things we have today that people didn't have in 1900.
2. As a class, or in small groups of six or seven, make a list of the different kinds of things written down in step 1. Then group them under major headings like *Transportation, Household Equipment,* and so forth.
3. Talk about how the things you listed may affect our health.

    If you had trouble imagining life in 1900, the rest of this section may give you ideas to add to your list and talk about.

In 1900, people traveled on horseback and horse-drawn vehicles, on bicycles, and on steam-driven trains and ships; or they just walked. The internal combustion engine was just starting to be used in automobiles. Lighting came mostly from kerosene and gas lamps. People still questioned the discoveries of Louis Pasteur and Joseph Lister, a British surgeon, that **microorganisms,** or germs, caused certain diseases.

The United States, still a young nation, welcomed the poor and homeless from other countries at the rate of almost a million a year. These immigrants became farmers, miners, factory and construction workers,

You and Your Health

teachers, doctors, and scientists. As a group, they helped to develop this nation's vast lands and other resources, which at the time were considered endless. More people at the turn of the century still lived on farms than in cities. In Table 2.2 you can see the steady movement of the population from rural areas to urban centers.

Table 2.2: Population Shifts in the United States, 1790–1970

Year	Rural	Urban
1790	3.7 million	.2 million (202,000)
1830	11.7 million	1.1 million
1900	45.8 million	30.2 million
1930	53.8 million	69.0 million
1960	53.7 million	124.7 million
1970	53.9 million	149.3 million

Adapted from *Statistical Abstract of the United States, 1975* (Bureau of the Census).

In 1900, around 30 million Americans lived in cities, but the cities were small and they were surrounded by farms, not suburbs. Those who lived on farms worked long hours to grow their own food as well as crops for sale. Workers in factories, mills, and mines put in 10-hour days or longer. Laborers worked on railroads, highways, bridges, and communication lines linking East, West, North, and South. And household chores were unending.

Heavy machines were used in factories, but at home people did most work by hand. They had no convenience foods or permanent-press fabrics. Few had ever tasted store-bought bread; bread was something one baked at home. People scrubbed dirty clothes by hand on washboards, hung them up to dry on clotheslines or bushes, and then pressed the wrinkles out with an iron heated on a wood- or coal-burning stove. They chopped wood for the stove by hand or carried coal in a bucket from the coal pile. As you can see, getting enough exercise was one health problem most of those people didn't have.

Only a few well-off people had indoor plumbing or hot water from faucets. This made good personal hygiene difficult. Without bathtubs and water heaters as we know them, taking a bath took time and effort. The following exercise will give you some idea of *how much time and effort:*

YOUR PART

Start timing as you imagine yourself performing the following steps:

1. Haul into the kitchen a metal tub large enough to sit in or stretch out in. (Some of the fancier ones were over 5 feet, or 1.5 meters, long.)

2. If the stove isn't going, build a fire. Heat enough water to fill the tub. How much water? For one bath, the average person today uses about 15 gallons (56 liters) of hot water.
3. Bask in the warmth as long as you can, because you're going to have to bail out and get rid of the dirty water when you're through. Carrying out a tub of water that size might bring about other health problems.

Figure 2.2. A bath in the year 1900.

End timing. From start to finish, about how long did your 1900 bath take?

Figure 2.2 shows how you might have looked. The time and effort are not shown.

The Leading Cause of Death in 1900   Bathing was merely one health problem. There were many others more important. People weren't as careful about public sanitation as they are today. They allowed garbage and other refuse, including human and animal wastes, to litter streets and alleys. Such conditions provided ideal breeding places for insects, rats, and other disease-spreading animals.

As a result, great epidemics of *communicable diseases*—diseases caused by germs and easily passed from one person to another—such as *smallpox*, *diphtheria* (dif-THIR-ee-uh), *influenza*, *bubonic plague* (PLAYG), and *typhoid* (TY-foyd) *fever*, swept through cities and towns, causing widespread sickness and death. Whole families became ill, and people died by the thousands, even millions (refer again to Table 2.1, page 16). The normal activities of entire cities came to a halt. In 1900, communicable diseases were the leading cause of death.

BEGINNING HEALTH PROGRAMS   Recognizing the need to decrease human suffering and early death in epidemics, federal, state, and local governments increased their programs to improve health conditions. New knowledge contributed by health scientists provided the foundation for community health programs.

18

Figure 2.3. Disease fighters: *(left)* Paul Ehrlich discovered
Salvarsan 606, a chemical to cure syphilis; *(right)* Emil von
Behring discovered a vaccine that immunizes against
diphtheria.

In 1857, Louis Pasteur developed the **pasteurization** (pas-chuh-ruh-
ZAY-shun) process, by which heat greatly reduces the number of bacteria
that cause wine to spoil. Today, we use pasteurization to reduce the
number of undesirable bacteria in milk. In 1908, Chicago passed the first
pasteurization law in this country. Joseph Lister introduced **antiseptic,** or
germ-free, surgery in 1865. In 1886, Ernst von Bergmann introduced the
use of steam for making instruments **sterile,** that is, germ-free. This soon
became a standard practice in hospitals.

Between 1890 and 1895, Paul Ehrlich and Emil von Behring (see
Figure 2.3), both German bacteriologists, did laboratory work to find
chemicals that would cure diseases. They also developed disease-
preventing vaccines. Injections (or shots) of vaccine are also called **immunizations** (im-yoo-nuh-ZAY-shunz). Each vaccine keeps the body safe
from, or immune to, a different disease. Von Behring's vaccines and those
of other scientists made possible the mass immunization programs of the
twentieth century.

Let's Pause for Review

In 1900, communicable diseases were the leading cause of
death. Poor public sanitation encouraged the spread of
epidemics. Health scientists like Pasteur, Lister, Ehrlich, von
Bergmann, and von Behring laid the foundation for modern
health programs.

Health Problems in the Future

Soon we will reach the turn of another century and begin the 21st century. No doubt our lives will change as much by that time as they have since 1900. Not all of the changes will be beneficial. According to one of today's experts from the U.S. Department of Agriculture, humanity's protein need is now 70 million tons a year and by the year 2000 will be about 140 million tons a year. Will agriculture as we have practiced it be able to supply that much food? Probably not, many experts say.

POPULATION GROWTH World population has been increasing at an alarming rate. In 1975, the population of the United States was over 212 million. Table 2.3 shows estimates of population growth for the United States alone from 1980 to the year 2000.

Table 2.3: Estimates of U.S. Population, 1980–2000

Year	Population
1980	236,797,000
1985	256,980,000
1990	277,286,000
2000	320,780,000

Adapted from Reader's Digest Almanac, 1976.

One population estimate for the year 2020 is 440,253,000—over twice the number of people in the United States today. The increase for the world as a whole may well be even more alarming. By the middle of 1976, world population was about 4 billion. At a growth rate of 2 percent a year, by the year 2006 world population could double to more than 7 billion.

YOUR PART

1. Write down five ways in which you think life will be different in the year 2000.
2. As a class or in small groups, find out how many different kinds of changes the class thought of, and group them under major headings like Institutions, Food, Leisure, and so forth.
3. Talk about how the things you listed may affect health.

If you had trouble thinking about changes in the future, consider the following questions. As the population grows larger, will people have enough food to eat, pure water to drink, and clean air to breathe? What

You and Your Health

will be the main source of fuel and energy in the year 2000? What about cities? Will we plan and build them in new and different ways? Where will we live? Scientific advances may open up regions uninhabitable today, such as deserts, ice caps, areas beneath the sea, and outer space. What health challenges lie ahead as a result of all these changes?

Focusing on Health Today

On the whole, Americans today are healthier, receive better medical care, and have more time for recreation than any previous generation. We will probably live longer, as well (see Figure 2.4). The dip in 1918 was caused in great part by the influenza pandemic cited in Table 2.1, page 16.

Yet many health problems still remain, both in the United States and in the rest of the world. In other parts of the world, communicable diseases have not come under complete control. In our own country, mass immunizations are still sometimes necessary, for example, when water supplies become impure as a result of floods or hurricanes. As another example, in 1976 the federal government began a mass immunization program throughout the United States against a feared outbreak of swine influenza—the same disease that caused millions of deaths during the pandemic of 1918.

Our advancing technology has brought both benefits and problems.

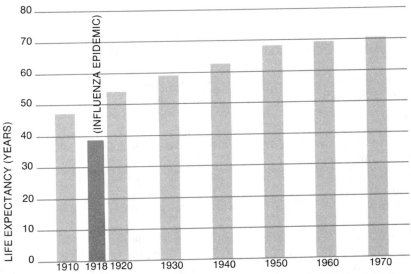

Figure 2.4. Estimated life expectancy at birth in the United States from 1910 to 1970.

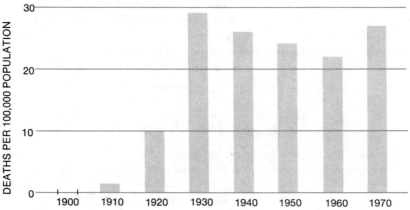

Figure 2.5. Death rate from motor vehicle accidents in the United States from 1900 to 1970.

Industrialization gave us almost unlimited possessions and food—and, at the same time, worldwide air and water pollution, land stripped of beauty, and the energy shortage. The airplane and automobile gave us almost unlimited freedom to travel—and smog, unbearable noise, and an increase in accidents (see Figure 2.5).

Laborsaving devices, such as washing machines, vacuum cleaners, and power lawn mowers, have given us more leisure time. But too many of us spend this extra time in inactivity, neglecting to get proper physical exercise.

A CLOSE LOOK   Let's take a close look at some of the major problems facing our country today. Health records show that heart disease, cancer, and accidents—in that order—are the leading causes of death today. Tooth decay, vision and hearing difficulties, and emotional illness are major health problems, too. There is also evidence that many people eat too little of the right foods and too much of the wrong foods.

The misuse of drugs endangers many lives. People who smoke run a higher risk than nonsmokers of developing diseases of the heart and lungs. Large numbers of people live or work in areas where noise, air, and water pollution may be serious threats to health. And two curable communicable diseases, *syphilis* (SIF-uh-lis) and *gonorrhea* (gahn-uh-REE-uh), are still not conquered.

Throughout your life, you will have to make decisions that affect your health and the health of members of your family and community (see Figure 2.6). Will you smoke or drink? Will you diet? As an adult, will you jog or golf or hike? As a consumer, will you buy throwaway cans and bottles or those that you can recycle? What size car will you buy, and how safely will you drive it? Will you use public transportation when you can and thus save energy?

You and Your Health

Of course, you must have the facts before you can answer such questions intelligently. Health education can give you some of the scientific facts, the basic knowledge that will enable you to prevent or solve many personal, family, and community health problems.

Looking Back

From a health point of view, this generation is better off than earlier generations. Both basic and applied sciences bring many changes for the better, but changes often bring new health problems, too. The study of health can give you much of the information you need to make intelligent decisions that can prevent or solve health problems for yourself, your family, your community, and the world.

Figure 2.6. A neighborhood scene, before and after. Will the decisions of your generation make your community a cleaner, healthier one to live in?

MODIFIED TRUE-FALSE QUESTIONS

1. Polio is a _communicable_ disease.
2. Most people in the United States today live in _rural_ areas.
3. Today, there are vaccines available to _cure_ influenza.
4. Advances in science and technology have _increased_ health problems related to communicable diseases.
5. There were _few_ opportunities for daily physical exercise in 1900.
6. One health problem that was prevalent in 1900 was _inadequate_ public sanitation.
7. Before milk is sold in supermarkets, it must be _homogenized_ to reduce the number of undesirable bacteria in it.
8. Between 1926 and 1930, hundreds of thousands of people in India died as a result of _smallpox_.
9. Allowing garbage to accumulate in streets and alleys provides conditions favorable for the breeding of _germ-spreading_ animals.
10. Widespread injections of _antiseptics_ can safeguard the human population from many epidemics.

MATCHING QUESTIONS

	Column A		Column B
1.	Lister	a.	polio vaccine
2.	Sabin	b.	antiseptic surgery
3.	noise	c.	surgical use of steam sterilization
4.	pandemic	d.	worldwide influenza epidemic
5.	von Bergmann	e.	milk processing
		f.	pollution

COMPLETION QUESTIONS

1. The Salk vaccine is used to prevent _____.
2. A disease that affects large numbers of people in a community is called a (an) _____.
3. A disease that spreads over a very large area and kills many people is said to be _____.
4. The disease that killed the largest number of people in the early 1900's was _____.
5. It is now an established fact that communicable diseases are caused by _____.
6. Communicable diseases are controlled today by _____ programs.
7. The world population will probably double by the year _____.
8. The leading cause of death today is _____.

9. Smokers run a higher risk than nonsmokers of developing diseases of the
   _____.

10. A serious environmental problem facing the entire world is _____.

MULTIPLE-CHOICE QUESTIONS

1. Before 1910, which of the following diseases was responsible for millions
   of deaths?
   a. bubonic plague   b. typhus   c. influenza   d. smallpox
2. It is estimated that by the year 2020 the population of the United States
   will
   a. decrease   b. stay the same   c. double   d. triple
3. From what you read in the daily paper, which communicable disease
   appears to remain a widespread problem?
   a. typhoid fever   b. syphilis   c. smallpox   d. diphtheria
4. By the year 2000, it is estimated that the world's need of protein will be
   a.   70 million tons   c.   280 million tons
   b.   140 million tons   d.   560 million tons
5. Figure 2.5, page 22, indicates that the death rate from motor vehicle
   accidents in the United States between 1900 and 1970 appeared to
   a.   rise steadily after 1930
   b.   decline steadily for 30 years after 1930
   c.   remain the same for 40 years
   d.   decline after 1960

THOUGHT QUESTIONS

1. Using the data in Figure 2.4, page 21, answer the following questions.
   a.   What accounted for the decline in life expectancy in 1918?
   b.   What was the life expectancy in 1910? 1960?
   c.   How can you explain the gain between 1910 and 1960?
2. What are some of the health benefits and health problems that have come
   with advanced technology?
3. How can health education help you prevent or solve personal, family,
   and community health problems?

Looking Ahead

The next five chapters of Unit Two describe how your body
works. Chapter 3 begins with a discussion of cells. Since your
own body, now containing billions of cells, grew from a
single cell, you will be interested to learn how these tiny
living units work.

How Health Practices Are Changing   25

Unit Two: HOW YOUR
BODY WORKS

Look in a mirror. Are you the same person you were a year ago? Of course not. Countless inner and outer changes have taken place. They will continue to take place throughout your life, though not at the rate they do during your growing years. It's no wonder that everyone asks, at some time or another, "Who am I?"

The answer is that you are a unique individual, one of a kind. Of course, like other people, you have skin, hair, arms, and legs. Like

In this typical family photo, do you recognize many similarities? Differences?

Students of approximately the same age. What is the normal height for this age group?

others, you must eat, sleep, learn, and play. You feel love, pain, joy, and sorrow. But no one else is exactly like you in face or body build, in fingerprints or voiceprints. Even your individual cells, tissues, and organs are a little different from those of other people, even those who are most closely related to you.

Look around you at your classmates. All of you may be about the same age, but notice the individual differences in height, weight, and body build. Everyone is growing according to his or her own pattern, controlled by his or her own physiological "growth clock," which determines when, how fast, and how much each part of the body will grow. Therefore, when we say a boy or a girl is of average height or weight, we do not mean that average is normal. The students who are shown at the top of this page are all normal in height, though few are average.

The individual differences that make each person special are determined by heredity and environment. We cannot change our heredity; it is built into every cell of our bodies. But if we know enough about how our bodies work, we can do a great deal to encourage good effects and reduce possible harm from our environment. The five chapters of Unit Two will introduce you to the important parts of the human body and will help you to understand how they function.

How Your Body Works

Chapter 3: Cells, Tissues, and Organs

Every human being begins as one fertilized egg cell formed by the union of one male and one female reproductive cell. The fertilized egg grows by dividing into two cells. Those two cells divide into four cells, and so on, until an adult's body contains approximately 60 thousand billion, or 60 trillion (60,000,000,000,000), cells.

How do all of these rapidly dividing cells grow into the many different kinds of cells a body needs? How do they become skin cells, blood cells, or bone cells? Amazingly enough, each one of these 60 trillion cells carries hereditary information directing its growth and development. Like a traveler with a road map, each cell carries its own plan along with it.

Moreover, each cell is a tiny factory that takes in nourishment from the bloodstream, changes this food into cell material, and gives off waste. Let's look at a single cell to see how it manages to do all of these things.

A Single Cell

A living cell is made up of a jellylike material called **protoplasm** (PROH-tuh-plaz-um). The protoplasm includes the **cell membrane, cytoplasm** (SYT-uh-plaz-um), and **nucleus** (NYOO-klee-us). Figure 3.1 shows a cell and its parts.

THE CELL MEMBRANE A membrane is a thin, soft sheet that acts as a covering or lining. The delicate cell membrane that surrounds each cell

Figure 3.1. A cell.

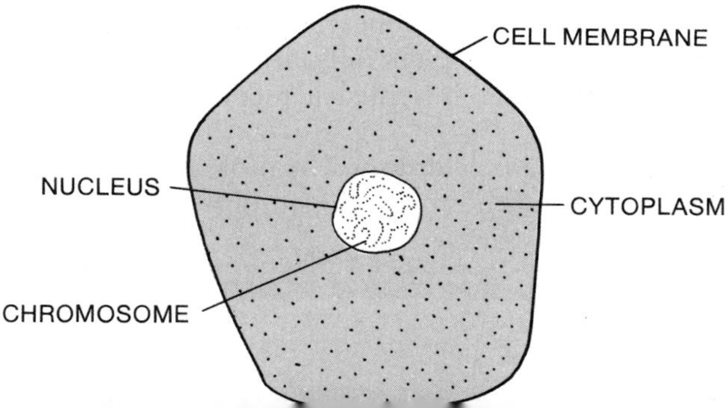

NUCLEUS

CELL MEMBRANE

CYTOPLASM

CHROMOSOME

allows food to enter and waste material to leave through it. The cell membrane also gives the cell its distinctive shape. Cells come in different shapes and sizes according to the job they do.

THE CYTOPLASM   Cytoplasm occupies most of the space in a cell. If you look at a cell under a microscope, you can see that the cytoplasm is almost colorless. The very thin line that surrounds the cytoplasm is the cell membrane. The large, oval, dark spot near the center of the cytoplasm is the nucleus, which is surrounded by its own membrane.

THE NUCLEUS   The nucleus is the most important part of the cell and controls many of its activities, such as growth and division. If the nucleus dies, the cell dies. Red blood cells, for example, lose the nucleus as they mature. The cells die within a few months. Other kinds of cells would die much sooner without a nucleus. Inside the nucleus of most cells are 46 tiny threadlike parts called **chromosomes** (KROH-muh-sohms) (refer again to Figure 3.1). Mature red blood cells, of course, have no chromosomes, and sex cells (see page 247) have only half as many chromosomes as other cells. Chromosomes are made up mainly of a chemical compound called **DNA.**

    DNA   DNA is an abbreviation for **deoxyribonucleic** (dee-AHK-sih-RY-boh-noo-KLEE-ik) **acid.** This substance is apparently the basic storage place for all hereditary information. Every cell in your body contains its own DNA, which carries the plan for your growth and development.

    Genes   Chromosomes are divided into smaller parts called **genes** (JEENZ). Each gene is composed of a certain amount of DNA. Each of your genes is related to a particular trait you possess, such as the color of the skin, eyes, and hair, and the shape of your nose. Genes come in pairs, with one of each pair coming from the mother and the other coming from the father. You received one gene for each hereditary characteristic from each of your parents. There are about 30,000 genes in the nucleus of most of your cells.

    Dominant and Recessive Characteristics   In a pair of genes for any characteristic, one gene may be **dominant** and the other **recessive.** A dominant gene overshadows, or hides, a recessive gene. Thus, the trait carried by the dominant gene usually appears. If the genes of a pair are both dominant, the dominant trait will appear, just as when one dominant and one recessive gene are present. Generally, if a recessive trait appears in a person, she or he must have inherited a recessive gene from both the mother and the father.

Most hereditary traits are determined by more than one pair of genes, often by a large number of them. But to simplify your understanding of

How Your Body Works

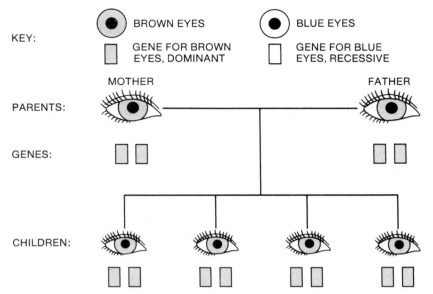

Figure 3.2. Children of two brown-eyed parents.

heredity, let us assume that only one pair of genes is involved in the inheritance of eye color. The gene for brown eyes is dominant. The gene for blue eyes is recessive.

Inheritance of Recessive Characteristics Suppose a brown-eyed woman, all of whose ancestors were also brown-eyed, marries a brown-eyed man of similar ancestry. All of their children will have brown eyes because there are no blue-eye genes present (see Figure 3.2).

Figure 3.3. Children of a brown-eyed mother and a blue-eyed father.

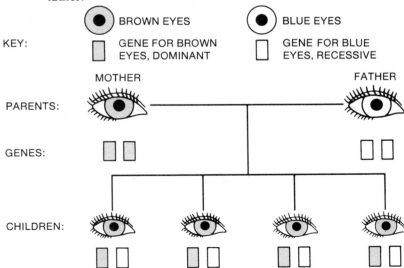

Now, instead, suppose the same brown-eyed woman marries a blue-eyed man. All of their children will have brown eyes because the brown-eye gene received from their mother is dominant (see Figure 3.3). How-

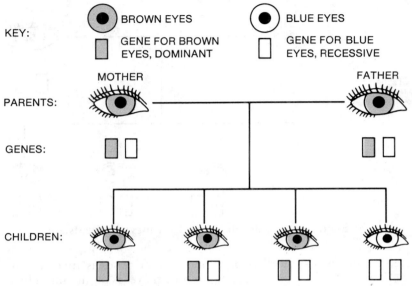

Figure 3.4. Children of parents each having a brown-eye gene and a blue-eye gene.

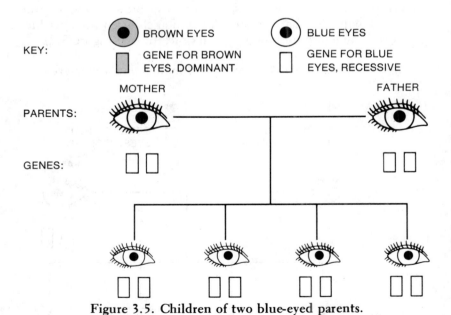

Figure 3.5. Children of two blue-eyed parents.

How Your Body Works

ever, all of these children will carry a gene for blue eyes received from their father. When two such people with both a brown-eye gene and a blue-eye gene have children, some of the children may have blue eyes, as Figure 3.4 shows.

A blue-eyed man, with his two recessive blue-eye genes, carries none of the dominant brown-eye genes, for if he did, his eyes would be brown. If he marries a blue-eyed woman, all of their children will have blue eyes (see Figure 3.5).

Observations of large numbers of people reveal that dominant traits appear more often than recessive traits. How much more often, do you think? The following activity will help you answer this question:

YOUR PART

1. Work with a partner. You and your partner will each need 50 dry red beans (to represent dominant traits), 50 dry white beans (to represent recessive traits), and a bowl.
2. Mix your 50 red and 50 white beans thoroughly together in one bowl. Have your partner do the same, using the other bowl. Label one bowl of 50 red and 50 white beans *Mother's Traits* and the other bowl of 50 red and 50 white beans *Father's Traits*.
3. Without looking, pick a bean from each bowl, and record the combination you picked on a separate chart, ruled like the following model. (**Note:** Sample tally marks are shown in the upper left column, showing a count of six.)

	Red-Red	Red-White	White-White
You	~~HHH~~ /		
Your partner			
Totals			
Class totals			

4. Continue until all of the beans are gone. Enter your team totals for

each of the three columns (you and your partner should have picked 100 combinations in all).

5. Using the chalkboard, compute the totals of all class teams, including your own. Record the results on the bottom line of your chart.

6. Referring to your own team totals, answer the following questions: *(a)* Which combination turned up most often? *(b)* How often? *(c)* How often did each of the other combinations turn up?

7. Referring to class totals, answer the following questions: (a) How often would dominant (red) traits actually appear in individuals resulting from these combinations? *(b)* How often would recessive (white) traits appear?

As you soon discovered, the red-white combination turns up more often than either red-red or white-white. If you were able to do this experiment hundreds of times, you would find the red-white combination turning up almost exactly twice as often as either red-red or white-white. This means that dominant traits would actually appear *three times as often* as the recessive traits produced by the white-white combination only.

Let's Pause for Review

All living things are built of cells. Cells are made up of protoplasm. The outer boundary of the cell is called the cell membrane. Inside the cell membrane is the jellylike material called cytoplasm. Imbedded in the cytoplasm is the nucleus. The nucleus is the most important part of the cell. Inside each nucleus are 46 chromosomes divided into smaller parts called genes. Both genes and chromosomes contain DNA, a chemical compound that stores hereditary information. The characteristics that appear in us are a result of the dominant and recessive genes we inherited from our parents.

Mitosis

As you know, all life develops from an individual cell, and, in order for an organism to grow, its first cell must divide and redivide many times. The body also needs new cells to replace worn-out cells and to repair injured body tissues. The name given to the way in which the nucleus of a cell divides as new cells are formed is **mitosis** (my-TOH-sis).

Figure 3.6 shows how a cell divides. The nucleus starts to change. Its membrane disappears. In Figure 3.6, for simplicity the cell is shown with

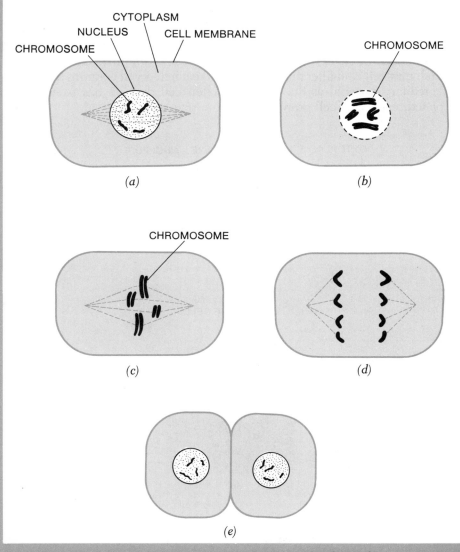

CYTOPLASM

NUCLEUS   CELL MEMBRANE

CHROMOSOME

(a)

CHROMOSOME

(b)

CHROMOSOME

(c)

(d)

(e)

Figure 3.6. How a cell divides: *(a)* cell before dividing; *(b)*
duplicated chromosomes are visible, and nuclear membrane
begins to disappear; *(c)* duplicated chromosomes line up; *(d)*
duplicated chromosomes move apart; *(e)* two cells with identical
sets of chromosomes.

four chromosomes. Remember that a human cell has 46 chromosomes.
The 46 chromosomes (each made up of duplicate halves) line up in the
center of the cell. The duplicates separate into two sets of 46 chromosomes
each. One set moves to one end of the cell, and the other set moves to the

Cells, Tissues, and Organs

other end. Each group of 46 chromosomes bunches up into a new nucleus, which develops a membrane.

Finally, the cell pinches in at the middle until it divides into two equal parts. Each nucleus is exactly like the nucleus of the first cell. Although each new cell is smaller than the original, each new cell contains the same hereditary material as the original. When cell division has been completed, each new cell grows to the same size as the original.

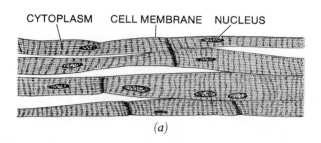

(a)

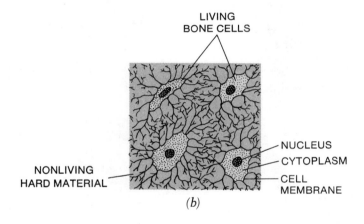

(b)

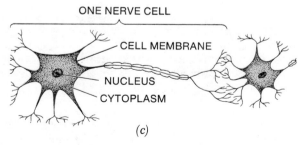

(c)

Figure 3.7. Some types of human tissue: (a) muscle tissue from the heart; (b) bone tissue; (c) nerve tissue.

How Your Body Works

Cells Form Tissue

Groups of cells together form the various **tissues** of the body. A tissue is a group of similar cells that work together. The body is made up of several types of tissues (see Figure 3.7).

You can see one type of tissue by looking at your hand. Its outer covering is made up of a group of cells called **epithelial** (ep-uh-THEE-lee-ul) **tissue.** This kind of tissue serves as a protective cover or lining. Other kinds of epithelial tissue cover the inside of the cheeks, the lining of the **trachea** (TRAY-kee-uh), or windpipe, and other surfaces and linings of the body. The cells of epithelial tissue fit together in such a way as to prevent foreign materials from reaching the cells beneath.

Tissues Form Organs and Organ Systems

The tissues of the body occur in special groups called **organs.** An organ is a part of the body that does a special job. Your stomach, heart, lungs, and brain are examples of organs.

Organs that work together as a group and do the same kind of work are called **organ systems,** or systems, for short. One of the systems of the body is the circulatory system, made up of the heart, blood vessels, and blood.

YOUR PART

1. By yourself or as part of a small group, list as many organ systems as you think there are.
2. For each organ system you listed in step 1, name all the organs you think belong within that system.
3. As a class, compare your lists of organ systems and their organs.

If you succeeded in listing all nine systems, your list includes the skeletal, muscular, nervous, circulatory, endocrine, respiratory, digestive, urinary, and reproductive systems.

Although we group the body's structures into separate organ systems, these systems are not independent of one another. They work together and meet all of the body's needs, and to work well each one depends on the others. For example, a heavy cold, which affects the respiratory system, can keep you from playing a good game of tennis, because your muscular system is dependent upon your respiratory system for oxygen.

Looking Back

All living things are built of cells, which are composed of cytoplasm, a cell membrane, and a nucleus. Within the nucleus of most cells are 46 chromosomes made up mainly of DNA, which stores hereditary information. Chromosomes are made up of smaller units called genes. Each gene is part of the DNA and may be dominant or recessive. Cells divide to form new cells. When the nucleus of a cell divides by mitosis, the same hereditary information passes to the new cells. New body cells are needed for growth, to replace worn-out cells, and to repair injured parts of the body. Cells in the body are grouped into tissues; groups of tissues form organs; organs are grouped into organ systems. These systems work together to meet all of your body's needs.

MODIFIED TRUE-FALSE QUESTIONS

1. The basic unit of life is the _cell._
2. Cell growth and division are controlled by the _cytoplasm._
3. The nucleus of a cell divides by the process of _mitosis._
4. A group of similar cells working together is called _an organ._
5. _Genes_ determine our inherited characteristics.
6. All material in a cell is called _protoplasm._
7. _A recessive_ trait can appear in a family in which both parents have a dominant trait.
8. Most hereditary traits are determined by _one_ pair(s) of genes.
9. The nucleus of most cells in the body carries _48_ chromosomes.
10. A person's heredity _cannot_ be changed.

MATCHING QUESTIONS

Column A	Column B
1. cell membrane	a. controls cell activity
2. cytoplasm	b. substance that stores hereditary information
3. nucleus	
4. DNA	c. acts as a covering
5. pair of genes	d. occupies most of the space in a cell
	e. related to a particular trait in an individual
	f. a dominant trait

How Your Body Works

COMPLETION QUESTIONS

1. Organs performing the same kind of work are grouped into _____.
2. The outer portion of your skin is made up of a group of cells that together form a (an) _____.
3. Genes that overshadow other genes are known as _____ genes.
4. Genes that are overshadowed by other genes are known as _____ genes.
5. The name given to the way in which the nucleus of a cell divides is _____.

MULTIPLE-CHOICE QUESTIONS

1. Tissues are to organs as organs are to
   a. cells b. systems c. cytoplasm d. protoplasm
2. Food and oxygen enter a cell through the
   a. nucleus b. DNA c. chromosomes d. cell membrane
3. The number of genes in the nucleus of most human cells is about
   a. 1500 b. 30,000 c. 150,000 d. 300,000,000
4. The number of chromosomes in most cells of the human body is
   a. 13 b. 23 c. 46 d. 92
5. The brain is an example of
   a. a system b. an organ c. a tissue d. a cell
6. The circulatory system is made up of the
   a. brain, eyes, and nerves
   b. bones, nerves, and muscles
   c. heart, blood vessels, and blood
   d. stomach, heart, and lungs
7. The number of cells in each adult's body is approximately
   a. 60,000 b. 600,000 c. 600,000,000 d. 60,000,000,000,000

THOUGHT QUESTIONS

1. Explain why parents who both have brown eyes may have brown-eyed and blue-eyed children.
2. You have a deep cut on your finger. Your physician tells you that the wound will heal properly and that you will hardly know that the finger had been cut. Explain what will happen during the healing process.
3. Why is it unlikely that two different people will look exactly alike?
4. Write a short composition entitled "Who Am I?" Include mention of those characteristics that you feel make you different from your classmates.

Cells, Tissues, and Organs

5. Using examples, compare cells, tissues, and organs.
6. On a separate piece of paper, label the parts of a cell, as indicated in the illustration that follows.

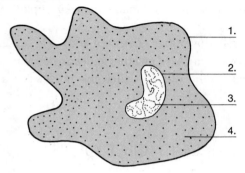

1.

2.

3.

4.

Looking Ahead

In Chapter 4, you will explore two body systems—the skeletal and muscular systems. You will learn how bones and muscles work together to make all of the moves that your body can make, from the most powerful to the most delicate.

Chapter 4: The Shape of Your Body

Your **skeletal** (SKEL-uh-tul) and **muscular** (MUS-kyuh-lur) **systems** and the skin that covers them give your body its shape and erect posture, making it possible for you to move like a human being instead of a jellyfish. Erect posture also frees your hands to do all the skillful things that human hands can do. An intelligent animal like the dolphin might like to play tennis or strum a guitar, but it doesn't have the right bones and muscles.

The Skeletal System

Your skeleton, like the one in Figure 4.1, page 42, has 206 bones, in four main shapes: long like your arm and leg bones, short like your finger bones, flat like your ribs, and irregular like the bones of your skull and spine. Bones furnish the framework for your body. They also protect your brain, heart, lungs, and other internal organs.

Bones have an ivorylike outer wall, which is surrounded by a thin, tough membrane. This wall is composed mainly of mineral matter, such as calcium and phosphorus salts. Blood vessels in the membrane supply materials for building and repairing bones. By using these materials, bone cells heal **fractures,** or broken bones.

Blood Cells From Bone

A substance called **marrow** fills the central part of the long bones of your arms and legs, the flat bones of your ribs, and your **sternum,** or breastbone. Within the marrow of these bones, red and most white blood cells are manufactured. You can see bone marrow in Figure 4.2, page 42.

Cartilage and Fibers

The ends of most bones are covered by a smooth, springy, tough material called **cartilage** (KAHR-tuh-lidj). This material provides a smooth surface

41

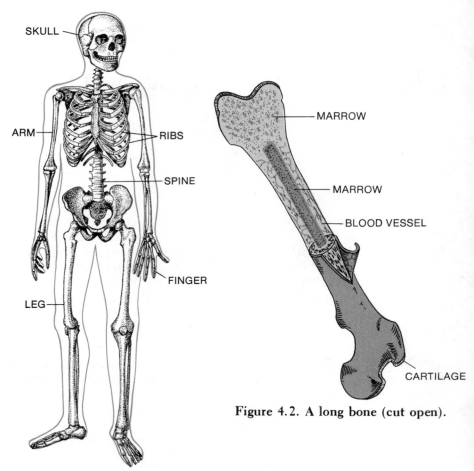

Figure 4.2. A long bone (cut open).

Figure 4.1. Human skeleton.

for easy movement of bone against bone. It also acts as a shock absorber against sudden jolts to the skeleton. Your outer ear, nose, and some ribs are composed mainly of cartilage.

Strong fibers run through bones and help them resist stress. The following activity will help you to see the value of these fibers:

YOUR PART

1. Obtain two chicken leg bones.
2. Soak one chicken leg bone in a jar of vinegar for 48 hours.

How Your Body Works

3. Just before you remove the leg bone from the vinegar, place the other leg bone in a pan and put the pan in an oven at 500 degrees Fahrenheit (260 degrees Celsius) for 1 hour
4. Remove the leg bone from the vinegar. Try to break it.
5. Remove the second leg bone from the oven and *allow it to cool.* Try to break it.
6. Account for any differences.

As you saw, the chicken bone from the oven broke easily whereas the bone soaked in vinegar wouldn't break at all. But perhaps you could not explain this difference. What happened was that the vinegar dissolved much of the calcium in the first chicken bone, leaving only the tough, flexible fibers. The second chicken bone, on the other hand, became more brittle (easily broken) because the oven heat destroyed the usually flexible fibers.

Immovable and Movable Joints

Joints are the places where your bones connect or meet. Some joints, like those of the skull, do not move. They are called *immovable joints. Movable joints,* on the other hand, may move (1) in a limited way like those of the spine, or (2) freely like the ball-and-socket joints of the shoulder and hip, the hinge joints of the elbow and knee, and the gliding joint of the wrist. The movable doll in Figure 4.3 has a ball-and-socket shoulder joint somewhat like yours.

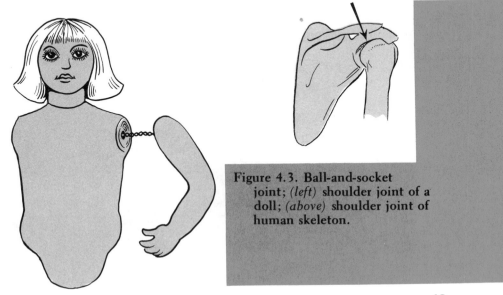

Figure 4.3. Ball-and-socket joint; *(left)* shoulder joint of a doll; *(above)* shoulder joint of human skeleton.

The Shape of Your Body

Ligaments and Tendons

Bands of tough tissue called **ligaments** hold joints together. You can feel ligaments at the sides of your knees. Ligaments are what you stretch or tear when you sprain an ankle. If you have ever made a puppet, you have probably given it ligaments by fastening pieces of cloth to both sides of each joint.

Bands of tissue called **tendons** connect muscles to bone. You can feel a tendon on the inside of your elbow as you bend your arm, or at the back of your ankle. Figure 4.4 shows a ligament and tendons of the hand and wrist.

YOUR PART

1. Write down the locations of ligaments in your body.
2. Write down at least five places where you have tendons.
3. As a class or in small groups, compare your answers.

If you used an illustrated reference book in making your list, you were probably surprised at the number and variety of ligaments and tendons. Your list should show ligaments at the various joints and tendons where muscles are attached to bones.

The Muscular System

Bones cannot move by themselves. They must have help from the muscles. When muscles contract (become shorter and thicker), they pull on

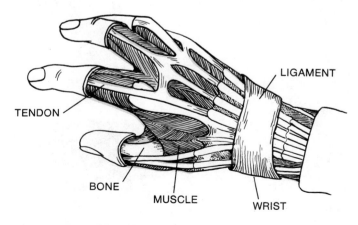

Figure 4.4. Tendons and ligaments of the hand and wrist.

How Your Body Works

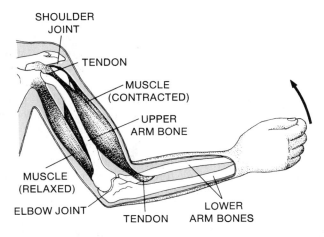

Figure 4.5. Muscle action on bone.

bones and cause them to move. Bend your arm at the elbow. Notice what happens to the muscle in the upper arm. Figure 4.5 shows how muscle can move bone.

VOLUNTARY AND INVOLUNTARY MUSCLES   Your body has two main kinds of muscles. **Voluntary muscles,** like those in your arms and legs, work when you want them to. **Involuntary muscles,** like those in the walls of the heart and stomach, keep working day and night, whether you think about them or not. And a good thing, too. You can control some involuntary muscles, like those that do your blinking and your breathing, but usually only for short periods of time. (Scientists are beginning to learn that, with special training, people can control some involuntary muscles, like those that affect the size of the blood vessels.)

YOUR PART

1.   Involuntary muscles do important work for us. List the major jobs they do in your body.
2.   For help in making your list, refer again to the list of organ systems on page 37.

You found nine organ systems listed on page 37. Fortunately for us all, involuntary muscles do most of the work of seven of those systems. The two exceptions are the skeletal and the nervous systems, which do not contain muscles.

MUSCLES AND EXERCISE Remember John Gordy, the professional football player quoted at the beginning of Chapter 1, page 3? He said he could look forward to a better year if he first built up good **muscle tone** by working out in the off-season. John Gordy isn't the only one. Good muscle tone—muscular vigor, elasticity, and strength—is important to you, too.

Almost half your body mass is muscle. Your all-important heart is largely muscle. The improved circulation that comes with muscular exercise will benefit your whole body.

Now may be the best time in your life to try new games and exercises in your gym classes and elsewhere and to find out which ones you like best. Then, as you grow older and wish to keep in shape, you will already have the habit of playing the games and doing the exercises you enjoy.

YOUR PART

1. List sports, games, and exercises you can continue to take part in into your adult years.
2. Circle your current favorites. Underline those that you think you might like if you tried them.
3. What exercises can people continue to take after retirement?

Looking Back

Your skeleton contains 206 bones, which provide a framework for your body. Bones also protect internal organs. Some bones manufacture blood cells in the bone marrow. Cartilage helps your bones move easily; fibers help them resist stress. Ligaments connect your bones at the joints. Tendons connect muscle to bone. With the aid of your muscles, bones allow you to stand erect, bend, and move.

The two main types of muscles are voluntary muscles, which you control, and involuntary muscles, which work without conscious control. A long-term program of exercise will help you keep good muscle tone throughout your life.

How Your Body Works

MODIFIED TRUE-FALSE QUESTIONS

1. The bones of the body are of _the same_ shape(s).
2. _Involuntary_ muscles keep working day and night, whether you think about them or not.
3. _Bones_ allow you to stand erect, bend, and move.
4. We usually cannot control our _voluntary_ muscles.
5. _Tendons_ connect bones.
6. _Ligaments_ connect muscle to bone.
7. Joints that do not move are located in the _skull._
8. Vigor and strength depend upon good _bone_ tone.
9. When strongly heated, a bone becomes _more_ flexible.
10. When muscles contract, they become _longer_ and thicker.

COMPLETION QUESTIONS

1. As you bend your arm and hold a finger in the crook of your elbow, you can feel a (an) _____ on the inside of your elbow.
2. The material that the body uses to heal fractures comes from _____.
3. A substance that fills the central part of most bones is called _____.
4. Stomach movements are carried on by _____ muscles.
5. When you sprain a wrist, you stretch _____.

MULTIPLE-CHOICE QUESTIONS

1. The skeletal system
   a. helps bones to move
   b. makes cartilage become brittle
   c. provides a frame for the body
   d. helps us digest food
2. Red and most white blood cells are manufactured in the
   a. marrow   b. ligaments   c. tendons   d. muscles
3. It is possible to move the shoulder freely because its joints are
   a. limited   b. hinged   c. ball-and-socket   d. gliding
4. Easy movement of the bones at the knee joint is aided by
   a. cartilage   b. marrow   c. calcium   d. involuntary muscle
5. The number of bones in the skeletal system is
   a. 103   b. 206   c. 416   d. 932
6. The type of bones located in the arms and legs is
   a. long   b. short   c. flat   d. irregular

THOUGHT QUESTIONS

1. What is the relationship between muscle tone and "working out" regularly and "warming up" before engaging in athletic activities?
2. How is the health of your skeleton related to the calcium in your diet?
3. Why can you move the bones of your finger but not the bones of your skull?
4. Why is a torn ligament a threat to the professional life of an athlete?

Looking Ahead

In Chapter 5, you will study the five parts of the circulatory system: the heart, the blood vessels, the blood, the lymph vessels, and the lymph. You will learn both how this system nourishes and cleanses your body cells and how it fights infection.

How Your Body Works

Chapter 5: Circulation: The Care and Feeding of Cells

You have thousands of billions of cells in your body. Every single one of them must take in nourishment and oxygen and get rid of waste materials. Your **circulatory** (SUR-kyuh-luh-taw-ree) **system** does the job. It carries to the cells oxygen from the lungs and nourishing substances absorbed from the digestive system. It removes waste materials from the cells and carries the waste materials to the organs that discharge them from the body.

A Five-Part System

The circulatory system has five parts: the **heart**, the **blood vessels**, the **blood** itself, the **lymph** (LIMF), and the **lymph vessels**. The first three parts of the system are familiar to you. The lymph, or body fluid, is carried by lymph vessels. We will discuss them in detail later.

THE HEART The chief organ of the circulatory system is the heart (see Figure 5.1). The heart is a hollow, muscular pump. Figure 5.2 shows you

Figure 5.1. Shape and location of the heart.

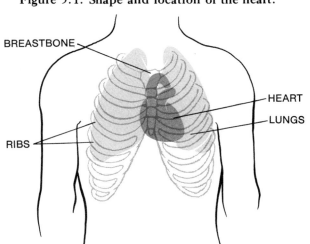

BREASTBONE

HEART

LUNGS

RIBS

the four *chambers*, or compartments, into which the heart is divided. The two upper chambers are called **auricles** (AWR-ih-kulz), **atriums** (AY-tree-umz), or **atria** (AY-tree-uh). The two lower chambers are called **ventricles** (VEN-trih-kulz). When the heart muscles contract, blood is pumped out of the ventricles; when the heart muscles relax, returning blood flows into the auricles. This heart action is also referred to as the *heartbeat*. When the body is at rest, the heart usually beats 60 to 80 times a minute. To get an idea of how much work your heart does, try the following:

YOUR PART

1. Figure out and write down approximately how many times your heart beats in 24 hours.
2. How many times does it beat in a year?
3. Time yourself to see how long you can bend your arm at the rate of 60 times a minute (once a second) before fatigue makes you stop.

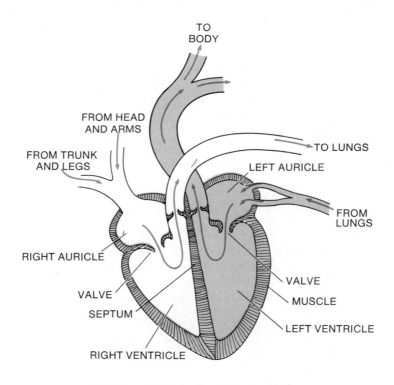

Figure 5.2. The heart (cut open).

How Your Body Works

Because you now know that your heart beats approximately 30 to 40 million times a year, don't get the idea that making it work hard is bad. Like all muscles, your heart thrives on the right kind of exercise.

The Heartbeat in Detail   The right and left sides of the heart do different jobs. In a normal heart, the two sides are separated by the **septum,** a wall with no openings. Blood returning to the heart from all over the body carries waste products, one of which is called *carbon dioxide*. This returning blood flows into the right auricle. The right auricle pumps it into the right ventricle, which then pumps it to the lungs. In the lungs, the carbon dioxide in the blood is exchanged for *oxygen*, a life-giving gas.

From the lungs this *oxygenated* (AHK-sih-jun-nay-tud) blood flows into the left auricle. The left auricle pumps it into the left ventricle. The left ventricle then pumps the oxygenated blood out of the heart, through blood vessels, and to all the cells of the body, except those in the lungs. The openings between the auricles and ventricles are guarded by **valves,** which normally allow the blood to flow in one direction only.

YOUR PART

1.   The muscular walls of the ventricles are thicker than those of the auricles. Try to figure out why, and write down your reason. For help, reread the preceding paragraph.
2.   When you visit your doctor for a medical checkup, your blood pressure is measured and recorded. A normal blood pressure reading looks something like this:

$$\frac{120 \quad \text{(systolic)}}{80 \quad \text{(diastolic)}}$$

(a) Which number represents pressure during the heart's contraction? (b) During the heart's relaxation? Write down your answers and your reason.
3.   As a class, compare your answers in steps 1 and 2.

No doubt, when you compared notes on step 1, you agreed that ventricle walls are thicker than auricle walls because ventricle walls do the job of pumping blood to all the body, whereas auricle walls pump blood only into the ventricles. You probably decided that, in step 2, **systolic** (sis-TAHL-ik) **blood pressure** refers to the pressure during heart contractions, when pressure throughout the circulatory system would naturally be greatest. You probably also decided that **diastolic** (dy-uh-STAHL-ik) **blood pressure** is the opposite—the pressure during heart relaxations, when pressure throughout the circulatory system would be least.

Circulation: The Care and Feeding of Cells

Now, if the necessary materials are available, do the following activity, which will allow you to see for yourself the parts of the heart that you have been reading about:

YOUR PART

MATERIALS

You will need the following:

- One or more beef hearts
- A *scalpel* (small, thin-bladed knife)
- *Forceps* (tweezers)
- Two *probes* (thin, pointed rods)
- A labeled diagram of the heart (see Figure 5.2, page 50).

PROCEDURE

Your teacher will show you how to do the *dissection,* or cutting apart for scientific examination. Then groups of two to four students will dissect beef hearts (one heart to a group), following these steps:

1. With the probes, follow the line of blood flow from the major blood vessels returning blood to the heart.
2. Still using the probes, follow the line of blood flow from one chamber to another, and through the vessels removing blood from the heart for recirculation.
3. Cut across the heart through the septum. Observe that the heart is actually two pumps in one.
4. Observe the four chambers and the various valves. *(a)* How do the upper and lower chambers differ? *(b)* How do the left and right sides differ? *(c)* How do the valves differ?
5. Now write down on a separate piece of paper your answers to these questions. If necessary, refer to the diagram of the heart:

   a. Through what blood vessels does blood return to the heart from the arms and legs? Is this blood oxygenated or does it lack oxygen?
   b. Which side of the heart receives the blood from the arms and legs?
   c. Which blood vessels carry oxygenated blood to the heart and to the rest of the body?
   d. Name the four chambers of the heart, and tell what job each chamber does.
   e. How do the valves control the flow of blood through the heart?
   f. Using a reference book, find out how the size and structure of a beef heart compare with the size and structure of a human heart.

How Your Body Works

BLOOD VESSELS   Your heart pumps blood through tubes of various sizes, called blood vessels. Your body has thousands of miles of these blood vessels, which are of three major types: **arteries, capillaries** (KAP-uh-ler-eez), and **veins** (VAYNZ).

Arteries carry blood away from the heart. They keep getting smaller, like the branches of a tree, until they finally connect with the tiniest blood vessels, the capillaries.

Capillaries do the real work of supplying your cells with food and oxygen and removing waste materials from them. Arteries and veins transport, but the capillaries deliver needed materials and pick up wastes. After the capillaries exchange food and oxygen for wastes, the blood returns to the heart through the veins.

Veins carry blood back to the right auricle of the heart. In Figure 5.3, you can see how arteries, capillaries, and veins are connected. It may take your blood only about 20 seconds to complete one round trip through the body.

All of the blood in your blood vessels is red. **Venous** (VEE-nus) **blood**

Figure 5.3. Path of blood throughout the body.

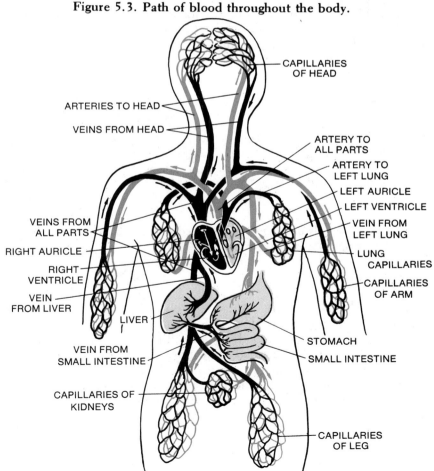

carrying carbon dioxide through your veins to the right auricle is dark red. **Arterial blood** carrying oxygen through your arteries to body cells is bright red.

BLOOD LIQUID: PLASMA   The average adult human body contains about 12 pints (almost 6 liters) of blood. About 55 percent of blood is **plasma,** the liquid portion. Plasma is 90 percent water. By itself, plasma is thin and almost colorless.

BLOOD SOLIDS: BLOOD CELLS AND PLATELETS   The red color of blood comes from the blood solids that float in the plasma. Blood solids, also called *blood cells* or *blood corpuscles* (KAWR-puh-sulz), make up about 45 percent of the blood.

The three main types of blood solids are **red blood cells, white blood cells,** and **platelets** (PLAYT-luts). Red blood cells carry oxygen to the body cells, where they pick up some carbon dioxide and return it to the lungs. (The rest of the carbon dioxide is picked up by the plasma.) White blood cells fight infection. Some white blood cells digest, or break down, foreign material, such as germs. Others surround and consume the foreign material. Platelets help the blood to clot when the body is injured and blood vessels are broken. Without platelets, a person might bleed to death from a cut. In Figure 5.4, you can see microscopic views of the various kinds of blood cells.

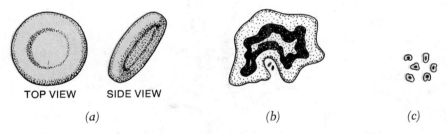

TOP VIEW   SIDE VIEW

(a)   (b)   (c)

Figure 5.4. Kinds of blood cells: *(a)* red blood cells; *(b)* white blood cells engulfing germs; *(c)* platelets.

A Blood Cell Count   Amazingly enough, a lab technician can estimate the total number of blood cells in your body by counting the cells in a very small drop of your blood (1 cubic millimeter) under a microscope. This procedure is called a *blood cell count*. Doctors often order such a blood count as part of a patient's physical checkup. A normal red cell count of about 5,000,000 would indicate, among other things, that a patient doesn't have **anemia** (uh-NEE-mee-uh), a blood deficiency. A normal

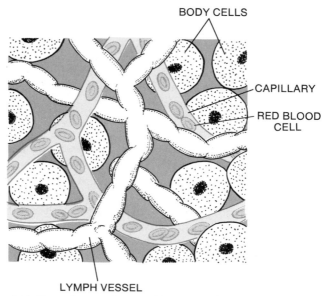

Figure 5.5. Lymph vessels, capillaries, and body cells.

white cell count, between 5000 and 9000, would indicate the absence of serious infection. A normal platelet count, between 200,000 and 400,000, would show normal clotting power.

Is All Blood the Same?   Except for blood type differences, the blood of all healthy people of the same age has the same general makeup. Racial and religious differences are therefore not considered when a person requires a blood transfusion.

LYMPH AND LYMPH VESSELS   Your circulatory system nourishes and cleanses your cells and fights infection. Part of this work is done by the **lymphatic** (lim-FAT-ik) **system,** composed of your lymph and lymph vessels. Lymph is a liquid that comes mainly from blood plasma. Lymph flows through thousands of miles of thin-walled lymph vessels (see Figure 5.5). Like blood vessels, lymph vessels branch all over your body.

Unlike blood vessels, however, lymph vessels are not connected to the heart. There is no "pump" for lymph as there is for blood. Lymph moves along in your lymph vessels whenever your body muscles are active.

The Body's Exchange Agent   Lymph from the blood plasma within capillaries filters through the walls of the capillaries. It fills the spaces between cells and bathes them. Food and oxygen from the blood pass through the lymph on their way to the cells. Carbon dioxide and other wastes pass from the cells through the lymph into the blood. Because this vital activity takes place in the lymph, it could be called the exchange agent of the body.

Built-In First Aid   Lymph gives first aid within the body by flowing to injured places and bathing them. The fluid you see in a blister is lymph. All lymph, including the lymph found at injured places, must circulate in order to be regularly purified. Lymph can either filter back to the blood through capillary walls or enter lymph vessels, which return to the bloodstream.

Lymph Glands (Nodes)   As it flows along through the lymph vessels, lymph passes through structures called **lymph glands** or **nodes**. Figure 5.6 shows you the location of major lymph nodes in your body. These nodes manufacture some of your white blood cells.

Lymph nodes do another vital job. They filter out and destroy impurities and germs that may invade the body. When fighting germs or infection, lymph nodes may become sore and swollen. Have you ever had swollen glands at the sides of your neck? They were probably swollen lymph nodes. **Tonsils** and **adenoids** (AD-uh-noyds), located in the throat

Figure 5.6. Lymph vessels and lymph nodes.

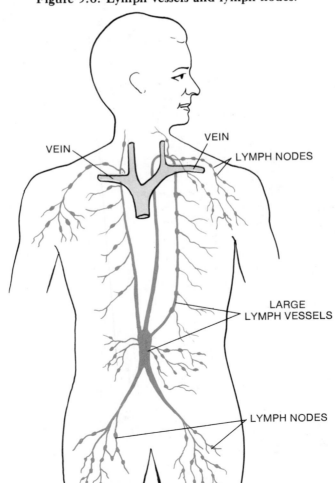

VEIN

VEIN

LYMPH NODES

LARGE
LYMPH VESSELS

LYMPH NODES

area, are lymph nodes, too. If yours have been removed, don't worry. You have plenty of other lymph nodes to take over their work of cleansing and purifying.

Looking Back

The circulatory system carries food and oxygen to the cells and waste products away from them. It cleanses body tissues and fights infection. This system has five parts: the heart, the blood vessels (arteries, capillaries, veins), the blood, the lymph, and the lymph vessels. Blood is composed of a liquid called plasma and three types of blood solids: red blood cells, which transport oxygen and carbon dioxide; white blood cells, which fight infection; and platelets, which aid in clotting. Lymph comes chiefly from plasma. Lymph bathes cells and fills the space between them. Lymph vessels pass through lymph nodes. Lymph nodes manufacture some white blood cells. They also filter out and destroy impurities and germs.

MODIFIED TRUE-FALSE QUESTIONS

1. The lower chambers of the heart are called <u>ventricles</u>.
2. Blood discharges carbon dioxide and receives oxygen in the <u>lungs</u>.
3. Our <u>heartbeat</u> is the result of the squeezing together and relaxing of the heart, as it pumps.
4. Valves control the <u>amount</u> of blood flow.
5. Arterial blood carrying oxygen is <u>darker</u> than venous blood.
6. The <u>lymphatic</u> system helps the body fight infections.
7. The action of <u>heart</u> muscles makes lymph move in lymph vessels.
8. The heart is <u>a muscle</u> and thrives on the right kind of exercise.
9. Blood may complete a trip around the body in 20 <u>minutes</u>.
10. A <u>lymph</u> count, done as part of a health examination, can tell the doctor whether the patient has an infection.

MATCHING QUESTIONS

Column A		Column B
1. artery	a.	carries blood away from the heart
2. heart	b.	carries blood back to the heart
3. vein	c.	helps the blood to clot
4. capillary	d.	manufactures some white cells
5. lymph nodes	e.	delivers food and oxygen to lymph spaces
	f.	main pump of circulatory system

Circulation: The Care and Feeding of Cells

COMPLETION QUESTIONS

1. Blood returning to the heart flows into a chamber called a (an) _____.

2. When muscles of the ventricles contract, blood is pumped out of the _____.

3. The liquid portion of the blood, made up largely of water, is called _____.

4. Blood cells, or corpuscles, make up about _____ percent of the blood.

5. The blood particles that help blood to clot are called _____.

6. A fluid that fills spaces between cells, bathes them, and comes chiefly from blood plasma is called _____.

7. Systolic pressure represents pressure when the heart _____.

8. The system that transports materials through the body is the _____ system.

9. The number in a blood-pressure reading that represents the pressure of the heart when relaxed is called the _____ pressure.

10. Some white blood cells are manufactured in the parts of the circulatory system called _____.

MULTIPLE-CHOICE QUESTIONS

1. Liquids and solids that make up the blood do *not* include
   a. plasma   b. white blood cells   c. red blood cells   d. lymph

2. Dark red blood carrying carbon dioxide is described as
   a. lymphatic   b. arterial   c. oxygenated   d. venous

3. The upper chambers of the heart are called
   a. auricles   b. ventricles   c. valves   d. capillaries

4. The number of pints of blood in the average human adult body is
   a. 6   b. 12   c. 18   d. 24

5. A normal white cell count would be an indication of
   a. anemia
   b. normal clotting power
   c. a normal systolic pressure
   d. the absence of serious infection

6. A main job of the lymphatic system is to
   a. cleanse and nourish cells
   b. help blood to clot
   c. provide a framework for the body
   d. carry blood

7. Red blood cells
   a. help blood clot
   b. fight infection
   c. carry oxygen to cells and pick up carbon dioxide
   d. fill the spaces between cells

How Your Body Works

8. Blood vessels that carry blood containing carbon dioxide are
   a. capillaries   *b.* veins   *c.* arteries   *d.* lymphatics
9. Blood vessels that carry blood rich in oxygen are
   a. capillaries   *b.* veins   *c.* arteries   *d.* lymphatics
10. A normal red blood cell count is approximately
   a. 1,250,000   *b.* 2,500,000   *c.* 5,000,000   *d.* 7,500,000

THOUGHT QUESTIONS

1. The results of a blood test indicate that the patient's blood will not clot properly and that the patient is fighting an infection. How has the doctor determined this from the patient's blood count report?
2. What would the lymph nodes look like if they became infected?
3. Why can tonsils and adenoids, which are lymph tissues, be removed without an adverse effect on the patient and without interfering with the patient's ability to fight infection?
4. In cases of emergency, when blood is not immediately available, why is plasma used?
5. If it takes the blood about 20 seconds to make a round trip through the body, how many trips does it make in *(a)* 1 minute? *(b)* 1 hour? *(c)* 24 hours?
6. Why is the continued loss of blood serious?
7. If you are in good health, will it hurt you in any way to serve as a blood donor? Explain your answer.
8. Why is it a good idea to rest before having a blood pressure reading?
9. Does the blood pressure of a given individual always remain the same? Explain your answer.
10. Should people of the same age always have the same blood pressure? Explain your answer.

Looking Ahead

You have been learning how the circulating blood transports food, oxygen, and wastes. But where exactly does the nourishment come from, and where do the wastes go? In Chapter 6, you will find out how your body changes solid food into material the blood can carry. You will also learn how waste materials are eliminated from the body.

Chapter 6: Nourishment and Waste

You can bite into a hamburger, but your cells can't. This chapter will tell how your **digestive** (dy-JES-tiv *or* duh-JES-tiv) **system** changes the solid food you eat into a nourishing liquid that your cells can absorb from the bloodstream through capillary walls. It will also discuss how the **respiratory** (RES-puh-ruh-taw-ree *or* rih-SPY-ruh-taw-ree) **system** helps "burn" this liquid fuel, and how the **urinary** (YUHR-uh-ner-ee) **system** disposes of cell wastes.

The Digestive System

If you tried to make a big meal of solid food into a digestible form *outside* the body, you would begin as your digestive system does—by chopping, mashing, and stirring. To complete the process, you would need to add many chemicals. Your digestive system does the same thing: it chops, churns, dissolves, and chemically changes your food. During this process, **fats** become **fatty acids** and **glycerin** (GLIS-uh-rin), a syrupy substance also known as *glycerol* (GLIS-uh-rawl). **Proteins** (PROH-teenz) become **amino** (uh-MEE-noh) **acids. Carbohydrates** (kahr-boh-HY-drayts), which are sugars and starches, become **glucose** (GLOO-kohs), or blood sugar.

THE ENZYME IN SALIVA   First, your teeth, with help from the tongue, chop and stir your food. At the same time, *taste buds* in your tongue send a signal that soon reaches your **salivary** (SAL-uh-ver-ee) **glands** located under your tongue, below your lower jaw, and below your ears. The signal makes your mouth "water," which means that the salivary glands are pouring **saliva** (suh-LY-vuh) onto your food. Saliva contains an **enzyme** (EN-zym) that begins the digestion of starches. Enzymes are chemicals produced by the body that allow chemical reactions to take place rapidly at body temperature. If you chew your food too briefly, you don't give the enzyme in saliva a chance to do its work. The following experiment will help you to see why:

60

MATERIALS

Each experiment team in the class will need the following items:

- Two slices of raw potato.
- A paring knife.
- Two 1-pint (500-cubic centimeter) jars with covers. Number each jar.
- Two test tubes standing in a test-tube rack. Number each tube.
- A measuring cup.
- A 4-inch (10-centimeter) square piece of cheesecloth.
- A small funnel.
- A medicine dropper.
- Some tincture of iodine.

Potatoes are a starchy food. Iodine, which is a dark red-brown color, reacts with starch to produce a blue-black color.

PROCEDURE

1. Cut one slice of potato into four chunks. Put them into jar 1. Cut the second potato slice into thin strips, and cut the strips into many tiny pieces. Put them into jar 2. Pour 2 ounces (10 cubic centimeters) of water into each jar. Cover both jars. Shake each jar for 1 minute.
2. Set the cheesecloth over the funnel to act as a strainer. Set the funnel in the mouth of test tube 1. Shake jar 1 again and pour only half of its liquid into test tube 1. Wash the funnel and cheesecloth and set them in the mouth of test tube 2. Shake jar 2 again and pour only half of its liquid into test tube 2.
3. With the medicine dropper, squeeze two drops of iodine into each test tube. Take test tube 1 from the rack and, with your hand over its mouth, shake the tube gently a few times. Do the same to test tube 2.

On a separate piece of paper, answer the following questions:

4. What color is the liquid in test tube 1? In test tube 2? Explain the difference in color.
5. Let the test tubes stand for 30 seconds. Now how do they look? In which tube has more starch settled to the bottom? Is there any difference in the color of the starch at the bottom of the two tubes?
6. How do you think thorough chewing helps you to digest starchy foods?

As you observed, more starch was available in test tube 2, both immediately and at the end of 30 seconds, to react with the iodine and produce a blue or blue-black color. This occurred because each time you cut the potato, you opened some starch-containing potato cells.

The more cuts you make, the greater is the amount of starch that oozes out of the potato. Thus, more starch was available because the potato in test tube 2 was cut into smaller pieces. In a similar way, thorough chewing of food also makes more starch available for interaction with digestive enzymes.

THE ESOPHAGUS   You swallow your food when the muscles of your tongue and throat push it into the **esophagus** (ih-SAHF-uh-gus), a 1-inch-wide (2.5-centimeter-wide) tube that carries food to the stomach. Figure 6.1 shows you the esophagus and other portions of the digestive system.

Fortunately, you don't have to rely on gravity to pull food down to your stomach. If you did, you would have trouble drinking from a drinking fountain or eating in bed during an illness. In reality, wavelike motions of the muscular walls of the esophagus push food down to the stomach. This motion, called **peristalsis** (per-uh-STAHL-sis), moves food along throughout the digestive system.

THE STOMACH   As you have learned, an enzyme in saliva helps digest starch. In other parts of the digestive system, your body manufactures other enzymes, each of which helps digest a different food substance. In the stomach, for example, food mixes with a digestive juice containing an enzyme that helps digest protein. Food in the stomach becomes a thick liquid. This liquid enters the **small intestine** a little at a time until, at the end of about 4 hours, the stomach is empty of food.

THE SMALL INTESTINE REGION   Most digestion takes place in the small intestine, which is about 20 feet (6 meters) long. More digestive juices, manufactured by glands in the walls of the small intestine, the **liver,** and the **pancreas** (PANG-kree-us), pour onto the food and mix with it, completing the job of digestion. For example, **bile,** manufactured by the liver and stored in the **gallbladder,** helps digest fats. (Since the gallbladder merely stores extra bile, it can safely be removed surgically if it is diseased.) Juices from the pancreas aid in breaking down carbohydrates, proteins, and fats. When digestion is complete, the resulting amino acids, fatty acids, glycerin, and glucose are absorbed into the bloodstream. Blood vessels in the walls of the small intestine pick up these nourishing substances, or **nutrients,** and deliver them to the cells.

THE LARGE INTESTINE   With digestion complete, some food material that your body cannot use remains. The unusable material now passes into the **large intestine,** which, though only 4 or 5 feet (1.2 or 1.5 meters) long, is bigger in diameter (across) than the small intestine. The **appendix,**

How Your Body Works

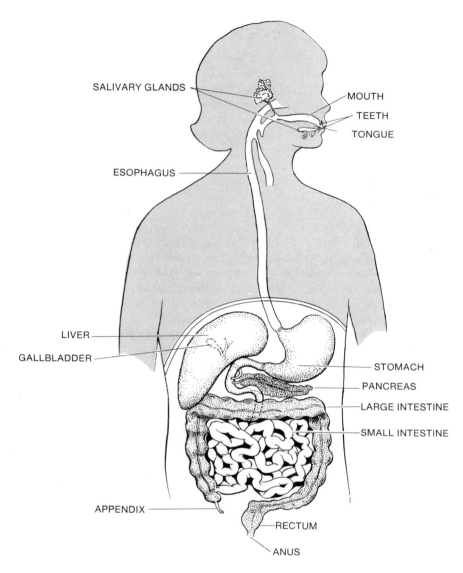

Figure 6.1. The digestive system.

which is attached to the large intestine, has no digestive function. The large intestine removes most of the water from the waste material. The thick mass that remains is pushed along by peristalsis until it reaches the lower end of the large intestine, the **rectum.** This solid waste material, made up of unusable substances, bacteria, and dead body cells, is called **feces** (FEE-seez). It is expelled through an opening, the **anus** (AY-nus).

Let's Pause for Review

The digestive system changes your food into nutrients that your blood can carry and your cells can use. Your mouth, esophagus, stomach, liver, gallbladder, pancreas, and small and large intestines work together to complete digestion. An enzyme in saliva begins the digestion of carbohydrates. Other enzymes in the stomach and small intestine help digest fats, proteins, and carbohydrates. The large intestine prepares solid waste materials for removal from the body.

Oxidation

"She really burns up a lot of energy," you might say of an active friend. You would be exactly right. Like a campfire, your body needs fuel. In fact, that's what people need oxygen for—to burn up, or *oxidize* (AHK-suh-dyz), the food nutrients, or the fuel, provided by the digestive system.

Oxidation (ahk-suh-DAY-shun) is the union of oxygen and some other substance. In this process, energy is released. In a campfire, oxidation releases energy in a burst of heat and light. In your body cells, energy is released gradually in the form of heat and chemical energy. The chemical energy is used for growth, activity, maintenance, and repair.

The Respiratory System

The digestive system provides fuels such as glucose, which are oxidized in your cells. The respiratory system provides the oxygen and also gets rid of carbon dioxide, which results from the oxidation of glucose. Ordinarily, oxygen in the air enters your body through your nose when you breathe in, or inhale.

NOSE   The upper section of your nose contains the **olfactory** (ahl-FAK-tuh-ree) **nerve,** which allows you to smell, or sense odors. As air passes through your nose, it picks up moisture, which helps to keep the moving air from drying out the delicate tissues of the lungs. Tiny hairlike structures in the lining of the nose capture dust particles and keep them out of your lungs. Passage through the nose warms the air as well. If you breathe through your mouth, you lose the advantages of admitting cleaned, warmed, moisturized air into your lungs.

TRACHEA AND EPIGLOTTIS   Inhaled air flows through the nose and throat, past the vocal cords, and into the **trachea** (TRAY-kee-uh), or windpipe. A little flap of tissue, the **epiglottis** (ep-uh-GLAHT-is), usually keeps swallowed food out of the trachea (see Figure 6.2a). However, when

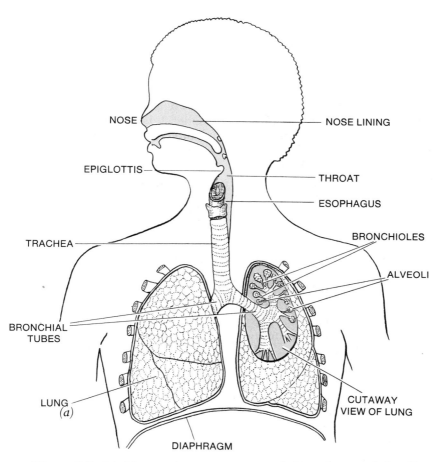

Figure 6.2. *(a)* The respiratory system, and *(b)* a cluster of alveoli.

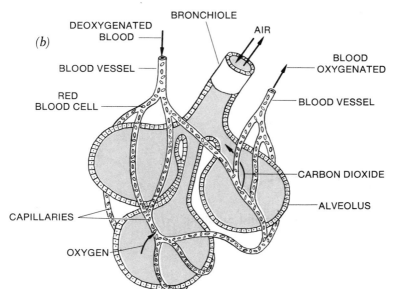

65

the epiglottis closes a split second too late, you cough automatically and usually expel wrongly swallowed food from the trachea.

BRONCHIAL TUBES AND ALVEOLI   In the chest, the trachea divides into two smaller branches, called **bronchial** (BRAHNG-kee-ul) **tubes,** which lead directly into the lungs. These tubes branch and divide within the lungs into smaller and smaller tubes, called **bronchioles** (BRAHNG-kee-ohlz). At the end of each bronchiole is a cluster of tiny air sacs, the **alveoli** (al-VEE-oh-lye), shown in Figure 6.2*b*. Here, the actual exchange of oxygen and carbon dioxide takes place between the millions of alveoli and the capillaries that surround them. Blood vessels carry the oxygenated blood back to the heart. After holding the carbon dioxide for a short time, the lungs exhale it, or breathe it out.

THE DIAPHRAGM   Your lungs cannot inhale and exhale without help from your muscles. When you inhale, muscles in the chest and back lift your ribs and expand your chest cavity. A large flat muscle called the **diaphragm** (DY-uh-fram) separates the chest cavity from the cavity below, which contains the stomach and intestines. As your chest and back muscles lift your ribs, the diaphragm contracts (see Figure 6.3) and enlarges the chest cavity still more. Air rushes in to fill the partial vacuum created in the chest cavity. The more deeply you breathe, the more your chest cavity expands.

When you exhale, your chest and back muscles relax, lowering your ribs. The diaphragm relaxes and pushes upward against the lungs. Together, these actions force air out of the lungs. The power of a hiccup, which is a sharp contraction of the diaphragm, will give you an idea of how powerful the diaphragm muscle is.

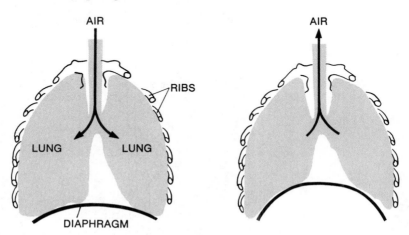

Figure 6.3. Inhaling and exhaling: *(left)* **inhaling — chest cavity enlarges;** *(right)* **exhaling — chest cavity decreases.**

How Your Body Works

By comparing your chest size when you breathe normally with your chest size when you breathe using only your rib muscles or your diaphragm, you will get a better idea of how your muscles help you breathe:

YOUR PART

1. Study your breathing as follows:
    a. Put your hands on your ribs and observe what happens when you breathe normally.
    b. Put one hand on the soft central part of your body just below your breastbone (this is the region of your diaphragm). Again, observe what happens when you breathe normally.
    c. With your hands on your ribs, try to breathe without moving your ribs or shoulders at all; that is, breathe using only your diaphragm.
    d. With a hand on your diaphragm region, breathe using only your ribs.

2. Choose a partner of your own sex. Have your partner exhale and hold this position while you measure your partner's chest size with a tape measure. Record this measurement—this measurement is the control—and allow your partner to breathe normally.
3. Now have your partner inhale using the diaphragm only, without moving the ribs. As this position is held, measure and record the chest size. Allow your partner to exhale.
4. After your partner takes two normal breaths, have your partner inhale with the ribs only, without moving the diaphragm. As this position is held, measure and record the chest size. Allow your partner to exhale.
5. After your partner takes a few normal breaths, have him or her hold the breath after inhaling fully. As this position is held, measure and record the chest size. Now your partner can inhale and exhale normally without interruption.
6. Repeat steps 2, 3, 4, and 5 as your partner measures your chest size in each step.
7. Was chest size greatest in step 3, 4, or 5? Normally, your chest size changes when you inhale and exhale. Write down why. Describe the best way of breathing, and defend your answer.

As you observed in making the measurements, there is considerable body movement when people breathe normally. When they exercise, they breathe far more deeply because they use more of their breathing muscles.

Let's Pause for Review

Your respiratory system takes in oxygen and expels carbon dioxide. Your nose, mouth, epiglottis, trachea, bronchial tubes, and lungs are all part of this system. Bronchial tubes lead into the lungs and divide into smaller tubes called bronchioles, which end in tiny clusters of air sacs called alveoli.

The capillaries surrounding the alveoli pick up oxygen from the lungs and leave carbon dioxide behind to be exhaled. The diaphragm and other muscles in the chest and back help you to breathe.

The Urinary System

As your blood circulates, it picks up waste material from every cell. Except for the carbon dioxide exhaled from the lungs, most of this waste is eliminated in the **urine** (YUHR-un), which is formed by the **kidneys.** You have two kidneys, one on each side, deep in your body just in front of the lowest ribs in your back (see Figure 6.4).

FILTERS FOR THE BLOOD   Approximately a million tiny filters in each kidney strain out waste materials from the circulating blood. The kidneys work quickly, purifying the blood over and over each day. Kidneys turn waste materials into urine by mixing the wastes with enough water to flush them out of the body. With the urinary system in mind, consider the following:

Figure 6.4. The urinary system, viewed from the front.

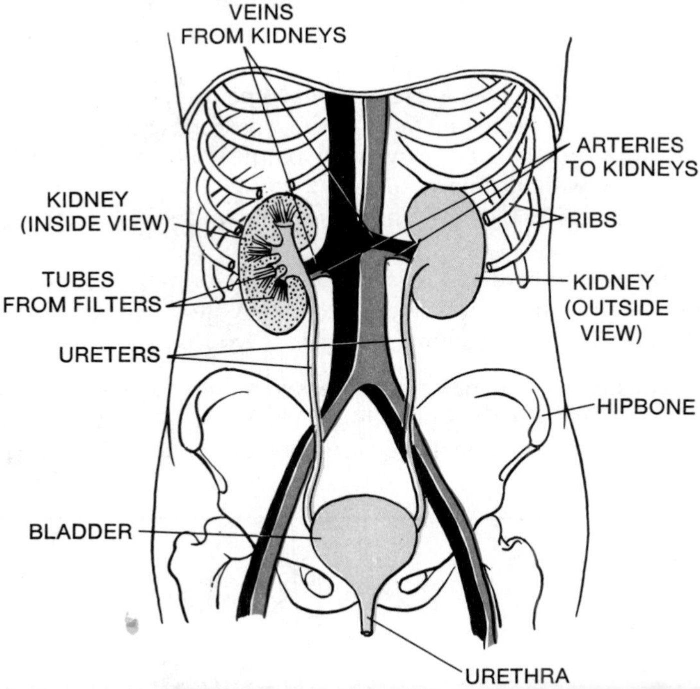

1. "Drink plenty of fluids." Perhaps when you had a cold or the flu, you received this advice from your doctor. Why do you think the doctor advised this?
2. What additional wastes might exist in a body that is fighting an infection?
3. Compare your answers with those of the rest of the class.

When you compared notes, you probably agreed that extra fluids help the body get rid of ordinary cell wastes, wastes produced by germs, dead germs, and dead germs killed by the body itself. All these wastes would be eliminated in the urine.

From each kidney, a tube called a **ureter** (YUHR-uh-tur) carries the urine to a muscular bag called the **urinary bladder.** The bladder is thin-walled and elastic and stores urine until it is passed from the body. In urination (yuhr-uh-NAY-shun), urine leaves the bladder through another tube, the **urethra** (yuhr-EE-thruh).

Looking Back

Together, your mouth, esophagus, stomach, liver, gallbladder, pancreas, and small and large intestines make up your digestive system. Enzymes and other digestive juices manufactured within the system break down and change nutrients such as fats into fatty acids and glycerin, proteins into amino acids, and carbohydrates into glucose. The blood can carry these products, and the cells can use them. In the cells, glucose is oxidized by combining with oxygen supplied by the respiratory system, and energy is released.

The respiratory system takes in oxygen and expels carbon dioxide. Your nose, mouth, trachea, bronchial tubes, and lungs make up your respiratory system. Within the lungs millions of tiny clusters of air sacs called alveoli, aided by the capillaries that surround them, exchange oxygen for carbon dioxide. The diaphragm and other muscles in the chest and back help you to breathe.

The urinary system, consisting of the two kidneys, the urinary bladder, the two ureters, and the urethra, filters most wastes from the blood, mixes them with water, and flushes them out of the body.

MODIFIED TRUE-FALSE QUESTIONS

1. The _nose_ helps filter and warm the air we breathe.
2. Chewing food _slowly_ aids digestion.
3. During digestion, fats become _amino acids._
4. The small intestine has _a shorter_ length than the large intestine.
5. The solid waste we expel is made up of _usable_ substances.
6. The _epiglottis_ usually keeps swallowed food out of the trachea.
7. To _exhale_ means to breathe in air.
8. Our bodies burn up, or oxidize, substances to provide _energy._
9. The _kidneys_ filter waste materials from the circulating blood.
10. A hiccup is a sudden, strong contraction of the _diaphragm._
11. Nourishing substances in the bloodstream are called _enzymes._
12. A branch of the _esophagus_ is called a bronchial tube.

MATCHING QUESTIONS

Column A	Column B
1. enzyme	a. a flap of tissue
2. bronchioles	b. tiny air sacs in the lungs
3. alveoli	c. a body-produced chemical
4. diaphragm	d. tiny tubes found in the lungs
5. kidneys	e. a muscle that aids in respiration
	f. turn cell wastes into urine

COMPLETION QUESTIONS

1. The wavelike motion of the muscular walls of the digestive system is called _____ .
2. The process that takes place in the body to provide energy for growth, activity, maintenance, and repair is termed _____ .
3. The system that chops, softens, dissolves, and chemically changes food in the body is the _____ system.
4. The digestion of sugar and starches starts in the _____ .
5. Bile manufactured in the liver is stored in the _____ .

MULTIPLE-CHOICE QUESTIONS

1. The exchange of carbon dioxide and oxygen takes place in the
   a. esophagus   b. trachea   c. bronchioles   d. alveoli
2. The waste product formed in the kidneys is
   a. saliva   b. carbon dioxide   c. urine   d. feces

How Your Body Works

3. Urine is expelled from the body through the
   a. urethra b. ureters c. bladder d. kidneys
4. Most of the liquid wastes in the blood are filtered out in the
   a. circulatory system   c. digestive system
   b. respiratory system   d. urinary system
5. Another name for blood sugar is
   a. glycerin b. glucose c. fatty acids d. amino acids

THOUGHT QUESTIONS

1. Explain why it is important to replace fluids lost by the digestive, respiratory, and urinary systems.
2. "Chew your food slowly" is a common expression. Why is this advice sound?
3. Describe what happens when you try to hold your breath, and tell why it happens.
4. A good health practice is to eat regularly. Why?
5. Compare food as a fuel for your body with oil as a fuel for heating your home.
6. A piece of food accidentally becomes lodged in your trachea. Describe what normally happens in the body to dislodge the food.
7. What is a kidney machine?
8. Describe the passage of a piece of cheese through the digestive system.
9. One good health practice involves deep-breathing exercises. Why?
10. Explain how your kidneys are like pieces of filter paper.

Looking Ahead

In Chapter 7, you will investigate two other body systems—the nervous system and the endocrine system. The nervous system provides the body with rapid communication and intelligent control. The endocrine system assists the nervous system in its job of control.

Nourishment and Waste

Chapter 7: The Nervous and Endocrine Systems: Communication and Control

Huge computers direct the flights of satellites and manned capsules into outer space. A small computer inside your body directs your movements down a ski slope, your play in a basketball game, or the delicate mental and physical moves you make in working a tough mathematical problem. This personal computer is your **brain,** which is connected to your **spinal cord** (directly below your brain) and **nerves** (throughout your body). In Figure 7.1, you can see a technician checking the wires of a large factory-made

Figure 7.1. The largest computers made can do only a few of the things that your brain can do.

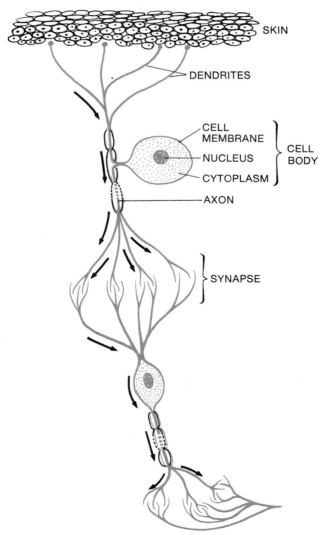

SKIN

DENDRITES

CELL
MEMBRANE

NUCLEUS

CYTOPLASM

CELL
BODY

AXON

SYNAPSE

Figure 7.2. Two nerve cells of a chain.

computer. Yet it isn't large enough to do the many things your brain can do.

Your Own Computer

Say that a space scientist in a mission control center receives a message that some part of an orbiting space capsule isn't working properly. The computer then considers all possible actions, decides on the best one, and sends a message back to the capsule, directing the astronauts inside to take this action. Your brain works in the same way, receiving information from all parts of your body, thinking it over, and sending back orders to your muscles and glands.

Three Kinds of Nerves

In your body, *nerves* carry messages, or **nerve impulses,** to and from the brain. Just as a cable is a thick bundle of wires, a nerve is a bundle of tiny, sensitive nerve fibers. **Sensory** (SEN-suh-ree) **nerves** gather and relay information to the brain or spinal cord about sensations, such as heat, pressure, darkness, and light. **Motor nerves** (motor means movement) carry messages from the brain and spinal cord, which tell the muscles and glands how to act. **Mixed nerves,** like those in your face and those attached to your spinal cord, contain fibers both of sensory and of motor nerves.

Figure 7.2, page 73, shows two **neurons** (NYUR-ahns), or *nerve cells,* of a chain of nerve cells. Each has its own **cell body, axon** (ACK-zahn), and **dendrites** (DEN-dryts). The cell body contains the cell nucleus and a mass of cytoplasm, surrounded by the cell membrane. Dendrites, which are branching, treelike fibers, carry messages into a neuron. The axon carries messages out of the neuron.

Jumping the Gap (Synapse)

Suppose that the ends of the dendrites sense that the skin is getting cold. A message travels along the dendrites, through the cell body, to the axon at

Figure 7.3. Testing the knee-jerk reflex. A tap below the knee joint starts the message that goes to the spinal cord and back to the muscles used to straighten the leg.

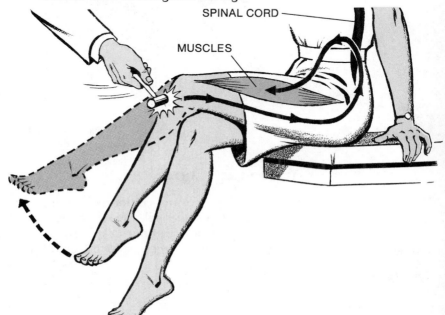

SPINAL CORD

MUSCLES

the other end. But now what? In Figure 7.2, you can see that the two neurons don't quite touch each other. How does the message get from one neuron to the other? The answer is that the message jumps the gap.

The gap is called a **synapse** (SIN-aps). Nerve impulses cause electrical and chemical changes to occur in the neuron and at the synapse. These changes allow messages to jump across the synapse. And they jump quickly—far more quickly than you can read about it. Some nerve fibers may carry messages at a speed of 20 feet (6 meters) per second. Others may carry them as fast as 400 feet (120 meters) per second. No wonder you can react to sensory messages instantly when you need to.

Reflex Reactions

Speaking of speed, your **reflex** (automatic) reactions to pain are some of your speediest. One reason is because they are controlled, not by the brain, but by the spinal cord. If your hand touches a hot stove, the message to withdraw your hand does not travel to the brain. It travels only to the spinal cord and back to the muscles that jerk your hand away. You can see another reflex reaction, which automatically straightens the leg, illustrated in Figure 7.3. However, most of the marvels performed by your nervous system are controlled by your brain.

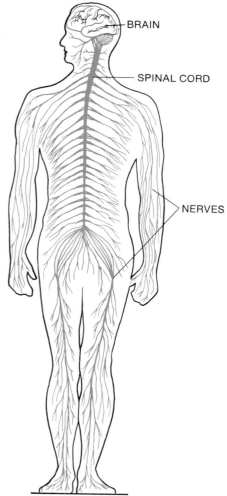

Figure 7.4. The central nervous system and some of the nerves that carry messages throughout the body.

The Brain in Detail

Millions of nerve cells make up your brain. Your bony skull protects them. Just inside the skull, a layer of fluid surrounds and cushions your brain. Three membrane layers wrapped around the brain provide further protection. As you can see in Figure 7.4, your brain and spinal cord, or **central**

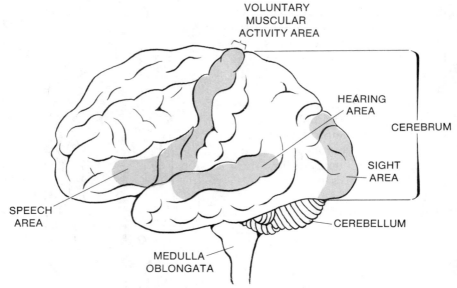

Figure 7.5. Major parts of the brain.

nervous system, join without any sort of break. It's not surprising, then, that the same fluid and membrane layers that protect the brain surround and protect the spinal cord as well.

THE CEREBRUM: THE LARGEST PART OF THE BRAIN   The cerebrum (suh-REE-brum *or* SER-uh-brum) does most of the brain's work (see Figure 7.5). The cerebrum remembers, learns, plans, reasons, wills, creates, decides, and sends orders to the voluntary (controlled by the will) muscles to act. Generally, nerve fibers carrying messages into or out of the cerebrum cross over from the left side of the body to the right side, and vice versa. That is why a severe injury to the right side of the cerebrum can interfere with movement of the left side of the body, and the reverse.

The Cerebral Cortex: The Outer Layer   The cerebral cortex (suh-REE-brul KAWR-teks) is the outer layer of the cerebrum. The surface of this layer has been partially mapped, as you can see in Figure 7.5. Over the years, scientists have learned which areas control speech, hearing, sight, and voluntary muscular activity. Only about one-third of the cerebral cortex has been mapped, however. The special work of the remaining two-thirds is not yet known.

THE CEREBELLUM   The cerebellum (ser-uh-BEL-um) is much smaller than the cerebrum and lies beneath it (refer again to Figure 7.5). The cerebellum automatically coordinates voluntary muscular activity

76   **How Your Body Works**

and helps balance your body. When you walk, for example, the cerebellum helps you to keep your balance and move smoothly without thinking. Answering the following questions will help you distinguish between the work of the cerebrum and the cerebellum:

YOUR PART

1. List three activities that your cerebellum coordinates.
2. List three activities that your cerebrum controls.
3. List three activities that require the participation of both the cerebrum and the cerebellum.
4. Write down whether you are right- or left-handed. Now write down which side of your brain controls the hand you use to write.
5. As a class, compare your answers.

Undoubtedly, you thought of many activities coordinated by your cerebellum, like guiding food to your mouth, walking, running, sitting, standing, and dancing, plus many sports activities at which you are skilled.

Anything you have to think about belongs on your list of activities controlled by the cerebrum.

Your third list might, if you cared to extend it, be almost endless, because most activity requires help from both the cerebrum and the cerebellum. For example, you think up an English composition with your cerebrum. But you use your cerebellum, too, since the act of writing, once mastered, is an automatically coordinated activity.

You were correct if you answered that the actions of your writing hand, left or right, are controlled by the opposite side of your brain.

THE BRAIN STEM: MIDBRAIN, PONS, MEDULLA OBLONGATA

Messages to and from the cerebrum and cerebellum pass through the **brain stem.** Figure 7.6, page 79, shows the parts of the brain stem: the **midbrain, pons** (PAHNZ), and **medulla oblongata** (muh-DUL-uh ahb-lawn-GAHT-uh). Each part of the brain stem has a different job.

The midbrain handles automatic reactions to sound and light, such as the contracting of the pupils when light strikes the eyes.

The pons, which means bridge, is the passageway for nerve impulses going back and forth between the various parts of the brain.

The medulla oblongata helps regulate the action of vital organs like the heart and lungs. It is here that the nerve fibers cross over on their way to the cerebrum.

The Nervous and Endocrine Systems

Two Nervous Systems: Voluntary and Involuntary

So far, we have been talking about parts of the central nervous system —the brain and the spinal cord. This nervous system controls most of our conscious, or voluntary, activities. But we have another nervous system, which is connected to the medulla oblongata and the spinal cord by special nerves. This second nervous system is called the **autonomic** (aw-toh-NAHM-ik) **nervous system.** Autonomic means independent, and this system works independently of the cerebrum. It controls most of our unconscious, or involuntary (not controlled by the will), activities.

Remember that your body contains many muscles that work without conscious control, like the muscles of your heart, breathing apparatus, and digestive system. Remember, too, that your body contains glands that work without thought on your part. All of this automatic, involuntary work is controlled by the autonomic nervous system. The central nervous system, on the other hand, provides conscious control of voluntary activity.

Of course, your two nervous systems work together. In an emergency, for example, the central nervous system guides the actions of your muscles. At the same time, the autonomic nervous system speeds up or slows down your heartbeat, breathing, and energy production as necessary.

Let's Pause for Review

Your brain includes the cerebrum, which controls thought, the cerebellum, which controls coordination and balance, and the brain stem, which controls many involuntary, automatic acts. Nerves are groups of nerve fibers that carry messages from all parts of the body to the brain (or spinal cord) and back again. Nerve messages jump the synapse, or gap, between individual neurons.

You have two nervous systems. Together, they regulate and control all of your body's activities. Your brain and spinal cord make up your central nervous system, which controls all voluntary activity. Special nerves attached to your spinal cord and the medulla oblongata in your brain stem make up your autonomic nervous system, which guides actions not consciously controlled.

The Endocrine System: The Hormone Factory

The nervous system regulates, coordinates, and controls bodily activity, but not alone. It gets help from the **endocrine** (EN-duh-krun) **system,** which consists of several special glands. A **gland** is an organ that *secretes*, or produces, some material that is useful to the body. For example, salivary glands secrete saliva, which aids in digesting carbohydrates; the liver is a gland that secretes bile, which aids in digesting fats.

78   **How Your Body Works**

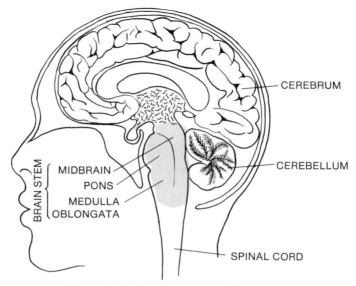

Figure 7.6. Brain (cut in half).

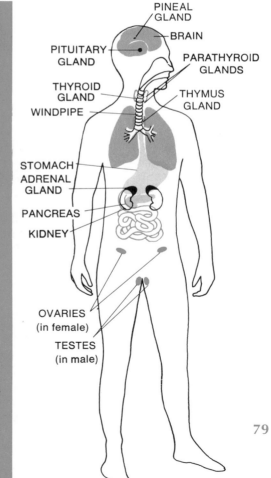

Figure 7.7. Locations of endocrine glands.

DUCTLESS GLANDS   Glands like the salivary glands and the liver pour their **secretions** out through tubes, or **ducts.** But the endocrine glands have no such ducts or other openings; they are ductless. The endocrine glands pour their secretions, called **hormones** (HAWR-mohnz), directly into the bloodstream. Each endocrine gland produces a different hormone, which does a special job. As they circulate in the bloodstream, the hormones influence growth, energy production, repair and replacement of body tissues, and the development of sex characteristics. In Figure 7.7, you can find the location of each of the endocrine glands you will now learn about.

THE PITUITARY GLAND: THE MASTER GLAND   The **pituitary** (puh-TYOO-uh-ter-ee) **gland** is a pea-sized gland at the base of the brain. Because its hormones control the activities of other endocrine glands, the pituitary gland is often called the *master gland* of the body. (Recent research has shown that the pituitary gland itself is controlled by a small part of the brain.) We know that this important gland produces at least eight different hormones. Here are four of them:

1. The hormone that regulates growth. This hormone keeps you growing until you reach adult size. Too much of this hormone can produce a giant. Too little can produce a midget or a dwarf. In Figure 7.8, you can see the effects of different amounts of the growth hormone. When the pituitary gland is no longer needed for growth, it continues to assist in life-maintaining processes.
2. The hormone that controls the development of the sex glands. This hormone stimulates the sex glands (see page 82) at **puberty** (PYOO-bur-tee), when the sex glands become active.
3. The hormone that helps control the amount of water in the tissues.
4. The hormones that influence other endocrine glands by slowing them down or speeding them up.

THE THYROID AND PARATHYROID GLANDS   The **thyroid** (THY-royd) **gland** is located at the base of the neck in front of the trachea (windpipe). It produces the hormone **thyroxin** (thy-RAHK-sin), which regulates the speed of energy production in body cells. Too much thyroxin makes a person jumpy and nervous. Too little may make a person listless and drowsy. Even worse, a lack of thyroxin in children may cause mental retardation and arrested growth.

To produce thyroxin, the thyroid gland needs a regular supply of iodine. Too little iodine in the diet causes a disturbance and swelling of the thyroid gland, called **goiter** (GOYT-ur). A good way to prevent goiter is to use iodized table salt.

The four tiny **parathyroid** (par-uh-THY-royd) **glands** are embedded in the back of the thyroid gland. They produce a hormone that is necessary for

How Your Body Works

Figure 7.8. *(below)* Dwarfs; *(right)* giant, shown with man of average height.

the body's use of calcium. An inadequate supply of this hormone will produce *spasm* (sudden contracting) and trembling of the muscles.

THE ADRENAL GLANDS: THE EMERGENCY GLANDS

Adrenal (uh-DREE-nul) means near the kidney, and that is where the **adrenal glands** are—just above the kidneys. When you become frightened, angry, or excited, the inner layer of your adrenal glands secretes the hormone commonly called **adrenaline** (uh-DREN-uh-lin). Adrenaline is sometimes called the "fight or flight" hormone because, in emergencies, it prepares your body either to fight or to run away quickly. It does this by making the heart beat faster, increasing the breathing rate, tensing the muscles, increasing the ability of the blood to clot, and providing extra energy. The extra energy comes from glucose (blood sugar), released into the bloodstream by the liver as soon as the adrenaline reaches the liver.

The outer layer of the adrenal glands produces several other hormones, which control the salt and water balance in your body. They also regulate the use of proteins and sugars. One of them, **cortisone** (KAWR-tuh-sohn), is often used as a medicine to help reduce inflammation, such as the painful joint inflammation of **arthritis** (ahr-THRY-tis).

THE PANCREAS   As you remember, the pancreas produces digestive juices. But part of the pancreas serves the endocrine system, too. Scattered groups of cells within the pancreas, known as the **islets** (EYE-luts) **of Langerhans** (LAHNG-ur-hahnz), secrete the hormone **insulin** (IN-suh-lin). Insulin regulates the body's use of sugar. A normal insulin output keeps the amount of glucose at a fairly constant level. Too small an output of insulin or the inability of some body cells to use insulin usually allows the amount of glucose in the blood to rise to abnormal levels. The resulting disease, **diabetes** (dy-uh-BEE-teez), can usually be controlled by injections of insulin or by oral medication that has a similar effect. (For more on diabetes, see Chapter 24, pages 423–425.)

THYMUS AND PINEAL GLANDS: THE MYSTERY GLANDS
The **thymus** (THY-mus) **gland,** located behind the sternum (breastbone), is relatively large in infancy but begins to shrink long before adulthood. Its function has long been a mystery. Only recently, scientists have discovered that certain cells derived from the thymus gland and a secretion from it in early life help the body fight infection.

The **pineal** (PIN-ee-ul) **gland,** located in the center of the brain, continues to puzzle scientists. Its function in human beings is still unknown.

OVARIES AND TESTES: THE SEX GLANDS   **Ovaries** (OH-vuh-reez) produce **ova,** or egg cells, and **testes** (TES-teez) produce **sperm cells;** both cells are used in reproduction. But since these glands also produce hormones, they serve the endocrine system, too. When stimulated to do so by the pituitary, these glands secrete hormones that trigger the onset of puberty. Ovaries, located in the abdomen of females, produce the female hormones responsible for the onset of menstruation and the appearance of breasts, rounded body contours, and other female sex characteristics. The testes, located in the **scrotum** (SKROH-tum), a sac suspended from outside the lower abdomen of males, secrete the male hormones that cause voices to lower, beards to grow, muscles to enlarge, and other male sex characteristics to appear.

Many endocrine glands and their products have been described so far. Before they get jumbled in your mind, try the following:

YOUR PART

1. In a vertical column on a separate piece of paper, write down the names of as many endocrine glands as you can remember.
2. Next to each gland write what it does for the body.
3. Compare your answers with those of the rest of the class to see if, as a group, you remembered all the glands.

You can check the completeness of your list by referring again to pages 78–82.

Looking Back

Your nervous systems provide your body with rapid communication and intelligent control. The central nervous system, made up of brain and spinal cord, controls your voluntary actions. The autonomic nervous system guides those actions you do not control consciously. The brain includes the cerebrum, the cerebellum, and the brain stem. All parts of the brain help with its computerlike work. At great speed, nerves carry messages from all body parts to the brain or spinal cord and back again. The nervous systems run things, so to speak, but not alone.

Your endocrine system assists your nervous systems by providing chemicals that regulate and stimulate much bodily activity. The endocrine system is made up of a number of separate glands. Each gland secretes one or more chemicals called hormones, which affect the activities of specific organs and tissues. Because these glands are ductless, they secrete directly into the bloodstream.

The master gland is the pituitary because its hormones control the activities of the other endocrine glands. The thyroid regulates the speed of energy production in cells. The parathyroid hormone enables your body to use calcium. The adrenal glands produce adrenaline, which gives you an extra burst of energy when you are frightened, angry, or excited. Other adrenal hormones control the body's salt and water balance, and the body's use of proteins and sugars. The adrenal hormone cortisone helps reduce inflammation. Insulin, manufactured in the pancreas, regulates the amount of glucose in the blood. Diabetes results when there is insufficient insulin or insulin cannot be used by certain body cells. Female hormones from the ovaries and male hormones from the testes trigger the onset of puberty.

MODIFIED TRUE-FALSE QUESTIONS

1. Most of the reactions performed by the nervous system involve the _brain_.

2. The _cerebellum_ does most of the work of the brain.

The Nervous and Endocrine Systems   83

3. Neurons consist of cell bodies, axons, and _synapses_.
4. The _nervous_ system enables us to react to our environment.
5. _Motor_ nerves gather and relay information about sensations.
6. The _pituitary_ gland is also known as the master gland.
7. Chemicals secreted by the endocrine glands are called _enzymes_.
8. The endocrine glands are _duct_ glands.
9. The gland located at the base of the brain is the _thyroid_ gland.
10. The use of iodized salt helps prevent _goiter_.
11. _Adrenalin_ prepares the body for emergencies.
12. The nervous system controls body activity with help from the _digestive_ system.
13. The _ovaries_ and testes produce hormones that trigger the onset of puberty.
14. The _thymus_ produces a hormone that regulates growth.
15. Hormones are carried throughout the body by the _circulatory_ system.
16. Unconscious actions are controlled by the body's _autonomic_ nervous system.
17. The passageway for nerve impulses between parts of the brain is the _pons_.
18. The _cerebrum_ controls coordination and balance.
19. The _parathyroid_ glands are located just above the kidneys.
20. Little is known about the function of the pineal gland and the _thymus_ gland.

MATCHING QUESTIONS

Column A	Column B
1. axon	a. spinal cord
2. dendrite	b. passageway for nerve impulses between the cerebrum and cerebellum
3. synapse	
4. brain stem	c. used to help reduce inflammation
5. medulla oblongata	d. branch of a nerve cell that receives messages
6. hormone	
7. parathyroid	e. helps body to fight infection
8. cortisone	f. fiber that sends messages out of a nerve cell
9. pancreas	
10. thymus	g. gap between nerve cells
	h. chemical secreted by an endocrine gland
	i. helps regulate action of vital organs
	j. helps body use calcium
	k. location of islets of Langerhans

COMPLETION QUESTIONS

1. The communication system of the body is called the _____ system.
2. The disease often caused by undersecretion of the islets of Langerhans is _____ .
3. A higher than normal rate of energy production is usually due to an overactive _____ .
4. Salt and water balance is controlled by the _____ glands.
5. The part of the brain that remembers, learns, plans, reasons, creates, and decides is known as the _____ .
6. The outer layer of the brain is called the _____ .
7. The part of the nervous system that works independently of the brain is the _____ system.
8. The brain can best be compared to a (an) _____ .
9. The _____ nerves gather and relay information about sensations.
10. Muscles associated with the skeletal system are directed by _____ nerves.

MULTIPLE-CHOICE QUESTIONS

1. Hormones secreted by a ductless gland are carried around the body by the system known as
   a. circulatory   b. digestive   c. urinary   d. nervous
2. The hormone that controls the development of the sex glands is produced in the gland called
   a. thyroid   b. parathyroid   c. thymus   d. pituitary
3. A person suffering from diabetes may have too little
   a. thyroxin   b. adrenalin   c. cortisone   d. insulin
4. The gland that may be responsible for mental retardation and arrested growth is the
   a. parathyroid   b. thyroid   c. thymus   d. pineal
5. The gland that is both a duct and ductless gland is the
   a. pituitary   b. parathyroid   c. pancreas   d. thyroid
6. Thinking is controlled by the
   a. brain stem   b. spinal cord   c. cerebellum   d. cerebrum
7. Voluntary muscular activity is controlled in the
   a. cerebral cortex   b. brain stem   c. medulla oblongata   d. pons
8. Automatic acts, such as the heartbeat and breathing, are
   a. voluntary   b. involuntary   c. reactions   d. habits

THOUGHT QUESTIONS

1. Describe the protections of the central nervous system.
2. Explain why an injury to the right side of the cerebrum can interfere with movement of the left side of the body.

The Nervous and Endocrine Systems   85

3. Describe how the duct and ductless glands carry on their functions.
4. Explain what can happen if the following glands secrete too little of their hormones: (a) parathyroid; (b) pituitary; (c) thyroid.
5. After a physical examination, Mary's doctor recommends that she see an endocrinologist. What might Mary's examination have revealed that would account for her doctor's recommendation?

Looking Ahead

Now you are ready to learn about how your senses and your nervous system work together. In Chapters 8 and 9, you will study two of your most precious senses, eyesight and hearing. You will learn how your eyes and ears work and what you can do to keep them working well.

How Your Body Works

Unit Three: HOW YOU SEE AND HEAR

What makes my eyes see?
What causes blindness?
How can I keep my eyes healthy, so I won't need to wear glasses?
Why does reading give me a headache sometimes?
Is it true that listening to rock music can make you deaf?
Why do I get dizzy when I spin around fast?
Why do my ears feel funny when I go up in an airplane?

Like most young people, you probably ask questions like these about your eyes and ears—two of the five sense organs that provide you with knowledge about your environment. Your environment includes light, heat, air, buildings, autos, trees, flowers, animals, and, of course, other people.

Sense organs are really extensions of the nervous system. They help the brain and other parts of the nervous system inform you that you are *you* and that there is a world outside your body.

Involuntary activities, such as digestion and circulation, go on inside your body without your being conscious of them. Such activities are controlled automatically by a special branch of the nervous system. At the same time, many things happen all around you, and your sense organs send this information to your brain. That is how you learn to adjust to the world outside your body. Most such adjustments are the results of voluntary brain-controlled actions.

Your sense organs help you in two major ways. First, they supply you with information about the environment. Second, they enable you to protect yourself against conditions in the environment that threaten your safety.

We have already described the sense organs of taste and smell in Chapter 6, pages 60 and 64. In this unit, we will concentrate on the eyes and ears. We will discuss the skin in Unit Four.

Chapter 8: You and Your Eyes

Everybody treasures the delights and the knowledge that eyesight brings. But not everybody knows for sure just how eyes work. To understand this, we need to know something about light.

How Light Behaves

The first thing to remember about light is that it can easily be made to **focus,** or form clear pictures. The second thing to remember is that, unless something bends light, it travels in a straight line. If it can't go through an object, light bounces off in the same way, and at the same angles, that a handball or a tennis ball bounces off a backboard. The bouncing off is called *reflection*. Light from the sun is reflected from everything around you, lighting up objects so that you can see them and cameras can photograph them.

HOW A PINHOLE CAMERA WORKS   If you have ever made a pinhole camera (see Figure 8.1), you probably understand the seeing process rather well. A homemade pinhole camera has only a tiny pinhole

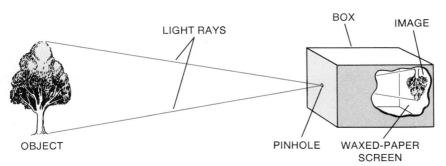

Figure 8.1. Homemade pinhole camera.

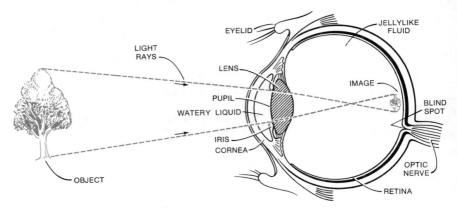

Figure 8.2. Formation of an image in the eye.

opening in the front to let in light. Only those light rays that are traveling in just the right direction can enter. Inside, those light rays do a strange thing. Within a short distance they form a clear picture, or **image,** on a screen at the back of the camera. (In a photographer's camera, the image is formed on film at the back of the camera.)

Light rays from the treetop in Figure 8.1 form the lowest part of the image. Light rays from the bottom of the tree trunk form the top of the image. This happens not because light turns things upside down, but because light travels in a straight line.

BENDING THE LIGHT   Light entering your eyes does the same thing, with one important difference. Light entering your eyes is bent so that it focuses in a much shorter distance than it does in a pinhole camera. Without this bending, your eye would have to be as big as a pinhole camera.

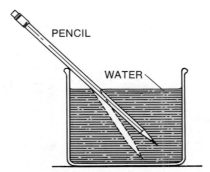

Figure 8.3. Bending of light by water.

How You See and Hear

Lens, Cornea, and Liquid

What bends the light? Three things do. The first is the **cornea,** a curved, transparent tissue in front of the eye (see Figure 8.2). The second is the **watery liquid** that fills the space behind the cornea. The third is the transparent **lens,** whose shape and placement bend light rays to a focus (see Figure 8.2). The cornea, the watery liquid, and the lens act together. As Figure 8.3 will remind you, you are already familiar with the way that a liquid bends light. To gain the same familiarity with the way a lens bends light, do the following:

YOUR PART

1. Inspect a magnifying glass. If you can't tell its shape by looking at it, use a tissue to protect the glass while you feel its shape. Write down whether its shape is the same as or different from the lens in Figure 8.2.
2. During daylight hours, find a white wall (or attach a sheet of white paper to a wall) that is opposite a window. Choose a window through which you can see something—a tree or building, for example. If the day is not cloudy, make sure that direct sunlight does not hit the magnifying glass, as you hold it about 6 inches (15 centimeters) away from the wall. Move the magnifying glass back and forth until an image forms on the wall. Write down what the image is and how it looks.

When you looked at or felt the magnifying glass, you found it was shaped like the lens in Figure 8.2, opposite. When you moved the glass back and forth, you found one point at which the light focused, or formed a clear image. This image was the same as the object (tree or building) outside of the window, except for one thing. The image on the wall was upside down.

The Retina

In the demonstration you just finished, light was focused on a wall. In a camera, light is focused on film at the rear of the camera. This light chemically affects the film. In your eye, light is focused on the **retina** (RET-uh-nuh *or* RET-nuh) (refer again to Figure 8.2, opposite) at the rear of your eyeball and affects the nerve cells there. These nerve cells, which are too small to be seen in the figure, are called **rods** and **cones** because of their shapes. Bright light and colors affect the cones. With them you see bright, colored things in sharp focus. (Color blindness, an incurable, inherited inability to see certain colors, usually results from some defect of the cones.) The rods are affected by dim light but not by color. With them you see only colorless shapes in a darkened room, for example. Owls and other night hunters rely more on their rod vision than human beings do.

The Optic Nerve

Nerve impulses travel from the retina to the brain by way of the **optic nerve.** In interpreting the impulses, your brain turns the image right side up, as you see it. In Figure 8.2, page 90, you can see where the optic nerve leaves the retina. At that point, there are no nerve cells to sense light. As a result, you have a small blind spot. To find your blind spot, do the following:

YOUR PART

1. On a separate piece of paper, draw a circle about the size of this O. About 2 inches (5 centimeters) to the right of it, draw a square about the same size. Fill both in so that they are easy to see.
2. Hold the paper at arm's length, with the circle directly in front of your right eye. Cover your left eye. As you bring the paper toward you, keep looking at the circle. Write down what happens.
3. Repeat the process, with the square in front of your left eye and with your right eye covered. Write down what happens.

As you brought the paper toward your face in step 2, the square should have disappeared for a moment. As you followed step 3, the circle should have disappeared. Your blind spots were responsible for the disappearances.

Protection for Your Eyes

For the most part, your precious eyes are protected by the bones of your skull. Your eyebrows, lashes, and eyelids keep things like dust out of your eyes. Look at Figure 8.2, page 90, again. In front, you see the cornea—the curved, transparent tissue that lets light into the eye and helps focus the light. The cornea is continuous with the tough white of the eye, which helps give the eyeball its shape and protects its inner structure. The space in the center of the eye is filled with a clear, jellylike liquid, which also helps give the eyeball its shape.

In Figure 8.4, you can see a gland that manufactures tears—not just when you cry or get something in your eyes, but all the time. When you blink, you spread the tears, which protect your eyes by bathing them and keeping them moist.

How You See and Hear

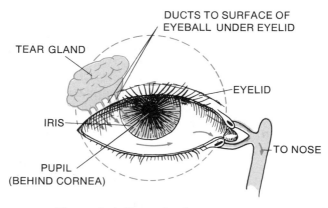

TEAR GLAND

DUCTS TO SURFACE OF
EYEBALL UNDER EYELID

EYELID

IRIS

PUPIL
(BEHIND CORNEA)

TO NOSE

Figure 8.4. Tear gland.

Light enters your eye through the cornea and then passes through the **pupil,** which looks dark because it is a hole leading into a dark chamber. Unlike the hole in a pinhole camera, this hole changes size. The **iris** (EYE-ris), the colored part of your eye, surrounds the pupil and does the changing to help protect your eye from too much light. In bright light, the muscles of the iris make the pupil's opening smaller. In dim light, they open the pupil wide to let in as much light as possible. To watch your iris at work, do the following:

YOUR PART

1. With a mirror and a small flashlight handy, sit for a moment in a dark room.
2. As you turn the flashlight on, watch your irises and pupils in the mirror. Write down what happened.
3. Now, still watching your irises and pupils, shine the flashlight in your eyes. Write down what happened.

As you turned the flashlight on, you watched your pupils contract, or shrink. Then, when you directed the beam of the flashlight into your eyes, you watched the pupils shrink again as the irises drew together still more.

HOW YOU CAN HELP   Clearly, your eyes have a good many built-in protectors, but you can help, too. When you read or otherwise work your eyes hard, look up now and then, and blink your eyes to rest and moisten them. Use enough light for reading—at least 100 watts. Sit with the light

You and Your Eyes

behind you and far enough to the side to keep shadows off the page. Sharp contrast, like that between bright light and dark shadow, tires the eyes. For this reason, when you read or watch TV, the rest of the room should be at least dimly lighted. In the daytime, avoid glare (uncomfortably bright light). Never look directly at the sun, even if you are wearing sunglasses. The sun's ultraviolet rays can permanently damage your retina.

Now do the following matching exercise to see how well you understand what you have read:

YOUR PART

By writing the correct pairs of numbers and letters on your paper, match these two lists:

Eye		Ordinary Camera	
1.	lens	a.	camera case
2.	pupil	b.	film
3.	retina	c.	diaphragm (regulator of opening)
4.	eyelid	d.	lens
5.	skull	e.	shutter
6.	iris	f.	aperture (opening)

Let's Pause for Review

Light bounces off objects in the world around you. Some of this bouncing light passes through your pupils. (The muscles of the iris enlarge or reduce the size of the pupil, as necessary, to control the amount of light entering.) Inside the eye, the cornea, the thin liquid behind it, and the lens bend the light so that it is focused on the retina. Nerve impulses travel to the brain by way of the optic nerve. Your brain interprets the impulses, and you see. Your skull, eyelids, lashes, and eyebrows protect your precious eyes. The white of the eye and the jellylike liquid at the center of the eye further protect and shape it. Tears, which are spread by blinking, help keep eyes clean and moist.

You can help protect your eyes. Use at least 100 watts to read by. Look up from your work and blink a few times to rest and moisten your eyes when you work them hard. Avoid sharp contrast by partially lighting the rest of the room when you read or watch TV. Avoid glare (uncomfortably bright light). Never look directly at the sun.

How You See and Hear

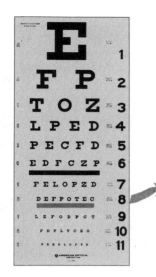

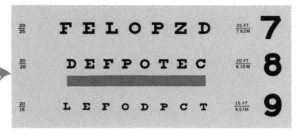

Figure 8.5. Reduced Snellen eye chart.

Testing Your Eyes

Your school may give eye tests regularly. Some school authorities recommend giving yearly tests, because most students who experience eyestrain, or unusual tiredness of the eyes, find it hard to concentrate on schoolwork. Another reason for yearly testing is that your eyes can change from year to year as long as you are growing.

Both schools and eye doctors often use a Snellen chart to test eyes (see Figure 8.5). At the end of each line on the chart, tiny numbers give the distance—in feet, and often in meters, too—at which normal eyes are able to read the line. If, at a distance of 20 feet (6.10 meters), you can read the line marked 20, you have normal vision. That is what 20/20 vision means. If you have 20/30 vision in one eye, you can barely read a line at 20 feet (6.10 meters) that you should be able to read at 30 feet (9.14 meters); vision in that eye is not quite as good as it should be.

WHEN YOU LEARN TO DRIVE   When you apply for a driver's license, you will probably have to take a Snellen eye chart test. Some states also test for **tunnel vision,** a defect that allows a person to see only what is looked at directly, as though through a tunnel. Normal eyes see many things on both sides of what they focus on, and this side vision is important to drivers. You can do the following test for tunnel vision yourself:

YOUR PART

1.   Hold your arms straight out in front of you and look straight ahead. Keeping arms at shoulder level, bring your arms back, as if you

were doing the breaststroke, until they are straight out from your sides. Wiggle your fingers as you move your arms.

2. Write down how long you were able to see your hands and wiggling fingers.

Even though you looked straight ahead, you could probably see your hands until your arms were almost straight out from your sides.

SEEING IN STEREO   Some states also test driving applicants to see how well they judge distance. You can judge both distance and depth (the relationship of objects at different distances) because you see with two eyes. This is something like listening to a stereo, which gives you a rich blend of sounds from two different sources. Your brain blends what is seen from two viewpoints—that of each eye—into one image. To see how this works, do the following:

YOUR PART

1. Put a narrow-necked bottle on a table at arm's length. Close or cover one eye. From a height of about 4 inches (10 centimeters), try to drop a paper clip into the bottle. Now try again with the other eye closed. With both eyes open, try it again.
2. Write down what happened in all three cases.

As you discovered, with both eyes open you easily judged the bottle's position correctly. With either eye closed, you probably missed the bottle, at least on the first try.

Muscles move your eyes in all directions. Sometimes, because of muscular imbalance, the eyes don't move as a unit, and they should. One eye or both may turn inward or outward. A person with one defective eye favors the image received by the better eye. In time, that person may lose some of the ability to see with the unused or underused eye. That is why it is important to correct such defects in early childhood, with exercises, glasses, surgery, or other corrective treatment.

Your Own Eyesight

Eye problems among students are very common, as reported by Dr. Benjamin Kogan in his book *Health: Man in a Changing Environment* (New York: Harcourt Brace Jovanovich, 1970). Dr. Kogan cites an earlier

How You See and Hear

study by Walter H. Fink, which showed that of 200,000 Philadelphia school children, nearly one in five was found to have eye problems of some kind. Such problems produce eyestrain whenever the eyes work hard. Here are some signs of eyestrain to watch for:

1. You squint or frown over your schoolwork.
2. The print blurs when you read.
3. You have trouble seeing the chalkboard.
4. You have many headaches.
5. Your eyes are often watery, or your eyelids are often crusty.
6. Your eyesight seems to be changing.
7. Your eyes bother you in any continuing way.

You should see your doctor if you suffer from one or more of these signs of eyestrain.

You should also see your doctor if you notice any unusual redness or discharge from either eye. If so, you may have **pinkeye,** or **conjunctivitis** (kun-junk-tih-VY-tis). Pinkeye is an inflammation of the lining of the eyelids and the covering of the front of the eyeball. Germs usually cause pinkeye, and it is often *contagious*, or catching. To help prevent infection, touch your eyes as little as you can.

Eyewash and Eye Makeup

Eyewashes may be helpful in clearing up mild cases of conjunctivitis and other conditions. However, eyewashes should not be used without consulting your doctor first. Some eyewashes contain drugs that can be harmful to some people.

In general, eye makeup is not harmful if it does not contain substances to which you may be *allergic* (sensitive). However, although makeup may not harm your skin or eyelashes, you must be careful to keep the makeup from getting into your eyes. Even substances that do not affect other parts of the body can be very irritating, if not harmful, to the eyes.

Three Kinds of Eye Specialists

Ophthalmologists (ahf-thal-MAHL-uh-jists), **optometrists** (ahp-TAHM-uh-trists), and **opticians** (ahp-TISH-unz) are all concerned with vision. An ophthalmologist, also called an **oculist** (AHK-yuh-list), is a medical doctor who treats diseases of the eye, measures vision, prescribes glasses, and performs eye surgery. An optometrist measures vision, prescribes glasses, and often makes and fits them to the patient; he is *not* a medical doctor. An optician grinds lenses, fits them into frames, and adjusts them to the wearer. The following activity will help you to remember which eye specialist is which:

1. Make three columns on your paper, one for each of the three eye specialists. List (by letter only) in the correct column each of the problems described in step 2.
2. Which eye specialist should be seen about the following problems:

    a. Your teachers say you hold books too close to your eyes when you read.
    b. Your ophthalmologist has given you a prescription for glasses.
    c. You blink all the time because your eyes bother you.
    d. Your family doctor has told you that you need glasses.
    e. When reading, you cover one eye to see more clearly.
    f. You have lost your new glasses.
    g. Your cousin's eyes cross when he is tired.
    h. Someone in your family needs eye surgery.
    i. The school nurse finds that you have pinkeye.

You probably put *(b)* and *(f)* in either the optician's or the op-tometrist's column, *(d)* in the optometrist's column, and all the rest in the ophthalmologist's column. However, you might choose to see your family doctor before you see an ophthalmologist. Then, if necessary, your doctor would refer you to the proper specialist.

Defects That Glasses Can Correct

Remember the experiment with the magnifying glass (refer again to page 91)? You found one point at which light from the window was focused perfectly and formed a clear picture. If you moved the glass backward or forward, the picture got fuzzy. The objects seen by the eyes can be fuzzy, too, and for the same reason—the light is being focused in the wrong place. You would probably need glasses to correct the following defects: near-sightedness, farsightedness, and astigmatism (see Figure 8.6).

NEARSIGHTEDNESS   In normal eyes, light is focused on the retina (refer again to Figure 8.2, page 90). In nearsightedness, or **myopia** (my-OH-pee-uh), the eyeball is too long from front to back, and light from distant objects is focused in front of the retina. A nearsighted person sees close things clearly, but faraway things are blurred.

FARSIGHTEDNESS   In farsightedness, or **hyperopia** (hy-puh-ROH-pee-uh), the eyeball is too short from front to back, and light from close objects strikes the retina before the light is focused. That is, the point of sharp focus would be behind the retina. A farsighted person sees distant things clearly. Near things are blurred.

The farsightedness that often develops in middle age has a different cause. The lens in a normal eye doesn't focus light by moving back and forth, as did the magnifying glass in the experiment on page 91. Instead, eye muscles attached to the lens change its shape for proper focus. In middle age, the lens sometimes stiffens and changes shape less easily. Small objects and near objects become harder to see.

ASTIGMATISM   In **astigmatism** (uh-STIG-muh-tiz-um), the cornea or the lens is curved unevenly. Some light is focused on the retina, some is focused in front of it, and some is focused behind it. A person can be nearsighted or farsighted and still have astigmatism.

Figure 8.6. Eye defects and their corrections: (a) **nearsightedness;**
(b) **farsightedness;** (c) **astigmatism.**

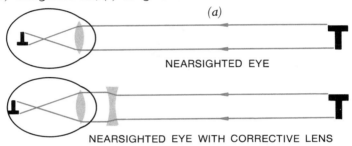

NEARSIGHTED EYE

NEARSIGHTED EYE WITH CORRECTIVE LENS

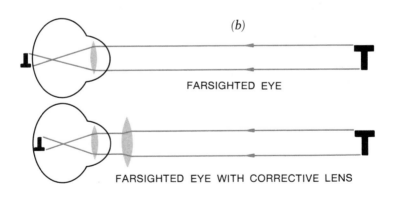

FARSIGHTED EYE

FARSIGHTED EYE WITH CORRECTIVE LENS

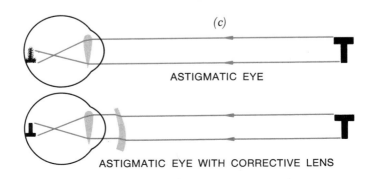

ASTIGMATIC EYE

ASTIGMATIC EYE WITH CORRECTIVE LENS

WEARING GLASSES OR CONTACT LENSES Remember that glasses do not *cure* eye defects. They merely help the eye to focus sharper images on the retina. You should wear your glasses for as long as they have been prescribed for you.

It is also important to remember one other thing about glasses. An eyeglass prescription is a tailor-made remedy for one person's eye defects. If you need glasses to see better, wear only the ones prescribed for you, and do not borrow glasses or lend your glasses to others.

In recent years, eye doctors have been prescribing *contact lenses* in place of eyeglasses for certain people in special situations. These lenses, unlike eyeglasses, are worn directly on the cornea. Contact lenses require great care in their use and are more expensive than regular glasses. Whether you should wear contact lenses or regular eyeglasses is a decision only your eye doctor should make.

Accidents

Students often ask what causes blindness. Among people who become blind during the teen years, accidents are the most common cause. Preventable accidents injure the eyes of more than half a million Americans every year. Blows to the eye seem to be the leading cause of accidental blindness. Injury with sharp objects seems to be the second greatest cause.

Remembering these facts, you won't want to take chances with your own eyes or the eyes of others. Keep sharp things away from your eyes. Follow the safety rules in home economics and shop classes and everywhere else they are posted. Take the time to put on safety glasses if you work at something that could be dangerous to your eyes.

Cataract

Out of every 100 blind people, about 3 are blinded accidentally, about 12 are blinded from unknown or unreported causes, about 25 are born blind (or become blind soon after birth), and about 60 become blind in middle or later life as a result of certain diseases such as **cataract** (KAT-uh-rakt) and **glaucoma** (glow-KOH-muh *or* gloh-KOH-muh). Cataract is the leading cause of blindness among people born with normal eyesight. With cataract, the eye lens, which is normally clear, becomes clouded. Fortunately, surgeons can usually remove a badly clouded lens. Glasses with corrective lenses are then worn to replace the lost lens or lenses. Eye specialists also recommend contact lenses following cataract surgery.

Glaucoma

The second greatest cause of blindness among people born with normal sight is glaucoma. Of every eight blind Americans, one is a victim of glaucoma. Glaucoma causes an increase of liquid pressure inside the eyeball, which damages it. When glaucoma develops suddenly, it is painful; people realize they must see a doctor right away. But when glaucoma develops slowly, only a doctor can recognize its early signs. Glaucoma can usually be controlled if discovered in time. You can see that regular eye examinations are important, especially after age 40, when glaucoma is most common.

Looking Back

Light enters your eyes and is bent and focused on the retina by the cornea, the liquid behind it, and the lens. Nerve impulses travel from the retina to the brain by way of the optic nerve. Your brain interprets the impulses, and you see. You can help protect your sight by having regular eye examinations, by using enough light when you read, by avoiding contrast and glare, by resting and blinking your eyes occasionally when you work, by touching your eyes as little as possible, and by doing all you can to avoid accidents. You can also help by seeing your doctor if you notice signs of eyestrain or infection, such as: squinting, frowning, blurring of the print, many headaches, unusual wateriness, redness, or discharge from the eyes.

There are three kinds of specialists to help you. Ophthalmologists (or oculists) are medical doctors who can perform eye surgery and treat eye disease, as well as measure vision and prescribe glasses. Optometrists are not doctors, but they can measure vision, prescribe glasses, and make and fit them. Opticians grind lenses, fit them into frames, and fit the frames and lenses to the wearer.

Nearsightedness, farsightedness, and astigmatism are eye defects in which light is not properly focused on the retina; all three defects can be corrected (but not cured) by eyeglasses.

Ophthalmologists can remove the clouded lenses of patients with cataract. They can also treat the increased liquid pressure inside the eyeballs of people with glaucoma, if the disease is discovered in time.

MODIFIED TRUE-FALSE QUESTIONS

1. An image appears upside down on the retina because light travels in <u>a straight</u> line.
2. Color blindness is usually inherited and results from some defect of the <u>rods.</u>

3. Frequent headaches and blurring of print may be symptoms of _eye-strain._

4. Wearing other people's eyeglasses is _an acceptable_ health habit.

5. The _eye_ is very much like a camera.

6. If light rays focus _in front of_ the retina, the individual has normal vision.

7. _A myopic_ person can see things clearly from a distance but not things that are up close.

8. _Tears_ protect eyes by bathing them and keeping them moist.

9. The dark part of the eye, which acts as an aperture, or opening, is known as the _iris._

10. A person who has _normal_ vision cannot see what is happening on either side of him or her.

11. The _iris_ regulates the amount of light entering the eye.

12. We can judge depth and _distance_ because we see with two eyes.

13. The white part of the eye gives the eyeball its _shape._

14. A defective eye that is not used gets _better_ as a person grows older.

15. _Glaucoma_ is the leading cause of blindness among people born with normal eyesight.

16. An increase in liquid pressure in the eye can cause _cataracts._

17. Another name for pinkeye is _astigmatism._

18. Contact lenses are worn directly on the _cornea._

MATCHING QUESTIONS

Column A		Column B
1. blind spot	a.	helps us see bright, colored things
2. rod vision	b.	upside-down image
3. cone vision	c.	helps us see in dim light
4. pinhole camera	d.	curved, transparent tissue
5. cornea	e.	disappearing circles and squares
	f.	"hole" in the eye

COMPLETION QUESTIONS

1. Nerve impulses travel from the retina to the brain by way of the _____.

2. Light enters the eye through the _____.

3. Because there are no nerve cells to sense light where the optic nerve leaves the _____, you have a blind spot there.

4. What we see with two eyes is formed into one image by the_____.

5. The medical doctor who specializes in diseases of the eye is known as a (an) _____.

MULTIPLE-CHOICE QUESTIONS

1. Of every eight blind Americans, one is a victim of
   a. glaucoma   *b.* birth defects   *c.* cataract   *d.* accidents
2. Pinkeye can be described as
   a.   a clouding of the lens of the eye
   b.   an increase of liquid pressure inside the eye
   c.   an astigmatism
   d.   an inflammation of the inner lining of the eyelids and the outer lining
        of the eyeball
3. A cataract is
   a.   a clouded lens of the eye
   b.   an increase of liquid pressure inside the eye
   c.   a crusty eyelid
   d.   an inflammation of the eyelids
4. An optician
   a.   treats diseases of the eye
   b.   measures vision and prescribes glasses
   c.   grinds lenses, fits them into frames, and adjusts frames
   d.   is a medical doctor
5. People who see close objects better than distant ones are likely to have
   a. astigmatism   *b.* hyperopia   *c.* cataracts   *d.* myopia

THOUGHT QUESTIONS

1. Explain what is meant by the expression, "You see with your brain and
   not with your eyes."
2. The Snellen chart is an instrument commonly used to test the vision of
   schoolchildren. If a reading of 20/20 is considered good vision, how can
   the following readings be interpreted? *(a)* 20/40 right eye, 20/20 left eye;
   (b) 20/15 right eye, 20/20 left eye; *(c)* 20/50 right eye, 20/50 left eye.
3. List five ways to keep your eyes healthy.
4. Describe when it is most advisable to consult an *(a)* optician; *(b)* optometrist; *(c)* ophthalmologist.
5. Suppose you are a basketball player who is nearsighted and wears glasses
   prescribed by your eye doctor. You decide you would prefer to use
   contact lenses in place of your regular eyeglasses. Indicate which eye
   specialist you would consult, and defend your choice.

Looking Ahead

One of the greatest pleasures in life is listening—to music, to
natural sounds, or to the conversation of friends. In Chapter 9,
you will study the sense of hearing—how sound travels to
waiting ears and how hearing works. Also, you will learn how
your inner ear helps your balance.

Chapter 9: Your Ears: Hearing and Balance

It would be difficult to decide whether sight or hearing is more precious. You can't deny that many of the sounds around you are either a source of pleasure, an important warning device, or a means of learning and communication.

Unfortunately, today's world is noisy and full of unpleasant sounds, too. Over a period of time, loud noises, even those you like, can make you lose some of your ability to hear. Rock musicians who use electrical amplifiers (see Figure 9.1) often wear earplugs to protect their own hearing. As we shall see, doctors now believe that those who listen to rock music may need protection, too.

YOUR PART

1. Choose a partner, and then decide on a listening post. It may be your home, a bus stop, the school cafeteria, or anywhere else.
2. Have your partner prepare a description sheet with four column heads: *Natural Sounds; Machine-Made Sounds; Location Sounds;* and *Warning Sounds.*
3. Close your eyes and listen for at least 3 minutes to the sounds around you.
4. Tell your partner each sound you hear so that she or he can write it down on the description sheet.
5. Bring your list to class the next day, and compare it to your classmates' lists.

You may have been surprised to realize how much your ears alone tell you about the world every moment of your life. You are so used to this constant stream of information about what goes on around you that you hear most of it without even realizing it. How does hearing work? How are sounds produced, and how do they reach your brain?

Sound Vibrations

Sound begins when something—a bell, a drum, a motor—makes particles of air *vibrate*, or quiver. If you ring a large gong and then touch it, you will feel its vibrations. It makes the air around it vibrate, too. Vibrations travel through the air to listening ears. The human ear can hear sounds that vibrate from about 16 times to 20,000 times per second. If you have ever dropped a stone in a pool of water, you have seen something very much like the wave motion of sound vibrations in the air.

YOUR PART

1. Fill a tub with water. Drop a coin into it. Write down what happens to the waves as they spread across the tub.
2. Remove the coin and put your hand into the water close to one side of the tub. Keep your hand in the water and, when the surface is still, drop the coin in again. Write down what happens when the waves reach your hand.
3. Bring your answers to class for comparison with those of your classmates.

Doubtless you agreed that the waves got larger but weaker as they spread, and that they bounced off your hand when they hit it.

Sound waves behave like the waves you created in the experiment. *Sonar* is an invention that uses special bouncing sound waves to find things such as the depth of the ocean floor or the presence of submarines under water.

Figure 9.1. Loud music played by groups like this can damage your hearing.

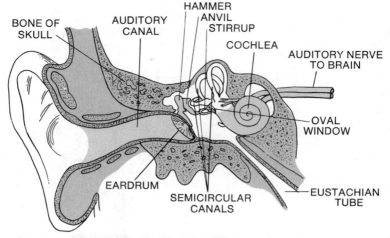

Figure 9.2. Parts of the ear.

The Outer Ear

When you refer to your ear, you usually mean one of the fan-shaped flaps attached to the sides of your head. Like an old-fashioned, funnel-like ear trumpet, each flap collects the sound waves that reach you and directs them into an inch-long tube called the **auditory** (aw-duh-TAW-ree) **canal** (see Figure 9.2). Both the fan-shaped flap and the auditory canal make up the outer ear. The auditory canal ends at the **eardrum, or tympanic** (tim-PAN-ik) **membrane,** which vibrates, like the drumhead it resembles, when sound vibrations reach it.

The Middle Ear

Beyond the eardrum lies the middle ear, a small chamber almost completely protected by surrounding bone. The three smallest bones in your body—the **hammer,** the **anvil,** and the **stirrup** (STIR-up)—stretch across the middle ear in a chain. If you look again at Figure 9.2, you can see that these little bones were named for their shapes.

The handle of the hammer is attached to the eardrum. When the eardrum vibrates, the little bones do, too, and in the same manner. They not only pass the sound vibrations on, they *amplify,* or increase, the force of the vibrations. Part of the last bone, the stirrup, rests on a membrane that covers an opening to the inner ear. This opening, or hole, is the **oval window.**

The Inner Ear

Within the inner ear lies the **cochlea** (KOH-klee-uh), which means snail shell. The vibrating stirrup sets in motion fluid within the inner ear. Nerve

How You See and Hear

endings within the cochlea sense the vibrations and send them on as nerve impulses, or signals, to the brain by way of the **auditory,** or hearing, **nerve.** The brain interprets these impulses as sound.

All of this happens very fast. Here is an activity to show you how fast:

YOUR PART

1. Watch carefully as a classmate claps hands once, pauses, and then claps again.
2. Was there any time lapse between the time you saw your classmate clap and the time you heard the sound?

In all likelihood, all of you heard the sound the same instant that your classmate made it. If the sound were made from far away, though, you would see the making of it before you heard it, because sound travels more slowly than light.

Let's Pause for Review

Sound begins when something—a bell, for example—vibrates. Sound vibrations cause air particles to move in ever-widening circles until some of them reach you. Your outer ear collects the vibrations and directs them to your eardrum. The vibrating eardrum moves the three little bones in the middle ear, thereby increasing the sound. The stirrup sets fluid in motion within the inner ear. Nerve endings in the cochlea change these vibrations into nerve impulses, which travel to the brain by way of the auditory nerve. When these impulses reach the hearing center of your brain, you are aware of hearing the bell.

Balance and the Inner Ear

The inner ear does more than help you to hear. In addition to the cochlea, the inner ear contains three **semicircular** (sem-ee-SUR-kyuh-lur) **canals,** which help you keep your balance (refer again to Figure 9.2, opposite). These canals contain both a liquid and some nerve endings. As you whirl, bend, pivot, or somersault, the liquid inside the canals also moves. Sensing the movement of the liquid, the nerve endings send impulses to the brain. The brain decides what muscles need to move to help you keep your balance. The following demonstration will help you understand how the semicircular canals do their job:

1. Fill a test tube half full of water. Put a stopper in the top. (Or use a tall, slender jar that has a cover.) Turning the test tube (or jar) in your hands, note how quickly the water copies any movement you make.
2. Now, hold the test tube (or jar) in one hand and turn it on its side. Balance the tube by making sure that the water is perfectly level. If the test tube were lined with nerve endings, you can see that they would sense the slightest imbalance at once.
3. On a broad table, lay the test tube on its side. Note the normal water level at rest. Spin the test tube around. Note that it takes a little time for the water to return to normal after the spinning has stopped. How does this explain the momentary dizziness you sometimes feel after spinning around or straightening up suddenly?

You probably noted that water doesn't return to its normal level immediately after rapid motion. Sometimes the liquid in the semi-circular canals doesn't adjust immediately either, and you can feel briefly dizzy as a result.

Two Kinds of Hearing Loss

Partial or complete hearing loss is of two main kinds: *conduction deafness* and *nerve deafness*. In conduction deafness, sound waves can't be passed along to the inner ear. Something has blocked the auditory canal, harmed the eardrum, or damaged the chain of bones in the middle ear. In nerve deafness, nerve impulses are either absent or they are blocked or changed on their way from the cochlea to the brain.

NERVE DEAFNESS AND LOUD SOUNDS   Even at low levels, continuous noise (unpleasant sound) has an unfavorable effect on the circulatory and nervous systems. When noise is very loud, it can cause nerve deafness. A very loud sound heard just *once* can bring about hearing loss. More often, though, damage to hearing is a result of repeated or continuous exposure to loud sound.

Loud sound causes hearing loss by destroying the tiny, sound-sensing nerve cells in the cochlea. Such hearing loss is likely to be permanent, and it may gradually worsen over a lifetime. No existing hearing aid can help a person with this kind of hearing loss, because there is no known way to pass sound impulses along to the brain, once the nerve cells are destroyed.

Decibels   Doctors have long recommended devices such as earplugs to people exposed to noise on the job (see Figure 9.3). But now doctors are

108   **How You See and Hear**

Figure 9.3. Ear covers protect the hearing of people who work in noisy places.

finding something new—hearing loss among young people continuously exposed to electrically amplified music. The relative loudness of sound is measured in **decibels** (DEHS-ih-bels). Decibel counts work this way: A 10-decibel sound is 10 times as loud as a 1-decibel sound. A 20-decibel sound is 100 times as loud as a 1-decibel sound. And a 30-decibel sound is 1000 times as loud as a 1-decibel sound.

How can you tell when music and other sounds are too loud? Table 9.1, page 111, gives the decibel (db) counts of many common sounds.

Warning Signals and Precautions   How can you protect your hearing from sounds of more than 100 decibels? Of course, the best way is to avoid them. Most people can avoid the noise of jet takeoffs, at least on a regular basis. But for young people, rock music may be a harder temptation to resist. Keeping this in mind, read and remember the following list of warning signals:

1. After listening to loud music, you have a ringing in your ears.
2. You have a "full" feeling or a sense of pain in your ears (only some of us are lucky enough to have this built-in warning).
3. It's hard or impossible to talk and listen to others.
4. After the music has stopped, you have a lingering feeling that your hearing is dulled.
5. You know that you make a regular habit of listening to very loud music.

These warning signals indicate exposure to sounds loud enough and prolonged enough to damage your hearing.

Do you have to give up the music you like? Not at all. But here is a list of listening suggestions you would be wise to follow:

1. If you work in a band or in a place where loud music is unavoidable, get yourself some ear molds or protective muffs. They can reduce the noise to less dangerous levels.
2. When playing your stereo, at the first painful or "full" sensation, turn the volume down.
3. If you like your music loud, take a 5-minute break every 30 minutes.
4. Give up headphones.
5. Have your doctor test your hearing at least twice a year.

In addition, remember to wear earplugs if your work consistently exposes you to loud noise. And if auto mechanics is your hobby, always test noisy engines out in the open where sound waves won't bounce off walls and hit your ears a second time. (Also, you won't feel the effect of the exhaust fumes if the engine is running outdoors.)

CONDUCTION DEAFNESS: BLOCKED SOUND WAVES

Various things can block the auditory canal. A wax buildup there is common. Removing this wax is a job for your family doctor or for an **otologist** (oh-TAHL-uh-jist), a physician who specializes in problems of the ears. You, yourself, should never do more than clean your outer ears daily with a soft, soapy washcloth.

Conduction Deafness and Infection Diseases like mumps and scarlet fever, sinus infections, and colds often cause temporary hearing loss by producing swelling within the ears. If such an infection gives you an earache, see your doctor right away. An infection in the middle ear can damage the chain of bones there, keep them from moving freely, or fill the area with **pus**, the thick yellowish fluid produced by infection, which contains germs, dead cells, and body fluid. You can help prevent infection of the middle ear by blowing your nose properly when you have a cold. Leave both nostrils open and blow gently. In this way, you probably won't force infectious material from the nose or throat into the middle ear.

The Eustachian Tube The **Eustachian** (yoo-STAY-shun or yoo-STAY-kee-un) **tube** leads from an opening in the middle ear to the back of the nose and throat (refer again to Figure 9.2, page 106). This tube keeps the eardrum from being burst by changes in air pressure. Most of the time, the Eustachian tube is closed, but you have felt it open up. That is what happens when your ears "pop" as you drive up a steep mountain road, ride the elevator to the top of a skyscraper, take off or land in an airplane, or go scuba diving. At such times, as you swallow or yawn, the tube opens and equalizes pressure on both sides of the eardrum.

When you have a cold or sore throat, swelling may keep the Eustachian

Table 9.1:   Decibel Counts of Common Sounds

Sound	Decibels
Hearing threshold	
Deepest bass pipe on organ	10 db
Rustling leaves	20 db
Normal whisper	30 db
Softly playing radio	40 db
Soft speech	50 db
Threshold of annoyance	
Normal conversation	60 db
Group conversation	70 db
Narrowing of arteries, rise in blood pressure	
Vacuum cleaner	80 db
Electric mixer	82 db
Garbage disposal	84 db
Range vent fan	88 db
Food blender	90 db
Loud orchestral music	90 db
Possible hearing damage from continuous exposure	
Jet plane at 1000 feet	105 db
Jet plane taking off	110 db
Rock music	110 db
Supersonic transport (SST) taking off	120 db
Threshold of pain	
Amplified music	130–140 db
Possible hearing damage from brief exposure	
Cap pistol	163 db

tube from opening freely into your throat. If possible, at such times you should avoid airplane trips and other activities involving changes in air pressure. Never hold your nose and force air pressure into your ears. Like violent nose blowing, such an action can drive infectious material into the middle ear.

Conduction Deafness and the Eardrum   A pressure change, a sharp blow, or an untreated infection can burst the eardrum. "Cleaning" the ears with hairpins or matchsticks can puncture it. When it heals, the

Your Ears: Hearing and Balance   111

(a)   (b)   (c)

Figure 9.4. Types of hearing aids: (a) over-the-ear type; (b) eyeglass type; (c) in-the-ear type; (d) on-the-body type.

eardrum may be scarred, and the sound vibrations that it passes on may not be normal. Protect your eardrums. Have infections treated, and if you take part in a sport that could be dangerous to the ears, wear the proper headgear.

Conduction Deafness and Otosclerosis   The tendency to develop **otosclerosis** (oh-tuh-skluh-ROH-sis) seems to be inherited. In this type of deafness, an abnormal growth of bone within the inner ear interferes with movement of both the stirrup bone of the middle ear and the oval window. Otosclerosis usually begins to develop in the teens and progresses until middle life. Fortunately, surgeons in recent years have learned how to do a delicate operation that often cures this type of deafness.

Except for hearing loss due to loud noise, all of the examples just given involve conduction deafness. To get an idea of how a person with a conduction hearing loss might still be helped to hear, try the following experiment:

YOUR PART

1. Take a flat-handled stainless steel table fork, hold it by the handle, and strike the *prongs* against a solid object. Quickly bring the prongs close to your ear. Write down what you hear.
2. Now strike the prongs again and quickly place the tip of the fork *handle* against your teeth. Write down what you hear now. Write down how you think this second sound reached your brain.

Health scientists have made hearing aids based upon what you have just observed: namely, that bones can pass sound vibrations along. This

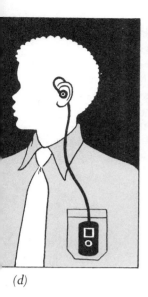

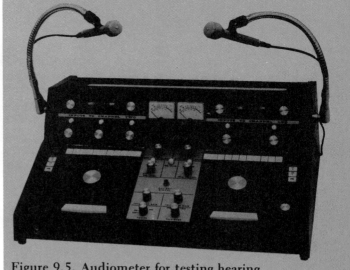

Figure 9.5. Audiometer for testing hearing.

(d)

type of aid, called a bone conduction hearing aid, uses the bones of the skull to pass sound waves along until they reach the nerve endings in the cochlea. In this way, sound can bypass the outer and middle ear and still reach the brain. Figure 9.4 shows you some of the hearing aids (for conduction hearing loss) available today. When surgery, medical treatment, or hearing aids are not effective, a deaf person can still get along well enough by learning how to read lips.

The Audiometer

If you suspect a hearing loss, see your doctor, especially if the hearing loss follows an infection of the nose or throat. If, after examining and treating you, your doctor thinks it necessary, he or she will have you take an easy, pleasant test, using an instrument called an **audiometer** (aw-dee-AHM-uh-tur). An audiometer (see Figure 9.5) tells your doctor exactly how much hearing loss has occurred.

Looking Back

Your ears enable you to hear and to keep your balance. Sound vibrations collected by your outer ear are passed along by the eardrum and the bones of the middle ear to the fluid in the cochlea of the inner ear. Nerve endings in the cochlea sense these vibrations and send them as nerve impulses to the brain,

Your Ears: Hearing and Balance

which interprets them as sound. The inner ear also helps you keep your balance by means of three small canals; they contain a liquid whose movement is sensed by nerve endings that send motion messages to the brain.

You can protect your precious hearing in many ways. Avoid loud noises when you can, or muffle them by means of ear coverings. Never poke anything into your ears. Clean them with a soapy washcloth. Take care of nose and throat infections. Don't spread infections to the inner ear by blowing your nose violently or with the nostrils closed. See your doctor if you have an earache or suspect a hearing loss.

MODIFIED TRUE-FALSE QUESTIONS

1. The loudness of noise in the environment is measured in _decibels._
2. A good way of cleaning an ear is to use _a matchstick._
3. _All_ forms of deafness can be helped by hearing aids.
4. _Inner_ ear infections are frequently caused by improper blowing of the nose.
5. Pressure changes on the eardrum are equalized by the _Eustachian tube._
6. Blasting music generally has a decibel rating of _under_ 100 decibels.
7. The _auditory_ nerve is the nerve of hearing.
8. Wax in the auditory canal can cause _temporary_ deafness.
9. _Air_ vibrations are responsible for the sounds we hear.
10. The three _smallest_ bones in the body are found in the ear.

MATCHING QUESTIONS

Column A	Column B
1. Eustachian tube	a. responsible for our sense of balance
2. cochlea	
3. semicircular canals	b. leads from middle ear to back of nose and throat
4. tympanic membrane	
5. audiometer	c. nerve endings for hearing are found in this snail-shaped organ
	d. detects hearing loss
	e. resembles a drumskin
	f. collects sound waves

114

COMPLETION QUESTIONS

1. The middle ear is separated from the outer ear by the _____ .
2. The hammer, the anvil, and the stirrup are found in the _____ ear.
3. Nerve endings that sense vibrations and send them on to the brain along the auditory nerve are found in the _____ .
4. The tube leading to the eardrum is the _____ .
5. The physician who specializes in problems of the ear is the _____ .

MULTIPLE-CHOICE QUESTIONS

1. The hammer, the anvil, and the stirrup conduct vibrations from the eardrum to the
   a. outer ear   b. inner ear   c. middle ear   d. brain
2. A bone found in the middle ear is the
   a. Eustachian tube   b. tympanic membrane   c. cochlea   d. stirrup
3. The air pressure in the middle ear is normally kept equal to the air pressure in the outer ear by the
   a. tympanic membrane   c. Eustachian tube
   b. cochlea   d. auditory nerve
4. An inherited type of deafness, which usually begins in the teens and progresses to middle age, is
   a. conjunctivitis   b. otitis   c. otosclerosis   d. myopia
5. Some hearing aids pass sound waves along the bones of the
   a. ear   b. skull   c. throat   d. nose

THOUGHT QUESTIONS

1. You have a friend who always listens to blasting music. What advice can you give your friend to help prevent hearing loss?
2. Discuss the following statement: "Improper blowing of the nose can cause ear problems." Include in your answer a description of the proper method of blowing the nose.
3. Why do doctors usually specialize in ear, nose, and throat rather than in only one of these structures?
4. Would you expect a person with inflamed semicircular canals to perform well as an acrobat? Give a reason for your answer.
5. You awake one morning, aware that you cannot hear through one ear. What should you do before seeking the advice of your doctor?
6. Is it possible for certain animals to hear sounds that humans cannot? Defend your answer.

Looking Ahead

Sight and hearing enable you to adjust to your environment, but they are not alone in this respect. Your skin, like your eyes and ears, senses the world around you. At the same time, it protects you from it. Moreover, as the largest organ of your body, your skin and its condition will determine how you look to others. Can you be attractive if your skin, hair, and nails aren't attractive, too? It's hard to see how. Good looks and good health begin with clean, healthy skin, hair, and nails. In Chapter 10, you will read about the functions of the skin. You will also learn about the kind of daily personal care that can make you feel and look your best.

How You See and Hear

Unit Four: THE APPEARANCE, CARE, AND FEEDING OF YOUR BODY

How can you keep skin nice?

Why do people get cavities?

Is there any way that I can prevent losing my teeth when I get older?

Will it hurt if I have my teeth straightened?

What is a good diet for losing weight?

How much sleep do I need?

How can you keep yourself looking attractive?

These are some of the questions that students ask about their personal appearance and health. Few people realize that the way they impress others depends on two factors. One of these is appearance. Is the person clean and neat in all observable respects? What is the condition of the skin, eyes, teeth, hair, nails, and clothing? The second factor is the impression the person gives of good health—mental and emotional, as well as physical. Does the person appear to be physically fit, alert, vigorous, clear-eyed, and stable?

Many people do not realize that good health and looking good (appearance) generally go together. A good appearance is often an important outward sign of good health.

Good health depends on more than avoiding certain diseases. It depends primarily on building a strong body that can resist disease. Such a body is the result of proper diet and eating habits, regular medical and dental care, regular exercise, and sufficient daily rest. Once a person's body is healthy, it will be physically trim. Then proper daily care of the skin, hair, nails, and teeth will add to the person's attractiveness.

What decisions will you make regarding your health and appearance? Will you choose to be as attractive, trim, and healthy as you possibly can be? Soon, all health and grooming decisions will be yours. The chapters in this unit are designed to help you in making those decisions.

The Appearance, Care, and Feeding of Your Body

Chapter 10: Skin, Hair, and Nails: The Outward Signs of Good Health

Young people today deserve congratulations. They like what is natural. As a result, young skin nowadays is rarely caked with heavy makeup. Hair is no longer as heavily greased or sprayed as it was in the past. Instead, today's natural tastes and styles are responsible for the beautiful hair and skin we see everywhere. This chapter will discuss what your skin, hair, and nails do for you, as well as what you can do to care for them. As an added bonus, every bit of care you give them makes you look better.

Your Skin and Your Nervous System

Your skin is actually the largest organ in your body. It does many jobs. Like your eyes and ears, your skin senses conditions outside your body and sends the news to your brain by way of nerves. The nerve cells in the skin and other organs that receive outside impressions are called **receptors.**

In Figure 10.1, you can see that the skin receptors differ according to the job they do. Pain, heat, and cold receptors, for example, warn you of

Figure 10.1. Receptors in the skin.

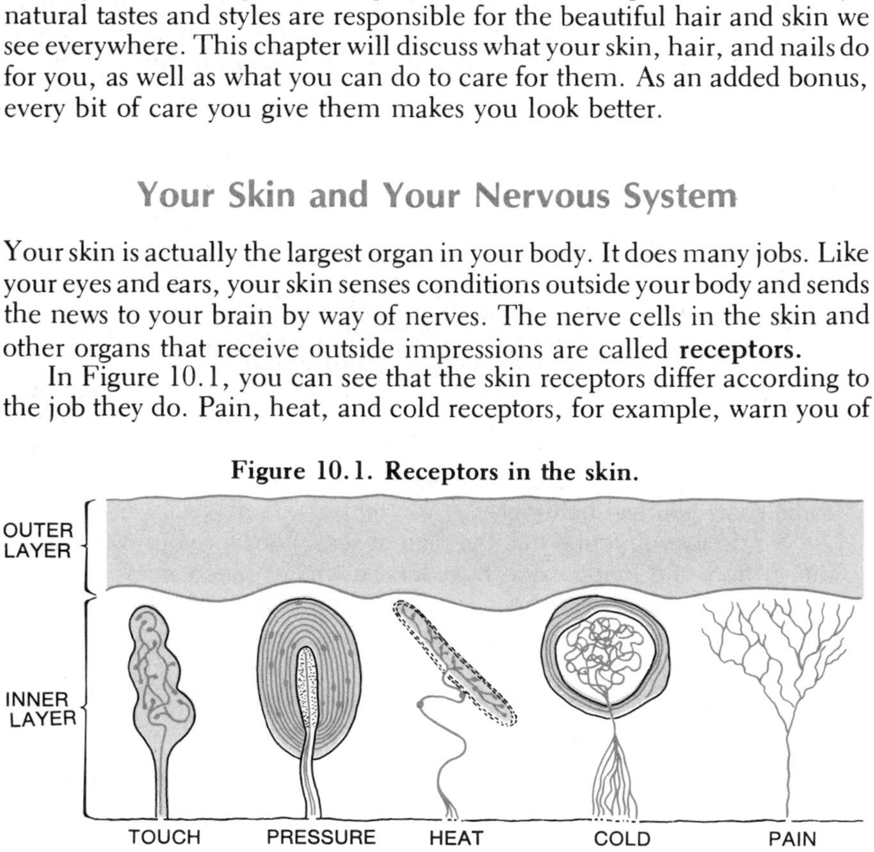

OUTER LAYER

INNER LAYER

TOUCH PRESSURE HEAT COLD PAIN

danger and discomfort. The various kinds of touch receptors help you tell the difference between things by their shapes, sizes, and surfaces. Even when things look alike to your eyes, your touch receptors may tell you that (1) they are really unalike or (2) they feel different to different parts of your skin. You can map the receptors in your hand by doing the following activity:

YOUR PART

MATERIALS
You will need a ball-point pen, some colored pencils (green, red, blue, black), a ruler, and a toothpick.

PROCEDURE
1. Choose a partner.
2. With the pen, draw a 1-inch (2.5-centimeter) square on the back of your hand. Draw four 1-inch (2.5-centimeter) squares on a piece of paper, labeling them *Heat, Cold, Pressure, Pain.* Make 20 evenly spaced dots inside each square, including the one on your hand. Have your partner do the same.
3. Keep your eyes closed as your partner presses a pencil point lightly against the first dot on your hand. Care should be taken not to puncture the skin. If you feel the pressure of the pencil, but no pain, tell your partner, who will color the corresponding dot green in the pressure square on your paper. If you feel a brief warm flash, the dot in the heat square should be colored red. If you feel a brief cool flash, the dot in the cold square should be colored blue. If you feel nothing, no dot should be colored.
4. Repeat this procedure, using a toothpick and pressing firmly. If you feel a brief sharp pain, the dot in the pain square should be colored black.
5. Repeat steps 3 and 4 until all 20 spots have been tested.
6. Open your eyes and carry out steps 3, 4, and 5 on your partner.

Isn't it strange that the same pencil point feels different on different spots of your skin, and that the point of a toothpick is painful on some spots and not on others? In some spots you felt warmth, in some coolness, in some pressure, and in some pain. It is even possible that in some spots you feel nothing!

No doubt you found that the map of sensations for your own skin differs from the maps made by your classmates. Such maps are as different as fingerprints.

If you try similar experiments on your fingertips and the middle of your back, you will find that maps of these areas are also very different. The skin

The Appearance, Care, and Feeding of Your Body

receptors of the fingertips are closer together and more numerous than those of the back. This explains why the fingertips are so sensitive. How would you explain why the lips are even more sensitive than the fingertips?

Your Skin and Your Body Temperature

Your skin receptors constantly give you the latest weather report of the region around your body. Blood vessels and sweat glands in your skin help your body to react to those weather reports. In Figure 10.2, you can see the tiny capillaries that supply the skin with blood. In hot weather, the capillaries expand, enlarging their surface areas. More body heat is given off from these enlarged surfaces.

In cold weather, the capillaries contract, or draw together. Less body heat is lost from their reduced surface areas. **Erector muscles** (shown in Figure 10.2) pull on the skin hairs. As these muscles work, they release a little heat and help keep the body warm. You can tell these muscles are working, for example, when you get "goose bumps" on your arms, and the tiny arm hairs stand on end. Perhaps you have seen a growling dog with its hackles, or neck hairs, erect. Your "goose bumps" and hair standing on end can be caused by fear, too.

Your Skin Eliminates Wastes

You have more than two million **sweat glands** like the one you can see in Figure 10.2. In hot weather, they give off more moisture than in cold weather. That moisture, drying on the skin, cools it. In addition, in hot weather and cold the sweat glands help the kidneys by collecting waste

Figure 10.2. Cross section of skin.

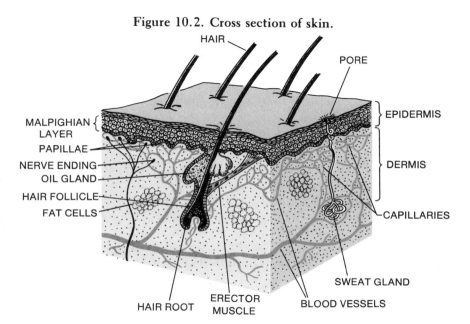

materials from the blood. This liquid waste, called **perspiration** (pur-spuh-RAY-shun), or sweat, leaves the body through openings in the skin called **pores** (PAWRZ).

The quart or so (about 1 liter) of perspiration given off by most of your body every day is almost odorless in itself. However, the perspiration given off by some sweat glands, such as those in the armpits, has a distinct odor. As soon as perspiration reaches the skin's surface, bacteria there begin to act upon it. This action produces more odor. Anything that increases perspiration—exercise, emotional stress, hot weather—can increase odor, as well.

(a)

DEODORANTS AND ANTIPERSPIRANTS   Many underarm sweat glands first become active in adolescence. For this reason, it is in adolescence that people usually begin to use *deodorants* (dee-OH-duh-runts) and *antiperspirants* (an-tih-PURS-puh-rents). Both preparations disguise perspiration odor. In addition, antiperspirants slow down or stop underarm perspiration. Deodorants do nothing to stop perspiration, but some of them slow down or stop bacterial action. If these preparations irritate your skin, try other brands. Frequent bathing and the use of talcum powder also help control perspiration odor.

Your Skin Protects

Inside your body, blood and lymph circulate, bathing cells and organs. Your skin covers and protects your moist inner body from germs, from chemicals, and from physical attack. Even when cut, your skin can usually fight off infections before they reach the inner body.

The Epidermis: Surface Skin

Your skin is made up of layers. The outer layer (refer again to Figure 10.2, page 121) is called the **epidermis** (ep-uh-DER-mis). Dead skin cells make up the surface layer of the epidermis. If these outer cells were moist living cells supplied with blood vessels, they would be too delicate to do their protective work. Beneath the dead cells, the **Malpighian** (mal-PIG-ee-un) layer of the epidermis constantly forms new cells to replace the surface cells as they wear off, wash off, or sunburn and peel off.

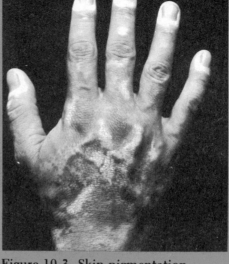

(c)

Figure 10.3. Skin pigmentation
conditions: *(a)* albino; *(b)* freckles;
(c) vitiligo.

(b)

YOUR SKIN AND THE POLYGRAPH   Dead cells or not, your outer skin tells much about you. A doctor can tell much about your health from the condition of your skin. Your friends can find out things about you, too. At times, you may be hiding your feelings successfully when a blush—a sudden rush of blood to the skin—gives you away. You may become red-faced with anger or sweaty-handed and pale with fear. A *polygraph* (PAHL-ee-graf), or lie detector, makes use of these involuntary emotional reactions by recording changes in skin moisture as well as changes in blood pressure, pulse, and respiration.

SKIN COLOR AND THE MALPIGHIAN LAYER   Three main coloring agents color skin. One of these agents is simply the color of blood, showing pinkly through the tiny blood vessels in the skin. The Malpighian layer contains two other coloring agents, or **pigments**—carotene (KAR-uh-teen) and **melanin** (MEL-uh-nun). Carotene is yellow or yellowish red. Melanin is brownish and often covers up the pinkish cast to a greater or lesser degree.

   An **albino** (al-BY-noh), who can be of any race, is born without skin pigments of any kind (see Figure 10.3a). An uneven sprinkling of melanin in the skin causes **freckles** (see Figure 10.3b). For some unknown reason, some people develop unpigmented patches of skin. This condition, called **vitiligo** (vit-uh-LY-goh), is shown in Figure 10.3c. Moles are raised, often pigmented skin imperfections that you are born with but which may not develop until later in life. Moles are usually harmless, but if they grow larger or bleed, you should consult a doctor.

Skin, Hair, and Nails   123

Melanin and Suntan   Skin melanin helps give protection from the sun. In general, people who live where the sun's rays are strong have more protective melanin than those who live in regions where the sun's rays are weaker. The deeply pigmented skin of Eskimo people might seem to be an exception to this rule; however, ice and snow reflect sunlight brightly. Skiers (and Eskimos) need protection from sunburn just as sunbathers do. Even people who normally have little melanin in their skins temporarily develop more when they are exposed to direct sunlight. To put it another way, their skins tan.

Sunburn   Sunburn is different. Like any other burn, sunburn actually injures the skin, often making it peel. The best way to avoid sunburn is to get your tan little by little. Start by sunning yourself early or late in the day. Stay out of the midday sun until you have some tan already. And use a protective lotion every time you sunbathe. Several studies have shown that lotions containing *PABA* (paraminobenzoic acid) protect best.

Even if you tan slowly and use lotion, you can still overdo sunning. Many doctors now believe that overexposure to the sun causes skin to age long before it should. They also warn that the development of some skin cancers is encouraged by overexposure to the sun.

A layer of gases, called the **ozone layer,** is present high above the earth. This layer protects us by absorbing most of the injurious rays of the sun. Certain pollutants discharged into the air by automobile and airplane exhausts and spray cans eventually reach the ozone layer and affect it adversely. Scientists inform us that if the ozone layer were ever to be reduced markedly, we could expect the number of cases of severe sunburn and skin cancer to increase.

Let's Pause for Review

Your skin is the largest organ in your body. The skin senses outside conditions, regulates body temperature, eliminates wastes, and protects the inner body. The condition of your skin gives clues to your health and your feelings. The epidermis, or outer skin, has a surface layer of dead cells. Beneath the dead cells, the Malpighian layer constantly manufactures new cells to replace surface cells as they are worn off. The Malpighian layer also contains pigments that color the skin and protect it from strong sunlight.

The Dermis

Beneath the epidermis lies the lower layer of the skin, the **dermis** (refer again to Figure 10.2, page 121). The dermis is the working layer of the skin. It contains the sweat glands that both cool the body and eliminate

The Appearance, Care, and Feeding of Your Body

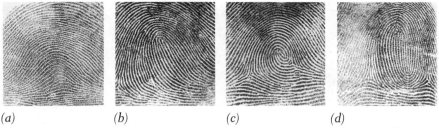

Figure 10.4. Types of fingerprints: (a) arch; (b) loop; (c) whorl; (d) double loop whorl.

waste; the erector muscles that help provide body heat; the nerves that sense conditions in the outside world; and the capillaries that nourish the skin. The dermis also contains projections called **papillae** (puh-PIL-ee), which point upward toward the epidermis, and **sebaceous** (sih-BAY-shus) **glands** (oil glands), which help smooth and soften the outer layer of skin and hair.

FINGERPRINTS AND THE DERMIS   Refer again to Figure 10.2, page 121, and locate the papillae. In the hand, the epidermis covers these inner projections to form the pattern for your fingerprints.

YOUR PART

1. Using an ink pad, fingerprint yourself at home. After washing your hands, label your prints to correspond with your fingers.
2. Compare your prints with those in Figure 10.4. Are they similar to any of those shown?
3. Bring your prints to class for comparison with those of your classmates.

    You may have found fingerprint patterns similar to your own, but, of course, you found none exactly the same. When you stop to think that fingerprints are like maps of the tiny papillae beneath the skin, it's not so surprising that no two people have the same prints.

THE SEBACEOUS GLANDS   Like many of the sweat glands, the sebaceous glands become more active during the teen years. They send oil, or **sebum** (SEE-bum), to the surface of the skin by way of the hair pockets, or **follicles** (FAHL-ih-kulz). This is normal. But sometimes the sebaceous glands work abnormally hard. No one knows exactly why; since the overactivity of the sebaceous glands begins just after puberty, it is thought to be related to the glandular changes that bring about sexual maturity.

Skin, Hair, and Nails   **125**

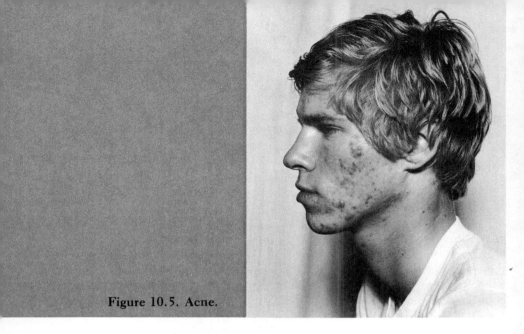

Figure 10.5. Acne.

When the sebaceous glands work overtime, they fill follicles and pores with sebum, which sometimes gets very thick. Sebum plugging a pore turns black when it is exposed to the air. This darkening—not dirt—is what gives blackheads their color. Whiteheads form when excess oil is trapped just beneath the skin. Pimples are clogged pores or follicles that have become infected. Pimples should never be squeezed, because breaking the skin can allow the infection to enter the bloodstream and spread. This is especially true of the area around the nose and mouth. From this area, infection can spread to the brain.

ACNE   If a number of pimples form around blackheads—and especially if infection spreads over the affected area—**acne** (ACK-nee) (see Figure 10.5) may result. Acne isn't caused by careless washing. However, since oil causes much of the trouble, some of the oil can be removed by washing three times a day with mild soap and water. A complexion brush does a better job than a washcloth. After washing, close your pores with a cold-water rinse or with a commercial *astringent* (uh-STRIN-junt), a liquid that helps close pores. You can also buy special blotting tissues to remove oil during the day, when you can't wash. Wash your hair often, too, especially if you style your hair so that it touches your face.

Since oil is the enemy, don't add oil to your face by using cold cream, oily lotions, or makeup with an oil base. Choose makeup with a water base instead. Acne often lessens in the summertime. So try moderate sunning, and see if it helps. Avoid fatty foods (butter, fried foods, and sweets, especially chocolate), which may make your acne worse. Where no pimples are present, you can safely remove blackheads with a blackhead remover purchased at the drugstore.

The Appearance, Care, and Feeding of Your Body

When Acne Is Severe   A person with severe acne should see a **dermatologist** (der-muh-TAHL-uh-jist), a doctor who treats skin problems. Dermatologists can help keep acne from spreading. They often prescribe a drying lotion, effective cleaning methods, and a special diet. (In addition to fatty foods, some people find that they must also avoid carbohydrates and foods containing iodine.) Dermatologists can also sometimes remove the scars that severe acne may leave.

Good-Looking Skin

Whether you get your advice on skin care from a dermatologist or from a teen or adult magazine, you will hear repeated over and over again the same two requirements for attractive skin: Keep your skin clean, and take care of your health. If you have ever looked in the mirror after a long walk in the fresh air, you know what good circulation and regular exercise can do for skin. So get a moderate amount of sunshine, exercise regularly, eat a balanced diet, and get plenty of sleep. As your doctor will tell you, only basic good health keeps skin fresh and glowing.

COSMETICS   Today's light, natural-looking makeup is flattering to most people, old and young. What's more, it doesn't clog pores, as heavy makeup does. Trying new cosmetics that may help you look your best can be fun. When you feel attractive, you are happier and more confident. Remember, though, that you may not know what is in the cosmetics that you use. According to a recent Food and Drug Administration (FDA) ruling, cosmetic ingredients must be listed on all new packagings manufactured. This will help you identify ingredients to which you are allergic or abnormally sensitive. Cosmetics may contain germs and other impurities, as well. (See Chapter 26, pages 464–466, for advice on buying cosmetics and other grooming aids.)

WHEN YOU USE A NEW PRODUCT   Usually, you can safely use cosmetics if you follow a few simple rules:

1. Read and follow directions on the package.
2. Keep cosmetics out of your eyes. Take special care not to touch your eyeball with eye makeup or makeup brushes. Never dye eyelashes or eyebrows with hair dyes. As their packages warn, these products can cause blindness.
3. Before trying a new product, do a *patch test.* Put a dab of the cosmetic somewhere other than on your face, such as on the inside of your forearm; leave it uncovered and undisturbed for 24 hours. If any redness, burning, itching, swelling, or other abnormal reaction results, don't use the product. Either you are allergic to it, or it is strong enough to cause **contact dermatitis** (duhr-muh-TYT-tis), or inflammation of the skin on contact.

Contact Dermatitis   You may already be familiar with the contact dermatitis produced by poison ivy. Other plants, detergents, cleansers, plastics, clothing, and cosmetics can cause it, too. Avoid such irritating substances, if you can. If it is too late for that, wash the affected skin immediately. If the inflammation doesn't clear up in a day or so, see a dermatologist.

Skin Infections

Infection means the successful invasion of the body by tiny organisms like **bacteria, viruses** (VY-rus-uz), and **fungi** (FUN-jy) or **funguses** (FUNG-guh-sez); all are often called germs. Part of good skin care is the prompt treatment of infection. For example, if you take care of pimples (by washing them gently and following the washing with a dab of **antiseptic,** or germ killer, such as 70 percent alcohol), they rarely become worse.

BACTERIAL INFECTIONS   A neglected pimple can get bigger and more infected and turn into a **boil.** The many germs in a boil can spread the infection, and **carbuncles** (KAHR-bung-kulz), which are large, deep boils, can result. Often, boils and carbuncles form where clothing rubs against a pimple, irritating and spreading the original infection. A person with a boil or carbuncle should see a doctor, because germs from these infected areas can get into the blood.

Another infection for which you should see a doctor right away is **impetigo** (im-puh-TEE-goh *or* im-puh-TY-goh). This cluster of blister-like sores later forms scabs or crusts. Impetigo is easy to catch from another person. Untreated, it spreads fast, but a doctor can cure it quickly with medication.

VIRUS INFECTIONS   Viruses cause many infections, among them **warts,** or solid raised sections of skin. People sometimes pick up this kind of virus as they walk around public swimming pools. As a result, a certain kind of wart can develop on the soles of the feet. If you have warts on the feet or elsewhere, and they bother you, see a doctor, who has several ways of removing them. Warts, like moles, are usually harmless, but if they bleed or grow noticeably larger, you should see a doctor about them.

Viruses also cause **fever blisters,** or **cold sores,** which usually go away by themselves in a few days. Some people never get cold sores. Others get them regularly. The virus responsible for cold sores can also cause serious eye damage, so if you are one of those people who get cold sores, take care not to spread the infection to your eyes.

FUNGUS INFECTIONS   **Athlete's foot,** or **ringworm** of the foot (see Figure 10.6), is a fungus infection. Like mold and mildew, which are also funguses, ringworm does well in warm, moist places. You may be able to prevent it by wearing sandals around swimming pools and in shower rooms. You can fight it by keeping your feet clean and dry, by wearing clean, dry socks, and by using medicated liquids and powders. If, in spite of your good care, your athlete's foot gets worse, see a doctor. Like any other infection, athlete's foot, if neglected, can become serious.

Ringworm of the scalp is the same kind of infection in a different place. If round patches of scaly skin on the scalp or elsewhere make you suspect ringworm, see your doctor right away.

Let's Pause for Review

The dermis is the working layer of the skin. Its surface papillae shape your fingerprints. The dermis contains sweat glands, erector muscles, the nerves of touch, blood vessels that nourish the skin, hair growing out of hair follicles, and sebaceous glands that oil up and soften surface skin and hair. Overactive sebaceous glands can clog pores and follicles with sebum, which turns black when exposed to air. Acne results when a number of pimples form around blackheads and infection spreads over the affected area. People with severe acne should see a dermatologist.

The two basic rules for attractive skin are (1) keep your skin clean, and (2) take care of your health. Cosmetics can help you look your best. But remember to use them with care. Treat skin infections promptly. See a doctor for boils, carbuncles, impetigo, annoying warts, or ringworm of the foot or scalp.

How Hair Grows

As you already know, hair grows outward from follicles in the dermis. Hair is part of your skin. It grows at the same rate whether you cut it often or

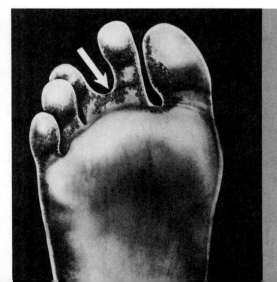

Figure 10.6. Athlete's foot.

Figure 10.7. Cross sections of hair types: *(left)* curly; *(right)* straight.

not—about 6 to 8 inches a year. The hair on your head grows for about four years, rests a few months, and then falls out. (Other body hair grows for a shorter period before being shed.) You lose 25 to 100 hairs a day, but new growth (at your age, at least) continually replaces the lost hair. Hair lost during an illness usually grows back. The hair that is lost to hereditary baldness does not.

HAIR AND HEREDITY   The baldness that comes with age is hereditary, as is the color, straightness, texture, and amount of your hair. Straight hair is stronger than curly hair and, as you can see in Figure 10.7, looks different in cross section. Hair color comes from melanin and other skin pigments that are transferred to the hair. For some unknown reason, pigment stops forming in hair as the years go by. That is why, as people age, hair first turns gray and then white.

Removing Unwanted Hair

Fortunately, visible hair, like surface skin, is made up of dead cells that can be painlessly styled, curled, shaved, or cut. Some girls use **depilatories** (duh-PIL-uh-taw-reez), liquids or creams that remove small amounts of unwanted hair. Others use warm wax instead. When it cools, the wax is pulled off, and the hair comes with it. When people want such hair removed permanently, they should go to someone licensed to perform **electrolysis** (ih-lek-TRAHL-uh-sis), a process that destroys the hair root electrically.

Since depilatories are too strong for daily use, boys learn to shave when, between ages 12 and 20, their beards begin to grow. Most girls also shave legs and underarms. If you use a safety razor, you will want to soften hair first with warm soapy lather or shaving cream. With practice, you can soon learn to do a good job with most razors. If you keep cutting yourself, however—perhaps because you hurry—you may want to try an electric shaver. You may not get as close a shave, but the job goes faster, and it's easier to avoid nicks and cuts.

130   **The Appearance, Care, and Feeding of Your Body**

Products That Color, Straighten, or Curl

Dead hair cells can also be painlessly colored, bleached, straightened, or curled. However, chemicals in the products that do these jobs can damage the hair and scalp. Normally, the sebaceous glands provide enough oil to keep hair shiny. But damaged hair usually needs extra oil, as well as a rest from the chemicals that did the damage. Cream rinses and products that promise to recondition damaged hair usually provide this extra oil in an easy-to-use form.

Products for home use that straighten or curl hair are much kinder to hair and scalp than they used to be. They are also easier to use. But they still contain strong chemicals. If you use these products, keep them away from your eyes, follow directions, and first take the recommended patch tests.

Scientists now believe that ingredients in some hair dyes may cause cancer. Until more is known about this possibility, if you want to change your hair color, use one of the natural coloring agents, such as henna.

Some Problems Caused by Long Hair

Long hair is often silky and beautiful. It is often also tangled and hard to comb. If you have this problem, you can probably find a commercial, after-shampoo rinse that will help you.

Head lice (see Figure 10.8) are another problem that seems to be on the increase now that hair is longer and harder to keep clean. Lice lay eggs, or **nits,** in the hair and feed on the blood they draw by biting the scalp or skin elsewhere on the body. The bites itch, turn red, and sometimes look like a rash.

The presence of lice can be serious. When they bite, they can pass on several diseases, including *typhus* (TY-fus) *fever.* In the past, people with lice had to saturate their hair and scalp overnight in such preparations as

Figure 10.8. The head louse is about ⅛ inch (3 millimeters) long, shown here magnified approximately 20 times.

131

kerosene, dissolved in oil. But today, drugstores carry a number of preparations that kill lice much more simply. It is best to have a doctor recommend one to you.

Dandruff

Normal dandruff is just the flaking off of dead scalp cells mixed, sometimes, with sebum. The cure for normal dandruff is thorough, regular shampooing. You can use a dandruff shampoo if it seems to help and doesn't irritate your scalp. However, if your scalp itches a great deal and your dandruff is abnormally heavy, see your doctor for help in getting rid of it.

Good-Looking Hair

The prime rule for skin and hair care is the same: Keep it clean. Clean your hair with the kind of shampoo (oily, normal, dry) that suits it. Shampoo often if your hair is oily, and remember that, in later years, the same troublesome oil will keep your hair and skin looking young. If your hair is dry, add extra oil in the form of after-shampoo rinses. Brush and comb your hair often enough to keep it well groomed and tangle-free. Nothing responds faster than hair to good care. Nothing does more for your looks than beautiful hair.

Fingernails

Fingernails, like hair, are part of your skin. Of the visible nail, only the little half-moon at the base of the nail is made up of living cells. Figure 10.9 shows you that more living cells are hidden beneath the nail. Therefore, you risk infection if you fail to keep your nails clean and unbitten. Other than that, nails don't need much care unless you like to polish them.

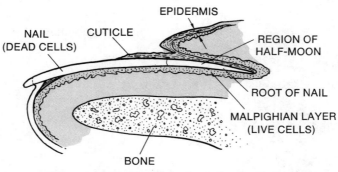

Figure 10.9. Cross section of a fingertip.

The Appearance, Care, and Feeding of Your Body

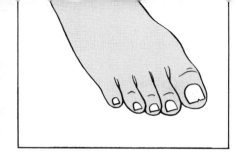

Figure 10.10. Toenails correctly cut, with notch (big toenail) to reduce pressure on ingrown nail.

Once a day, when you are washing your hands, use a nailbrush to clean your nails. Then, use the towel you dry with to push back the **cuticle** (KYOO-tih-kul), or hardened skin, around the nails.

Your nails also need trimming since they grow about ¹⁄₁₆ of an inch a week. (If you injure and lose a nail, it takes about six months to grow a new one.) You can use a small scissors, fingernail clippers, or the same clippers you use to trim your toenails. If you like polish, however, you will probably want to shape your nails more carefully, using an emery board for the nails and an orange stick for the cuticles. If a bit of cuticle comes loose from the nail, cut it off before it tears and becomes a painful, possibly infected, hangnail.

Ingrown Toenails

Tight shoes, socks, and stockings can cause short toenails, especially rounded ones, to turn and grow toward the skin. If neglected, ingrown toenails hurt and may become infected. But prevention is simple. Be sure your shoes, socks, and stockings (especially the stretch kind) are big enough. Cut toenails straight across without removing the corners. If a toenail is slightly ingrown, cut a little *v* in the nail (see Figure 10.10) to reduce pressure on the ingrown ends. If an ingrown toenail causes your toe to become quite painful and, possibly, inflamed, see your doctor or a **podiatrist** (puh-DY-uh-trist), also called a **chiropodist** (kih-RAHP-uh-dist), a person who specializes in care of the feet.

Looking Back

Your skin is a sensing organ that also regulates body temperature, eliminates wastes, and protects your inner body. Your skin gives clues to your feelings and your health. That is why, for good-looking skin, hair, and nails, you need exercise, some sunshine, good food, and plenty of sleep. Hair and nails grow out from and are part of the skin.

Visible skin, hair, and nails (except for the little half-moon) are made up of dead cells. Skin and hair need oil to stay smooth and soft. The sebaceous glands that supply this oil sometimes work overtime during the teen years. Acne results if sebum clogs pores and follicles, if infection is present, and if the infection spreads. People with severe acne should see a dermatologist. Others should wash hair and skin often, get a moderate amount of sun, and avoid adding oil to the skin—with cold cream, for example, or with cosmetics that have an oil base.

Whether your skin and hair are oily, normal, or dry, good looks start with cleanliness. Cosmetics can help you look your best, as long as you choose them to suit your special needs and use them with care.

Fingernail care is easy, if you don't bite your nails. Then, you need only clean them, trim them, and, after washing your hands, push back cuticles with a towel every day or so. To prevent ingrown toenails, wear shoes, socks, and stockings of the proper size, and trim toenails straight across.

MODIFIED TRUE-FALSE QUESTIONS

1. The skin is the _largest_ organ of the body.
2. Overactive sebaceous glands may cause the skin to become excessively _dry_.
3. Blackheads are caused by skin oil that has been exposed to _dirt_.
4. Infected follicles are called _pimples._
5. Athlete's foot is related to _a virus._
6. Normally, dandruff is _harmless_ to the body.
7. The skin condition called _impetigo_ is related to excessive skin oil during the teen years.
8. Warts are _a bacterial_ infection.
9. Pimples often result from _enlarged_ pores.
10. A liquid waste given off through the skin is called _urine._
11. Fever blisters, or cold sores, can cause serious _eye_ damage.
12. _Warts_ may develop on the soles of the feet.
13. Excessive exposure to _astringents_ can cause skin cancer.
14. With longer hair, the tendency is for head lice to _increase._
15. The dermis is made up of _dead_ skin cells.
16. The hair and _nails_ are part of the skin.
17. _Acne_ is caused by a buildup of oil in the sebaceous glands and infection.
18. The _chiropractor_ is a doctor who specializes in the care of feet.
19. Blushing is caused by a sudden rush of _blood_ to the skin.
20. "Goose bumps" form when _erector_ muscles straighten skin hairs.

The Appearance, Care, and Feeding of Your Body

21. Sweat glands give off _more_ moisture in cold weather than in hot weather.
22. The _skin_ helps control the body temperature.
23. Skin receptors are very close together on the _lips_.
24. It is a good health practice to acquire a tan _quickly_.

MATCHING QUESTIONS

Column A	Column B
1. dermatitis	a. cluster of sores caused by bacteria
2. fever blister	b. inflammation of the skin
3. impetigo	c. a large, deep boil
4. carbuncle	d. absence of skin pigment
5. ringworm	e. virus infection around nose and mouth
	f. round patches of scaly skin

COMPLETION QUESTIONS

1. The doctor who treats skin problems is a (an) _____.
2. The condition in which unpigmented patches of skin develop in some people is referred to as _____.
3. A person born without skin pigment is known as a (an) _____.
4. A commercial product that aids in closing the skin pores is called a (an) _____.
5. Hair can be permanently removed by _____.
6. Hair can be temporarily removed by using a commercial chemical product known as a (an) _____.
7. _____ are ineffective in stopping perspiration.
8. Seventy percent alcohol, used to slow down or stop bacterial action, is referred to as a (an) _____.
9. An uneven sprinkling of melanin in the skin causes _____.
10. Raised, pigmented skin imperfections we are born with are called _____.

MULTIPLE-CHOICE QUESTIONS

1. The outer layer of the skin is the
   a. dermis   b. fatty layer   c. epidermis   d. follicle
2. Whiteheads form when
   a. excess oil is trapped just beneath the skin
   b. an oil-plugged pore is exposed to air
   c. a follicle gets infected
   d. a pimple is squeezed

3. You can use cosmetics safely if you do all of the following, *except*
   a. read and follow the directions on the label
   b. keep them away from your eyes
   c. do a patch test before trying new products
   d. buy the most expensive ones
4. New skin cells to replace dead surface cells are constantly formed in the
   a. sebaceous glands   b. epidermis   c. Malpighian layer   d. blood
5. A condition of the scalp caused by the flaking of dead cells is
   a. dermatitis   b. dandruff   c. ringworm   d. impetigo

THOUGHT QUESTIONS

1. Hair continues to appear on various parts of your body, and you are considering removal of some of it. List four methods of hair removal and explain the disadvantages of each.
2. Your brother, who is 13 years old, has a bad case of acne. He has a very oily skin. His diet is lacking in fruits and vegetables and is excessive in sweets and fried foods.

   a. Discuss the possible causes of his problem.
   b. What can he do to improve this condition?
   c. If the condition worsens, what should be done?

3. You have been bothered by hangnails and ingrown toenails. What causes these conditions, and how can they be prevented?
4. Why is a healthy skin a vital part of good health?
5. Why don't two people ever have the same set of fingerprints?
6. Is maintaining a year-round tan a good health practice? Explain.
7. Your parents want you to cut your overly long hair. How would you react to this and still keep peace in the family?

Looking Ahead

In Chapter 11, you will learn about another part of the body that contributes to your health as well as your appearance— your teeth and gums. Most cavities are formed between the ages of 8 and 18, so it is important for you to learn now how to guard against tooth decay, and how to care properly for both teeth and gums. In addition, now may be the best time in your life to straighten and reposition teeth that require this treatment.

The Appearance, Care, and Feeding of Your Body

Chapter 11: Your Teeth and Gums: Daily Care for a Lifetime of Use

Circus performers hang by them. You may catch a plane by the skin of yours, or sink them into a good steak. After death, they are one of the most durable parts of the body. Some have been found in centuries-old skeletons. Yet during life, they are quite susceptible to decay. What are they? Teeth, of course, and they are important to your health and happiness all your life.

Once, people resigned themselves to losing many, perhaps all, of their teeth as they grew older. Fortunately, those days are past. As you will learn, if you visit the dentist regularly, eat the right foods, and properly clean your teeth carefully every day, you have a very good chance of completely preventing dental disease and thus keeping your permanent teeth permanently. Decide now to keep yours. Begin with the kind of good, daily care that will be discussed later in this chapter.

Baby Teeth: Your First Set (of Twenty)

Remember when you were about six years old and your front teeth loosened and fell out? Those teeth belonged to your set of *primary teeth*, *baby teeth*, or "milk teeth," as you may have called them. Those first teeth began to form eight months before birth. In most babies, all 20 of them stay hidden in the jaw for about six to eight months after birth. Then they begin to push through the gums. By the age of three, most children have a full set of 20 baby teeth.

Permanent Teeth: Your Second Set (of Thirty-Two)

Your second set of teeth also took many months to develop in the jaws before pushing through the gums. Each tooth has a **crown,** which shows

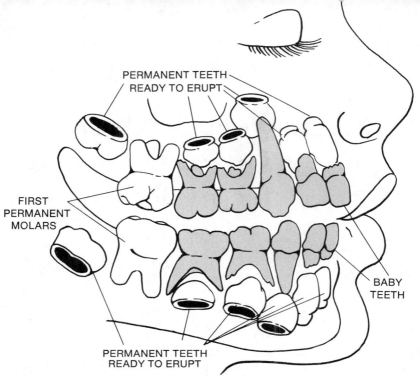

PERMANENT TEETH READY TO ERUPT

FIRST PERMANENT MOLARS

BABY TEETH

PERMANENT TEETH READY TO ERUPT

Figure 11.1. This child has baby teeth and first permanent molars, with other permanent teeth ready to erupt.

above the gum, and one or more **roots,** which anchor the tooth in the jawbone. As the crowns of the *permanent teeth* grow larger, the roots of the baby teeth are broken down gradually into material that the blood carries off and delivers elsewhere. As this takes place, the roots shrink away from the jawbone.

Figure 11.1 shows permanent teeth ready to come in and baby teeth ready to fall out. As you can see, at this stage a baby tooth has lost its root completely. The rootless crown becomes loose and falls out—or, more likely, is wiggled out by an eager child. This is why people sometimes think that baby teeth have no roots.

Early dental care is important because a permanent tooth is sometimes ready to come in before the baby tooth in its place has completely lost its root. In such cases, it is important to have a dentist remove the baby tooth so that the permanent tooth can line up in its normal position.

NEW MOLARS: TEETH THAT MUST LAST   By the age of 12, most people have 28 permanent teeth. Twenty of these replace baby teeth. Eight are new grinding teeth, or **molars** (MOH-lurs), for which the growing jaw now has room. In fact, your first permanent teeth were molars, too, which came in when you were about six and grew behind the last baby teeth on each side of your upper and lower jaws. You can see why early dental care is

The Appearance, Care, and Feeding of Your Body

important. If new molars develop cavities, they must be filled or these permanent teeth may be lost.

For a few years, no more teeth appear. Then, usually between ages 18 and 21, your third molars, or **wisdom teeth,** come in. With these four new teeth, your set of 32 permanent teeth is complete (see Figure 11.2).

YOUR PART

1. Take a mirror and count the teeth in your own mouth. Do you think you have any small baby teeth left?
2. Write down how many permanent teeth you have.
3. Which permanent teeth do you still need to give you a full set of 32?

You probably found that you have 28 permanent teeth, all of which, with good care, you hope to keep. You probably need only your wisdom teeth to complete the set.

FOUR KINDS OF TEETH In Figure 11.2, you can see four kinds of teeth: **incisors** (in-SY-zurz), **cuspids, bicuspids** (by-KUS-pids), and **molars.** Incisor means cutter. A cusp is a raised part, so a cuspid is a tooth with one raised part, and a bicuspid is a tooth with two. Cuspids are also called **canines** (KAY-nynz), because they look like dog teeth, and **eyeteeth,** because people used to think that the roots of the upper cuspids went all the way up to the eyes. Incisors and cuspids have single roots; bicuspids may have one or two roots; and molars may have two or three.

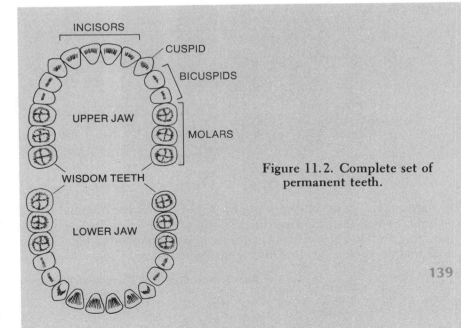

Figure 11.2. Complete set of permanent teeth.

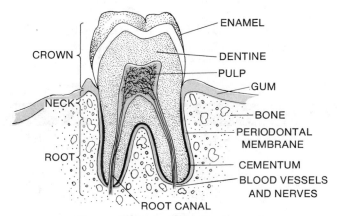

Figure 11.3. Structure of a tooth.

1. Bite into a flat sheet of softened dental wax (or into a stick of sugarless chewing gum) in such a way as to leave an imprint of your teeth.
2. Can you see imprints of four kinds of teeth? Each kind of tooth does a different job in chewing. Try to figure out what the different jobs are, and write them down.

Although you may have used different words, you probably decided that *(a)* incisors cut food, *(b)* cuspids tear and shred it, *(c)* bicuspids both tear and grind it, and *(d)* molars crush and grind it between their broad surfaces.

Let's Pause for Review

Everyone gets two sets of teeth, 20 baby teeth and 32 permanent teeth. Teeth cut, shred, tear, crush, and grind food, according to their shapes. Early dental care is important to protect permanent teeth, which start to come in by age 6.

A Tooth in Detail

In Figure 11.3, you can see the four tissues that make up each tooth: **enamel, cementum, dentine** (DEN-teen), and **dental pulp.** Enamel is the shiny material that covers the crown. It is the hardest material in the body and the tooth's first line of defense against decay. Cementum is the bonelike material covering the root. Dentine is another bonelike substance, which forms the body of the tooth under the enamel; it is somewhat softer than enamel. Dental pulp occupies the space in the center of the tooth; it is the softest part of the tooth. It contains the nerves and the blood and lymph vessels that enter the tooth through a tiny opening at the end of each root and reach the pulp through a narrow channel. This channel is called a **root canal.**

Each tooth is anchored in its own *socket* in the jawbone. Covering the root and lining the wall of the socket is a delicate tissue called the **periodontal** (per-ee-oh-DAHN-tul) **membrane.** This membrane helps hold the tooth in its socket and also acts as a shock absorber when your teeth meet as you chew. In a moment, you will see what happens to these tissues when a tooth decays.

Is Tooth Decay Inevitable?

One of the most surprising things to be said on the subject of tooth decay is that so many people still believe it is unavoidable. In fact, proper home and professional care can almost completely prevent the problem. But you must be willing to take the time and make the effort that good dental hygiene requires if you are going to avoid the unpleasantness of decay, tooth fillings, and other unnecessary dental damage.

After we have taken a brief look at the increasing damage that tooth decay can cause, we will discuss what you can do about it before it begins. You will probably decide for yourself that early preventive care of your teeth is the best routine for a lifetime of comfort.

Tooth Decay

Not everything is yet known about the causes of tooth decay, or **dental caries** (KAR-eez). But scientists have learned that decay begins when **lactic** (LAK-tik) **acid** eats away a tooth's protective enamel at some point. Where does this destructive acid come from? The answer is **plaque** (PLAK), a sticky, colorless substance that forms constantly on everyone's teeth. Plaque contains bacteria that act upon the foods you eat—and, in particular, sugar—to produce the decay-causing acid. The bacteria in plaque can change some sugars into acid within minutes. For other foods, the process takes longer. In either case, plaque not only produces dangerous acids but also holds them in contact with the teeth, prolonging the acid attack on tooth enamel and irritating the surrounding gum tissue (a subject we will discuss later in this chapter). Continued acid action on tooth enamel can produce a small hole, or **cavity.**

WHERE DECAY STARTS   When plaque is not regularly removed from teeth by proper cleaning methods, decay usually begins in a pit or small crack in the enamel, or in an area that is hard to clean, such as the surfaces between teeth or at the **neck** of the tooth along the gum line (refer again to Figure 11.3, page 140). Nearly all molars have pitlike flaws, and other teeth may have them, too. Some dentists paint a layer of plastic enamel over such flaws to make them more resistant to decay.

THE TOOTH BECOMES SENSITIVE   If decay in the enamel isn't soon treated by a dentist, the decay and the bacteria that produce it will move into the dentine. At this point, the tooth usually becomes sensitive, or uncomfortable, when touched by anything hot, cold, or sweet. Since dentine is softer than enamel, decay goes faster there, until finally the pulp is exposed. This exposure usually produces a toothache. If still untreated, the decay will destroy the nerves in the pulp. Then the pain will stop, but decay will go on eating away the structures of the tooth.

AN ABSCESSED TOOTH   When decay exposes the root canal, the invading infection can cause an **abscess** (AB-ses) to form at the tip of the tooth's root. Since an abscess is like an internal boil, it often hurts. Sometimes, if the infection worsens, the pain may pulsate, or come and go in waves, and the face may swell. It is dangerous to leave an abscess untreated, because the infection can travel through the bloodstream to other parts of the body.

EVERYBODY'S PROBLEM   The most common disease in the United States today is dental caries, or decay. At some time, 98 out of every 100 Americans experience decay. Right now, half of the two-year-olds in this country have one or more decayed teeth. By the time they reach school age, these same children will average three or more decayed baby, or primary teeth. You, yourself, are living through the years (from 8 to 18) when most cavities are formed. By age 16, the average student already has seven decayed, missing, or filled teeth, and less than 4 percent of high school students are free of decay.

WHAT YOU CAN DO ABOUT DECAY   How can you cut down on the amount of decay-producing acids in your mouth, strengthen your tooth enamel, and keep decay from entering the dentine or the pulp of your teeth? To put it very briefly, you can keep your mouth clean, cut down on sugar and sweet snacks, see your dentist regularly, and support community **fluoridation** (fluhr-uh-DAY-shun) programs (see page 145).

As mentioned earlier, with proper home and professional dental care, most dental diseases can be completely prevented.

Brush After Meals and Snacks   As you already know, whenever possible you should brush your teeth *soon* after eating. Remember that lactic acid is formed by plaque within minutes. Only by thorough and immediate brushing can you remove most food particles before plaque bacteria can change them into acid. You may find it refreshing to rinse your mouth after eating, but rinsing doesn't remove plaque and is, therefore, an ineffective substitute for brushing.

Use Dental Floss Once a Day for Plaque Control Plaque control is something rather new in the fight against decay. In addition to regular brushing, dentists now advise using dental floss at least once a day to remove decay-causing plaque, particularly between the teeth and near the gum line. Flossing for plaque control has a secondary benefit as well: when plaque is not removed as soon as it forms, minerals from saliva will be deposited in it, hardening it into **tartar.** Tartar is so hard that only a dentist or **dental hygienist** (hy-JEEN-ist), a trained assistant, can remove it.

Disclosing Agents Disclosing **agents** are tablets or solutions that color the plaque in your mouth so that you can see it. If you or your teacher can obtain some disclosing agents, do so. They will make the first of the following activities more interesting, and they are necessary for performing the second one:

YOUR PART

MATERIALS
You will need a toothbrush, dental floss, and, if possible, disclosing agents.

PROCEDURE
Tonight when you are at home, go through the following brushing and flossing steps. (These steps are recommended for plaque control by the American Dental Association.) If you are able to obtain disclosing agents, use them as directed in the package, both before you begin and after you have ended the activity:

1. Place the head of your toothbrush alongside your teeth, with the bristle tips angled against the gum line (see Figure 11.4).

Figure 11.4. The correct angle for toothbrushing of *(left)* side teeth and *(right)* front teeth.

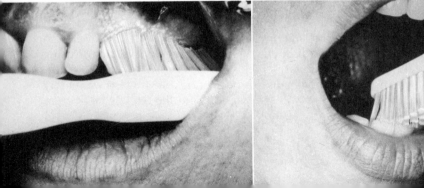

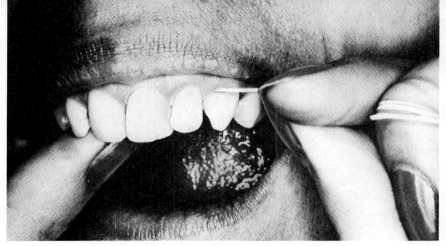

Figure 11.5. Correct flossing procedure.

2. Move the brush back and forth with *short* (half-a-tooth-wide) strokes several times, using a gentle "scrubbing" motion.
3. Brush the outer surfaces of each tooth, uppers and lowers, keeping the bristles angled against the gum line.
4. Use the same method on all of the inside surfaces of your teeth except for front teeth.
5. For the front teeth, brush the inside surfaces by tilting the brush and making several gentle up-and-down strokes with the front part of the brush over the teeth and gum tissue (see Figure 11.4).
6. Break off about 18 inches of dental floss and wind most of it around one of your middle fingers.
7. Wind the rest of the floss around the same finger of the opposite hand. This finger can "take up" the floss as it becomes soiled.
8. Use your thumbs and forefingers, with an inch of floss between them, to guide the floss between your teeth.
9. Holding the floss tightly (there should be no slack), use a gentle sawing motion to insert the floss between your teeth. Never "snap" the floss into the gums! When the floss reaches the gum line, curve it into a C-shape against one tooth and *gently slide* it into the space between the gum and the tooth until you feel resistance.
10. While holding the floss tightly against the tooth, move the floss away from the gum and back toward it by scraping the floss against the side of the tooth (see Figure 11.5).
11. Repeat this method on the rest of your teeth.

If this was your first attempt at plaque removal, it may have taken some time. But don't be discouraged. After a few days' practice, flossing will take just a few minutes.

If you are able to obtain disclosing agents, you will also want to try the following activity. It will let you compare the effectiveness of *(a)*

The Appearance, Care, and Feeding of Your Body

rinsing your mouth and *(b)* brushing and flossing your teeth as means of removing harmful plaque:

1. Get up one morning and *do not* brush and floss your teeth.
2. Rinse your mouth as thoroughly as possible.
3. Use the disclosing agent.
4. If the plaque has been colored by the disclosing agent, brush and floss your teeth, following the instructions in the preceding activity.
5. Use the disclosing agent again.

It is clear from this activity that rinsing alone is not an effective way to remove plaque. The only way to remove plaque and prevent dental decay is to brush and floss in the prescribed manner.

Your Diet Can Help Prevent Decay   Every time you chew gum, eat cookies, candy, and cake, or drink a sugar-sweetened soft drink, your teeth are attacked, at least a little, by destructive acid. Every time you cut down on sugar-sweetened foods, you are doing your teeth a favor. Another thing you can do is to choose the best time to eat sweets. The best time is when you can brush your teeth immediately afterward.

The chewiness of food is important, too. Hard or chewy foods, like crusty bread or roast beef, give your chewing muscles and gums the exercise they need.

Although there is no specific "dental diet," calcium is essential to the formation of teeth and the maintenance of strong bones, including the jawbone. This means that, even after your permanent teeth are completely formed, you will continue to need calcium for good, strong bone tissue. Milk is an excellent source of calcium. Other foods needed for general health also promote healthy gums, teeth, and the bones that support them. You will be learning more about foods needed for health in Chapter 12, page 155.

Fewer Cavities Through Fluoridation   Some years ago, scientists observed that in areas where the water contained natural minerals called **fluorides** (FLUHR-eydz), children had strong teeth that resisted decay. By adding fluorides to other water supplies, the scientists discovered that children who drank fluoridated water from birth had 65 percent fewer cavities than children whose water did not contain fluorides. Adults also benefited, though not as much. We now know that fluorides make tooth enamel harder and more resistant to acid attack (see Figure 11.6, page 146).

If Your Water Lacks Fluorides   If your community does not fluoridate its water, your family can buy bottled fluoridated water for use at home. In addition, your dentist can apply fluoride directly to tooth surfaces

Your Teeth and Gums   145

regularly during your growing years. Although these applications will help prevent further decay, they are not as effective as fluorides in drinking water.

Look for the ADA Seal of Acceptance　You can also use a fluoride toothpaste found acceptable by the American Dental Association (ADA). Not all fluoride toothpastes work equally well. Each one must be tested. When a toothpaste really helps prevent decay, the ADA allows the manufacturer to put the ADA Seal of Acceptance on the label of each tube (see Figure 11.7). Look for the seal when you buy toothpaste.

See Your Dentist Twice a Year　Brushing, flossing, and fluoridation are the primary preventive measures in the fight against tooth decay. The responsibility for each of these aspects of mouth care is yours alone.

But regular visits to your dentist are important, too, for several reasons. First, your dentist can keep you up to date on the newest techniques of dental hygiene for you to follow at home. Second, if given the chance, your dentist will remove decay before it can penetrate the enamel and then fill your cavities. When caught in time, cavities need not be painful or

Figure 11.6. Dental condition of children living in Grand Rapids, Michigan, before and after water fluoridation.

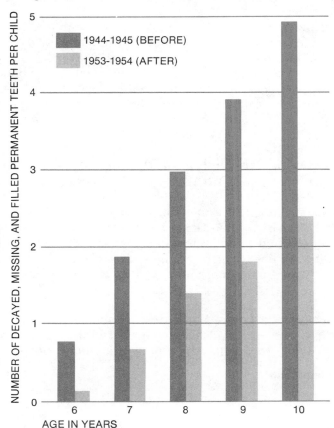

1944-1945 (BEFORE)

1953-1954 (AFTER)

NUMBER OF DECAYED, MISSING, AND FILLED PERMANENT TEETH PER CHILD

AGE IN YEARS

146

Figure 11.7. American Dental Association Seal of Acceptance, appearing on some tubes of toothpaste.

expensive to fill, and they will not lead to the formation of abscesses. Third, you also need regular professional cleaning to remove tartar, and you may need dental X rays to uncover hidden problems as early as possible.

Let's Pause for Review

Tooth decay begins when lactic acid destroys tooth enamel. Plaque bacteria, acting on sugars and other foods, produce lactic acid and carry on the work of decay. If left untreated, decay first penetrates the enamel, next the softer dentine, then the soft pulp of the tooth, and finally the root canal, where it produces an abscess at the tip of the tooth's root.

Tooth decay affects 98 out of every 100 Americans. You can help protect your teeth from decay by daily flossing and brushing after you eat (especially if you have eaten sweets), by limiting your diet of sweets, by drinking fluoridated water, and by seeing your dentist at least twice a year.

Impacted Teeth

The jaws of modern people often don't have enough room for all 32 permanent teeth. As a result, one or more teeth may become **impacted,** or wedged between the jaw and another tooth. An impacted tooth can't erupt (push out through the gum) normally. Figure 11.8, page 148, shows an impacted wisdom tooth. Many impacted teeth can be safely left alone. But if they cause pain and swelling, or if they grow the wrong way (pointing toward the cheek, for example), they require a dentist's attention.

Good Bite or Bad?

Your teeth do four jobs. They chew your food thoroughly. They help you speak clearly. They hold your other teeth in place. And they help you look

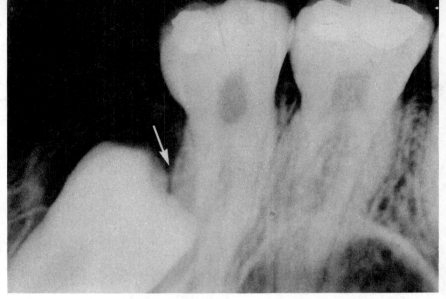

Figure 11.8. Enlarged X ray of impacted wisdom tooth.

your best by supporting your facial features and giving you an attractive smile. If your teeth are lined up well in their proper positions, they do these four jobs well. They meet in a "good bite" or *normal occlusion* (uh-KLOO-zhun). Occlusion means closing.

CAUSES OF MALOCCLUSION   Sometimes, however, teeth meet in a bad closing, or **malocclusion** (mal-uh-KLOO-zhun) (see Figure 11.9). Such teeth may have been pushed out of place by thumb sucking or by sleep habits that put pressure on the jaw. They may have moved slowly out of place when teeth next to them were lost. (A dentist can put in a space maintainer to prevent this from happening.) Maloccluded teeth may have pushed in crookedly ahead of or behind baby teeth that were slow in loosening and falling out. (A dentist can remove such baby teeth.) Or maloccluded teeth may simply result from overcrowding in too small a jaw.

RESULTS OF MALOCCLUSION   Malocclusion has many causes, but its result is that the teeth do their four jobs less well. From 30 to 50 percent of American schoolchildren have malocclusion. They may have problems with chewing and pronunciation. Because teeth can push facial features out of place, these children's faces may be affected, also. Fortunately, dentists can do something about all of these problems.

CORRECTION OF MALOCCLUSION   You should be especially interested in these problems now, because the teen years are usually the best time in life to correct malocclusion. Your jaw structures are almost fully grown, so that later growth will not push the straightened teeth out of line. At the same time, the jaw structures can still be remolded by teeth that are slowly and gently pushed into new positions.

The Orthodontist   For extensive work of this kind, the dentist will refer you to an **orthodontist** (awr-thuh-DAHN-tist), a specialist in the treatment of malocclusion. The orthodontist fits *braces* of wire and springs, designed specifically for each patient's problems. In Figure 11.10, page 150, you can see the result of such work.

It is not only in youth that your regular dentist or an orthodontist can help you look well. All of your life, these professionals can help you look your best by replacing lost teeth with false teeth or implants, and by preserving your other teeth.

Periodontal Diseases

Periodontal means around the tooth, and **periodontal diseases** are diseases of the gums and other supporting structures of the teeth. Although young people are sometimes troubled by periodontal diseases, such serious dental disorders are much more common among older people. After age 35, in fact, the chief cause of tooth loss is periodontal disease.

GINGIVITIS   Gingivitis (jin-juh-VYT-is) is an inflammation (swelling, heat, redness, pain) of the gums. Once again, the main culprit is plaque. We have already seen how plaque buildup not only attacks tooth enamel but also inflames gum tissue. As the plaque hardens into tartar, gum inflammation increases, and gingivitis begins.

The condition may be further worsened by incorrect toothbrushing that injures the sore gums, by food becoming packed between the teeth,

Figure 11.9. Casts showing five kinds of malocclusion.

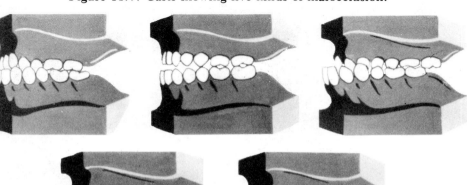

and by a poor diet. To prevent gingivitis, brush and floss daily, eat a good diet, and visit the dentist regularly for tartar removal.

PERIODONTITIS **Periodontitis** (PER-ee-oh-dahn-TY-tis), sometimes called **pyorrhea** (py-uh-REE-uh), is a more severe gum inflammation, which usually begins as gingivitis. If tartar is not regularly removed, additional plaque accumulates on top of it, spreading gum inflammation and drawing the gums away from the teeth to form pockets that fill with bacteria and pus (see Figure 11.11). A gum abscess can form, as can a tooth abscess if the infection reaches the tip of a tooth's root. If treatment is not begun early, periodontitis can eventually cause teeth to be lost.

VINCENT'S INFECTION: TRENCH MOUTH **Vincent's infection** is often called "trench mouth" because many soldiers suffered from it during World War I when they spent long periods in trenches at the front. This disease attacks the gums and other parts of the mouth and throat. Its symptoms are severe inflammation and soreness of the gums. The gums may also bleed and smell bad.

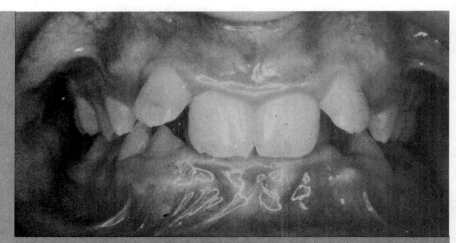

Figure 11.10. What an orthodontist can do for malocclusion: *(above)* **before and** *(below)* **after.**

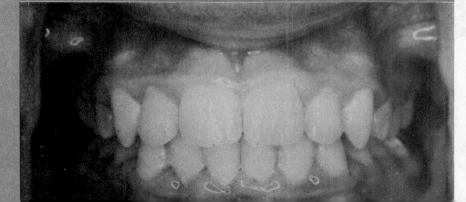

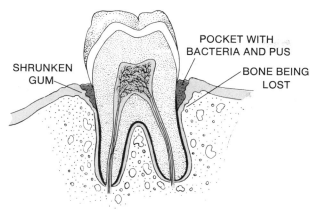

POCKET WITH
BACTERIA AND PUS

SHRUNKEN
GUM

BONE BEING
LOST

Figure 11.11. Periodontal disease. Compare the tissue around this
tooth with that in Figure 11.3, page 140.

If you have any bleeding, soreness, swelling, or other unusual condition of the gums that does not disappear in a day or so, consult your dentist.
She or he can detect gum disease early, when treatment is most effective.

Looking Back

Tooth decay affects 98 out of every 100 Americans. Decay
begins when plaque bacteria produce lactic acid, which destroys tooth enamel. If left untreated, decay next penetrates the
dentine, then the pulp, and finally the root canal, where it can
result in an abscess at the root of the tooth. You can protect
yourself from decay, abnormal development of the teeth, and
periodontal disease (of the gums and other supporting structures of the tooth) by the following measures: (1) brush after
eating to remove plaque, especially if you have eaten sweets;
(2) floss daily; (3) drink fluoridated water or use fluoridated
toothpaste; (4) eat healthful foods and, as much as possible,
avoid sugar and sweet snacks; and (5) see your dentist twice a
year—and, if necessary, an orthodontist, as well. They can
detect and treat any dental diseases or malformation you may
have and help you prevent further dental troubles in the future.

MODIFIED TRUE-FALSE QUESTIONS

1. _Lactic acid,_ a sticky substance, builds up on teeth and contributes to the
   formation of cavities.
2. Tooth decay begins on the _inside_ of a tooth.

3. The hardest substance in the human body is _dental enamel._
4. By the age of _six,_ most children have a full set of baby teeth.
5. The first permanent teeth are _molars._
6. Dentine in the tooth decays _faster_ than enamel.
7. An infection at the tip of the root of a tooth is called _a cavity._
8. A "good bite" is referred to as _normal occlusion._
9. _Braces_ are often used to correct problems of malocclusion.
10. _Iron_ is essential to the formation and maintenance of strong bones and teeth.

MATCHING QUESTIONS

Column A	Column B
1. malocclusion	a. tooth shock absorber
2. periodontal membrane	b. improper alignment of the teeth
3. dentine	c. under enamel
4. dental caries	d. hardened plaque
5. trench mouth	e. gum disease
	f. tooth cavities

COMPLETION QUESTIONS

1. An adult normally has _____ teeth.
2. The permanent teeth that come in first are the _____.
3. The doctor who specializes in the care of teeth is a (an) _____.
4. The doctor who specializes in problems of malocclusion is a (an) _____.
5. Decay begins when the protective covering of the tooth is damaged by _____.
6. The last permanent teeth to erupt are the _____ teeth.
7. The most common chronic disease in the United States today is dental _____.
8. Lactic acid is produced by _____ acting on sugars and other foods in the mouth.
9. A severe disease of gums, mouth, and throat is _____.
10. The thin tissue surrounding a tooth is called the _____ membrane.

MULTIPLE-CHOICE QUESTIONS

1. The hard outer covering of the tooth is the
   a. dentine   b. enamel   c. cementum   d. pulp

The Appearance, Care, and Feeding of Your Body

2. For good dental care, clean regularly and see the dentist
   a. when you find a cavity
   b. when you have a toothache
   c. on a regular basis
   d. when your breath is bad

3. Teeth should be cleaned by a dentist regularly in order to
   a. kill all bacteria   c. remove tartar
   b. make them shiny   d. eliminate bad breath

4. A lost tooth should be replaced chiefly because
   a. it is needed for chewing
   b. other teeth will decay
   c. it looks better
   d. adjacent teeth may shift into the vacant spot

5. Teeth with cavities
   a. frequently heal themselves
   b. always produce pain
   c. can be restored by removal of decay and then filled
   d. should be extracted

6. The dentist uses X rays to
   a. help keep teeth clean
   b. stop bacterial decay
   c. spot dental problems that the eye cannot see
   d. prevent tooth decay

7. The teeth that help us cut food are
   a. incisors   b. cuspids   c. bicuspids   d. molars

8. Teeth that tear and shred food are
   a. incisors   b. cuspids   c. bicuspids   d. molars

9. Molars
   a. cut food   c. tear and grind food
   b. tear and shred food   d. crush and grind food

10. The bonelike material that covers the root of a tooth is
    a. dentine   b. enamel   c. cementum   d. pulp

11. The part of the tooth anchored in the jaw is the
    a. neck   b. enamel   c. crown   d. root

12. To reduce tooth decay, drinking water is treated with
    a. fluorides   b. chlorides   c. disclosing tablets   d. lactic acid

13. Malocclusion can cause all of the following, *except*
    a. mispronounced words   c. facial distortions
    b. chewing problems   d. plaque

14. Most periodontal diseases occur
    a. at infancy   c. during middle age
    b. during early childhood   d. during old age

15. A disclosing tablet will
    a. whiten teeth   c. show up dental plaque
    b. remove decay   d. cause decay

THOUGHT QUESTIONS

1. Why is it dangerous to leave an abscessed tooth untreated?
2. "If you are unable to brush your teeth, a thorough rinsing of the mouth is a good alternative." Discuss this statement, giving facts to support your point of view.
3. Explain the relationship between diet and healthy teeth.
4. Jan's diet is high in sweets. She has not received fluoride treatments. She rarely brushes her teeth and never flosses them. At her last dental examination, she had several cavities, and her teeth were covered with tartar. Discuss the following statements: (a) sweets have little effect upon Jan's teeth; (b) fluoride treatments may be beneficial for Jan; (c) Jan's brushing and flossing habits are less dangerous than her diet preferences; (d) cavities are only a minor problem, and neglect of the teeth will have little or no effect on Jan's general health.
5. Refer again to Figure 11.3, page 140, and tell what you think root canal treatment might mean.
6. Why is dental treatment more painless today than it was 25 years ago?
7. Why is the cost of orthodontic treatment generally high?

Looking Ahead

Your diet also contributes to your health and to your appearance. When you look at the older people around you, you see the results of the food choices they have made over the years. Of course, you want to be one of those who choose food wisely and who stay healthy and trim as the years go by. In Chapter 12, you will learn how to choose the foods you need to grow properly, to stay healthy, and to maintain your ideal weight.

The Appearance, Care, and Feeding of Your Body

Chapter 12: A Varied Diet for Health and Weight Control

First of all, look again at the title of this chapter and think about how the word *diet* is used in it. Did it occur to you that this word really has *two* important meanings? In one sense, your diet is the amounts and kinds of food you normally eat. In another sense, your diet could be a careful, conscious attempt to restrict amounts and kinds of food that cause over-weight. Both meanings are suggested in the chapter title, and both meanings will be investigated in the pages ahead.

Oxygen, hydrogen, carbon, and nitrogen—these elements serve as building blocks that make up most of the world around us. It is mainly these elements that form (1) rivers and seas, (2) the part of soil that is fertile for growing plants, and (3) living bodies—plant, animal, and human. As you can see in Table 12.1, these four elements make up about 96 percent of your own body.

Table 12.1: Elements in the Body (Approximate Percentages)

Element	Percentage	Element	Percentage
Oxygen	65.0	Sulfur	0.2
Carbon	18.5	Magnesium	0.04
Hydrogen	9.5	Cobalt	Trace
Nitrogen	2.7	Copper	Trace
Calcium	1.5	Fluorine	Trace
Phosphorus	1.0	Iodine	Trace
Potassium	0.3	Iron	Trace
Chlorine	0.2	Zinc	Trace
Sodium	0.2		

Every day you need a new supply of carbon, hydrogen, and oxygen to provide you with warmth and energy. Every day you need these three

Figure 12.1. Energy foods: *(a)* **foods rich in carbohydrates;** *(b)* **foods rich in fats.**

elements plus nitrogen to provide materials for growth and for replacement of worn-out and injured cells. You get these elements from your food.

Of course, you don't sit down to a meal of oxygen, hydrogen, carbon, and nitrogen. Combinations of these elements are present in food in the form of **carbohydrates, fats,** and **proteins.** (For a quick review of the way your body digests these food substances, reread pages 60–64.)

Carbohydrates: Quick-Energy Foods

As you might partly guess from the word itself, carbohydrates are made up of carbon, hydrogen, and oxygen. You can see some foods high in carbo-hydrates (sugars and starches) in Figure 12.1a. Your body can change them into *glucose*, which is the main source of your warmth and energy. The following activity will show you how quickly this change takes place in the mouth (most carbohydrate digestion takes place in the small intestine):

The Appearance, Care, and Feeding of Your Body

1. Chew a bite of starchy food (use a bite of soda cracker or a piece of raw potato) for a few minutes without swallowing—until the taste changes.
2. Write down what happened.

Most likely, you noticed that, after a short time, the starchy food began to taste sweet. An enzyme in your saliva had rather quickly changed the starch to sugar.

Fats: Long-Lasting Energy Foods

Fats, too, are made up of carbon, hydrogen, and oxygen. But it takes you longer to digest them than carbohydrates. You can see foods rich in fat in Figure 12.1*b*. The longer it takes for something to be digested, the less hungry you feel. So, for example, the orange juice and toast you had for breakfast might help you through first-period math, but the milk, scrambled eggs, and bacon would probably keep you going through fourth-period gym. When you eat more carbohydrates or fats than your body needs, the extra amount is stored away in fat cells under your skin and around body organs. When you lack energy because you have not eaten for some time, some of this fat is oxidized and used up.

Proteins: Cell-Building Foods

But your body needs more than warmth and energy. It also needs materials called **amino acids** to build cells with. Proteins, which contain carbon, hydrogen, oxygen, and nitrogen, along with a few other elements, provide these materials. During digestion, proteins are broken down into various amino acids. Your body uses these amino acids to build the protein part of each body cell. Without amino acids, your body could not build or replace muscle tissue, the protein parts of the digestive enzymes, the internal organs, the lymph, or the blood. Even the **antibodies** that form in your blood to fight off infection are made of body protein.

THE ESSENTIAL AMINO ACIDS   Scientists have identified over 20 amino acids. Your body can manufacture 12 of these. But it is essential, or necessary, that you get the others from the food you eat. Animal proteins, from milk, cheese, poultry, and fish, contain large amounts of all the essential amino acids (see Figure 12.2*a*, page 158). Plant proteins don't supply all of the essential amino acids (see Figure 12.2*b*). For this reason, animal proteins are called *complete*, and plant proteins are called *incomplete*. To check your own protein intake, do the following:

A Varied Diet for Health and Weight Control

(a)

(b)

Figure 12.2. Proteins in animal and plant foods: *(a)* **foods containing complete proteins;** *(b)* **foods lacking complete proteins.**

<hr>

YOUR PART

1. With the help of Figure 12.2, list your favorite protein foods, both complete and incomplete.
2. Do you think protein foods make up about $\frac{1}{10}$ to $\frac{1}{8}$ of your daily diet? If not, estimate (and write down) how much of your food is protein.
3. You are the family cook, and there is a *vegetarian* coming to dinner. A vegetarian does not eat meat. Referring to Figure 12.2, decide if you are able to provide your guest with complete protein.

You probably decided that you could provide your vegetarian guest with complete protein by serving milk products or eggs. But be warned: some vegetarians regard these foods as animal-related and will not eat them. Chances are, you yourself like a variety of protein foods. If so, you should have no trouble making sure that $\frac{1}{10}$ to $\frac{1}{8}$ of your diet is protein, as it should be. (At least half of that should be complete protein.)

Minerals

In addition to energy foods and proteins, your body needs small amounts of at least 17 **minerals**. You already have enough calcium in your body to provide your classroom with chalk for 5 months, enough sodium and chlorine (KLAW-reen) to make enough salt to fill a small salt shaker, and enough iron to make a nail. These and other minerals make up about 4 percent of your body weight.

You need minerals to help build body tissue and to help regulate various body processes. Calcium, for example, not only helps build bones and teeth; it also helps in blood clotting. Iodine is essential for the working of the thyroid gland. Without iron in your blood, oxygen could not be carried to your cells. Like enzymes, minerals also help with the digestion and oxidation of the food you eat.

American diets are often short on calcium, iron, and iodine. Table 12.2 shows you which foods contain these minerals. If you eat a good

Table 12.2: Your Body's Need for Minerals

Mineral	Good Sources	Needed For
Calcium	Milk, dairy products, green vegetables	Building bones and teeth; blood clotting; maintaining normal heart, muscle, and nerve activity; regulating use of other minerals by cells
Phosphorus	Milk, dairy products, meat, liver, eggs, beans, peas, oatmeal, whole wheat	Building bones, teeth, and nerve tissue; energy production by cells
Iron	Liver, eggs, meat, green vegetables, whole-grain cereals	Carrying of oxygen by red blood cells; use of oxygen by all cells
Copper	Liver, mushrooms, shellfish, green vegetables, cocoa, bran	Forming oxygen-carrying compounds in red blood cells
Iodine	Vegetables grown in soil near the sea, seafoods, iodized salt	Manufacture of thyroxin by the thyroid gland

Adapted from *How Your Body Uses Food,* National Dairy Council.

mixed diet of such foods, you will get the other minerals you need, as well. This is because many minerals are present in one food. For example, a glass of milk and a raw green salad salted with iodized salt will give you all the minerals listed in Table 12.2. If you would like to see for yourself some of the minerals present in food, do the following:

YOUR PART

1. Use a small amount of mashed fruit, vegetable, or powdered milk. Put it in a test tube or porcelain evaporating dish.
2. Holding the test tube or dish with a pair of tongs, heat the food over a high flame until it has stopped smoking and very little remains. (Do not touch the hot container directly.)
3. Describe what is left and write down what you think it is.

You may have written that the gray or white ashes that remained after heating were minerals present in the food. (Minerals like salt and iron do not burn.)

Water and Other Liquids

The teens are years of rapid growth. During these years you need 4 cups of milk a day (1 quart or about 1 liter) to provide the calcium you need for bones and teeth. Since your body is three-quarters liquid, and since you lose 4 to 8 cups of that liquid every day, you will usually need more liquid than that provided by your milk. Your food contains some liquid. How much more do you need? Your thirst is a good guide. In general, 2 to 4 glasses of water in addition to your milk will give you the liquid you need.

Vitamins

Before our century, carbohydrates, fats, proteins, minerals, and water were the only known nutrients, or nourishing substances. Scientists in our century have discovered many more. Among these are the **vitamins** A, C, D, E, and K, plus several B vitamins. Table 12.3, pages 162–163, gives their names and sources.

Like enzymes and minerals, vitamins help in the functioning of various body processes. Vitamin B_1, for example, helps maintain the nervous system in good condition. In addition, a lack or shortage of vitamins in the diet can cause **deficiency** (dih-FISH-un-see) **diseases** to develop.

DEFICIENCY DISEASES   In 1906, a British physician and chemist, Frederick Hopkins, fed pure fats, carbohydrates, proteins, minerals, and water to healthy rats. The rats stopped growing, lost weight, and died. Something vital was missing from their diet, as Dr. Hopkins' experiment had proved. A deficiency is a lack or shortage. We know today that Dr. Hopkins' rats died of a vitamin deficiency.

FOODS THAT PREVENT DEFICIENCY   As early as 1747, James Lind, a doctor in the British Navy, did an experiment proving that scurvy (SKUR-vee) could be prevented on long voyages if sailors ate some citrus fruit each day. (Table 12.3 describes the symptoms of scurvy as well as those of other deficiency diseases.)

Similarly, in the nineteenth century, two Dutch doctors learned that people who ate only white rice (with the brown hulls, or coverings, removed) developed **beriberi**. The doctors learned that something in the discarded rice hulls could prevent beriberi. It remained for twentieth-century scientists to find out that the something was vitamin B_1, or thiamin.

Scientists in our century have given vitamins their names, discovered their exact chemical makeup, and learned how to produce *synthetic* (sin-THET-ik), or artificially made, vitamins in laboratories. This last development is important because synthetic vitamins can be distributed cheaply and can easily be added to foods that lack such vitamins. Few scientific stories are more dramatic than those telling how vitamins were discovered. To investigate these discoveries, do the following:

YOUR PART

1. Volunteer to report to the class on one of the following people or subjects:

    a.   Elmer V. McCollum and vitamins A and D
    b.   Marguerite Davis and vitamin A
    c.   Joseph Goldberger, **pellagra** (puh-LAY-gruh), and niacin
    d.   Conrad Elvehjem and niacin
    e.   Paul Gyorgy and riboflavin
    f.   Robert R. Williams and thiamin
    g.   Christiaan Eijkman, Gerrit Grinjns, beriberi, and thiamin
    h.   Kanekiro Takaki, beriberi, and thiamin
    i.   Roger J. Williams and folic acid
    j.   Mary Shorb, Edward Rickes, and vitamin B_{12}
    k.   James Lind, scurvy, and vitamin C
    l.   Herbert Evans, K. Scott Bishop, and vitamin E
    m.   The deficiency disease **rickets** and vitamin D
    n.   The deficiency disease **kwashiorkor** (kwah-SHEE-awr-kawr), sometimes called protein deficiency.

A Varied Diet for Health and Weight Control   161

Table 12.3: Vitamin Sources

Vitamin	Promotes	Sources	Results of Deficiency
A (body converts carotene to vitamin A)	Good vision in dim light; resistance to skin infections	Carrots, other yellow vegetables; whole milk, butter, eggs; leafy green vegetables, peas; fish-liver oils	Nightblindness; eye infections; increased likelihood of infections of nose, throat, and skin
B Vitamins B₁ (thiamin)	Appetite, oxidation of foods; normal action of nervous system	Whole-grain cereals and enriched bread; beans and peas; yeast; milk; lean beef, liver, pork, poultry	Loss of appetite; beriberi (exhaustion, paralysis, heart disease)
B₂ (riboflavin)	Healthy skin, especially around lips and eyes; oxidation of foods	Yeast; lean beef, liver; milk, eggs; green vegetables; whole wheat; prunes	Lip and tongue inflammation; dim vision
P-P (niacin)	Digestion; healthy skin; normal action of nervous system	Lean beef, liver; milk, eggs; leafy green vegetables, tomatoes; yeast	Pellagra (skin irritation, tongue inflammation, digestive and nervous disturbances)
B₁₂ (cobalamin)	Normal blood formation; growth; normal action of nervous system	Liver, kidney; fish	Pernicious anemia; retarded growth; disorders of the nervous system
Folic acid	Normal blood formation	Leafy green vegetables; yeast; meat	Some types of anemia

Table 12.3 (concluded)

Vitamin	Promotes	Sources	Results of Deficiency
C (ascorbic acid)	Adhesion of body cells to one another	Citrus fruits (oranges, grapefruits, lemons, limes); leafy green vegetables, tomatoes	Scurvy (soft and bleeding gums, loose teeth, swollen painful joints, bleeding under the skin)
D (calciferol, made in skin if exposed to sunlight)	Growth of teeth and bones	Fish-liver oils; milk; eggs	Rickets (bowlegs, knock-knees, swollen joints, especially wrists and ankles); badly formed teeth
E (tocopherol)	Benefits unknown in humans	Wheat germ; leafy green vegetables; meat; whole-grain cereals	Sterility (inability to reproduce) in rats, and possibly in humans
K (phylloquinone)	Blood clotting	Leafy green vegetables	Hemorrhage (excessive bleeding, even from minor wounds)

As you gave and listened to the reports on vitamins, you probably noticed one thing. People who eat a wide variety of foods don't get deficiency diseases. Only those who limit their diets in some way get them.The beriberi sufferers ate only white rice with the vitamin-rich hulls removed. Scurvy sufferers avoided or couldn't get fresh fruits and vegetables.

Pellagra sufferers ate only corn, instead of a variety of grains, and couldn't afford to eat enough good protein food.

Perhaps you limit your diet in some unnecessary way. To get an idea of how habit and personal tastes can affect diet variety, do the following:

YOUR PART

1. List your ten favorite everyday foods. Add two favorite foreign foods, for a total of 12.
2. As a class or in small groups, tally the lists to find the groups' 12 favorite foods. Compare these favorites with your own.
3. At home, list the 12 favorite foods of each member of your family. Write down how your favorites differ from theirs.

You probably found that your list was not matched by anyone else's, not even within your own family. Some classmates undoubtedly were more adventurous in their food choices than others. A taste for variety is a sign that you are growing up into the kind of adult who feels at home in the world—who enjoys the people, customs, and foods of many regions and many nations. As for your diet, variety means that you get the nutrients you need.

ORGANIC FOODS AND PROCESSED FOODS   Perhaps because vitamins are a fairly recent discovery, people disagree about them. Many people take extra vitamins. Others shop only in health food stores. Such people pay high prices for fruits and vegetables that are *organically grown*—without chemical fertilizers and insect killers, also called **insecticides** (in-SEK-tuh-sydz) and **pesticides** (PES-tuh-sydz). It is true that some fertilizers and insect killers affect our foods for the worse (see Chapter 25, pages 450–451). So do some of the chemicals that are commonly added to processed food by manufacturers (see page 457). We need more controls to guard against harmful side effects from both of these sources.

On the other hand, some people live almost entirely on *processed foods* (foods that go through many or most of the steps of preparation before they reach the home). Most processing destroys some vitamins. Therefore, many of your foods should be freshly prepared.

No matter how fresh fruits and vegetables are grown, they are still full of vitamins. However, many of these precious vitamins are lost each additional day that the food is stored and not eaten. Heat and oxygen destroy vitamins, too, especially vitamin C. So it is important to buy really fresh fruits and vegetables and to use them fairly promptly. And when it is necessary to cook them, cook them in a small amount of water. The water in which vegetables and fruits have been cooked contains important nutrients, and this leftover liquid can be used in soups and gravies.

Let's Pause for Review

Every day you need oxygen to "burn up" your food and water to replace lost liquid. In addition, your body needs (1) the oxygen, hydrogen, and carbon present in carbohydrates and fats (for warmth and energy) and (2) the oxygen, hydrogen, carbon, and nitrogen present in proteins (to build the protein parts of body cells). The minerals in food are needed to build bones and teeth and to regulate various body processes. Vitamins assist body processes and prevent deficiency diseases. The best way to avoid any diet deficiency is to eat a wide variety of foods, both cooked and raw. To get the most from vitamin-rich foods, use them promptly and eat them raw, if possible. If such foods must be cooked, cook them quickly in a small amount of water, and add the leftover liquid to other foods in your diet.

Choosing a Balanced Diet

How can you be sure of getting all the vitamins, minerals, proteins, and energy foods you need each day? A good way is to choose foods from each of the four food groups recommended by the federal government (see Figure 12.3, pages 166–167).

THE MILK GROUP: A QUART A DAY   Milk is your best source of calcium and a good source of other minerals, vitamins, and proteins. You need a quart (about 1 liter) a day during your teens. This can be skim milk (milk from which cream has been removed) if you are watching your weight. If you prefer to drink less milk, make up for it with servings of cheese, ice cream, or other milk products.

THE MEAT GROUP: TWO SERVINGS A DAY   The meat group includes not only meat, fish, and poultry, but also other protein foods such

(a)

(b)

Figure 12.3. The four food groups for good nutrition: (a) the milk group; (b) the meat group; (c) the fruit and vegetable group; (d) the bread and cereal group.

as eggs, dried beans, peas, nuts, and peanut butter. A serving means 2 or more ounces (about 60 grams) of meat, two eggs, a cup of dried beans, or 4 tablespoons of peanut butter. Remember that half your protein should be of the complete type (animal protein).

THE FRUIT AND VEGETABLE GROUP: FOUR SERVINGS A DAY Because cooking destroys many vitamins, try to include two servings of raw fruits or vegetables daily—a leafy green salad and a glass of orange juice, for example. Since your body can't store vitamin C, be sure to include one good source of that vitamin daily. As a check on your vitamin C intake, do the following:

(c)

(d)

1. Which of your usual foods provide you with vitamin C? Write down the answer, describing the size of the usual serving.
2. Ask class volunteers to look up in a nutrition book or table exactly how many milligrams (mg) of vitamin C various food servings provide.
3. When the volunteers report their findings, listen to see if your daily serving actually provides you with the amount of vitamin C you need each day during your teens. Write down the result.

You may have been surprised to learn that one serving only of foods rich in vitamin C (a medium orange, half of a grapefruit, a tomato) may not give you the amount you need each day.

THE BREAD AND CEREAL GROUP: FOUR SERVINGS A DAY When choosing from this group, remember that whole-grain breads and cereals, such as whole-wheat bread, wheat germ, oatmeal, and brown rice, are naturally rich in vitamins. On the other hand, many available foods in this group are processed in such a way that some of the original vitamins are lost. This is true of bakery products made from bleached or refined flours and cereals that have been dried, flavored, and sometimes sugarcoated. So, if you like to eat white bread, dried-flake cereals, instant rice, and such foods, be sure they are *enriched* (with vitamins added to replace those lost in processing). In general, when you can, choose foods from natural rather than processed sources.

The Most Important Meal

Why is breakfast so often called the most important meal of the day? First of all, by the time you wake up in the morning, your body has been without food for 10 or 12 hours. If you miss breakfast, you add 4 or 5 hours to that total. Then, the warmth and energy you need as you begin a new day must be supplied by borrowing from body cells. Second, studies have shown that people who miss breakfast are usually less alert and get less done, especially when they are performing mental activity such as schoolwork. Third, other studies have shown that by skipping breakfast (or some other meal) you don't lose weight; you usually gain, instead. You get so hungry when you go without a meal that you *more* than make up for it the next time you sit down to eat. The fourth reason for having a good breakfast is that, even though you may eat a big lunch and dinner, you may forget to make up for the missed vitamin C serving (orange juice), the missed protein serving (eggs), and the missed whole-grain serving (toast or cereal) that breakfast would have provided.

Snacks

While you are still growing, especially if you are getting a healthy amount of exercise, you often need snacks to keep you going. If you choose a soft drink or other sweet snack, it will give you energy, but no vitamins, minerals, or proteins. So, if you are not getting any of the necessary daily food servings, you can make up for them at snack time by eating peanuts, cheese, or fresh fruit, and by drinking fruit juice or milk. To see if you are choosing a good mixed diet, do the following:

YOUR PART

1. Plan (and write down the menus for) a whole day's food (three meals and two snacks). Include four servings from the milk group,

two from the meat group, four from the fruit and vegetable group, and four from the bread and cereal group. Consult the vitamin chart (refer again to Table 12.3, pages 162–163). If necessary, add servings to provide any missing vitamins. Bring these menus to class the next day and save them for later use.

2. Beginning with your next meal, write down the menus of all your meals and snacks for the next 24 hours. Bring this list to class.

3. Compare your two menu lists. Write down whether the meals you planned or those you actually ate were more nourishing. Write down any servings you missed.

4. Spend some time thinking about the way you usually eat. Now write down the weaknesses in your usual diet. List the servings you often skip and the vitamins you may not always get.

Chances are you will find it easy to add any servings you have been skipping. Did you include coffee, tea, cocoa, or cola drinks in either menu list? Perhaps you, like most people, enjoy one or more of these drinks for their taste and for their **caffeine** (KAF-een), an ingredient that stimulates, or speeds up, the activities of the nervous system. Many people come to rely too much on the pick-me-up supplied by caffeine, sometimes with ill effects on their health. One or two cups (or glasses) a day of such drinks is plenty. Just remember not to let them take the place of the milk and fruit juice your body needs to stay strong and active.

Deficiency Diseases Today

Doctors today know how to prevent deficiency diseases. Yet, in the Orient beriberi still exists among people who don't know about or can't afford the right food. Children go blind in India because their parents don't know that certain foods rich in vitamin A can save their sight. Protein deficiency kills many children every year in Africa and India; starvation kills many more.

SUGAR AND VITAMIN DEFICIENCY   In our own country and in some European countries, however, most people have the opposite problem. Because plenty of food of all kinds is available, people eat too much. And the problem is not confined to the overeating of good food.

Recent medical studies suggest that the average American consumes more than 100 pounds of sugar a year. Sugar is a major ingredient in candy, soda pop, cakes, cookies, and sweetened chewing gum; it is also found in such foods as canned soups, potato salad, salad dressings, and baby food, among other things.

Dentists have long warned about what a taste for sweets does to teeth. We are now learning that sugar is probably responsible for other problems

A Varied Diet for Health and Weight Control   169

as well—and one of them is vitamin deficiency. Excess sweets and other foods with significant sugar content fill us up and make us lose our appetites for the vitamin-rich foods we need to stay healthy.

Hardened Fat and Heart Disease

Many people who overeat, eat too much fat, in particular. This has two results. Many people are overweight, and many are getting too much **saturated** (SATCH-uh-ray-tud), or hardened, **fat** in their diets. Studies have been done and continue to be done on the connection between diet and heart disease. There is no completely convincing proof that diet causes either heart or artery disease. However, there is no denying that *coronary* (heart) arteries clogged with **cholesterol** (kuh-LES-tuh-rawl) and other fatty material show up most often in people living in the United States, Germany, and Denmark, where fat intake equals about 40 percent of the diet. The blood moves with difficulty through artery channels narrowed by fat. This makes it easier for a clot to form, blocking such a channel and causing a heart attack. Healthy arteries are far more common in people with low-fat diets like the Japanese.

Table 12.4:   Calories You Need for Various Activities

Activity	No. of Calories per Hour per 2.2 Pounds (1 Kilogram) of Body Weight
Sleeping	0.9
Awake, lying still	1.1
Sitting, at rest	1.4
Sitting, reading aloud	1.5
Standing, relaxed	1.5
Sewing or knitting	1.6
Dressing or undressing	1.7
Singing	1.7
Ironing	2.0
Washing dishes	2.1
Carpentry	3.4
Exercise, light	2.4
Exercise, active	4.1
Exercise, heavy	6.4
Exercise, very heavy	8.6
Walking, slowly	2.9
Walking, moderately fast	4.3
Walking, very fast	9.3
Descending stairs	5.2
Ascending stairs	15.8

Adapted from the Los Angeles Junior High School *Instructional Guide in Health.*

So, although all of the facts are not yet in, doctors nowadays advise us to limit fat intake to about 25 percent of the diet. They also recommend that, whenever possible, people use unsaturated fats like salad oil, which do *not* harden even if allowed to stand, rather than saturated fats like beef fat, butter, cheese, and lard, which do. It's easy to substitute skim milk for whole, to cut fat off meat before cooking, and to limit hardened fat in the diet in other ways. Most doctors believe this small effort can lengthen lives.

Overweight

A second result of plentiful food is overweight. Insurance company records show that overweight people have more health problems and lead shorter lives than do others. Now is a good time for you to form eating habits that will allow you to avoid these problems.

Normally, hunger tells you when to eat just as thirst tells you when to drink. But everyone has eaten a favorite food just because it looked delicious. People often eat to please the person who did the cooking. Sometimes whole families overeat all the time just out of habit. If, for reasons like these, you are eating more food than you need, you will gain weight. Why? Because by overeating you are regularly taking in more food than your body needs. Your body will store the unused food as fat.

COUNTING CALORIES Doubtless, in your time, you have burned a few marshmallows you meant only to roast. If you had had the right equipment with you, you could have measured in this way the number of **Calories** of heat in one marshmallow. But you would have had to burn the marshmallow inside a sealed container of oxygen surrounded by water. If you had used a liter (about 1 quart) of water, and if the heat resulting from the burning marshmallow had raised the temperature of the surrounding water about 20 degrees Celsius, you would then have known that a marshmallow releases about 20 Calories of heat energy. (The amount of heat needed to raise the temperature of 1 liter of water 1 degree Celsius is a Calorie.) In this way, scientists have measured the Calorie values for almost every food.

Scientists have also found out how many Calories your body uses up for various purposes. Even if you were completely at rest, for example, you would need from 1000 to 1500 Calories a day just to keep your heart, lungs, and cells going. You need more Calories for every additional thing you do (see Table 12.4). Calorie need also varies with age, weight, sex, and environment. Thus, young, growing people require more Calories than others. Heavier people normally require more Calories than lighter people because heavier people have more body cells that use food. Males generally need more Calories than females. People in cold climates need more Calories to maintain normal body heat than those in warm climates.

To get a better idea of your own Calorie needs, do the following:

A Varied Diet for Health and Weight Control

Even at rest, your body uses 1 Calorie an hour for each kilogram (2.2 pounds) of body weight, or about 11 Calories per pound per day.

1. Figure, on a separate piece of paper, your own Calorie needs by either of the following methods:

    11 Calories per pound × body weight = daily Calories needed
    when at rest

    or

    $$\frac{\text{body weight}}{2.2 \text{ pounds}} \times 24 \text{ hours} = \text{daily Calories needed when at rest}$$

2. Now use the information in Table 12.4 to estimate how many *more* Calories you need to fuel up for your activities. Here is the method for figuring:

    $$\frac{\text{body weight}}{2.2 \text{ pounds}} \times \text{Calorie count per hour's activity (Table 12.4)}$$
    $$= \text{Calories needed for activity}$$

3. Now add:

    Total Calories needed daily to keep heart,
    lungs, and cells going: _____ Calories

    Total Calories needed for additional
    activities: _____ Calories

    Total Calories needed: _____ Calories

4. Using the menu list you made earlier (refer again to pages 168–169) and the Calorie counts shown in Table 12.5, figure out approximately how many Calories you take in daily.

5. You may also use additional charts from home and library, if they are available. Compare your total Calorie intake with your Calorie needs.

6. Write down whether you took in too many or too few Calories on the day you made the list.

Did you take in too much or too little? Perhaps a simpler way of finding out would be to look in the mirror. Do you look a bit under-nourished or too well fed? Try the pinch test. On the outside of your upper arm take a pinch of skin between your thumb and forefinger. If the pinch measures more than ½ inch (1.25 centimeters), you probably have more fat stored beneath the dermis of your skin than you need for health and warmth. If the pinch measures much less than ¼ inch (about .5 centimeters), you may be underweight instead.

Table 12.5: Calories in Common Foods

Food	Serving	Calories (Approximate)
Dairy Products	*(See end-of-table note)*	
Butter (and margarine)	1 tablespoon	100
Cheese, American	1 ounce	115
Cheese, cottage	1 ounce	30
Cheese, cream	1 ounce	105
Cheese, Swiss	1 ounce	105
Egg, boiled	1 large	80
Egg, scrambled	1 large	110
Ice cream	½ pint	295
Milk, chocolate-flavored	1 cup	190
Milk, malted	1 cup	280
Milk, skim	1 cup	90
Milk, whole	1 cup	165
Pudding, chocolate	¼ cup	100
Meats/Poultry		
Bacon	2 slices	95
Chicken, roasted	4 ounces	207
Frankfurter	1½ ounces	155
Ham, boiled	2 ounces	170
Ham, smoked, without bone	3 ounces	340
Hamburger	3-ounce patty	245
Lamb chop, thick, with bone	5 ounces	475
Roast beef (fatty)	3-ounce slice	420
Steak, broiled	3 ounces	375
Seafood		
Clams, raw	3 ounces	70
Fishsticks	8 ounces	400
Mackerel, broiled	3 ounces	200
Shrimp	3 ounces	110
Tuna, canned in oil	3 ounces	170
Nuts		
Cashew nuts	1 cup	770
Peanut butter	1 tablespoon	90
Peanuts, shelled	1 cup	840
Vegetables		
Asparagus, cooked	1 cup	35

Table 12.5 (continued)

Food	Serving	Calories (Approximate)
Vegetables (continued)		
Beans, lima, cooked	1 cup	260
Broccoli, cooked	1 cup	45
Carrots, cooked, diced	1 cup	45
Carrots, raw	1 carrot	20
Celery, raw	8-inch stalk	5
Corn, sweet	5-inch ear	65
Lettuce	2 large leaves	5
Peas, canned	1 cup	170
Peas, cooked	1 cup	110
Potato, baked or boiled	5 ounces	90
Potato, french-fried	10 pieces	155
Potato chips	10 chips	110
Spinach, cooked	1 cup	45
String beans, canned	1 cup	45
Fruits		
Apple, raw	1 medium	70
Banana	1 medium	85
Grapefruit	½ medium	50
Orange	1 large	70
Orange juice	1 cup	105
Peach, raw	4 ounces	35
Peaches, canned	1 cup	80
Pear, raw	1 medium	100
Raisins	1 cup	460
Tomato, raw	1 medium	30
Cereal Products		
Biscuits	1 biscuit	130
Bran flakes	1 ounce	85
Bread, white	1 slice	60
Bread, whole-wheat or rye	1 slice	55
Cake, angel food	$1/12$ of a cake	110
Cookies	3-inch cookie	110
Cornflakes	1 ounce	110
Crackers, graham	4 small	55
Crackers, soda	2 (2½-inch square)	45
Cupcake, without icing	1 cupcake	130
Doughnuts	1 doughnut	135

Table 12.5 (concluded)

Food	Serving	Calories (Approximate)
Cereal Products (continued)		
Layer cake	¹/₁₆ of a cake	490
Oatmeal	1 cup	150
Pancakes	1 cake	60
Rice, cooked	1 cup	200
Rolls, hard	1 roll	160
Sweets/Soda		
Candy, chocolate	1 ounce	145
Cola-type soda	1 cup	105
Jelly	1 tablespoon	50
Sugar	1 tablespoon	50

Note: Approximate equivalent servings in the metric system are:
1 tablespoon = 15 grams   ½ pint (1 cup) = 250 cubic centimeters (milliliters)
1 ounce = 30 grams   1 inch = 2.5 centimeters

ACTIVITY AND OVERWEIGHT Two things determine whether food is burned up or stored as fat. One is the amount of food. The other is the amount of activity. In a 1967 study of overweight, well-known nutritionist Dr. Jean Mayer showed a surprising thing. The overweight teenagers in the study actually ate slightly fewer Calories than their slimmer classmates. The important difference was that they exercised a *great deal less*. Feeling awkward, they avoided exercise. When some of them did exercises set to music in a class that emphasized poise and grace, they lost weight steadily. If you would like to be trimmer, such a class in gym or at the Y might be the answer.

TREATING YOURSELF TO FOOD Food treats are pleasant. Everyone enjoys them. But because snack food is now so convenient, some people form the habit of eating every time they want or think they deserve a treat. If you are inclined to gain weight easily, find treats other than food for yourself. Take an outing. Visit or phone a friend. Instead of eating when you aren't hungry (or eating more than you are hungry for), join a new group, ride a bike, or do something else that you will enjoy and that will take your mind off food.

IF YOU ARE OVERWEIGHT If you need to lose more than 10 pounds (about 5 kilograms)—especially if you want to lose more than a pound (about ½ kilogram) a week—you should see your doctor, who will supervise your dieting program. But if you are just a little overweight, study the menu list you made earlier. Foods that are mostly fat or sugar can be cut out of your diet without harm. They contain many Calories and few vitamins and minerals. If you eliminate just one high-Calorie snack, dessert, or second helping *every day*, you will lose weight gradually, and that is the only healthy way to lose weight.

Why Crash Diets Don't Work There are good reasons why weight loss should always be gradual. First, a too rapid change—a crash diet—puts a strain on your body. Second, as long as you are growing, you should not greatly reduce your food intake because you may cut out the very nutrients you need for growth. Third, you must change your exercise and eating habits if your weight loss is to be permanent, and habits change slowly.

Your present habits took a long time to form. When you lose weight slowly, you are gradually forming new habits that will keep you slim in the future. Are you thinking that you don't know exactly what your new habits should be? Gradually, as you work at it, you will discover the exercise you enjoy. Little by little, you will find out how often you can have a second helping or dessert without gaining weight. That way, by the time you reach your desired weight, you will have acquired habits to match.

Underweight

Perhaps the pinch test, the Calorie count of your menu, and the mirror all indicated that you are a little underweight. Be sure that you are getting enough sleep and that you eat regular, well-balanced meals plus nourishing snacks. If you still can't gain—especially if you don't feel your best— you should see your doctor. You should also see a doctor if you need to gain more than 10 pounds (5 kilograms). You may have an infection or other medical problem that is keeping you from gaining weight, or your doctor may assure you that you are naturally lean and perfectly well.

Looking Back

Every day you need (1) carbohydrates and fats for warmth and energy; (2) proteins to build the protein parts of body cells; (3) minerals to build and strengthen bones and teeth and to assist other body processes; and (4) vitamins to assist body processes and prevent deficiencies. A good mixed diet of foods, both cooked and raw, includes four servings from the milk group, two servings from the protein group, four servings from the fruit and vegetable group (including one citrus serving), and four servings from the bread and cereal group (either whole-grain or

The Appearance, Care, and Feeding of Your Body

enriched). To keep your heart and arteries healthy, you should reduce the amount of hardened (saturated) fat in your diet by cutting the fat off meat, by using skim-milk products, and by using unsaturated fats whenever possible.

See your doctor for help if you are more than 10 pounds overweight or underweight. If you are just a little underweight, you may be able to gain by getting more sleep and by eating regular, well-balanced meals. If you are just a little overweight, try adding to your daily schedule some regular exercise that makes you feel graceful and confident. Cut out just one or two sugary or fatty servings a day, and you will lose weight gradually. But never skip a meal, especially breakfast. Breakfast helps you to do your best at school, to get the nutrients you need, and to control your weight.

MODIFIED TRUE-FALSE QUESTIONS

1. Oxygen, hydrogen, carbon, and _nitrogen_ make up more than 96 percent of your body.
2. A liter equals approximately _4_ quart(s).
3. _Fats_ provide the materials needed to build body cells.
4. The body manufactures _all_ of the necessary amino acids.
5. _Skin_ tissue may show evidence of the increase of carbohydrates or fat in the diet.
6. Heart disease may be related to _overweight._
7. Vitamin _D_ is essential for the proper formation of teeth.
8. An underweight person consumes _more_ Calories than are necessary for good health.
9. Antibodies that form in the blood to fight infections are made of _fats._
10. When carbohydrates are digested, _starch_ is formed.
11. _Mineral elements_ make up about 4 percent of our body weight.
12. Temperature in the metric system is expressed in _Fahrenheit_ degrees.
13. Foods from all _four_ basic food groups are necessary for a balanced diet.
14. Like enzymes and minerals, _vitamins_ help with oxidation of food and other body processes.
15. Animal proteins are referred to as _complete_ proteins.
16. Lack of vitamin B_1 may affect the nervous system.
17. Teenagers usually need _more_ Calories daily than do their grandparents.
18. Foods containing proteins are best for _energy._
19. Your body _requires_ Calories even when it is at rest.
20. Skipping a meal, especially breakfast, is _a satisfactory_ way to control weight.

A Varied Diet for Health and Weight Control

MATCHING QUESTIONS

Column A	Column B
1. carbohydrates	a. contained in organically grown foods only
2. proteins	
3. fats	b. body needs very small quantities
4. vitamins	c. quick-energy foods
5. minerals	d. long-lasting energy foods
	e. cell-building foods
	f. calcium and iron

COMPLETION QUESTIONS

1. Carbohydrates are compounds containing _____, _____, and _____.
2. Proteins provide the body with growth materials called _____.
3. In addition to energy foods, proteins, and water, your body needs _____ and _____.
4. Foods grown without using chemical fertilizers and insect killers are commonly called _____ foods.
5. For the body to obtain energy from food, we need the gas _____.
6. Breads and cereals to which vitamins are added because of loss in processing are called _____.
7. The most important meal of the day is _____.
8. The amount of heat needed to raise the temperature of 1 liter of water 1 degree Celsius is known as a (an) _____.
9. Body structures that can be clogged by the deposit of a fatty material are _____.
10. Quick diets for losing weight are called _____ diets.

MULTIPLE-CHOICE QUESTIONS

1. A good guide to the amount of liquid you need is
   a. the amount of exercise you take
   b. your thirst
   c. your age
   d. the dryness of your skin
2. The four basic food groups are
   a. proteins, fats, carbohydrates, and vitamin products
   b. vitamins, minerals, fats, and protein products
   c. fruits, vegetables, milk, and meat products
   d. bread and cereals, fruits and vegetables, meat, and milk products
3. Lean meats are rich in
   a. carbohydrates   b. fats   c. oxygen gas   d. proteins

The Appearance, Care, and Feeding of Your Body

4. Protein contains carbon, hydrogen, oxygen, and
   a. sodium   b. chlorides   c. nitrogen   d. fluorides

5. A diet deficient in vitamin C can cause
   a. scurvy   b. kwashiorkor   c. pellagra   d. beriberi

6. The best source of calcium is
   a. meat   b. fruit   c. vegetables   d. milk

7. If a person is overweight, the best thing to do is
   a.   go on a crash diet   c.   exercise
   b.   take steam baths   d.   follow your doctor's advice

8. A Calorie is a unit used to express
   a.   heat   c.   weight
   b.   height   d.   girth (size around an object)

9. Vitamins are required to
   a.   prevent baldness   c.   provide warmth
   b.   provide amino acids   d.   prevent deficiency diseases

10. The best way to avoid any diet deficiency is to
   a.   eat very few raw vegetables   c.   drink lots of milk
   b.   eat raw meat   d.   eat a wide variety of foods

THOUGHT QUESTIONS

1. Discuss the importance of proteins, minerals, and vitamins in our daily diet, and include examples of foods containing each.

2. Why is water necessary for life?

3. There is a history of heart disease in your family. You consume a large quantity of fats and are slightly overweight. Explain why this can be potentially dangerous to your health.

4. List some arguments in favor of and opposed to the use of organic foods.

5. Write a brief composition on the following topic: All Illnesses May Be Traced to Faulty Diets.

6. Despite our superior knowledge of foods and food production, many people in the world are ill fed and suffer from deficiency diseases. How do you account for this apparent contradiction?

Looking Ahead

A program to insure good health involves developing proper attitudes toward sleep and exercise. In Chapter 13, you will investigate the many new discoveries about sleep and dreaming. You will also read about rest and fatigue, and explore the many benefits of regular exercise.

A Varied Diet for Health and Weight Control

Chapter 13: Sleep, Rest, and Exercise

In spite of the fact that we all spend roughly a third of our lives sleeping, sleep has always been a great mystery. Have you ever asked yourself some of the following questions?

I dreamed I went surfing in a hurricane—do dreams mean anything?
What does it mean if you dream in color?
Is it true that your eyes move when you dream?
How much sleep do I need?
Why do we dream?
What happens to our bodies while we sleep?
How long do dreams take?
Does everybody have trouble falling asleep once in a while?
Why do I always dream I'm late?
Does everyone dream?

Thanks to much active, recent research, many of the questions people have always asked about sleep can now be answered.

What Is Sleep?

Sleep is a regularly returning state of body and mind in which most of your body processes slow down. Your senses grow dull until you are no longer conscious of your surroundings. Your heartbeat slows down, lowering your blood pressure and your pulse rate. You breathe more deeply and slowly. Almost all of your glands produce fewer secretions. You often wake up with a dry mouth, for example, because you produce less saliva during sleep. You may also have noticed that, when you have a cold, you are most comfortable just after waking up because nasal secretions have also decreased during sleep.

In sleep, your muscles relax. Your inactive voluntary muscles do not need as much blood. More blood goes instead to your brain and to the surface of your body. Because very few impulses are being sent back and forth from your voluntary muscles to your brain, the part of your brain that handles these impulses rests.

As you learned in Chapter 4, page 45, your involuntary muscles work 24 hours a day. But during sleep they work more slowly. Less food is oxidized, for example, and less heat produced. Your body temperature drops slightly. To see how this works, do the following:

YOUR PART

1. For five nights in a row, just before going to bed, take your oral (mouth) temperature for 2 full minutes.
2. Take your temperature again when you first get up on the five following mornings.
3. Record all readings on a chart like the following:

Oral Temperature Readings

	Day 1	Day 2	Day 3	Day 4	Day 5
Bedtime temperature					
Morning temperature					

4. Bring your chart to class for comparison and discussion.

If you are like most people, your morning temperature was the lower one. Real night owls (people who work well at night and have trouble getting going in the morning) often have an unusually low morning temperature. On the other hand, people who tire early in the evening, but wake up quickly in the morning, often have a higher morning temperature than night owls do.

SOME PROCESSES SPEED UP   Not everything slows down during sleep, however. New skin cells, for example, are manufactured twice as fast during sleep. Repair and replacement of other worn-out cells speed up, as well. Your sweat glands often work harder. Some parts of your brain and nervous system become more active as you dream.

Sleep Research

In recent years, scientists have learned much that is new about sleep. Dr. Nathaniel Kleitman and his team at the University of Chicago pioneered in sleep research. Today, in university and hospital laboratories across the country, many more researchers are investigating the subject.

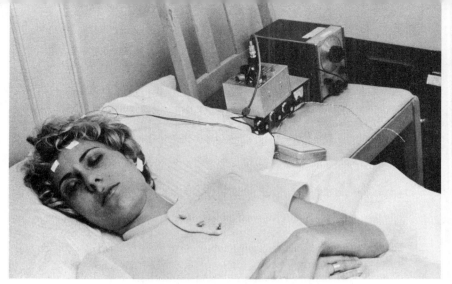

Figure 13.1. Recording brain waves during sleep.

A volunteer taking part in such sleep research often has wires attached above and beside the eyes to record any eye movements. The volunteer shown in Figure 13.1 has other wires attached to various parts of her scalp; by means of these wires, electric currents within her brain are recorded by an **electroencephalograph** (ih-LEK-troh-en-SEF-uh-luh-graf), a machine much used in sleep research. Its long name simply means electric brain recorder.

BRAIN WAVES AND THE EEG   As you remember from Chapter 7, page 75, nerve signals, or impulses, travel to the brain and back by means of electrical and chemical changes that take place within the nerve cells of the nervous system. These changes produce tiny electric currents in the brain called **brain waves,** which the electroencephalograph records. The resulting record of brain wave tracings is called an **electroencephalogram** (ih-LEK-troh-en-SEF-uh-luh-gram), or **EEG** for short. Figure 13.2 shows you some of these tracings.

THE FOUR STAGES OF SLEEP   Using the EEG, researchers have found that everyone dreams and that each night's sleep is really many sleeps. They have discovered that each sleeper goes through four different steps, or stages, as he or she sleeps, ending with the deepest sleep. The sleeper then comes out of, or emerges from, deep sleep and starts over again with stage one. Since this takes about 90 minutes, a sleeper can go through all four stages of sleep five or six times during a normal night's sleep.

Stage One: Light Sleep and REM Sleep   When you go to bed, you fall at first into a light sleep. Later, after the onset of sleep, you have **rapid eye movements,** or **REM** for short. Beneath your closed lids, your

The Appearance, Care, and Feeding of Your Body

eyes move as though you were watching a movie or play. Scientists believe you may be doing just that. But the movie, produced and directed by you, is your own dream. Have you ever watched your dog doze off to sleep? You may have seen signs of twitching and whimpering, the closed eyes moving in REM sleep as the dog followed some exciting dream.

Though REM sleep is light, your muscles relax, and your breathing and heartbeat speed up. If someone wakes you during REM sleep, you can almost always remember what you were dreaming. By waking hundreds of volunteers during REM sleep, dream researchers have established that everyone dreams every night, although most dreams are quickly forgotten.

Stages Two and Three   After the first REM period of stage one, stage two begins. Now your sleep is deeper, your body processes slower. Next you sink into the deeper sleep of stage three. Your slowing body processes slow further.

Stage Four: Your Deepest Sleep   During a night's sleep, the first time you reach stage four you stay there about ½ hour before returning to REM sleep. During this stage-four sleep, some people talk and sleepwalk. Deep sleep appears to give your body its most complete rest. As the night goes on and the cycle of four stages is repeated, you spend less and less time in stage four because your need for deep sleep has already been met. No matter when you go to bed, you get most of your deep sleep during the first few hours and most of your light sleep during the end of the sleep period.

Normally, you spend about 12 percent of your sleep time in deep sleep. But this percentage increases when you are making up for lost sleep. Researchers have found that volunteers who are kept awake for long periods make up for lost deep sleep first and for lost REM sleep only later on, when they are finally allowed to sleep normally. Sleepers wakened during stage four report few dreams. Sometimes they say their stage-four dreams are more like thinking than like the visual dreams of REM sleep.

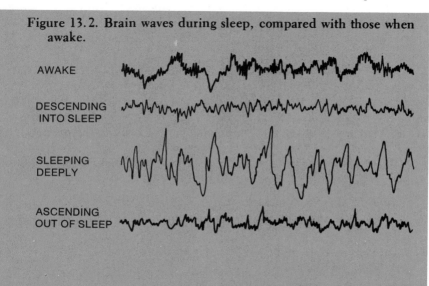

Figure 13.2. Brain waves during sleep, compared with those when awake.

AWAKE

DESCENDING
INTO SLEEP

SLEEPING
DEEPLY

ASCENDING
OUT OF SLEEP

ONE THOUSAND DREAMS A YEAR   Every night, you spend twice as much time in REM sleep as in deep sleep. You dream at least a thousand times a year. Scientists reason that all of this mental activity must have a function or functions. Many researchers are at work trying to discover what these functions are.

In the course of their work, scientists have disproven many old ideas. For example, dreams in color, once thought to be rare, are now thought to be the usual thing. At least 80 percent of the time, volunteers wakened during REM sleep said they were dreaming in color.

Another discovery is that dreams don't take place in a quick mental flash, as some once believed. Rather, a dream takes about as much time as it seems to take. For instance, if you dream of eating breakfast, the dream takes about as long as eating that dream breakfast would actually take.

In addition, outside events like loud noises seem to influence, but not to cause, dreams. In other words, you are going to dream anyway, even if there are no loud noises, no indigestion, no drafts from open windows, or other disturbances.

DO YOU NEED TO DREAM?   Dr. William Dement of Stanford University Medical School in California established that sleepers who are kept from dreaming make up for the loss with extra REM sleep when they are finally allowed to sleep normally. In fact, Dr. Dement had to stop his first experiment at the end of ten days, because, by that time, his volunteers fell back into REM sleep every time they were wakened. Since we always make up for lost REM time, scientists reason that our minds and bodies must need it.

THE USEFULNESS OF DREAMS   Some experiments suggest that dreaming helps to keep brain tissue in good working order. Other research indicates that people work out all kinds of problems while they sleep. The 19th-century Swiss naturalist Louis Agassiz (see Figure 13.3), who dreamed solutions to scientific problems, would have agreed. So would Robert Louis Stevenson (see Figure 13.3), who recorded many of his dreams. One such dream suggested the beginning of, and a later dream the ending for, his novel *Dr. Jekyll and Mr. Hyde*.

Some people find that they can set themselves problems at bedtime and wake up to find that they have the solutions wholly or partly in mind. The dream records of volunteers show that, in a sense, people often work on the same personal problem all night. That is, they return each time they dream to a different aspect of the same problem. Perhaps this is why people have always thought it wise to "sleep on" important decisions.

There are three kinds of social scientists who use dream interpretation to help people work out serious personal problems:

● The **psychiatrist** (suh-KY-uh-trist) is a medical doctor specializing in the treatment and prevention of mental illness.

Figure 13.3. Two men who made the most of their dreams: *(left)* Louis Agassiz, Swiss naturalist; *(right)* Robert Louis Stevenson, novelist.

- The **psychologist** (sy-KAHL-uh-jist) is a scientist who studies the mind and human behavior and is often licensed to treat mental disorders.
- The **psychoanalyst** (sy-koh-AN-uh-list), or analyst, may be either a psychiatrist or a psychologist specially trained to treat seriously disturbed patients by methods such as interpretation of dreams and behavior.

Such social scientists believe that dreams give us clues to our deepest, truest, though often most hidden, feelings, by dramatizing the dangers we face and the mistakes we may be making.

Dreams probably have all of the uses just mentioned, and more. Modern research should continue to tell us more each year.

Let's Pause for Review

Sleep is a regularly returning state of mind and body in which your muscles relax, your pulse and breathing speed up while you are dreaming and then slow down, and most of your glands produce fewer secretions. Cell repair and replacement speed up. Some parts of your brain and nervous system become more active as you dream. Sleep researchers have discovered four stages of sleep: (1) the onset of sleep followed by REM sleep, (2) and (3) deeper and deeper sleep, and (4) the deepest sleep. You go through all four stages five or six times each night. When you miss sleep, you make up for lost deep sleep first. Next you make up for lost REM sleep, the stage of greatest dream production. Your dreams, scientists believe, are useful and necessary in ways not fully understood.

Sleep, Rest, and Exercise   185

Falling Asleep Easily

You probably fall asleep easily. But if you don't, there are many remedies far better than sleeping pills for **insomnia** (in-SAHM-nee-uh), or sleeplessness. Let's say you are an athlete, and you know that worry and excitement keep you awake the night before a game or meet. Don't wait until that last night before you catch up on sleep. Be sure you get plenty of sleep for at least a week before the game. That way, even if you are wakeful the night before, you will know that your body is well rested, and you won't worry about it. Remind yourself that even though you may be wakeful, your body, lying quietly in bed, is resting.

CLEARING YOUR MIND   It's not just athletes who get the "night-before" jitters now and then. Life is full of excitement for everyone. So it's a good idea to develop now the ability to put all of your daily concerns out of your mind. This skill will help you all your life. With a little practice, you can learn to make your mind as blank as a sheet of clean paper when you want to sleep.

You can do a few things to ease your mind in preparation for a good night's sleep. First, take a few moments to set the stage. A quiet, dark room, comfortably loose bedclothes, and good ventilation help most people sleep well. So does a more or less regular bedtime. Like the people in Figure 13.4, you should have a regular bedtime routine. For example, you may go to sleep most easily after a little reading, a small snack, or a warm bath or shower.

EXERCISE   Another way to fight insomnia is to exercise every day. As already mentioned, muscular relaxation is an important part of sleep. Daily exercise leaves your muscles pleasantly relaxed and ready for sleep. People who take sleeping pills to relax their muscles, on the other hand, do not sleep or dream normally. Their EEG's show disturbed brain waves. This is why doctors advise against the habitual use of drugs for sleeping.

How Much Sleep Do You Need?

People vary in their need for sleep. For example, people in their teens need from 7 to 11 hours of sleep nightly. How do you know how much sleep is

Figure 13.4. These people have different, yet relaxing, routines that help them fall asleep readily.

right for you? You can easily find out by performing the following week-long activity:

1. Each morning for a week, write down how many hours you slept the night before. (Include any naps from the afternoon before.)
2. Each day, write down how you felt 1 hour after getting up.

Even though you feel sleepy when you first get up, you may still be getting enough sleep. Scientists say that it takes about an hour to wake up fully. If, at the end of the first hour after getting up, you feel well rested and good-natured, you have had enough sleep. If, however, you still feel tired, ill tempered, or quarrelsome, you probably need more sleep than you are getting.

FATIGUE Nine hours of sleep may be enough for you. A classmate may need only eight. Your sister, who is growing fast, may need eleven. But all of you may need extra sleep after a day of working or exercising unusually hard.

This is because prolonged muscular activity causes waste products, like carbon dioxide and lactic acid, to build up in the cells faster than these wastes can be removed. In addition, nourishing materials in the cells are used up. This condition is called **fatigue** (fuh-TEEG). A similar thing happens to brain cells after prolonged mental activity. But during rest, and particularly sleep, the blood is able to carry away all of the fatigue wastes and to supply new nourishment to the cells. To sample the feeling of fatigue, do the following:

YOUR PART

1. Rapidly open and close your hand, making a fist over and over. Count how many times you are able to make a fist. Write down the number.
2. Write down how your hand and arm felt just before you stopped.

Sometimes, as you just saw, fatigue wastes can build up so quickly in muscles that they will slow down and then stop muscular activity altogether. Athletes sometimes collapse from *exhaustion*, which is simply fatigue that affects most or all of the muscles. However, just as rest soon cured the fatigue in your hand and arm, rest fairly rapidly cures the exhaustion felt by fit, young athletes.

Sleep, Rest, and Exercise

WHEN TIRED FEELINGS LAST What if you still feel tired after rest and sleep? Everyone does once in a while. Remember that it takes a lot of energy just to grow. Make sure you are eating a good, mixed diet and are *regularly* getting enough sleep. If that doesn't help, you should see your doctor. Chronic, or lasting, fatigue can be a sign of illness. Besides, a person who is always tired isn't enjoying life. Often, too, the chronically fatigued person will develop more infections and have more accidents than do other people.

EMOTIONAL FATIGUE Sometimes, people say they are tired when they are really tired *of* something. If you are bored or dissatisfied, try to understand the reason. Ask yourself what you can do to make things better. Try making the effort to find a new hobby, new activities, and helpful new friends. Whenever you can, give variety to your day by including work, play, rest, and entertainment. After a good deal of brain work, do something athletic, and the reverse. Change-of-scene vacations help, too.

If your dissatisfactions are very strong, it often helps to talk them over with someone you can trust. Talking things out makes you feel better. It helps you to think more clearly, too. And clear thinking can usually help you solve your problems.

Exercise

Oddly enough, exercise, which can cause fatigue, can also help prevent it. This is because exercise makes your body more *efficient* (ih-FISH-unt), which means it is able to do more work with less effort and less fatigue. Let us say, for example, that you ask two friends to help you move your belongings when your family changes its residence. One friend, who exercises regularly, is strong and healthy. The other friend is flabby, weak, and out of shape. You are not surprised when your strong friend moves more furniture more quickly and is less tired at the end of the day.

A well-exercised body can do more work with less fatigue, because regular exercise actually makes the heart strong enough to pump more blood with every beat. Therefore, a strong heart can work harder with fewer beats per minute than a weaker heart. For this reason, a strong heart gets more rest.

The same thing is true of your lungs. With each breath, well-exercised lungs take in more oxygen and rid the body of more carbon dioxide than lungs that are out of condition. With efficient lungs, you can exercise harder and longer without getting out of breath. It is easy to see how regular exercise can help lengthen life. Over a lifetime, an efficient heart and lungs get more rest and work less hard on every job the body does.

EXERCISE AND HEALTHY ARTERIES Doctors also prescribe exercise to help prevent clogged arteries like those we discussed earlier (refer

Figure 13.5. These young people exercise regularly, developing grace and poise.

again to page 170). Exercise helps your body to remove fatty material from the bloodstream before it can be deposited inside artery walls. Even after a heart attack, most doctors advise some form of exercise, such as jogging.

EXERCISE AND INNER TENSION *Stress, strain, pressure, tension*—these are all words for that uptight feeling that is so much a part of modern life. As you learned in Chapter 7, page 81, your body, like that of a wild animal, gets ready for fight or flight when you are frightened or angry. But since you live in civilization, not in the wild, you can rarely fight or run away, much as you might like to. More often you must sit quietly and do nothing. This conflict—between what you must do and what you feel like doing—produces inner tension, or stress.

Exercise relaxes this tension in a healthful way. As exercise tires and relaxes your muscles, you relax, too, and begin to forget the worries, pressures, and disappointments that made you uptight in the first place. The daily release of tension is important to your health. Doctors believe that unreleased inner tension can help cause certain physical illnesses like stomach ulcers, as well as other problems like emotional fatigue.

EXERCISE AND GOOD LOOKS Exercise also helps your body develop properly and, therefore, more attractively during the years when you are growing fast. Enlarging muscles and lengthening arms and legs don't always work together smoothly without practice. But regular exercise brings skill, grace, and poise to the way you move (see Figure 13.5).

Exercise also gives your muscles *tone* (refer again to page 46), which means a healthy state of readiness to do, with vigor, whatever needs to be done. Thus, good muscle tone enables you to react quickly in an emergency and to complete your daily work in good time. As you may know, skiers in overall good condition suffer fewer injuries than do skiers in poor condition. And on the average, students who are physically fit do better work in school than those who are not. Well-toned muscles are slightly contracted, or shortened, and this contraction is what maintains good posture. To check your posture and muscle tone, try the following:

Figure 13.6. Positions for checking posture: *(a)* **side and** *(b)* **front.**

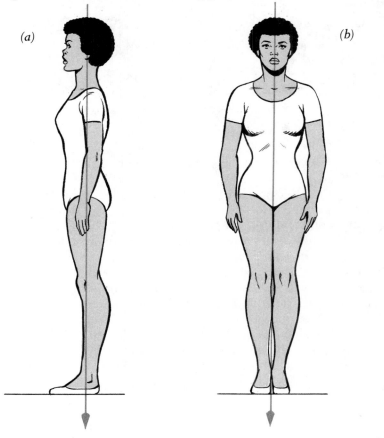

(a)

(b)

MATERIALS

You will need the following:

- A plumb line, which is a piece of cord or string from which a weight is suspended to insure that the line is straight. The cord should be about 6 feet (185 centimeters) long.
- A copy of the following chart:

Posture Checklist

	Yes	No	Comments
Plumb line used at side. Does string pass: In front of ankle joint? In back of kneecap? In center of hip joint? Through tip of shoulder? Through lobe of ear?			
Plumb line used in front. Does string pass: Between ankles? Between knees? Through navel? Through center of chest? Along bridge of nose? Between eyebrows? Through center of head?			

PROCEDURE

1. Working with a partner, check each other's posture. The partner being checked should stand against a wall with knees slightly bent while the other partner checks his or her posture from the side and front, using the plumb line and the Posture Checklist.
2. The partner doing the checking should hold the string at head height just above the other partner's ear but in the middle of the head. When checking from the front, hold the string in the center of the forehead at the level of the hairline (see Figure 13.6).
3. Exchange the finished Posture Checklists. As a further check on your posture, copy the following questions on the other side of your

Sleep, Rest, and Exercise

paper. Observing yourself in a full-length mirror, answer the questions:

    a. When you stand against a wall, does the small of your back touch the wall?

    b. When your feet are parallel and 2 or 3 inches (5 or 7.5 centimeters) apart, is your body weight borne equally on your heels and on the balls of your feet?

    c. Are your kneecaps directed straight ahead?

    d. Is your abdomen flat?

    e. Is your chest high?

    f. Are your shoulders held level and easy?

    g. Is your chin level and your head high?

4. A person with perfect posture would have answered yes to all of the questions in the Posture Checklist and in step 3. Did your answers show your posture to be good? Make a list of any areas that need improvement.

After you and your classmates have checked your posture, invite an exercise expert—an instructor in physical education, for example—to class to talk about posture and exercise and to answer questions about improving problem areas. Ask your expert, too, about community facilities for exercise, dance classes, and sports of all kinds.

Exercise is quite a bargain. That is, you get a big return for the effort you put into it. It helps you to control your weight and to release your inner tensions. In addition, exercise promotes sound sleep, good posture, and attractive muscular development as well as healthy arteries, heart, and lungs. You could hardly ask for more. Yet, all around you, you see adults who take no extra exercise at all. The reason seems to be that somewhere between childhood and adulthood, exercise changes from a delight into a rather unpleasant duty. But it doesn't have to be that way. If you make the effort to find the exercise that is right for you and also enjoyable, you can help yourself stay slim and trim for a lifetime.

YOUR PART

1. Do you have a favorite exercise for every season? If not, write down those seasons during which you get too little exercise.
2. Do you have a favorite carry-over sport—a sport you can continue to take part in as an adult—for every season? If not, write down the seasons for which you lack a carry-over sport.

The Appearance, Care, and Feeding of Your Body

Table 13.1: Exercises for Now and Later in Life

Partner/Team Exercises	Individual Exercises	Carry-Over Exercises
Badminton	Archery	Archery
Baseball	Bowling	Badminton
Basketball	Calisthenics	Bowling
Fencing	Cycling	Calisthenics
Football	Dancing (classical,	Cycling
Handball	modern)	Dancing (classical,
Hockey	Fishing	modern)
Ping-Pong	Gardening	Fencing
Soccer	Golfing	Fishing
Softball	Hiking	Gardening
Squash	Horseback riding	Golfing
Tennis	Isometrics	Hiking
Volleyball	Jogging	Horseback riding
Waterskiing	Jumping rope	Isometrics
	Rowing	Jogging
	Skating	Ping-Pong
	Skiing	Rowing
	Swimming	Skating
	Skin diving	Skiing
	Surfing	Softball
	Weight lifting	Squash
	Yoga	Swimming
		Tennis
		Volleyball
		Yoga

3. As a class or in small groups, share your ideas about exercise, including your likes and dislikes. Discuss exercises suitable to each season. Include things like dancing and yoga as well as the usual games and sports (see Table 13.1).

During the exercise discussion, you probably gave and received some good suggestions. As a result, you may be ready to try something new. If so, remember to take it easy at first, increasing your new activity gradually. If the exercise is strenuous, warm up properly. If you haven't had a medical examination in some time, check with your doctor before taking part in an unusually strenuous activity.

HOW MUCH EXERCISE IS TOO MUCH? You can tell if you occasionally overdo, because you may feel tired two or more hours after you have stopped exercising. Sometimes, the signs of extreme exertion—weakness, fatigue, and muscle aches—will show up only the next day. If so, you probably need to rest more and exercise less. As thirst tells you when to drink, fatigue tells you when to rest.

Looking Back

Sleep is a regularly returning state, during which your body rests and repairs itself. You are getting enough sleep if you usually feel alert and refreshed an hour after getting up. When tired feelings last in spite of a good diet and plenty of rest, you should see your doctor; there may be a physical cause for your fatigue. Fatigue can be emotional, too, indicating, perhaps, a need for change. It could also mean you need a better balance between exercise and rest, work and play, and time spent alone and time spent with other people. Normally, however, sleep and rest cure fatigue rather quickly by carrying away the waste materials that have built up in body cells.

Five or six times each night, you go through four stages of sleep, beginning with the light sleep and REM sleep of stage one (the period of greatest dream production) and ending with stage four (the period of deepest sleep). People who are kept awake for long periods make up for lost deep sleep first and for lost REM sleep second. Deep sleep appears to rest your body most completely. Dreams have many uses. They may dramatize and help you solve your problems; they may express your true, but hidden feelings; they may help keep brain tissue in good condition. Since normal sleep is necessary to health, doctors advise against the habitual use of sleeping pills, which, as EEGs show, interfere with normal brain waves during sleep.

Instead of relaxing your muscles with drugs, you can do the same thing by means of daily exercise. Exercise is also good insurance against long-lasting fatigue. Exercise can help lengthen life by making your heart and lungs more efficient and by keeping fatty material from being deposited inside artery walls. Exercise also gives your muscles tone, and well-toned muscles help maintain good posture. Regular exercise helps make you fit enough to do the things you want to do in life. Physical fitness helps people do better in school. In emergencies, physical fitness helps people avoid injuries. Now is a good time for you to form the exercise habit and to try out the carry-over sports that can keep you fit in the years to come.

The Appearance, Care, and Feeding of Your Body

MODIFIED TRUE-FALSE QUESTIONS

1. During sleep, blood pressure _increases._
2. When you have a cold, you are _more_ comfortable after you sleep.
3. As you sleep, your body temperature _rises._
4. New skin cells are manufactured _more_ quickly during sleep.
5. As you dream, parts of your brain and nervous system become _less_ active.
6. A tracing produced by an electric brain recorder is _an electroencephalogram._
7. Scientists say that you experience about _one thousand_ dreams a year.
8. During REM sleep, your heartbeat _slows down._
9. Teenagers generally need from 7 to _9_ hours of sleep nightly.
10. During fatigue, there is _more_ lactic acid in the body than at other times.
11. When _few_ muscles are tired, exhaustion sets in.
12. Well-exercised lungs take in more oxygen and release _less_ carbon dioxide than lungs that are out of condition.
13. All people require _the same_ amount of exercise.
14. When you exercise regularly, your heart becomes used to pumping _less_ blood with every beat.
15. The period of greatest dreaming occurs during stage _one_ of sleep.

MATCHING QUESTIONS

Column A	Column B
1. insomnia	a. tiny electric currents
2. unreleased tensions	b. excess sleep
3. exhaustion	c. collapse
4. REM	d. stomach ulcers
5. brain waves	e. sleeplessness
	f. sleep stage

MULTIPLE-CHOICE QUESTIONS

1. You get your deepest sleep
   a. during the first hours of sleep
   b. in the middle of a night's sleep
   c. just prior to awakening
   d. during the last hours of sleep
2. Scientific sleep research indicates that
   a. everyone dreams
   b. nobody dreams every night
   c. some people never dream
   d. we have only one dream a night

3. All the following are generally true about dreams, *except*
   a. dreams help solve problems
   b. in general, the same dreams always come back
   c. dreams do not take place in a flash
   d. dreams help to keep brain tissue in good shape
4. All of the following are professionals who help people work out serious emotional problems, *except*
   a. psychiatrists   b. psychologists   c. analysts   d. podiatrists
5. Your sleep is lightest during stage
   a. one   b. two   c. three   d. four

THOUGHT QUESTIONS

1. How can you tell how many hours of sleep you really need?
2. Explain the following statement: Exercise can cause fatigue, but it can also prevent fatigue.
3. You know you have an important math test the next day at school. Comment on each of the following possible preparations to meet this challenge:

   a. Getting to bed very early
   b. Watching a late movie on TV
   c. Taking a mild sleeping pill
   d. Exercising days before the test
   e. Skipping breakfast on the day of the test

4. What is the purpose of sleep research?
5. How can sleep researchers improve your health?
6. Why is mild exercise recommended for people recuperating from heart attacks?
7. Under what conditions is even mild exercise *not* recommended? Defend your choices.

Looking Ahead

Learning how to care for your own health and appearance is part of growing up. So is taking responsibility for your own safety. In Chapter 14, you will explore the many steps you can take to prevent accidents.

The Appearance, Care, and Feeding of Your Body

Unit Five: HEALTH THROUGH SAFETY

When you were a child, your parents took responsibility for your safety. They still try to keep you safe, of course. Your school and community also try to provide you with safe surroundings. But more and more, the responsibility for your safety is largely yours. It is a serious responsibility.

Every 3 seconds, an individual somewhere in the United States suffers an accidental injury. Every 5 minutes, an accidental death occurs. Accidents are the fourth most important cause of death. Among people between the ages of 1 and 38, accidents are the leading cause of death.

Fortunately, ways of preventing accidents can be learned. And whenever special care is taken, accident rates go down. For example, the National Safety Council compared statistics on accidents in companies that were members of their organization and in those that were not. (These companies were in the manufacturing and mining industries.) The member companies studied and practiced safety. The nonmembers did not. The National Safety Council found that members averaged about 70 percent fewer accidents than did nonmembers.

Knowledge can help prevent lasting injury and death in another way. In an emergency—an unexpected situation that calls for immediate action—a knowledge of first aid can help you take care of yourself and others. This unit is presented to give you the information you need to prevent accidents and to be helpful in emergencies.

Chapter 14:   Accident Prevention

The household stepladder was missing. Maria didn't want to waste time looking for it. She was in a hurry to change a light bulb in time for a party. She grabbed a handy three-legged stool, climbed up on it, and reached for the burned-out bulb over the back door. But the stool was too low. As Maria stood on tiptoe and reached up to unscrew the bulb from its socket, the three-legged stool tipped and Maria fell.

Gary earned money taking care of the lawn. When his father ordered a new power mower, Gary was delighted. One afternoon when Gary was home alone, the new mower arrived. Gary was eager to try it after a year of using a hand mower. With a friend's help, he unpacked the power mower, set it up, and went to work without first clearing the lawn of sticks and stones (see Figure 14.1). Before long, Gary's friend went limping home, his leg badly cut by a small, jagged rock that was picked up and thrown out by the power mower.

Figure 14.1. How could this accident have been prevented?

Table 14.1: Accidental Deaths From Falls

Age	Deaths
0–4	300
5–14	200
15–24	400
25–44	1,100
45–64	2,900
65–74	2,400
75 and over	9,600
	16,900 total

Adapted from National Safety Council graph.

What caused these accidents? A dangerous place? Dangerous equipment? A dangerous attitude on the part of the people involved? Answering the following questions should help you decide:

YOUR PART

1. Was Gary at work in a dangerous place? Was Maria?
2. What equipment were they using? Was it dangerous?
3. What attitude on Maria's part helped cause her accident? What attitude on Gary's part helped cause his?

Did you decide that since both Maria and Gary were working at home, both were at work in a safe place? As we shall see, more people injure themselves at home than anywhere else. You probably decided that Gary's lawn mower was more dangerous than Maria's three-legged stool. Falls cause so many injuries, however, that all stairways, ladders, stools, chairs, and the like deserve careful use (see Table 14.1).

You probably noted, too, that Gary was impatient to use the new lawn mower—too impatient to wait for permission, preparation, and instruction. Maria was also in a hurry.

People Cause Accidents

As in the cases of Maria and Gary, people who are impatient or in a hurry help cause many accidents. In fact, strong feelings of any kind—joy, fear, anger, or sadness—can keep you from paying attention to what you are doing and to the dangers around you. Knowing this, you should be on your

Health Through Safety

Figure 14.2. Why is "having a place for everything" a good safety precaution?

guard against taking foolish chances whenever your feelings are stirred up.

You should also take extra care when you are hungry or tired. Long ago, researchers in industry found out that most accidents happen either just before lunchtime or near quitting time, when hunger and fatigue make people careless. This is one reason why workers now get regular work breaks for rest and refreshment. Remember these facts whenever you are playing hard in the late afternoon or working late at some job requiring special care. It pays to know that accidents don't just happen—they are caused, and the causes usually start with people.

ACCIDENTS AT HOME   We have already seen how easily accidents may happen at home. It is true that accidents on the highway account for 48 percent of all accidental deaths, whereas the figure for accidental home deaths is 22 percent. However, people receive nonfatal injuries twice as often at home as they do either at work or in traffic accidents. Most of these accidents could have been avoided. To help protect yourself at home, note the following rules for home safety:

1. Practice good housekeeping. Because falls cause many home injuries, one of the best ways to prevent such accidents is by picking up things after you drop them.
2. Have a place for everything—especially knives and sharp tools (see Figure 14.2).
3. Store poisons in their original containers, out of the reach of children and away from food.
4. Ask your **pharmacist** (FAHR-muh-sist), or druggist, to put medicines for your family in bottles with safety caps. These caps are designed to be difficult for young children to open. Keep medicines in their original containers, out of the reach of children. Throw away outdated prescriptions (see Figure 14.3, page 202). But be sure, when you throw medicines away, that children cannot take them from your trash barrels.
5. Check household appliances and electrical equipment for frayed cords and broken plugs that need replacing. Electrical outlets should have safety covers if you have small children in your family.

6. Use power tools and equipment only when you have both permission and training. Wear shoes when you use a power lawn mower. Before clearing material away from the blades or making any kind of adjustment, turn the power off. Watch for rocks and other sharp objects; they can be picked up and thrown out by the mower with enough force to cause serious injury.

7. Be alert when you cook. Turn pot handles inward, away from the edge of the stove. Don't leave unattended liquids that can boil over. Use a mesh skillet cover to prevent grease from spattering. (Keep baking soda handy to smother small grease fires. The soda won't spoil the food.)

8. Check walkways, halls, and stairs for anything that might cause a fall: a loose brick, a slippery rug on a polished floor, torn carpet on a stairway, a broken handrail. Take corrective measures promptly.

9. When you need to reach for something high up, climb on a sturdy three- or four-legged stool or a stepladder rather than on a box, chair, or counter top. Before you climb, make sure the bottom of the ladder is level. Lean the ladder against the wall at a safe angle (with the foot of the ladder neither too far from nor too close to the wall). Wear shoes and don't reach farther than one arm's length when standing on a ladder (see Figure 14.4).

10. Light all areas in use at night (with switches placed so that they can be turned on before the area is entered).

11. Small children like to explore; they sometimes crawl into unused freezers, refrigerators, or old chests. Remove the doors from unused refrigerators and the like. Store plastic bags out of the reach of children.

12. Always treat firearms as if they were loaded. Firearms should be stored in a different place from their ammunition and locked up if there are young children in the home.

Figure 14.3. How can such situations be avoided?

Figure 14.4. He saved time, but what did he get?

13. Plan escape routes in case of fire. Each family member should know how to get out of the bedroom, for example, even if the doors and halls usually used are blocked. Plan how you would report a fire if you couldn't use your own phone.

14. Keep a list of emergency numbers near your telephone. You can probably be a real help to your family by doing the following:

YOUR PART

1. Make a list of emergency telephone numbers—fire department, doctor, hospital, ambulance, and so on—to keep near your phone. Bring your list to class.

2. Write down how people on the second floor of your home could escape from a fire that blocked the stairs.

3. Write down what you would do (and not do) if you came home from school and noticed a strong smell of gas in the house.

4. Write down what you would do (and not do) if, while you were cooking dinner, the grease in a frying pan caught fire.

5. As a class or in small groups, compare your emergency lists and your answers in steps 2, 3, and 4.

Was your emergency number list complete? Did you agree never to light a match when you smell gas? Did you agree to smother the grease fire (with a sprinkling of baking soda or by putting the lid on the frying pan) rather than use water to put it out?

Accident Prevention

ACCIDENTS IN PUBLIC PLACES   You will recall that more people hurt themselves at home than either at work or in traffic accidents. But accidental injuries in public places are the next most numerous. Public places include your school and most of the places you go for recreation.

School safety is a subject you know well. Fortunately, the same kind of behavior that keeps you safe at school (showing consideration for others, walking slowly when in a crowd, keeping to the right, watching your step) will keep you safe in other public places. Although school is a fairly safe place, some school activities do result in accidents. The greatest number of school accidents happen in physical education (on apparatus, in games, and in shower and dressing rooms).

A substantial number of accidents occur around the school building (in auditoriums and corridors and on stairs). As you might expect, *interscholastic* (in-tur-skuh-LAS-tik) *sports* (football, basketball, and other games played between schools) are responsible for accidents, too, as are shop and laboratory activities. But you can do your part to prevent accidents to yourself and to others, as we shall see.

Safe Recreation

When it comes to recreation, the most important thing is to keep your activity in line with your skill, whether you are hiking, skiing, swimming, or boating. Unfortunately, people engaged in recreation often take chances as a result of group social pressure—chances they would never take if they were alone. If you love water sports, the following groups of safety rules will be of special importance to you.

SOME RULES FOR SAFE SWIMMING

1. Never swim alone.
2. Unless you are a strong and practiced swimmer, admit your limitations and stay in shallow water, fairly close to shore or the pool's edge.
3. Know the water (depth, temperature, condition of the bottom) in which you are swimming or diving. Check diving boards before you use them, and watch a few experienced divers use them first.
4. Stay out of the water (or get out of the water) when you are tired, overheated, or chilled.

SOME RULES FOR SAFE BOATING

1. Wear a life preserver.
2. Be considerate of swimmers and of other boats.
3. Know the water—its currents and tides.
4. Watch for rocks and other hazards.
5. Unless weather conditions permit safe boating, stay ashore.

Health Through Safety

SOME RULES FOR SAFE WATERSKIING

1. Even if you are an excellent swimmer, wear a life preserver (waist or jacket type).
2. Keep both hands on the tow rope.
3. Ski only in uncrowded waters that are free of swimmers and as free of other boaters as possible.
4. Don't ski unless the tow boat has two people in it—one to steer and one to watch you.

SOME ADVICE FOR THE NONSWIMMER Even if you swim poorly or not at all, you can still help a swimmer in trouble if you stay calm and use your head. Most pool areas keep on hand special lifesaving equipment, which you can throw or otherwise use to reach a swimmer. If you are in a place with no equipment, look around for something that will float—a piece of wood or a large, sealed, empty plastic bottle or empty thermos jug—and throw it to the swimmer. If you are close enough, use a long stick, a rope, or knotted clothing to pull the swimmer ashore or to the boat. Whatever you do, *don't jump into the water* to try to save another person. It takes a strong swimmer to rescue another swimmer in trouble.

Let's Pause for Review

Accidents are the leading cause of death among persons between the ages of 1 and 38. However, when special care is taken, accident rates go down. You may need to take more care for your safety whenever you are hungry, tired, or emotionally keyed up (either pleasantly or unpleasantly). More nonfatal accidents take place at home than anywhere else. Next most numerous are accidents in public places, followed by accidents at work.

Most of these accidents can be prevented if people take the time and trouble to do things in a safe way (putting things away; using appliances and tools according to instructions; repairing walkways, appliances, and so on; keeping medicines, poisons, firearms, and other dangerous things away from children; lighting areas used at night; planning escape routes for all family members in case of fire; following the safety rules for recreation).

Highway Safety

Before long, you may be taking driver education, in which you will learn traffic laws, principles of good driving, and something about how cars work. This will be followed by driver training with you behind the wheel. Accident rates are lower among new drivers trained in school than among

Accident Prevention

other new drivers. This is why many states now require all students to take such training. You may or may not be looking forward to these classes.

Some students are eager to learn to drive. Others worry a bit about their ability to become good drivers. Either way, your current behavior can tell you something about the kind of driver you may become. Do you obey the traffic laws as a pedestrian, crossing safely where you should? Are you considerate of motorists, bicyclists, and other pedestrians? If you ride a bike, do you stay to the right of the roadway and ride single file? Do you keep your bike in good repair and well equipped (with a headlight visible for 500 feet [150 meters], a rear reflector visible for 300 feet [90 meters], and, possibly, reflector tape on the pedals)? As a car passenger, do you wear your seat and shoulder belts and try not to disturb the driver?

SAFETY AND THE LAW   If you can answer yes to the questions just asked, you are already law-abiding, considerate, and responsible as a pedestrian, bicyclist, and passenger. Chances are, you will be the same kind of driver. Obeying the law is important, not only in itself but also for your safety on the road. Lawbreaking plays a part in most of the fatal accidents caused by improper driving. Examples of such lawbreaking are driving while under the influence of liquor or drugs, driving too fast for road conditions, and failing to stop for traffic signs and signals.

In particular, driving while under the influence of alcohol is a major cause of death. At least half of all fatal accidents involve a drinking driver. (About 5 percent of all fatal accidents involve a drinking pedestrian.) Like other accidents, those caused by people who drink and drive can be prevented. In countries where laws against drinking and driving are strictly enforced, accident rates are much lower than they are in the United States.

SAFETY AND HIGHWAY CONDITIONS   Speeding is involved in 25 percent of all accidental deaths. However, it is not merely speeding that causes such accidents, but rather speeding when highway conditions are unfavorable. It is true that accident rates also go up because of darkness, heavy traffic, and bad weather. But in most cases, those conditions alone don't cause accidents. The real cause is the failure of drivers to slow down and drive more carefully when the road is slippery, crowded, or hard to see.

SAFETY AND THE CONDITION OF THE DRIVER   Fatigue and upset emotions help cause traffic accidents just as they help cause home accidents. Good drivers try to stay both alert and calm and to be considerate of others. Consideration seems to be especially important. Failure to yield the right of way is the leading cause of nonfatal traffic accidents.

THE YOUNG DRIVER   Young drivers are still perfecting their driving. They are still gaining experience and improving their judgment about many kinds of driving situations. For these reasons, perhaps, accident rates

206   **Health Through Safety**

are highest among drivers under the age of 25. Insurance rates are highest for these drivers, too. Although careful driving habits are important at all ages, young drivers probably need to drive with more patience, alertness, and care than any other drivers. Fortunately, young drivers generally hear and see well, react quickly, and have had good, recent driver training.

YOUR PART

1. Draw a map of the route you travel to and from school. Mark any special hazards on your route (dangerous intersections, railroad crossings, and the like) with an X.
2. List the traffic laws and safety rules you follow to protect yourself and others as you walk, bicycle, or ride a bus to school.

Looking Back

Most accidents are caused by people rather than by dangerous conditions or places. People need to be on guard against accidents whenever they are hungry, tired, or emotionally upset. When people take the time and trouble to do things in a safe way at home, at work, or when engaged in recreation, accident rates go down.

Accidents are the leading cause of death among people between the ages of 1 to 38. Of these deaths, about 48 percent result from traffic accidents. Lawbreaking is involved in most of these fatal accidents. Drinking drivers are involved in at least half of all fatal accidents. Speeding too fast for conditions at the time causes one-fourth of all such accidents. Consideration of others is important to traffic safety. Failure to yield the right of way is the leading cause of nonfatal traffic accidents. Because they are still perfecting their driving, young drivers (under 25) need to drive with special patience, alertness, and care.

MODIFIED TRUE-FALSE QUESTIONS

1. Distressing circumstances *increase* the likelihood of accidents.
2. Most accidents happen in *schools.*
3. Drinking and driving *always* create a safety hazard.
4. *Few* accidents can be prevented.
5. Most accidental deaths result from disregard of *safety rules.*
6. Safety belts *reduce* injuries from highway accidents.

Accident Prevention

7. An accidental injury occurs every <u>30</u> seconds in the United States.
8. The <u>fourth</u> leading cause of death in the United States is accidents.
9. Accidents are the leading cause of death for people between the ages of 1 and <u>38.</u>
10. Lawbreaking is involved to a large extent in most <u>on-the-job</u> accidents.

MULTIPLE-CHOICE QUESTIONS

1. Nonfatal injuries occur most frequently at
   a. school   b. play   c. home   d. work
2. Which of the following is *not* a good rule for safe swimming?
   a.   knowing the depth of the water
   b.   checking a diving board before using it
   c.   swimming when nobody is around
   d.   staying close to shore.
3. Accident rates are lower among drivers trained by
   a.   parents
   b.   school driver-training instructors
   c.   bus or truck drivers
   d.   friends
4. Which of the following is *not* a good rule for safe boating?
   a.   knowing the water, its currents, and tides
   b.   disregarding weather conditions
   c.   watching out for rocks and other hazards
   d.   wearing a life preserver
5. Most accidental deaths result from
   a. fires   b. drowning   c. traffic accidents   d. falls
6. Which of the following is *not* related to an increase in highway accidents?
   a.   bad weather   c.   darkness
   b.   heavy traffic   d.   cautious driving
7. A grease fire at home can be extinguished most quickly by
   a.   tossing water on it
   b.   fanning the flames
   c.   smothering it with baking soda
   d.   removing the grease
8. The best way to make an unused refrigerator safe is to
   a.   place it in a crate
   b.   tie a rope around it
   c.   remove the door
   d.   place it in a corner of the yard
9. Accidental poisoning is more likely to occur if poisons
   a.   are kept in their original containers
   b.   have been removed from their original containers
   c.   are kept out of the reach of children
   d.   are kept away from foods

Health Through Safety

10. Which of the following is *not* a safe procedure if you ride a bicycle?
  a. ignoring traffic laws
  b. staying to the right of roadways
  c. keeping your bike in good repair
  d. riding single file

THOUGHT QUESTIONS

1. You have a better chance of surviving during a fire by crawling and putting a bedspread or blanket over your head. Explain why these are good safety measures.

2. Using Table 14.1, page 200, answer the following questions:

  a. What age group has the most deaths from falls?
  b. How do you account for the differences between the various age groups?

3. Statistics show that in grades 7 to 9 fewer accidents occur in shop and laboratory classes, such as home economics, science, and industrial arts, than in other places. Yet, all these areas have more potentially hazardous equipment than is found in other areas including classrooms, lunchrooms, corridors, restrooms, and stairways.

  a. How do you account for these differences?
  b. List as many safety rules as you can that your school has and tries to enforce to prevent accidents.

4. List some important recreational safety rules.

5. Should safety education concentrate on eliminating all accidents? Explain your view.

6. Will imposing tough standards to limit the number of people who drive vehicles decrease the number of accidents? Explain your position.

Looking Ahead

Suppose you witness an accident. What should you do? People who keep calm and act correctly in emergencies often save lives. In Chapter 15, you will learn about calm and helpful behavior in an emergency and about how to give first aid effectively.

Accident Prevention

Chapter 15: First Aid

Johnson Reid's health class saw a film on first aid. In one scene, a small boy playing hide and seek found a perfect hiding place—an unused refrigerator stored in a friend's garage. The boy crawled inside, the door slammed shut, and he was trapped. By the time his playmates found him, he was no longer breathing. One of his friends ran to call a doctor. His other friends pulled him from the refrigerator and started **mouth-to-mouth resuscitation** (ree-sus-uh-TAY-shun).

"I don't believe it," Johnson said in the discussion that followed the film. "Kids that young wouldn't know how to give mouth-to-mouth resuscitation. At least, *I* wouldn't know how, and I'm older than they are."

"You shouldn't move an unconscious person," Linda Pérez said.

"What did you want them to do? He'd die in there!" Johnson said.

"If you do the wrong thing, you can do more harm than good," said Linda.

"But they did the right thing, and they saved his life. We should all know as much as they do about first aid," Johnson said.

Figure 15.1. Good first-aiders look things over and send for help at once.

Table 15.1: First Aid Kits

For Family Car	For Home
Roller bandages (in various sizes)	Same
Gauze pads (sterilized)	Same
Adhesive compresses (such as 1-inch, or 2.5 centimeter, Band-Aids)	Same
Absorbent cotton (sterilized)	Same
Triangular bandage (for a sling)	Same
Burn ointment	Same
Eye pads (sterilized)	Same
Tweezers	Same
Tourniquet	Same
Scissors	Same
Flashlight	Same
Matches	Same
Blanket	Syrup of ipecac (to induce vomiting) Universal antidote or activated charcoal

What Is First Aid?

The American Red Cross says that first aid is immediate, temporary care given to the victim of an accident or sudden illness until a doctor can take over. If you are to give first aid, you must (1) learn what to do and (2) train yourself to stay calm in an emergency. Another helpful thing you can do in preparation is to fit out two (or more) first aid kits—one for home use and one for the family car. Table 15.1 lists the necessary items for first aid kits for the home and for the family car. It is a good idea to check the contents of each kit regularly. In that way, you can identify items that have been used up and should be replaced.

FIRST STEPS   If you are one of the first people on the scene in a serious emergency involving injury, look the situation over to see what must be done. At once, send some reliable person to telephone for help (see Figure 15.1). In most areas, it is best to call the police for help in obtaining an ambulance or other emergency rescue unit. Ask the caller to report what the emergency is, where it happened, and how many people are involved.

REASSURING THE VICTIM   Then, if you can do nothing else, you can at least assure the victim that help is on the way and that she or he will be taken care of. Good first aid is more than caring for a particular injury or

Figure 15.2. Good first-aiders keep a victim warm, quiet, and flat, with legs raised.

illness; it should be consideration for the injured person's entire sense of well-being. Reassurance is part of first aid whenever the victim is conscious. In addition to reducing mental suffering, reassurance may help to lessen shock. We will explain what shock is later on in this chapter.

YOUR PART

1. Some people have proposed that phone companies set up a single emergency number to be dialed in all kinds of emergencies, in every part of the country. Would you favor such a proposal? What number would you dial for emergency medical help in your own neighborhood? In another city? Out on the highway? At a water recreation area? As a class or in small groups, discuss these questions.

2. Assign a different volunteer to look up the answer to each question and to report the answer to the class.

The answers to these questions vary across the country. When in doubt, you can usually get quick help by dialing "O" and asking the operator to reach the emergency service you need.

Health Through Safety

WHAT TO LOOK FOR IN AN EMERGENCY The Red Cross tells people to check first for (1) severe bleeding, (2) stoppage of breathing, and (3) signs of poisoning. These three conditions call for immediate action. But if you don't find severe bleeding, breath stoppage, or poisoning, your next job is to keep the injured person warm and resting quietly until a doctor or an ambulance arrives (see Figure 15.2).

MOVING AN ACCIDENT VICTIM Often, the most important thing you can do is to keep others from moving an accident victim. Unless life is threatened, an injured person should not be moved. If a person's back is injured, unskilled handling can injure spinal nerves and cause permanent **paralysis** (puh-RAL-uh-sis), or loss of the ability to move. If continued danger makes it absolutely necessary to move an injured person, the moving should be done by a team of experienced people who can lift and carry (or use a stretcher) without twisting or bending the victim's body (see Figure 15.3).

But what if you are alone? You may be able to work a blanket or overcoat carefully under the victim's body. Then you can use the coat or blanket to drag the person gently to safety without twisting or bending his or her body (see Figure 15.4, page 214).

TREATING FOR SHOCK **Shock** is an overall body reaction to injury. In cases of serious accidental injury, shock is always present to some extent, and shock can be fatal. Therefore, if you are giving first aid, you should treat for shock as soon as possible, that is, as soon as you have taken care of serious bleeding or breathing problems. You may lose an hour or more of valuable treatment time if you wait for the signs of shock to develop. The signs of shock are pale, cold, and clammy skin; a fast, weak pulse; dull, vacant eyes; abnormal breathing—irregular, perhaps, or shallow; listlessness and mental dullness; an upset stomach, perhaps followed by vomiting.

Figure 15.3. The three-person carry: one person supports the victim's head, neck, and shoulders; one supports the back and thighs; and one supports the knees and ankles.

Figure 15.4. How to drag a victim to a safe place.

Keeping the Victim Flat, Quiet, and Warm   In shock, blood pressure drops. Not enough blood circulates through the body, and many body processes slow down. Since too little blood is going to the brain and heart, your job in treating shock is to help the blood flow toward these vital parts. The victim should lie flat unless he or she has trouble breathing in that position or has suffered a head injury. The person's legs may be raised, as Figure 15.2, page 212, shows, unless this position hurts or makes it difficult to breathe.

Cover the person to insure warmth, but don't overheat the person or induce sweating. Don't add heat (with a hot water bottle or heating pad) except in the coldest weather. If it looks as though the injured person may vomit, gently turn the head to one side so that vomited material will not be breathed back into the lungs.

YOUR PART

1. Fainting is a common emergency that is sometimes confused with shock.

   a. What is the cause of fainting?
   b. What is the proper first aid for a person who feels faint?
   c. What is the proper first aid for a person who has fainted?
   d. Name three things that might make a person feel faint.
   e. Name three things that might produce shock.

   As a class, discuss these questions.

2. Assign a different volunteer to find the answer to each question and to report the answer to the class.

Your researchers probably reported that shock is a serious emergency, whereas fainting usually is not. A person who feels faint should sit with the head between the knees. Persons who have fainted should be rolled on their backs and allowed to remain in that position until they recover. Their faces may be bathed gently with cool water. If used cautiously, smelling salts may at times be helpful.

Fainting is a temporary, often partial, loss of consciousness that can be caused, for example, by too little food intake, sudden surprise, or fright. But unconsciousness can have many serious causes such as injury, severe shock. intoxication, insulin shock, stroke, heart attack, and epilepsy, among others. When you don't know what has caused a person's unconsciousness, you should call at once for medical aid and wait with the unconscious person until that aid arrives.

Severe Bleeding

If a major blood vessel is cut, blood loss can be fatal in from 1 to 5 minutes. The sudden loss of a quart or so (about 1 liter) of blood can sometimes be fatal; the loss of much more almost certainly will be. Therefore, if you find severe bleeding, you must act quickly.

DIRECT PRESSURE   Remove any clothing that hides the wound (a break in the skin). Firmly apply *direct pressure* to the wound with your hand. If the necessary equipment is at hand, before you press you can first

Figure 15.5. How to apply a flat bandage.

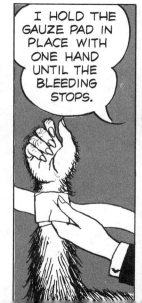

cover the wound with a sterile (germ-free) gauze pad from a first aid kit or with a clean handkerchief or other piece of clean cloth. But it is better to use your bare hand rather than waste precious time looking for a pad or piece of cloth. Sometimes it helps to raise a bleeding arm or leg.

Direct pressure often stops the bleeding, especially if a vein has been cut. (Cut veins bleed more slowly and steadily than cut arteries, from which blood flows in spurts.) If you can stop the bleeding, bandage a sterile gauze pad or piece of cloth in place. If the gauze or cloth becomes blood-soaked, apply more layers of gauze or cloth before you bandage (see Figure 15.5). Don't remove the blood-soaked pad, because the bleeding may have stopped under it and the bleeding may start again as you remove the pad.

ADDITIONAL PRESSURE AT PRESSURE POINTS   If direct pressure alone doesn't control the bleeding, you will have to apply additional pressure at what are called *pressure points* (see Figure 15.6). At these points, major blood vessels lie close to bone. Pressing the blood vessel against the bone sometimes helps to control bleeding. Remember, this is *additional* pressure. You should also continue to apply direct pressure to the wound with your other hand.

It's not easy to find pressure points for the first time, especially in an emergency. You can practice finding these points by doing the following:

YOUR PART

1. Invite a first aid expert to your class (your school nurse, perhaps, or a Red Cross representative) to demonstrate the location of pressure points.
2. Work with a partner, but practice on yourself first. After studying Figure 15.6, try to find the pressure points on your own face, neck, and arm (you should feel a pulse with your fingertips). When you are successful, try to find the same pressure points on your partner.

THE LAST RESORT: A TOURNIQUET   If pressure on an arm or leg wound and on pressure points fails to stop the bleeding, and the bleeding continues to be severe enough to threaten life, a **tourniquet** (TUR-nih-kut) may be used as a last resort. A tourniquet consists of (1) a small pad placed on an arm or leg pressure point between the wound and the heart, (2) a flat bandage wrapped twice around the pad and arm or leg, and (3) a thin, strong stick or rod. (Never use as the bandage wire, rope, or anything else that will cut into the arm or leg.) As you can see in Figure 15.7, the thin stick or rod is inserted between two knots tied on the outside

Health Through Safety

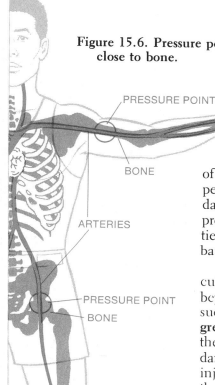

Figure 15.6. Pressure points showing blood vessels close to bone.

PRESSURE POINT

BONE

ARTERIES

PRESSURE POINT
BONE

of the tourniquet. The stick allows the person giving first aid to tighten the bandage just enough to stop the bleeding. To prevent the tourniquet from loosening, tie down one end of the stick with another bandage.

A tourniquet is dangerous because it cuts off the blood supply to the tissues beyond it. As a result, in time these tissues may die. Tissue death is called **gangrene** (GANG-green) and can result in the loss of an arm or leg. Because of this danger, you should attach a note to the injured person that shows the location of the tourniquet and the time it was put in place. Don't cover the tourniquet with clothes or blankets. Then, if you have to leave the victim's side, the doctor or ambulance attendant, on arrival, can see and read about the tourniquet.

At one time, experts, hoping to prevent gangrene, taught that a tourniquet should be released every 30 minutes. At present, however, the Red Cross advises those who give first aid to leave tourniquets in place until they can be removed by people with medical training. This is because the danger of fatal bleeding may still exist. Moreover, in many cases tourniquets have been left in place for 3 or 4 hours without causing gangrene.

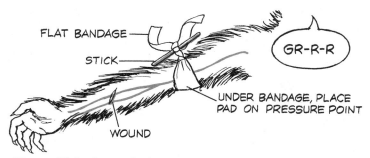

FLAT BANDAGE

STICK

GR-R-R

UNDER BANDAGE, PLACE PAD ON PRESSURE POINT

WOUND

Figure 15.7. Control of serious bleeding with a tourniquet.

Slight Bleeding

Fortunately, most wounds are small, and most bleeding slight. A small amount of bleeding helps to clean the wound. First aid in such cases is easy but still important. Proper care can help prevent infection, which is always possible whenever the skin is broken. First, wash your own hands. Then, clean the wound with soap and water. Finally, apply a dry, sterile dressing and bandage it in place.

Animal Bites and Scratches

Bites and scratches from dogs, cats, and other animals often break the skin. Like other wounds, human and animal bites and scratches should be thoroughly cleaned and covered with a sterile dressing. If an animal has done the biting, try hard to keep the animal under observation, or have someone else do so for you. Then get medical attention for the victim so that the danger of infection—and especially of **rabies** (RAY-beez), a nervous system disease caused by some animal bites—can be dealt with. Finally, report the bite (and the whereabouts of the biting animal, if you know it) to your local health department, and follow the procedure they recommend.

Four Kinds of Wounds

Figure 15.8 pictures and defines the four main kinds of wounds: **abrasion** (uh-BRAY-zhun), **puncture** (PUNGK-shur), **incision** (in-SIZH-un), and **laceration** (las-uh-RAY-shun). The following activity will give you a chance to learn more about them:

YOUR PART

This activity may take the form of a demonstration for the class or an experiment in which all take part.

MATERIALS

Each experimenter will need the following: *(a)* a tomato, *(b)* an emery board, *(c)* a nail, *(d)* a plastic knife with saw-toothed edge, and *(e)* some paper towels.

PROCEDURE

Write down your answers to all questions.

1. With the emery board, gently rub the tomato until the skin is rubbed off. What kind of wound is this? If this were human tissue, what would be affected? Is there oozing?
2. Stick the nail into another area of the tomato. When you remove the

Health Through Safety

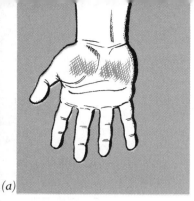

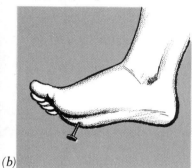

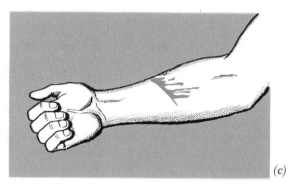

Figure 15.8. Types of wounds:
(a) abrasion — irregular wound
with skin scraped off;
(b) puncture — small hole made
by pointed object; (c) incision —
single, clean cut like that made
by a surgeon; (d) laceration —
jagged, irregular tearing of
tissues.

(a)

(b)

(c)

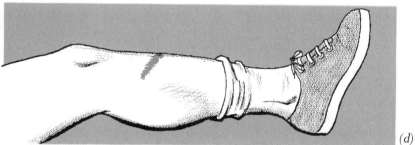

(d)

nail, what does the wound look like? What kind of wound is this? If this were human tissue, what would be affected? Is there oozing?

3. With the knife, cut into another area of the tomato. Examine the wound. What kind of wound is this? If this were human tissue, what would be affected? Is there oozing?

4. With your fingers, take hold of the skin where it was cut with the knife, and tear the skin back. What kind of wound is this? If this wound and the wound made in step 3 were equally deep, which do you think would heal more quickly? Why?

5. What do all four wounds have in common?

6. How might a person acquire these wounds?

7. For which kind of wound or wounds might you be likely to need a doctor?

First Aid

8. What is the best first aid treatment for each kind of wound?

You probably wrote that in all wounds the skin is broken, and that wounds should be cleaned with soap and water and covered, if necessary, with a sterile dressing that is bandaged in place. You may have said that you might need a doctor for any one of these wounds if it were deep or extensive, but that you would be sure to see a doctor for a deep puncture wound because of the difficulty of cleaning it to prevent infection.

TETANUS Tetanus (TET-nus), or lockjaw, is a serious, often fatal, disease, which develops when tetanus germs enter a wound and multiply there. Tetanus germs grow best in the absence of air, or oxygen. Therefore, it is especially important to consult a doctor when you suffer a severe puncture wound, which offers tetanus germs an ideal growing place. Once, tetanus killed many people, but today protective shots can prevent the disease. Most babies get protective tetanus shots during their first year of life, as well as additional booster shots in the later years to maintain that protection.

Let's Pause for Review

First aid is immediate, temporary care given to prevent further injury and lessen shock until a doctor can take over. If you are one of the first people on the scene of an emergency, look the situation over and send for help. Don't move (or let others move) the injured person unless life is in danger. If the person is safe in a given place, treat first for bleeding, breath stoppage, and signs of poisoning. Then treat for shock (keep the person flat, warm, quiet, and reassured). Continue to reassure the person, stressing that help is on the way.

To stop severe bleeding, cover the wound with a sterile dressing, a piece of cloth, or with your bare hand, and apply direct pressure. If additional pressure is needed, apply it on the appropriate pressure point with your other hand. A tourniquet can cause gangrene, so use one only when all other methods have failed to stop severe (possibly fatal) bleeding.

When bleeding is not severe, clean abrasions, punctures, incisions, and lacerations with soap and water, and cover them, if necessary, with a sterile dressing that is bandaged in place. Contact a doctor about deep puncture wounds, in which tetanus germs may grow easily.

Figure 15.9. Dr. Heimlich demonstrates the Heimlich Maneuver on newscaster Tony Guida of WNBC-TV's "Newscenter 4."

Choking

Choking occurs when some foreign object is breathed into the air passages. This is a common emergency. Usually, after a moment or two, the victim automatically coughs the object out. So the first-aider should keep calm, reassure the victim, and encourage coughing.

However, if the victim can't cough the object out within a moment or so, other procedures may be tried. If the victim is a child, the first-aider may turn the child over one arm and, using the heel of the hand, give the child two or three sharp blows between the shoulder blades in order to remove the foreign object. The same method may be used with adults who have first been turned onto their sides.

THE HEIMLICH MANEUVER   When a large food particle completely blocks the passage of air, a victim can neither breathe nor speak; such an emergency is very serious. A new first aid procedure, called the **Heimlich** (HYM-lik) **Maneuver,** has been introduced recently to treat severe choking (see Figure 15.9). To help a choking victim who is standing or sitting, proceed as follows (see Figure 15.10, page 222):

First Aid

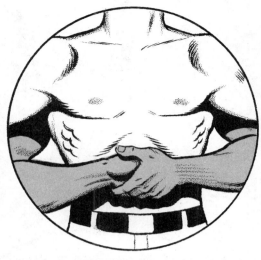

Figure 15.10. First aid for choking if victim is sitting or standing: *(left)* full view; *(above)* detail of hand position.

1. Get behind the victim and wrap your arms around his or her waist.
2. Grab one of your fists with your other hand. Place the fist against the victim's abdomen, slightly above the navel and below the ribs.
3. Press your fist into the victim's abdomen with a strong, *quick upward thrust*. Repeat this action a few times, if necessary.

To help a victim who is lying down, roll him or her over on the back and proceed as follows (see Figure 15.11):

1. Face the victim, and kneel with each knee outside the victim's hips.
2. Place the heel of one of your hands on the victim's abdomen slightly above the navel and below the ribs. Place your other hand over the first.
3. Press into the victim's abdomen with a strong, *quick upward thrust*. Repeat, if necessary.

If the victim vomits, place him or her on one side and wipe the mouth.

To help yourself if you are choking when you happen to be alone, press into your abdomen yourself or roll your abdomen against the edge of a sink, table, or other rigid object.

If these methods fail, if medical help is not yet available, and if the victim stops breathing, **artificial respiration** should be given. Details about this procedure follow.

Health Through Safety

ARTIFICIAL RESPIRATION A person may stop breathing for many reasons (electric shock, drowning, gas poisoning, choking, drug overdose, crushing injury to the chest). When a person's *respiration*, or breathing, stops completely, the victim must be helped to breathe in an *artificial* way, a way that imitates the natural way. The best procedure for doing this is for rescuers to force their breath directly into the lungs of victims. Another method involves moving a victim's upper *torso* (body part above the waist) so that the chest cavity can expand and contract. We will now examine these procedures.

The Best Method: Mouth-to-Mouth Resuscitation

From every point of view, mouth-to-mouth resuscitation is the very best way to resuscitate, or revive, a victim. First of all, it is the easiest method. A lone rescuer can keep it up for hours. This is important, because victims of breath stoppage have been revived after having received artificial respiration for as long as 4 hours.

Second, mouth-to-mouth resuscitation produces a flow of air most like natural breathing. How? The pressure provided inflates the lungs immediately, keeps the victim's air passages open, and moves much more air into the lungs than other methods do.

Third, mouth-to-mouth resuscitation allows the rescuer to see and hear how effective his or her efforts are. The rescuer can watch the rise and fall of the victim's chest and actually hear if an air exchange is taking place.

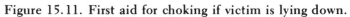

YOUR PART

1. Before you read the following directions on how to give mouth-to-mouth resuscitation, try to remember how it is done. (No doubt you have read or heard about it before.) Now imagine that someone has stopped breathing and that you are the only other person

Figure 15.11. First aid for choking if victim is lying down.

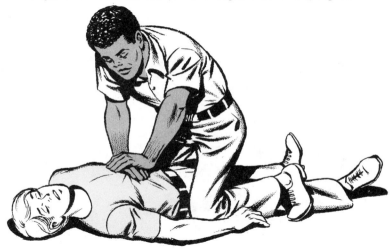

(a)   (b)

present. List five steps you would follow in giving mouth-to-mouth resuscitation.

2. Now read the directions in steps 3 and 4, and, if necessary, correct the directions in your own list.

3. Mouth-to-mouth resuscitation for an adult:

   a. Place the victim on his or her back and open the mouth.
   b. Clear the mouth of any foreign material.
   c. Tilt the victim's head back. (This pulls the tongue away from the back of the throat, opening the air passage to the lungs [see Figure 15.12a].)
   d. Pinch the victim's nostrils together to prevent air leakage, and place your mouth over the victim's open mouth. Blow air into the victim's lungs (see Figure 15.12b).
   e. When the victim's chest rises, remove your mouth and listen for the return flow of air from the victim's lungs (see Figure 15.12c).
   f. Repeat the process of blowing and listening about every 5 seconds (12 times a minute).
   g. Continue your efforts until the victim breathes regularly or until a doctor tells you to stop.
   h. Even when the victim's breathing returns to normal, stay with the victim in case breathing stops again before medical help arrives.

4. Mouth-to-mouth resuscitation for a child or baby:

   a. As for an adult, place the victim on his or her back, open the mouth, and clear it of any foreign material.
   b. Tilt the victim's head back slightly. Do not pinch the nostrils.
   c. Cover the victim's nose and mouth with your mouth (see Figure 15.13). Blow more gently than for an adult. For a baby, use only small, gentle puffs of air.
   d. Watch the victim's chest and listen for return flow of air, as for an adult.

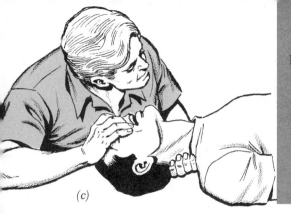

Figure 15.12. Steps in mouth-to-mouth resuscitation: (a) opening air passage; (b) blowing air into victim; (c) listening for return flow of air.

(c)

e. Repeat blowing and listening about every 3 seconds (20 times a minute).

f. Continue your efforts and stay with the victim, as for an adult.

The Silvester Method   You may feel that you do not want to put your mouth directly over the victim's. If so, you can put a handkerchief or thin piece of cloth over the victim's mouth and breathe through that. If, for some reason, you can't give mouth-to-mouth resuscitation, you can use the less effective method shown in Figure 15.14, page 226. This is the **Silvester Method,** which calls for applied chest pressure and arm lifts.

YOUR PART

1. Before you read the following directions for the Silvester Method, try to remember if you have ever seen or heard about artificial respiration by means of chest pressure and arm lift. Now imagine that someone has stopped breathing and that you are the only other person present. List five steps you would follow.

Figure 15.13. Mouth-to-mouth resuscitation for a young child, with child's mouth and nose sealed off by first-aider's mouth.

Figure 15.14. Silvester Method of artificial respiration: (a) tilting the position of the head; (b) applying pressure; (c) lifting and stretching the arms.

(a)

(b)

(c)

2. Now read the directions in step 3, and, if necessary, correct the directions in your own list.
3. The Silvester Method:

   a. Place the victim on his or her back.
   b. Clear the mouth of any foreign material.
   c. Tilt the head back (see Figure 15.14a).
   d. Kneel behind the victim's head; take the victim's arms and place them over the lower ribs. With your hands on the victim's wrists, rock forward and press almost directly downward (see Figure 15.14b). This forces air out of the victim's lungs.
   e. Slowly move the victim's arms outward, away from the body and upward above the head (see Figure 15.14c). This allows the lungs to expand and fill with air.
   f. Repeat the process—press, lift, stretch, and release—10 to 12 times a minute. The release should be as short as possible.
   g. Continue your efforts as in mouth-to-mouth resuscitation.

Health Through Safety

Quick Action Against Poison

Poisoning, like severe bleeding and breath stoppage, is an emergency that calls for immediate action. It is important both to get medical help and to give first aid immediately. If possible, have another person do the calling while you take care of the poisoned person. The caller should be ready to describe the victim's symptoms and give the name of the poison, if known.

WHERE TO CALL   In a poison emergency, you telephone others for two reasons. First, you want to get first aid advice. Second, you want to alert the doctor or hospital emergency room that you need an ambulance, so that they will be ready to care for the victim in transit and on arrival. Therefore, you may call your nearest well-equipped hospital emergency room. Or, you may call your own doctor for advice on what to do and where to go. In some areas, you may call the local poison control center.

The Poison Control Center   Every year new products containing poisons come on the market. Thousands of such products already exist. In many places, poison control centers have been set up to gather and store information on these products, as well as information on all known poisons and poisonous plants, insects, and reptiles. These centers are good sources of first aid information, especially if the poison taken is unusual or unknown.

DILUTING THE POISON   While someone is calling for help, you should try to *dilute* (duh-LOOT), or thin, the poison in the victim's stomach by giving her or him 1 or 2 glasses of milk or lukewarm water to drink. Use milk instead of water if you have it, because milk gives more protection to the digestive system. Then try to make the person vomit, unless a substance listed in Table 15.2, page 228, has been swallowed. During vomiting, gasoline and kerosene can be breathed or forced into the lungs where they can do serious harm. Chemical compounds such as strong **alkalis** (AL-kuh-lyz) and acids that have already burned the throat while being swallowed will burn it a second time if vomiting takes place. Of course, an unconscious person should never be made to vomit, since the vomited material will get into the lungs.

EMPTYING THE STOMACH   After giving milk and water, you may be able to make the victim vomit by slipping a finger or a spoon part way down the throat to make the person gag. Or, you may need to use an **emetic** (ih-MET-ik), a preparation that causes vomiting. You can use a homemade emetic—2 tablespoons of salt *or* baking soda *or* mustard stirred into a cup of warm water. (This emetic is advisable for adults but not for children, in whom salt poisoning can occur.) Or you can use the commercial emetic, syrup of **ipecac** (IP-ih-kak), recommended in Table 15.1, page 211, for your home first aid kit.

First aid experts stress the importance of consulting a poison control center, if at all possible, before making a victim vomit. This is because, as new findings about poisoning are made, recommendations for the best treatment against specific poisons are revised.

GETTING THE PERSON TO A DOCTOR   If you have managed to dilute the poison and empty the stomach within 10 minutes after the poison was swallowed, chances are you have saved the victim from serious harm. The next step is to get the person to a doctor without further delay (and via a preordered ambulance, if possible), taking the poison container and its contents with you.

ANTIDOTES   If, for some reason, medical help is not immediately available, you may be able to give the victim an **antidote** (AN-tih-doht), a preparation that counteracts the effect of a poison. Antidotes are often printed on the labels of poisonous household products, for example. Or, a poison control center can supply information on the correct antidotes.

Universal Antidotes   If an individual has swallowed an unknown poison, you must not make the victim vomit. And, as we've already learned, you mustn't make a person vomit substances like gasoline or kerosene, either. However, if medical help is not available, you can first dilute the poison and then give a **universal antidote**, a preparation that counteracts the effects of several kinds of poison. You can buy a universal antidote at the drugstore and keep it in your first aid kit. Or you can use activated charcoal—1 or 2 tablespoons in a glass of water.

Table 15.2:   Poisons That Should Not Be Vomited

Type	Source or Name
Strong acids	Toilet bowl cleaners
	Hydrochloric acid
	Sulfuric acid
Strong alkalis	Drain cleaners
	Sodium hydroxide (lye)
	Potassium hydroxide
	Trisodium phosphate
	(beet salt)
Petroleum products	Furniture polish
	Kerosene
	Gasoline
	Benzene (paint thinner)

Acids and Alkalis

If someone has swallowed a strong acid or alkali like lye or drain cleaner, tissue damage to the mouth and throat will begin almost at once and continue to get worse. Therefore, poison experts now doubt the value of diluting such substances. In addition, dilution may also cause injurious vomiting. (Petroleum products are a special case. Since such poisons may be very harmful if they enter the bloodstream, the doctor or poison control center you call may advise you to induce vomiting. Don't make this decision on your own.)

In general, the best procedure is to rush the victim of acid or alkali poisoning to a hospital or doctor's office, taking the poison container and its contents with you.

SAVING THE POISON CONTAINER Taking the poison container to the hospital with you helps the doctor to identify the poison and to start treatment more quickly. Saving the container is especially important if the person is unconscious and cannot tell you what he or she has taken. (Remember, you should never try to give an unconscious person anything to drink, because the victim may breathe the liquid into the lungs.)

Poisonous Plants

Most poisons enter the body through the mouth. Some plant poisons do, too. Because young children often nibble on plants, parents must warn children about poisonous plants near home. Table 15.3, pages 230–231, lists many wild and cultivated plants that are poisonous if eaten, and there are others. However, poison ivy, poison oak, and poison sumac (see Figure 15.15, page 231) affect the skin, as well.

Poison ivy is most often a vine. *Poison oak* is usually a low shrub. On both plants, the leaves grow in groups of three. Both plants have greenish white flowers and small gray berries. The leaves of both are green in summer and reddish in spring and fall. *Poison sumac* is a tall shrub or small tree that often grows in swampy areas in the eastern third of the United States. Its leaves are bright orange in spring, changing to dark green in late spring and summer, and becoming bright orange-red again in the fall.

Learn to recognize and avoid these poisonous plants when you are out walking. If you think there may have been contact, as soon as you get home wash with hot soapy water, sponge with rubbing alcohol, and change your clothes. If you do so, the symptoms—redness of skin, blisters, swelling, burning, itching, even fever—may not develop. However, if within hours or days the symptoms do appear, you can treat the skin with a commercial calamine lotion or with a solution of baking soda and water. If the symptoms are severe, see your doctor, who may recommend that, if you are especially sensitive, you go through a process of immunization for future protection.

Table 15.3: Plants That Are Poisonous If Eaten

Plant	Poisonous Parts	Symptoms
*Amanita mushroom	All parts	Sweating; wheezing; irregular breathing and heartbeat
*Azalea	All parts	Vomiting; paralysis; convulsions
*Baneberry	Root; sap; berries	Stomach irritation; nausea; diarrhea
*Bittersweet	Leaves and berries	Burning of throat; nausea; dizziness
Black locust	Leaves; bark; pods; young sprouts	Vomiting; diarrhea; paralysis
Bloodroot	Stems and roots	Intense burning of mouth, throat, and stomach; vomiting
Calla lily	All parts	Intense burning and irritation of mouth and stomach
*Castor bean	Beans	Vomiting; cramps; coma
*Daffodil, narcissus, jonquil	Bulb	Vomiting; diarrhea; convulsions
*Daphne	Berries	Burning and ulceration of digestive tract; diarrhea
Indian hemp (marijuana)	Leaves; flowers; resin	Hallucinations; mental depression
Iris	Leaves; root; fleshy stalk	Vomiting; diarrhea
Jerusalem cherry	Berries	Vomiting; diarrhea; weakness; collapse
*Jimsonweed (thorn apple)	All parts	Intense thirst; dilated pupils; delirium; rapid heartbeat; convulsions
Lantana	Berries	Vomiting; diarrhea; weakness; collapse
Lily-of-the-valley	All parts	Dizziness; vomiting
*Pokeweed	All parts	Vomiting; drowsiness; impaired vision; coma

Health Through Safety

Table 15.3 (concluded)

Plant	Poisonous Parts	Symptoms
Privet	All parts	Bloody vomiting; diarrhea; collapse
Rhubarb	Leaves	Vomiting; diarrhea; convulsions; coma
Wisteria	Pods and seeds	Vomiting; diarrhea; abdominal pain
*Yellow jessamine	All parts	Paralysis; respiratory failure

*Can be fatal.

Figure 15.15. Plants that affect the skin: (*a*) poison ivy; (*b*) poison oak; (*c*) poison sumac.

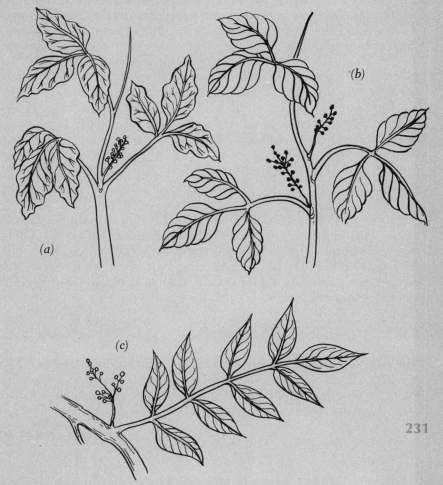

231

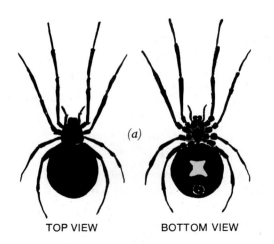

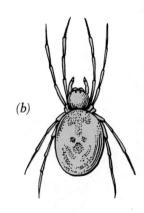

TOP VIEW   BOTTOM VIEW

Poisonous Spiders

In the United States, we have only two poisonous spiders. One is the *black widow* and the other is the *brown recluse,* or *violin spider* (see Figure 15.16). The black widow's bite hurts, reddens and swells the skin, but rarely kills. The victim feels weak, dizzy, and sometimes short of breath. The abdomen cramps, and the victim feels like vomiting. The brown recluse's bite gets very red and may result in chills, fever, joint pains, nausea, and vomiting. In a day or two, a rash may appear on the skin. In a week or two, the bite may become an open sore.

First aid is the same for both kinds of poisonous spider bites. Have the victim lie down (or in some other way keep the affected part lower than the heart). Reassure the victim. Call the doctor, or get the victim to a source of medical help.

Scorpions

Our only poisonous scorpions (see Figure 15.17) live in the Southwestern states. The sting from a scorpion's tail can sometimes kill a child. The sting tingles or burns. The victim becomes dizzy and may feel like vomiting. The victim also suffers abdominal cramping and may go into convulsions (a seizure or a fit). First aid is the same as for poisonous spider bites. Call a doctor right away.

Poisonous Snakes

We have four kinds of poisonous snakes in the United States (see Figure 15.18). Three of them—rattlesnakes, copperheads, and cottonmouth moccasins—are called *pit vipers* (snakes) because of the small pit between nostril and eye on each side of the head. The **venom** (poison) of pit vipers

Figure 15.17. Scorpion.

(a)

(b)

(c)   (d)

Figure 15.18. Poisonous snakes: (a) rattlesnake; (b) copperhead;
(c) cottonmouth moccasin; (d) coral snake.

affects the circulatory system, whereas the venom of the fourth poisonous snake—the *coral snake*—affects the nervous system.

When it comes to snakebite, prevention is better than cure. And prevention is simple if you follow three rules in snake-infested areas: (1) watch where you step, where you put your hands, and where you sit; (2) wear high boots—half of all bites are below midcalf; and (3) learn to identify poisonous snakes (refer again to Figure 15.18).

If a person is bitten, here is the recommended first aid routine:

1. Get medical care, or transport the victim to a source of medical treatment as quickly as possible. Call ahead, if possible, so that **antivenin** (an-tih-VEN-un), which counteracts venom, will be ready.

2. Keep the victim still, calm, and reassured. Make sure that the affected part is lower than the heart, even when the victim is being transported for medical treatment.

3. If you are going far into country where it may be difficult to reach medical help for many hours, carry a snakebite kit with you. and *know how and when to use it*. Then, if the victim begins to show serious symptoms (rapid swelling, severe pain, pinpoint pupils, slurred speech, convulsions), do the following:

   a. Make two *shallow* incisions over the fang marks with a sterile knife (see Figure 15.19). The incisions must cut through the skin only, so that muscles and nerves beneath the skin are not injured.

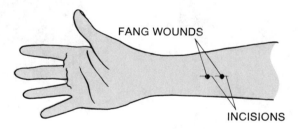
FANG WOUNDS

INCISIONS

Figure 15.19. Incisions for snakebite when symptoms are severe.

   b. Apply suction with the suction cup from your snakebite kit. Continue the suction for 30 to 60 minutes. After applying suction, wash the wound with soap and water, and dry it.

   c. Continue to reassure the victim, and get the victim to a source of medical treatment as soon as you can.

Stinging Insects

Bees and wasps inject venom, too. For most people, such venom is painful but not dangerous. However, to a few people who are highly allergic to

234   **Health Through Safety**

insect venom, wasp and bee stings can be fatal. Allergic people can get medication from their doctors to take if they are stung.

When an allergic person is stung, the victim may collapse or the affected area may swell. If you are present, give first aid and send for medical help right away. To give first aid, remove the stinger, if one is present. Lift it out with tweezers or scrape it off; by grasping it, you may inject the remaining venom into your fingers. Continue to reassure the victim that medical help is on the way.

Let's Pause for Review

Encourage a person who is choking to cough. Or else, use the heel of the hand to tap this person sharply between the shoulder blades. A new procedure, the Heimlich Maneuver, involves exerting quick, sharp pressure upon the abdomen, just above the victim's navel.

Use mouth-to-mouth resuscitation to revive a person who has stopped breathing. Quickly clear the mouth. Tilt the person's head back to open the air passage to the lungs. Except for a small child, pinch the victim's nostrils to prevent air leakage. Put your mouth directly over the victim's mouth and blow air into the lungs. Watch the chest to see that it rises. Turn your head aside to let the victim "exhale." Repeat 12 to 15 times a minute for an adult, 20 times a minute (more gently) for a child, and 20 times a minute (light puffs only) for a baby. Continue your efforts until either the victim starts to breathe or a doctor tells you to stop. Even if the victim starts to breathe normally, remain with the victim until medical care is available.

If mouth-to-mouth resuscitation is, for some reason, impossible to give, another less effective treatment is the Silvester Method, which involves applied chest pressure and arm lifts.

In cases of poisoning, it is important to be quick both in getting medical attention and in giving first aid. First, dilute the poison (if the victim is conscious) by giving several glasses of milk or lukewarm water. Second, identify the poison. Third, if the victim has not swallowed a strong acid, lye, gasoline, kerosene, or the like, make the person vomit. You can slip a finger or a spoon down the throat or have the victim drink an emetic, either homemade (2 tablespoonfuls of salt, baking soda, or mustard stirred into a cup of warm water) or commercial (syrup of ipecac). Then, rush the person to a doctor.

If you can't identify the poison or if the victim has swallowed a strong acid, alkali, or petroleum product, such as gasoline or kerosene, don't make the person vomit. Instead, dilute the poison and, if medical help will be delayed, give a universal antidote or activated charcoal in water. If the poison was acid, give milk or water, then milk of magnesia solution, followed by milk, egg white, or olive oil. For alkalis like lye, give the victim milk or water, then diluted vinegar or lemon juice, followed by egg white, olive oil, or more milk or water. Then rush the victim to a doctor. In every case of poisoning, take the poison container (including any remaining poison) to the doctor or hospital.

Warn children about plants around the house and garden that are poisonous if eaten. Learn to recognize and avoid poison ivy, oak, and sumac. After contact, wash with hot soapy water, and change clothes. If redness, itching, and blisters develop, treat them with calamine lotion or with a solution of baking soda and water. For severe cases, see a doctor.

For poisonous bites and stings, give first aid and get medical help. If a person is bitten by a poisonous snake, spider, or scorpion, keep the victim comfortable and reassured, with the affected part lower than the heart. To remove as much poison as possible from a serious snakebite when help will be long delayed, use a snakebite kit to cut small, skin-deep slits over fang marks and apply suction. In case of an allergic reaction to a bee or wasp sting, remove any stinger, and get help.

First Aid for Burns

Lightning, sunshine, chemicals, fire, hot liquids, steam—all of these can cause burns. The first aid you give depends upon the severity of the burn. **First-degree burns** redden the unbroken skin, **second-degree burns** blister the skin and break it to some extent, and **third-degree burns** destroy and often blacken, or char, the skin and its underlying growth cells.

SERIOUS BURNS A third-degree burn (or any extensive burn regardless of degree) is a serious and painful injury, which should always be treated by a doctor. The twin dangers of shock and infection are always present. When giving first aid for serious burns, the best rule is to keep it simple. Have the person lie down and treat for shock. If the person is conscious, you can give fluids to drink. If you expect a doctor or an ambulance soon, do nothing more.

If Medical Help Is Delayed If you know that medical help will be late in coming, you may be able to phone a doctor for advice. This is wise because ideas on the best treatment for burns keep changing. You don't want to do anything that will interfere with later treatment. For this reason, never put oil, butter, ointment, or any other medication on a serious burn.

Health Through Safety

The doctor will only have to remove the ointment or other medication before beginning professional treatment.

What if you know that medical help will be delayed, but you can't reach a doctor by phone? Don't peel away clothing that is stuck to the burn. But if a large burned area is exposed to the air, wash your hands and apply a thick, dry, sterile dressing to the burn. This should help prevent infection and lessen pain from contact with the air. If possible, help prevent shock by transporting the victim lying down.

MINOR BURNS   The best way to treat a minor burn is to cover it with cold water until it stops hurting. Often, no further treatment will be needed. If necessary, however, you can coat the burn with a lotion suggested by your doctor.

CHEMICAL BURNS   Fire is not the only cause of burns. Strong chemicals can burn body tissues, too. First aid in such cases consists of pouring water over the affected area. For example, if some burning chemical comes into contact with the eyes, the victim can put the head beneath a tap of running water so that the eyes can be easily and completely washed out. If this method can't be used for some reason, a first-aider can help by gently pouring water from a container into the victim's eyes.

If a strong chemical soaks into the victim's clothing, this clothing should be removed and the affected area flooded with water. After receiving first aid, a person with a chemical burn should see a doctor. There are specific antidotes for many chemicals, and a doctor can use these antidotes to prevent further harm and to speed healing.

First Aid for Frostbite

Frostbite (freezing or partial freezing of some part of the body) most commonly affects the ears, nose, hands, and feet. To treat frostbite, *quickly* warm the affected area by immersing it until it thaws in warm, but not hot, water. The water temperature should be about 102° to 105° (F 39° to 40.5° C), which is just a little warmer than normal body temperature. The first-aider can put his or her forearm in the water first to test its temperature. Don't rub, or put pressure on, the frozen part; frozen tissues are easily damaged. Therefore, all of the victim's constricting clothes or dressings should be removed, and the victim should not be allowed to bear weight on the affected area.

Broken Bones

Only a doctor can properly care for a broken bone, or **fracture**. But there are times when ordinary people must give temporary care to broken bones. This is because injured people must sometimes be moved out of life-

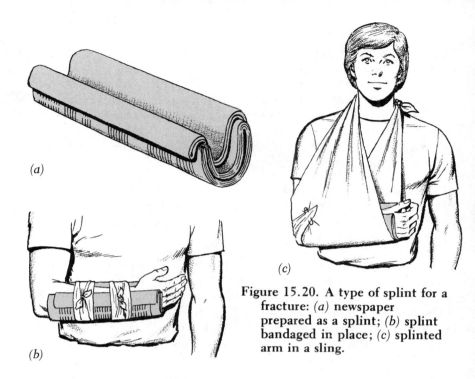

Figure 15.20. A type of splint for a fracture: (a) newspaper prepared as a splint; (b) splint bandaged in place; (c) splinted arm in a sling.

threatening situations, and, if it is at all possible, a broken bone should be put in a **splint** (see Figure 15.20) before such moving takes place.

How can you tell if a bone is broken? Sometimes the victims can tell you themselves. Sometimes you can see that an arm, for example, is swollen, crooked, or deformed when compared with the other arm. Sometimes, by very gently running your fingertips over the injured area, you can feel some unevenness beneath the skin. In the case of a **compound fracture** (see Figure 15.21), you can see the bone where it has broken through the skin.

Refer again to Figure 15.20, which shows you how to apply a splint. The purpose of a splint is to keep the broken bone and the nearest joints from moving, even though the victim is being moved. Note that you can prevent movement by using magazines, newspapers, a pillow, or a rug, if padded boards are not available. Remember, though, that unless splinting is necessary to save a life, a fracture victim should not be moved or splinted at all. You can help most by treating the victim for shock, by reassurance, and by remaining on the scene until medical help arrives.

Sprains, Strains, and Dislocations

The violent wrenching or twisting of a joint (shoulder, elbow, wrist, finger, hip, knee, ankle, toe) can cause sprains, strains, and dislocations. A **sprain** is an injury to the soft tissues (ligaments, tendons, blood vessels) of the

Health Through Safety

joint. A **strain** is an injury to the muscles that operate the joint. A **dislocation** displaces a bone from its normal connecting place with another bone.

Fractures often go along with sprains, strains, and dislocations. Therefore, when a sprain has occurred, it is wise to see a doctor and be X-rayed to make sure that no bones have been broken. It is always necessary to see a doctor for a dislocation. First aid for dislocations is the same as for fractures. Keep the joint and other affected parts from moving, and get medical attention.

First aid for sprains consists of applying ice bags or cold wet cloths to keep the swelling down. The sprained joint should also be supported to keep it from moving. First aid for strains, on the other hand, consists of warm applications and rest.

Looking Back

First aid is quick, temporary care given to prevent further injury and lessen shock until a doctor can take over. When giving first aid, look the situation over and send for help. Don't move an injured person unless the life of the victim is in danger.

Treat first for severe bleeding, breath stoppage, and poisoning. Then treat for shock by keeping the person flat, warm, quiet, and reassured.

To stop severe bleeding, apply direct pressure to the wound. Apply additional pressure on the appropriate pressure point. Use a tourniquet only when all other methods fail to stop what may be fatal bleeding.

For someone who is choking on food and cannot breathe or

Figure 15.21. Types of fractures: *(left)* **simple fracture;** *(right)* **compound fracture.**

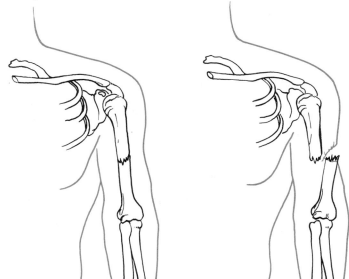

speak, use the Heimlich Maneuver. From behind the victim, wrap your arms about the victim's waist. Grab your fist and press into the victim's abdomen just above the navel. Apply the pressure with a quick upward thrust and repeat, if necessary.

Use mouth-to-mouth resuscitation to revive a person who has stopped breathing. Quickly clear the mouth. Tilt the person's head back. Pinch the victim's nostrils shut, if the victim is not a young child. Put your mouth over the victim's mouth and blow air into the lungs. Check to see that the chest rises. Turn your head aside after each breath to let the victim "exhale." Repeat 12 to 15 times a minute for an adult, 20 times a minute (gently) for a child, and 20 times a minute (light puffs only) for a baby. Keep it up until the person starts breathing or until a doctor tells you to stop. Even if normal breathing begins, stay with the victim until medical care is available.

In poisoning, it is important both to get medical help and to give first aid quickly. If the individual is conscious, dilute the poison by having the victim drink several glasses of milk or lukewarm water. Next, identify the poison. Make the victim vomit, unless a poison like gasoline, acid, or lye has been swallowed. Give a universal antidote to someone who has swallowed an unknown poison or a strong acid, alkali, or petroleum product. Give milk of magnesia solution and milk, egg white, or olive oil to someone who has swallowed acid. Give diluted vinegar or lemon juice and milk, water, egg white, or olive oil to someone who has swallowed a poison like lye.

Avoid contact with poisonous plants whenever possible. Wash and change clothes after contact. Treat symptoms with calamine lotion. See a doctor for serious cases.

For poisonous snakebites, send for medical help and, if a serious bite will not be treated for many hours, cut into the skin and apply suction to snakebite to remove poison. For poisonous spider bites, scorpion stings, and allergic reactions to bee and wasp stings, get medical help.

A victim of serious burns (third-degree burns or extensive burns of any degree) should be treated for shock and given fluids to drink if conscious. Then, medical care should be sought as soon as possible. Do nothing more without a doctor's advice, unless you know that medical help will be a long time in coming. In that case, you can protect the burned area from infection by covering it with thick, dry, sterile dressings. Cover a minor burn with cold water until it stops hurting. Chemical burns may result when strong chemicals come into contact with body tissues. To give first aid, flood the affected body part with water (under a running tap, if possible).

Treat frostbite by quickly warming the affected area, immersing it in warm, but not hot, water, if possible.

Treat fracture victims for shock. Move such victims only when doing so is necessary to save their lives. If the victim is to be moved, apply splints (padded boards, magazines, pillows) to keep the broken bone and the nearby joints from moving. Get medical help. Treat dislocations the same way.

Treat sprains with cold packs at first to keep swelling down. See a doctor for an X ray, if you suspect a fracture. Treat strains with warm applications and rest.

MODIFIED TRUE-FALSE QUESTIONS

1. First aid is immediate, temporary care given to the victim of an accident or illness until _a doctor_ arrives on the scene.
2. When you witness an accident, the first thing to do is to assist the _police._
3. In an emergency caused by an accident, check first for _stoppage of breathing._
4. Unless the life of an injured person is in danger, the person should _never_ be moved from the scene of an accident.
5. _Shock_ always accompanies serious injury.
6. During shock, blood pressure _drops._
7. A person in shock should be kept _cool._
8. Smelling salts may be used with caution in cases of _shock._
9. The loss of _a half-pint_ of blood may be fatal.
10. Blood from a cut artery flows in _spurts._
11. Direct pressure may control bleeding, especially if _an artery_ has been cut, until a doctor arrives.
12. Major blood vessels lie close to _bone_ at pressure points.
13. Failure to remove a tourniquet may cause _blood poisoning._
14. _A small amount_ of bleeding helps cleanse a wound.
15. Tetanus germs grow best in the _presence_ of air.
16. When breathing has stopped, the easiest way to revive the victim is to use _oxygen._
17. In cases of poisoning, the best thing to do first is to dilute the poison by having the victim drink _milk._
18. A preparation that counteracts a poison is called _an antiseptic._
19. Most poisons enter the body through the _mouth._
20. The venom of a rattlesnake affects the _digestive_ system.
21. A homemade emetic consists of baking soda or mustard mixed with warm _soap suds._
22. _Third-degree_ burns destroy the skin tissue.

23. In cases of frostbite, warm the affected area _rapidly_.
24. The Heimlich Maneuver is a first-aid measure for _choking_ on food.
25. The displacement of a bone from its normal connecting place with another bone is referred to as _a sprain_.

MATCHING QUESTIONS, GROUP 1

Column A	Column B
1. fainting	a. tissue death
2. shock	b. body reaction to injury
3. rabies	c. partial loss of consciousness
4. gangrene	d. lockjaw
5. tetanus	e. animal bite
	f. bee sting

MATCHING QUESTIONS, GROUP 2

Column A	Column B
1. laceration	a. skin scraping
2. puncture	b. sharp, clean cut
3. incision	c. small hole piercing the skin
4. abrasion	d. torn, jagged, irregular wound
5. emetic	e. settles stomach
	f. produces vomiting

MATCHING QUESTIONS, GROUP 3

Column A	Column B
1. first-degree burn	a. skin blisters
2. second-degree burn	b. use water
3. third-degree burn	c. skin and underlying growth cells destroyed
4. chemical burn	d. use suction
5. serious snakebite	e. use a tourniquet
	f. skin reddens but remains unbroken

MULTIPLE-CHOICE QUESTIONS

1. In an emergency situation involving injury, you should be concerned with all of the following, _except_
   a. severe bleeding
   b. stoppage of breathing
   c. signs of poisoning
   d. having the victim sit up

Health Through Safety

2. All the following are signs of shock, *except*
   a. abnormal breathing c. rapid weak pulse
   b. increased awareness d. cold and clammy skin
3. Unconsciousness is *not* related to
   a. severe shock c. heart seizure
   b. stroke d. first-degree burns
4. Of the following, which is *not* the accepted practice when giving first aid?
   a. check for severe bleeding
   b. use a hot water bottle or heating pad
   c. check for signs of poisoning
   d. keep the victim still and quiet
5. Shock can best be described as
   a. a slowing down of body processes due to failure of the circulatory system
   b. an increase in the blood flowing through the body
   c. a slowing down of body processes due to failure of the nervous system
   d. an increase in blood pressure
6. Which of the following is *not* a treatment for shock?
   a. keep the victim warm without overheating
   b. keep the victim lying flat unless there is difficulty in breathing
   c. warn the victim of possible consequences of movement
   d. keep the victim quiet
7. If a major blood vessel is cut, blood loss can be fatal within
   a. 1 to 5 minutes c. half an hour
   b. 15 minutes d. 1 hour
8. In adults, the recommended number of cycles per minute for mouth-to-mouth resuscitation is
   a. 5 c. 20
   b. 12 d. 25
9. Which of the following is a poison for which you would *not* encourage vomiting?
   a. acid c. charcoal
   b. ipecac d. antivenin
10. First aid for a poisonous snakebite involves all of the following, *except*
    a. keeping affected part lower than the heart
    b. using a suction cup
    c. making two shallow incisions over the fang marks
    d. applying warm packs to affected part

THOUGHT QUESTIONS

1. You are driving along a street and see a car strike a child in a crosswalk. The child is flung into the air, lands on the sidewalk, and is now unconscious. Describe, in order, the steps you should take in administering first aid.

2. You are planning a class field trip to the mountains. State three safety rules to follow in snake-infested areas, and explain why.

3. Your friend has just been stung by a bee and seems to be having an allergic reaction. Describe the symptoms of the reaction, and explain the first aid treatment that should be given.

4. You arrive on the scene and find someone suffering from third-degree burns. Describe the kind of burns from which the victim is suffering. What first aid treatment will you give?

5. Why should people who take first aid courses repeat these courses every few years?

6. Why should a first aid course include practical exercises, as well as textbook studies?

7. More people engage in recreational activities than ever before. Therefore, training in first aid has become essential if people are to continue to enjoy their increased leisure time with minimal injury. Make a list of first aid procedures that would be common treatment for all recreational injuries.

8. Suppose you have an accident and are able to help yourself. Should you administer first aid to yourself or should you seek help? Explain your view.

9. Many first aid practices have changed during the years. As a library project, seek out some practices that have changed, tell why they have changed, and describe what the new procedures are.

10. Why has the emphasis on first aid increased so sharply during the last decade?

Looking Ahead

In Chapter 16, you will read about the bodily changes that lead to physical maturity, particularly those changes that begin at puberty and lead to mature sexual development.

Health Through Safety

Unit Six: FIND OUT ABOUT YOURSELF

Researchers asked 5000 students in an Eastern state what they really wanted to know about growing up physically, emotionally, and socially. Here are some of the questions the students asked and some of the statements they made (from *Teach Us What We Want to Know*, Connecticut Board of Education):

Why do some kids act so immature?

Why do kids rebel against their parents?

How can you be sure of what and who you are?

I would like to understand myself.

How can you get popular?

How can you convince your parents you're old enough to make your own decisions (with exceptions and without being over-bold)?

How are values established?

How can I control my emotions?

How can I learn to cope with emotional problems?

How can I get more privacy? My brother is a nuisance.

How can I keep from yelling?

I have a ten-year-old sister, and I get blamed for what she does.

Some days I'm depressed and irritable. Why?

Why am I so ugly? Why don't people like me?

How do you overcome embarrassment?

What does it take to be a mature adult?

How can I achieve happiness?

How can I learn to get along with other people and with myself?

I want to know about other people.

Why do people judge others on superficial things, following fads, etc.?

I understand myself and am satisfied.

If you're a dud like me, how can you become graceful?

I would like to understand my personality.

I like to feel grown up but adults say, "You're only 12." Why do they do this? It hurts a lot.

Who am I?

Does acting mature at 12, 13, or 14 hurt your personality?

How can you overcome shyness?

What is right and what is wrong?

Is there any solution to picking friends well?

What is love, the kind that sustains a marriage for 40 or 50 years?

It is hard to concentrate on schoolwork and get good grades when you're really concentrating on boys.

Why can't I get anything done because of thinking of girls?

What does "going steady" mean?

Is it wrong to go out with a boy a year or two older?

At what age should you date?

I am not planning to marry. Should I date?

I hope someday we will have a real liking for one another; that we will understand people of different races and colors.

These questions and statements—and others you yourself may have—reveal that the growing-up process is more than just becoming broader, taller, or heavier. You probably realize that these questions have no final answers. You can't look up the meaning of complete living in a dictionary. And you can't find out in an encyclopedia how to overcome embarrassment. But that doesn't mean that you shouldn't ask such questions and try to find answers for them.

Complex physical, emotional, and social changes help prepare you for the responsibilities of womanhood and manhood. Using the foregoing student questions and statements, and others that are typical, we will discuss these changes in the three chapters of this unit. It is hoped that these chapters will provide some answers to the questions you may have about growing up and making a mature and satisfactory adjustment to life.

Chapter 16: You're Growing Up Physically

Every day of your life, some of your tissues, especially surface tissues like those of the skin, hair, and nails, reproduce by cell division (see page 34). But more than cell division is necessary to reproduce an entire individual. Each new human life begins, not when one cell divides, but when two cells join (one cell from the mother, one from the father), forming a fertilized egg cell.

As you may remember, most of your body cells contain 46 chromosomes which "program" your growth and development. But the *sex cells* (**egg cells** in female bodies, **sperm cells** in male bodies) contain only 23 chromosomes each. So, when a sperm cell from the father unites with an egg cell produced by the mother, the single new cell that is formed contains the 46 chromosomes needed to direct its growth.

This new cell then begins to develop on its own. After many cell divisions, the single cell has become a group of cells. And this group of cells is the developing **embryo** (EM-bree-oh), or unborn individual. At the end of about nine months, the new individual has completed the period of most rapid human growth and is fully developed and ready to be born into the world. After birth, the new individual continues to grow, becoming heavier, taller, and broader, until physical maturity has been reached.

What is puberty?

Puberty (PYOO-bur-tee) is the time during which boys and girls mature sexually and become able to have children of their own. At puberty, adolescence also begins. But puberty ends when a person becomes sexually mature, whereas adolescence doesn't end until a young person becomes an adult legally.

The organs that produce the sex cells—ovaries in girls, testes in

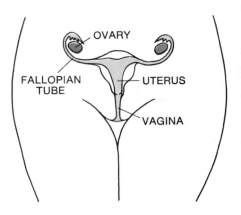

Figure 16.1. Female
reproductive system.

boys—were part of your body even before birth. But these organs do not produce sex cells until signaled to do so by the pituitary gland at puberty. Pituitary hormones stimulate the ovaries or testes and adrenal glands to produce hormones of their own, called *sex hormones*. All of these hormones working together bring about the momentous changes of puberty. Height increases dramatically, body shape changes, and the reproductive organs mature.

On the Way to Womanhood

The average girl begins to mature sexually at about age 10½ or 11, but it is quite normal for puberty to come earlier or later. At puberty, the organs of the female reproductive system begin to mature. Most of these organs are located inside the female body. They include the **ovaries,** the **Fallopian** (fuh-LOH-pee-un) **tubes,** the **uterus** (YOOT-uh-rus), and the **vagina** (vuh-JY-nuh). Figure 16.1 shows you how these organs look and where they are.

What is a menstrual period?

The thick lining of the uterus is richly supplied with blood vessels. If a fertilized egg is not present in the uterus, the lining will break down and be shed, and in the process some small blood vessels of the lining will break, too. About two weeks after an ovary has released an egg cell, the shed lining of the uterus, colored by a small amount of blood from the broken blood vessels, passes out of the body through the vagina, the passageway from the uterus to the outside of the female body. This monthly discharge of the unused uterine lining is called **menstruation** (men-struh-WAY-shun). The time required for menstruation, called a **menstrual** (MEN-struh-ul) **period,** usually takes from three to five days, but in some girls a six- or seven-day period is quite normal.

Find Out About Yourself

At what age does menstruation usually start?

Most girls begin to menstruate (men-struh-WAYT) when they are about 11 or 12. But some may start as early as age 9 and others as late as age 15 or 16. All of these starting times are normal. (However, if a girl has not menstruated by age 16, she should talk to her doctor about it.)

How and why does menstruation come about?

As a young girl reaches puberty, hormones from the pituitary gland cause the internal sex organs to grow and mature. As a girl's ovaries mature, the **ova** (singular, **ovum**), or egg cells, within the ovaries begin to mature, too. (These egg cells were part of each girl's body even before birth.) Once about every 28 days, a mature egg cell is released by one of the ovaries.

The ovaries usually take turns releasing mature egg cells. The process of releasing an egg cell is called **ovulation** (ahv-yuh-LAY-shun). Ovulation usually continues until age 45 or 50, at which time most women gradually stop ovulating and menstruating. This time, during which ovulation and menstruation gradually stop, is called the **menopause** (MEN-uh-pawz) or change of life. By then most women have released several hundred of the 400,000 egg cells their ovaries have contained.

If you look again at Figure 16.1, opposite, you will see the uterus—the hollow, muscular organ in which babies grow and develop before birth. You will also see that the Fallopian tubes open into the uterus at one end. At the other end, fingerlike projections lying near the ovaries receive the newly released egg cell. The egg cell now travels through a Fallopian tube toward the uterus. This journey takes from three to six days.

If a male sperm cell should enter the Fallopian tube at this time and join with the egg cell, a single new cell—a fertilized egg cell—would form. However, if no sperm cell joins the egg cell, the unfertilized egg cell breaks down and disappears. When no fertilized egg cell arrives, the uterus soon sheds its soft, thick lining. This special lining builds up again each month and is ready to receive and nourish a fertilized egg cell.

THE MENSTRUAL CYCLE After menstruation, another egg begins to mature in one of the ovaries. In about two weeks, ovulation will take place again. This maturing of an egg cell, buildup of the uterine lining, and later discharge of the unused lining is called the **menstrual cycle**. The cycle is counted from the first day of one monthly period to the first day of the next monthly period. Many girls and women have a 28-day cycle. But longer cycles (up to 35 days) and shorter cycles (as short as 21 days) are also normal for other individuals.

It is important to remember that menstruation is in no way a sickness. It is part of the normal work of a healthy female body. So a girl can go right ahead with her normal activities. In fact, the same things that help maintain general health—a positive outlook, a well-balanced diet, regular exercise, and plenty of sleep—help insure menstrual periods free from discomfort and tension.

Why do you sometimes skip a month?

When a girl first begins to menstruate, she is likely to be irregular because her hormone system has not settled down. She may skip a month or two, or menstruate a day or two early or late. After about a year, though, a regular pattern is established. (Menstrual periods can be missed or become irregular during times of stress, such as emotional upset, physical illness, worrying about exams, going away to college, and similar situations.) Sometimes, too, a girl may have mild cramps or aching on the first day or two of her period. But, like irregular periods, these discomforts usually disappear as the body adjusts itself more fully to physical maturity. A girl with severe cramps that interfere a great deal with her normal activities should see her doctor.

What about bathing and swimming during your period?

A girl should certainly bathe or shower each day of her period. Bathing in water that is neither too hot nor too cold will help her to stay fresh and odor-free. Similarly, if she swims, the water should not be so cold as to chill her. Many girls find they can swim comfortably while they are menstruating. Others find they are better off not swimming. So this is an individual matter, which each girl can decide for herself.

Also an individual matter is the form of protection that a girl chooses to use. Some girls protect their clothing from menstrual flow by wearing *sanitary napkins*, or pads. These gauze-covered pads come in different sizes and thicknesses according to need. They are worn with either sanitary panties or belts.

Another kind of menstrual protection is the *tampon*. This is a slim, tight roll of absorbent material that is worn inside the vagina. A piece of string is attached to the outside end for easy removal. There is probably less odor with a tampon since it is worn internally. For help in deciding on which form of protection to use, a girl can talk to her mother, an adult female friend, or her family doctor. Once her period is well established, a girl can soon discover how often she needs to change pads or tampons to prevent odor and absorb the menstrual flow.

What is pregnancy?

Menstruation gets its name from the Latin word *mensis*, meaning month, since females menstruate about once a month. However, if a woman becomes **pregnant**—that is, if a fertilized egg cell becomes implanted in

250   **Find Out About Yourself**

the lining of her uterus—she usually stops menstruating until her baby is born. During pregnancy, the uterine lining stays in place and nourishes the growing baby.

Let's Pause for Review

During puberty, height increases dramatically, the body changes shape, and the sexual organs mature so that young people become capable of parenthood. In girls, egg cells begin to mature and, once every 21 to 35 days (depending on the person), an egg cell is released from one ovary or the other. One of the two Fallopian tubes receives the released egg cell, which then journeys through the tube for three to six days. A male sperm cell entering the tube at this time may join with, or fertilize, the egg cell.

When the egg cell is not fertilized, however, it breaks down and disappears. The soft lining of the uterus, colored by a little bleeding from a few small blood vessels, also breaks down and leaves the body by way of the vagina in a process called menstruation. The menstrual process is a normal, healthy one. Therefore, the same measures that normally maintain good health (getting plenty of exercise, sleep, and good food) maintain health and comfort during menstruation, as well.

On the Way to Manhood

The average boy begins to mature sexually at about age 12½, which is one or two years later than the average girl's beginning puberty. And, of course, some boys begin later than age 12½. Remember that each person grows at his or her own rate, and a person who begins to mature later than classmates may be in every way just as tall and well developed as faster-growing friends when growth is complete.

Unlike a girl's sexual organs, a boy's are mainly on the outside of his

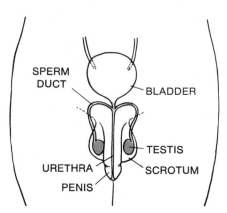

Figure 16.2. Male reproductive system.

251

body. These organs are the **penis** (PEE-nus) and two **testes** (TES-teez); the singular of testes is **testis** (TES-tis). The testes are also called **testicles** (TES-tih-kulz). Like other body parts, these organs vary in size from person to person. However, an early sign of puberty is an increase in the size of the penis and the testes. Figure 16.2 shows you how these organs look and where they are.

The testes, each about the size of a walnut, lie behind the penis in a small protective pouch called the **scrotum** (SKROH-tum). The testes correspond to a girl's ovaries. That is, the ovaries send out the egg cells, and the testes send out the sperm cells, each of which is necessary for reproduction. Sperm cells leave the testes by way of the **sperm ducts**. These ducts correspond to a girl's Fallopian tubes.

How do sperm cells and egg cells compare?

Sperm cells are more sensitive than egg cells to body heat. Sperm cells seem to need the cooler temperatures outside the body in order to grow and mature. And the protective scrotum helps the testes adapt to these outside temperatures. Muscles in the scrotum contract to draw the testes close to the body in cold weather and relax to let the testes hang farther from the body in hot weather.

Sperm cells are much smaller and more numerous than the egg cells. An egg cell is a bit smaller than the period at the end of this sentence. A sperm cell (see Figure 16.3) is very much smaller than an egg cell and cannot be seen without a microscope. Perhaps you remember that a female's ovaries contain about 400,000 egg cells. But within a male's testes, many millions of sperm cells mature every *month*. And there may be 400 to 500 million sperm cells in a single teaspoonful of the fluid in which they leave the body.

What is semen?

The testes are filled with about 1000 feet (300 meters) of tightly coiled, threadlike tubes in which, at puberty, sperm cells begin to grow and mature. As you saw in Figure 16.3, a sperm cell looks a little like a tadpole, with a head at one end and an energetic tail at the other. Like a tadpole, a sperm cell needs liquid in which to float or swim. A thick, white liquid is produced for this function by glands attached to the sperm ducts.

This thick white liquid with sperm cells floating in it is called **semen** (SEE-mun). Semen is *ejaculated* (ih-JAK-yoo-lay-tud), or sent forcefully out of the body, by the contractions of the tubes through which the semen reaches the **urethra** (yuhr-EE-thruh), another tube by which semen leaves the body.

If you look again at Figure 16.2, page 251, you will see that urine also leaves the bladder by means of the urethra, but this does not happen at the

Find Out About Yourself

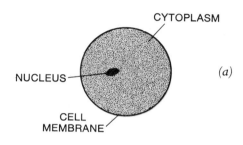

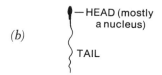

Figure 16.3. Egg cell and sperm cell compared: *(a)* egg cell; *(b)* sperm cell.

same time that semen leaves. When semen is being released, the opening from the bladder to the urethra closes, blocking the discharge of urine.

ERECTION, EJACULATION, AND EMISSION COMPARED   At puberty, a boy begins to have **erections** (ih-REK-shunz). That is, his penis, which is usually soft, becomes hard and erect at times. This happens when extra blood fills the many blood vessels within the penis and other blood vessels clamp temporarily shut to hold the extra blood in place. **Ejaculation** may or may not accompany an erection. However, after an erection or ejaculation, the penis again becomes soft.

Most boys experience their first ejaculations at about age 14. But these experiences can come earlier or later, and they may occur in a variety of situations. Boys often wake up in the morning with erections resulting from the pressure of a full bladder. But erections also result from sexually stimulating thoughts and experiences. In addition to erection, a stimulating dream may also trigger the release of semen during sleep.

To emit means to send forth, and *nocturnal* means at night. So, a nighttime release of semen is called a **nocturnal emission** (nahk-TURN-ul ee-MISH-un), a **seminal** (SEM-un-ul) (from the word *semen*) **emission,** or simply a "wet dream." Nocturnal emissions are completely normal. The semen released is surplus semen, and its loss is not harmful in any way. Some boys have many such emissions; other boys have few or none. These variations are normal, too.

Do boys experience anything like girls' menstruation?

Some people mistakenly think that nocturnal emissions are similar to

You're Growing Up Physically   253

menstruation. But, as this chapter shows, the two processes are entirely different. However, both processes do signal sexual maturity. Nocturnal emissions show that a boy has begun to produce mature sperm cells and that he is physically able to become a parent.

CIRCUMCISION   Loose skin, called the **foreskin,** covers the tip of the penis. The foreskin does not prevent the penis from freely enlarging during an erection. However, a small operation to remove the foreskin is often done soon after birth. This operation, called **circumcision** (sur-kum-SIZH-un), makes cleanliness easier. A boy who has not been circumcised needs to turn back the foreskin and bathe the area beneath it each time he bathes or showers. Except in the matter of cleanliness, it makes no difference to general health whether a boy is circumcised or not.

Let's Pause for Review

The average boy starts to mature sexually at about age 12½, but no boy should worry if his development comes earlier or later than that. An early sign of puberty is an increase in the size of the penis and the testes. Inside the testes the sperm cells necessary for reproduction begin to mature in very large numbers. Boys begin to have erections in a variety of situations. At about age 14, the average boy experiences his first ejaculation, in which semen (a thick, white liquid with sperm cells floating in it) is sent forcefully out of the body through the urethra. Sometimes, surplus semen is ejaculated during sleep. Such an experience is quite normal and harmless.

How Traits Are Passed On

A male sperm cell is deposited in the female's vagina. The sperm then enters the uterus and travels to a Fallopian tube. If a female egg cell is present, the sperm may fertilize, or join with, the egg cell (see Figure 16.4). The fertilized egg, containing hereditary information from both parents, soon begins to grow by dividing. This growing group of cells then travels to the uterus, where it becomes implanted in the soft, thick lining. There, in approximately nine months' time, the new cells develop into a new person, ready to be born into the world. Many of that new person's traits (sex, body size and shape, and hair, eye, and skin color, for example) were determined at the moment that the egg cell and the sperm cell joined.

As we learned at the beginning of this chapter, egg cells and sperm cells

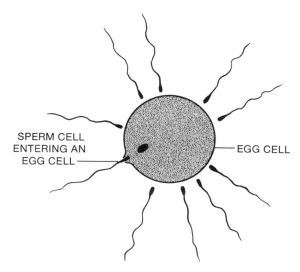

Figure 16.4. Many sperm cells surround an egg cell, but only one fertilizes it.

have 23 chromosomes each. When an egg cell and a sperm cell join, they form a single new cell with 46 chromosomes, containing all the hereditary information needed to direct the growth of a new human being (refer again to Chapter 3, page 30).

Figure 16.5. The sex chromosomes.

Y	X
SPERM CELL	SPERM CELL
+	+
X	X
EGG CELL	EGG CELL
↓	↓
XY	XX
BOY	GIRL

X AND Y CHROMOSOMES

The **X** and **Y chromosomes** are called sex chromosomes because they determine the sex of each new individual. Every egg cell has an X chromosome. But only half of all the sperm cells carry an X chromosome, whereas the other half carry a Y chromosome. Thus, it is the father's sperm cell that determines the sex of a baby. If a sperm cell carrying a Y chromosome happens to unite with an egg cell, the XY combination in the fertilized egg will produce a baby boy. If, on the other hand, the sperm cell that fertilizes the egg cell has an X chromosome, the combination of XX in the fertilized egg will produce a baby girl (see Figure 16.5).

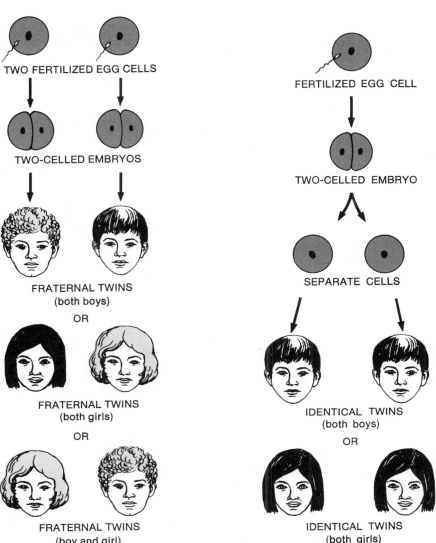

Figure 16.6. How fraternal twins are produced.

Figure 16.7. How identical twins are produced.

FRATERNAL TWINS Occasionally, a woman produces two or more egg cells at a time. Since sperm cells are so numerous, the chances are good that all of the eggs present will be fertilized. This is how many twins are produced. Such children are no more alike than brothers and sisters born at different times. Twins born from a union of different eggs with separate sperms are called **fraternal twins** (see Figure 16.6).

IDENTICAL TWINS Sometimes, for unknown reasons, a fertilized egg splits into two or more parts and develops into two or more embryos.

Find Out About Yourself

When a fertilized egg splits, each part that results has an identical set of 46 chromosomes. The children (twins, triplets, and so on) that develop from the separate cells, therefore, have identical chromosomes. So they look alike and are always of the same sex (see Figure 16.7).

From Egg to Embryo

At the moment when an egg cell and a sperm cell join, the baby-to-be is tinier than the period at the end of this sentence. But the fertilized egg soon starts to grow, dividing once within the first 24 hours after fertilization, and regularly thereafter (see Figure 16.8). Growth by cell division (refer again to Chapter 3, page 34) continues until a berrylike group of cells, or young embryo, forms. After about three or four days, this group of cells reaches the uterus, where it floats about for ten days or so before becoming implanted in the uterine lining.

By the time of implantation, the embryo looks like a disk. And it is from this tiny disk that all the many tissues of the human body develop. (Your eyes, ears, brain, nerves, muscles, and bones all grew from a small group of cells that seemingly were much alike.) After only one month's growth, for example, a heart and some blood vessels have formed, and the heart has begun to beat.

Structures that protect and nourish the unborn child are also formed from some cells of the original berrylike group of cells. These structures are the **umbilical** (um-BIL-uh-kul) **cord,** the **placenta** (pluh-SENT-uh), and the **amnion** (AM-nee-ahn). As you can see in Figure 16.9, page 258, the umbilical cord is attached at one end to the embryo's navel and at the other end to the placenta.

Food nutrients and oxygen from the mother's bloodstream seep through the placenta and are absorbed by the baby's bloodstream. The umbilical cord delivers additional food and oxygen to the baby and carries the baby's wastes back to the placenta, through which they seep into the

Figure 16.8. Early stages of an embryo.

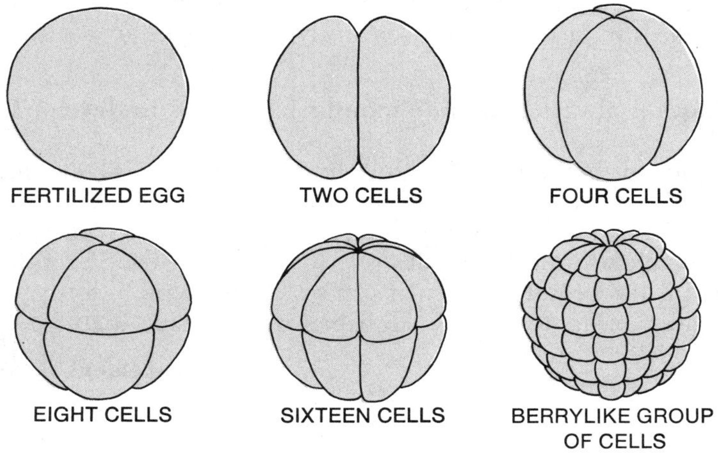

FERTILIZED EGG   TWO CELLS   FOUR CELLS

EIGHT CELLS   SIXTEEN CELLS   BERRYLIKE GROUP OF CELLS

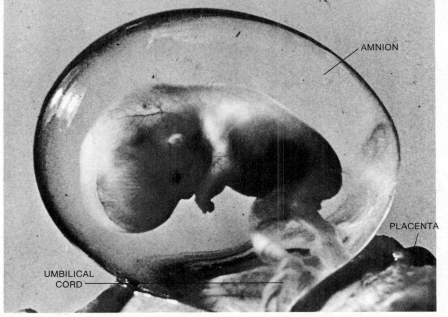

Figure 16.9. An embryo inside the amnion eight weeks after
fertilization.

mother's bloodstream. Thus, the mother-to-be breathes, eats, and gets rid
of wastes for the growing baby.

The embryo shown in Figure 16.9 floats within a fluid in the amnion.
This membrane is also called the "bag of waters." Though the mother may
bump into things or stumble and fall, the unborn baby, floating comfortably in the amniotic fluid, feels few of these discomforts. In fact, because
they are so well protected, unborn babies often come through even serious
accidents unharmed.

From Embryo to Fetus to Newborn Baby

For the first two months, the baby-to-be is called an embryo, after which it
is called a **fetus** (FEE-tus). After two months' growth, the fetus is less
than 2 inches (5 centimeters) long. But it has begun to look like a human
being, and its most important body structures have begun to grow.

Does it always take nine months for a baby to develop?

During the fourth month of life, the fetus begins to move about, and soon
its mother will begin to feel these movements. By the seventh month of its
development, the unborn baby's organs and other necessary structures are
fairly completely formed. The baby is 12 to 15 inches (30 to 38 centimeters)
long, and it has begun to fatten. Even so, a baby born at this age needs
special care in order to survive. All babies weighing less than 5½ pounds

(2.5 kilograms) are considered *premature,* or early, and should receive special care.

What is a normal pregnancy?

Normally, a baby spends a little more than nine months in the uterus, growing fatter, longer, and stronger in the last two months. A mother's body changes during pregnancy to accommodate this growth. Shortly before being born, the baby moves into birth position. In this position, it will be born head first, as most babies are.

HOW A BABY IS BORN   About nine months after the fertilization of the egg cell, the uterus has stretched to its fullest extent, the placenta now delivers less food, and the unborn baby is fully developed. It is time for birth to begin. If the mother has received regular *prenatal* (pree-NAYT-ul), or before-birth, *care,* she is likely to be in good health for the event. Because most American mothers now receive such prenatal care and most of their babies are born in hospitals, childbirth today is a very safe event, which women need not fear.

What is the labor period?

Labor refers to the work done by the uterus during birth. The uterus, being the largest, strongest muscle in a woman's body, is well able, by its contractions, to push the child out into the world. Birth begins with rhythmic contractions of the uterus (every half hour, for example). These contractions put pressure on the lower, narrow part of the uterus called the **cervix** (SUR-viks), which must open before birth can proceed. Once the cervix has opened, the uterine contractions become more powerful and push the baby through the birth canal, or vagina, and out into the world.

Are labor contractions and labor pains the same?

For centuries, labor contractions have been miscalled labor pains, but labor discomforts would be a better name. Fear of the unknown, however, can cause tension, and tension can change discomfort into pain. So it is wise for a fearful mother-to-be (especially a first-time mother) to change the unknown into the known. How? By attending classes (given by the Y and other groups) that provide preparation for childbirth.

In these classes, women learn just what to expect during every stage of childbirth. They do exercises to strengthen muscles that get extra use during pregnancy and childbirth. And they learn how to relax during the contractions of the first stage of labor. In other classes, hypnosis is used to achieve similar results. So there is no need for fear to mar the happy time when a baby is born. Figure 16.10 shows a newborn baby crying. The crying indicates that the baby has begun to breathe on his or her own. The doctor has clamped and cut the umbilical cord. This baby is about average in size, weighing close to 7 pounds (3 kilograms) and measuring about 20 inches (50 centimeters) in length.

Being a parent is a rewarding and happy experience when a man and woman want to have children and are prepared to provide them with the affection and security they need.

Let's Pause for Review

Egg cells and sperm cells have 23 chromosomes each. Human traits are passed on by means of these chromosomes. When an egg cell and a sperm cell join, the fertilized egg cell grows by dividing and soon becomes a group of cells. This cell group travels to the uterus, becomes implanted in the uterine lining, and grows in about nine months' time into a fully developed human baby. At birth, uterine contractions push the baby through the birth canal and out into the world. Childbirth today is a safe and normal event, which no woman need fear, especially when classes providing preparation for childbirth are available almost everywhere.

Changes in Body Shape

As the body matures internally and becomes capable of parenthood, it matures externally, too. In response to sex hormones circulating in the bloodstream, boys begin to look like men, and girls begin to look like women. Boys become more muscular, their shoulders broaden, and their beards appear. Girls' hips broaden, breasts grow and develop, and fat deposits beneath the skin give them a softer, rounder look.

The word *puberty* comes from a Latin word meaning fine, short hair. And an early sign of puberty in both sexes is the appearance of new hair beneath the arms and in the **pubic** (PYOO-bik) **region** (the triangular section that is the lowest part of the abdomen).

As vocal cords lengthen and the **larynx** (LAR-inks), or voice box, descends to a lower position in the throat, voices—and especially boys' voices—change. And, as you may remember from Chapter 10, page 125, at this time the skin of both boys and girls needs increased care as sweat glands and oil glands become more active.

THE ADOLESCENT GROWTH SPURT   Since most girls start their rapid growth ahead of boys (the average girl starts at age 10½, the average boy at age 12½), there is a time when many girls are taller than most of the boys in their classes. However, although boys start their rapid growth later,

260   **Find Out About Yourself**

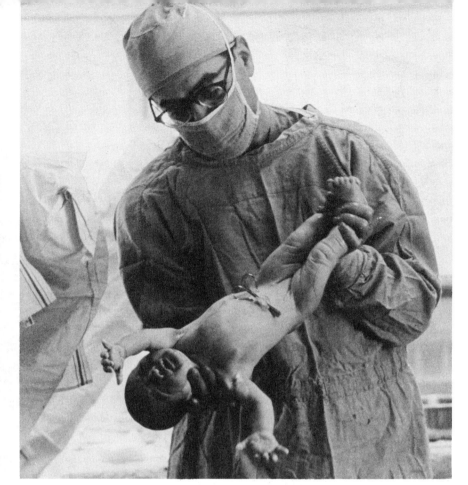

Figure 16.10. Just born!

they have a longer total growing time and end by being about 5 inches (13 centimeters) taller, on the average, than girls. Only in the nine months before birth and in the first year of infancy is growth more rapid than during the growth spurt of adolescence. No wonder that teenage appetites are good. In order to reach their greatest possible strength and height, young people need plenty of nourishing food.

ALL ARMS AND LEGS   Each part of the teenaged body grows at its own rate and time. This rapid growth is uneven but usually starts with the feet and hands. (So don't worry about big hands and feet; the rest of your body will catch up.) Next the legs and arms lengthen. Tall teenagers, in particular, may be high-waisted for a time and may feel as if they are all arms and legs. Finally, the lower trunk and the chest increase in size.

All of these unevenly growing body parts may be hard to coordinate (get to work together smoothly) for a while. Strength increases greatly in ad-

Figure 16.11. Facial change by the end of adolescence: *(above)* some people change a great deal; *(below)* others do not.

olescence, too, but often not in time to control the arms and legs when they first lengthen.

ALL NOSE AND CHIN At their own time and rate, the heart and other internal organs grow faster, too. Even the head's growth speeds up. Adolescent nearsightedness may develop as eyeballs grow and change. Facial features change as facial bones lengthen. Most chins and noses grow longer. Most foreheads expand and become more prominent (see Figure 16.11).

YOUR PERSONAL TIMETABLE Weight gains—about 45 pounds (20 kilograms) for the average boy and 35 pounds (16 kilograms) for the

Find Out About Yourself

average girl—may be uneven, too, making some young people chubby for a while before growth is complete. All of these changes vary greatly from person to person, as does the time at which growth is complete. Some people grow until they are age 20. Some people grow very, very slowly for much longer. However, most girls are about 98 percent fully grown by age 16½, and most boys by age 18.

How does your body know when puberty should begin? How does it know when to stop growing? Scientists aren't really sure. However, your body probably has ways of sensing your own level of growth, development, and readiness for sexual maturity. And it is your own "growth clock" that matters. You grow in accordance with your own inner timetable.

Why do some kids act so immature?

Some people just naturally grow slowly and reach puberty later than their schoolmates. The interests and behavior of these "late bloomers" may seem immature to their faster-growing classmates. But when growth is complete, these late maturers may be just as tall and well developed in every way as their faster-growing classmates. Albert Einstein and Winston Churchill, for example, developed slowly and were considered backward in childhood.

Fortunately, doctors nowadays can check to be sure that a late-maturing youngster is growing normally. Doctors do this by X-raying the hands and measuring the amount of cartilage present between the bones of the hands. In Figure 16.12a, page 264, spaces between bones are larger than in Figure 16.12b. Figure 16.12a is of a hand of a child with a bone age of 7. The spaces (cartilage) indicate that growth is not complete. Figure 16.12b is of a hand of a child with a bone age of 15. The smaller spaces indicate that growth is nearly complete.

Why do kids rebel against their parents?

When the internal changes of puberty are complete (in girls, when menstruation begins or within a year thereafter; in boys, usually by the time the voice deepens), young people are physically able to become parents. In simpler societies than ours, young people enter directly into manhood and womanhood not long after they are able to become parents. Impressive initiation (in-ish-ee-AY-shun) ceremonies usually mark the change. After their initiation into adulthood, these young people begin more and more to do the work of men and women. Before long, they marry and have families of their own.

Our society is very different, even though some of us do celebrate the time of puberty with special ceremonies. Our young people do not enter fully into adulthood for several years after they have reached sexual maturity. At age 18, a young person is legally adult in some ways, but in many

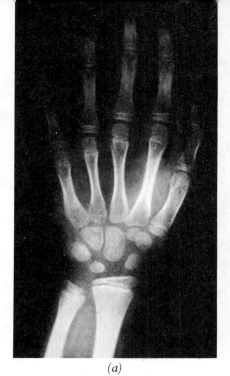 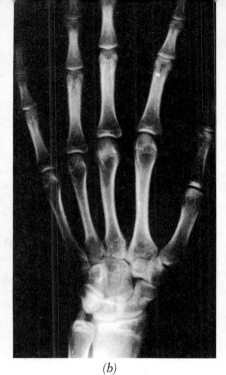

(a)   (b)

Figure 16.12. X rays used to determine whether bone growth is normal: (a) **bone age of 7;** (b) **bone age of 15.** *Courtesy of The New York Times.*

states he or she must wait until age 21 for other adult rights and responsibilities. And even then, if a young person is a college student, she or he may not yet be fully adult in the sense of being financially independent of parents.

YOUR PART

1. It takes longer for young people to become adults in our society than in simpler societies. Write down why you think this is so.
2. Our society prolongs childhood and keeps young people dependent on their parents longer than in simpler societies. This long dependence can cause trouble between parents and children. How? Why? Write down your answers.
3. As a class or in small groups, compare and discuss your answers.

Perhaps you noted that in simpler societies there are no brain surgeons, space scientists, ballet dancers, Supreme Court justices, or research chemists. You may have agreed that you have so much to learn before you can do the adult work of our society that you can't possibly learn it all by age 14, 15, or 16.

Find Out About Yourself

In simpler societies (or in past societies), a 15-year-old would be considered a young adult and would be so treated by parents and others. In our society, a 15-year-old is a financially dependent minor and is so treated. To make matters worse, puberty comes earlier than in the past. Each new generation of teenagers begins to grow taller—and, therefore, to appear more mature—earlier than the one before.

Young people know that they have much to learn in order to do the complicated jobs of our society, but they feel their adulthood, too, and sometimes resent their dependence. For parents, the long years of adolescent dependence can also be difficult. Mothers and fathers often wonder how to treat young people who are still regarded as minors but are in so many ways adult.

Looking Back

Throughout life, each person follows his or her own growth pattern, developing in accordance with an inner "growth clock." When young people are physically mature enough, pituitary hormones signal the ovaries, the testes, and the adrenal glands to make sex hormones. These hormones stimulate the body to (1) achieve sexual maturity and (2) achieve adult shape and size. Rate of adolescent growth varies from person to person. However, the average girl reaches puberty at about 10½ and, before long, begins to produce mature egg cells. The average boy reaches puberty at about 12½ and, before long, begins to produce mature sperm cells. The internal and external changes of puberty that make parenthood possible are usually complete by the time a girl menstruates, or within a year thereafter, and by the time a boy is capable of erection and ejaculation. External changes in body shape often take longer. However, by the time the average girl is 16½ years old, she has a rounded, womanly body and 98 percent of her adult height. By the time the average boy is 18 years old, he has the beard, voice, body hair, broad shoulders, and heavy muscles of a man, and he, too, has achieved 98 percent of his adult height. People vary, but usually the feet start their rapid growth first. The legs and arms follow, and the trunk lengthens last. Facial features may change as facial bones—especially those of the nose and chin—lengthen.

Young people in our society do not achieve full adulthood (financial independence, full legal rights and responsibilities) until long after they reach sexual maturity. The long period during which young people are partly adult, yet still financially dependent, can be difficult at times for both young people and their parents. Without this long dependence, however, our society would lack people with the knowledge, skills, training, artistry, and development that make our society what it is.

MODIFIED TRUE-FALSE QUESTIONS

1. New life begins to develop when _two_ sex cells join.
2. Most of your body cells contain _48_ chromosomes.
3. The monthly discharge of the unused uterine lining is called _a period._
4. At puberty, _adolescence_ begins.
5. Sex cells in the female are produced in the _uterus._
6. The production of sex cells is stimulated by the _thyroid_ gland.
7. Menstruation generally begins during _puberty._
8. The fertilized egg grows in the _stomach_ of the female.
9. Menstrual fluid consists largely of _blood_ and the cast-off lining of the uterus.
10. Sanitary napkins and _tampons_ are menstrual absorptive devices.
11. The _scrotum_ is a protective pouch that holds the testes.
12. Sperm cells manufactured in the testes are _less_ numerous than egg cells manufactured in the ovaries.
13. Semen leaves the body through the _ureter._
14. Removal of the foreskin from the penis makes cleanliness _easier._
15. An XY combination of chromosomes will produce a baby _boy._
16. _Identical_ twins develop from two fertilized egg cells.
17. The unborn baby receives food and nourishment from the mother through the placenta and _small intestine._
18. The work done by the uterus during birth is called _conception._
19. The birth canal through which the newborn baby enters the world is the _vagina._
20. The regularity of the menstrual periods is influenced by _emotional stresses._

MATCHING QUESTIONS

Column A	Column B
1. Fallopian tube	a. foreskin
2. urethra	b. male sex cell duct
3. ovum	c. egg cell
4. sperm	d. sensitive to body heat
5. testis	e. provides sperms
	f. opens into the uterus

Find Out About Yourself

COMPLETION QUESTIONS

1. During puberty, boys begin to look like men and girls begin to look like women in response to the action of _____ hormones.
2. Most girls begin menstruation when they are about _____ years old.
3. Most boys begin to mature sexually by the age of _____ .
4. In this country, although a young person may vote at the age of 18, he or she reaches legal adulthood in many of the individual states only at the age of _____ .
5. At maturity, the height of boys is generally _____ than that of girls.

MULTIPLE-CHOICE QUESTIONS

1. On the average, during adolescence, the weight of girls
   a. decreases
   b. decreases and then increases
   c. increases
   d. remains the same
2. On the average, during adolescence the weight of boys
   a. decreases
   b. decreases and then increases
   c. increases
   d. remains the same
3. Most young people have completed their growth and development by age
   a. 12   b. 14   c. 16   d. 18
4. The average girl starts puberty at about age
   a. 8½   b. 10½   c. 12½   d. 14½
5. The average boy starts puberty at about age
   a. 8½   b. 10½   c. 12½   d. 14½
6. On the average, by the end of adolescence the height of boys compared to the height of girls is
   a. somewhat less   c. somewhat greater
   b. about equal   d. double
7. The period of most rapid human growth occurs
   a. before birth
   b. during the first year of life
   c. during adolescence
   d. at about age 20
8. Humans carry their young internally for about
   a. 3 months   c. 9 months
   b. 6 months   d. 12 months
9. The gland that begins the production of hormones that trigger puberty is the
   a. pituitary   b. pineal   c. parathyroid   d. thymus

10. During puberty, more rapid growth usually first appears in the increased size of the
   a. chin and nose
   b. arms and legs
   c. lower trunk
   d. hands and feet

THOUGHT QUESTIONS

1. Explain why it is meaningless to compare your growth and development to that of any of your classmates.
2. Suppose, before your growth spurt, you were well coordinated and could excel in all sports. This semester, however, you do a lot of fumbling and misjudging. Explain why and how this is happening.
3. In our society, young people do not achieve full adulthood as soon as young people in less complex societies. Compare our society to a simpler society of your own choosing, with respect to *(a)* puberty rites, *(b)* legal rights and responsibilities, *(c)* financial dependence and independence, and *(d)* technological skills.
4. Identify the following changes caused by puberty by indicating if they occur in girls only, in boys only, or in both sexes. Use the symbols ♀ for girl only, ♂ for boy only, and ♀ ♂ for both:

   a. hips broaden
   b. shoulders broaden
   c. underarm hair grows
   d. voice changes
   e. skin changes
   f. sperm cells are produced
   g. egg cells are produced
   h. beards appear
   i. full breasts appear
   j. sweat glands become more active

5. Do young people today experience more "growing-up pains" than their fathers and mothers did? Take a position and justify it.

Looking Ahead

In Chapter 17, you will be reading about feelings of all kinds—joy, fear, anger, sadness. You will explore healthful ways of expressing your feelings and of meeting your emotional needs. You will also have a chance to think about what it takes to be an emotionally mature adult.

Find Out About Yourself

Chapter 17: You're Growing Up Emotionally

Physical growth is fairly easy to observe and to measure. Furthermore, physical growth speeds up during adolescence, then slows down and levels off as physical maturity is reached. But emotional growth is hard to observe and measure. And, unlike physical growth, emotional growth never stops. What does it mean to grow up emotionally? In part, it means learning to deal in a mature way with your feelings—love, hate, fear, anger, frustration, and disappointment, for example. Growing up emotionally also means learning to understand your emotional needs and to plan your life so that those needs are met.

Your Emotional Needs

Psychologists, who spend their working lives trying to understand themselves and other people, know that each individual is unique (like no other person). Yet most psychologists would agree that all human beings have the same basic emotional needs for *love, safety, freedom,* and *self-esteem,* which means a good opinion of oneself. Your physical needs for food, exercise, and sleep must be met if you are to be physically healthy. Your emotional needs must be met, too, if you are to be emotionally healthy (see Figure 17.1, page 270).

I would like to understand myself.

As a baby, you needed love and safety most of all. Everything had to be done for you. You needed complete protection from danger. You had to be fed and clothed. For the sake of your emotional health, you needed to be picked up, talked to, and held affectionately. (Babies who don't get this loving protection are less confident, less trusting, and less happy as adults than babies who do.)

269

Figure 17.1. Families have always helped meet their young people's needs for emotional health: *(a)* love; *(b)* safety; *(c)* freedom; *(d)* self-esteem.

YOUR NEED FOR LOVE AND FRIENDSHIP   You still need to feel safe and loved, but those needs have changed and grown. For example, you still need your family's love, but, more and more, you need the friendship and love of people outside your family, as well. Moreover, you need to *give* love and friendship as well as to receive them. You need to like both yourself and other people in an easy, confident way.

In fact, most psychologists seem to agree that liking and respecting other people may depend on liking and respecting yourself first. How well do you like yourself? Perhaps you have never stopped to think about it. If so, the following activity may help:

YOUR PART

1. In private, jot down all of the things you like about yourself physically, emotionally, and socially. Include skills, talents, feelings about people and things—any trait you are glad you have.
2. Now turn your paper over and list the things you don't like about yourself. Include things you would like to change or do away with.

Do your lists show that you like yourself fairly well? Did you find things you want to change? (Save your lists for use in Chapter 18, page 293.)

People often say, "You can't change human nature," and, "People never change." But the truth is that people change all the time. Look at a picture of yourself taken ten years ago. Try to remember how it felt to be yourself at that time. Most people have trouble remembering their feelings in the past, partly because they have changed so much.

How can I make myself more likeable?

It is healthy to expect to like most other people and to expect most other people to like you. At the same time, you need to realize that you can't please everyone and you needn't try to do so. Like most teenagers, sometimes you will probably try to please everybody, or try too hard to please certain people. It's not easy to be moderate (to avoid going to extremes) about friendship during adolescence.

How can you get popular?

Friendship is suddenly important in a different way. First of all, members of the opposite sex are more attractive to you now than they were in earlier years. Second, you are eager to gain approval for the new adult self you are building. Your friends' opinions help you judge your new behavior. Nevertheless, you should try to keep a balanced point of view about the approval of others. Remind yourself that your health and safety matter, too, and that your real opinion of yourself matters most of all.

Figure 17.2. During the Great Depression of the 1930's, people on breadlines such as this showed evidence of being insecure and without hope for the future.

YOUR PART

1. When your teacher tells you to do so, stand and wander slowly and aimlessly around the room. Observe the other students, but do not talk to them. When your teacher tells you to do so (after 2 or 3 minutes), return to your seat.
2. Write down your answers to the following questions:

   a. Why did you walk in the direction you did?
   b. Was there any pattern to your wandering? What was the pattern? Did other students follow a pattern?
   c. Did you sit down before being told to do so? Why or why not?
   d. Did you change your behavior because of what others did? How and why?
   e. What were your thoughts about students who talked, walked away from the group, returned early to their seats, or never took part in the activity at all?

In groups, most of our actions are strongly influenced by others. You may have changed your behavior because of what others did. You may have noted cooperative, considerate behavior on the part of some and individualistic (most interested in self) behavior on the part of others. And some students may have shown themselves to be most interested in the teacher's opinion (by carefully following or by refusing to follow directions).

YOUR NEED FOR SAFETY AND SECURITY   Your parents kept you safe as a baby. But now, your security (safety, confidence, freedom from worry) depends largely on forces beyond your parents' control. Citi-

zens cannot feel secure in a nation at war or in the midst of a depression (see Figure 17.2). And more and more, your security even in your personal life depends, not upon your parents, but upon yourself.

Your emotional security depends on your ability to get along with others and to form lasting ties and friendships. Your financial security depends on your ability to earn a living, to save your money, to use it wisely, and in other ways to behave as a responsible adult. Your feeling of security about life itself depends upon your beliefs. People are generally more secure when they believe that life makes sense and has some purpose.

Some people just feel in their bones that life makes sense. Others have faith in life because of their religious beliefs or as a result of study and experience. Such people feel at home in the world. Less secure are those who decide that life doesn't make much sense or that their efforts don't make any difference in the long run.

YOUR NEED FOR FREEDOM AND INDEPENDENCE Your needs for love and safety have been with you since birth. But now you have a strong and growing need for independence, too. You probably realize that no one is completely free. You still depend largely upon your family for emotional and financial support. You will always be somewhat dependent upon other people for emotional, and perhaps even financial, security. Nevertheless, you look forward to the day when you will be in charge of your own life.

> How can you convince your parents you're old enough
> to make your own decisions (with exceptions
> and without being overbold)?

The need for independence causes a good deal of conflict, not only with parents and friends, but also within yourself. You are probably eager to run your own life, but not quite so eager to take on the work and responsibility that go along with growing up (see Figure 17.3, page 274). Freedom and responsibility go together. Responsible people are usually given more

You're Growing Up Emotionally   273

freedom by parents and teachers—and later by employers—than less responsible people. How independent are you now? How responsible are you now? The following activity may help you answer these questions:

YOUR PART

Number your paper 1 through 15. Make three columns for your answers. Head the columns as follows: *Almost Always, Sometimes,* and *Never.* Put a check in the proper column opposite the number of the question you are answering. Be as honest as you can.

1. People can count on me to be on time.
2. I take full responsibility for keeping myself clean without being reminded to bathe, shower, shampoo, or wash my hands.
3. I take full responsibility for doing my homework without any reminders from my parents.
4. People can count on me to do a job if I say I will.
5. I can cook a meal for myself if I have to.
6. My family counts on me for some help around the house every day.
7. My family counts on me for some help around the house every weekend.
8. When I need extra money, I can earn it by my own work either at home or away from home.
9. When my parents are sick, I am willing and able to help with the shopping, the cleaning, and the laundry.
10. I know how to do the dishes and clean the kitchen after a meal.

Figure 17.3. Are you ready to accept responsibility and run your own life?

Figure 17.4. How is the self-esteem of these teenagers being given a lift?

11. If I am going to be late, I telephone to let people know.
12. I take full responsibility for cleaning that part of the house that is mainly mine (my bedroom or my part of a shared bedroom).
13. I pick up after myself at a self-service restaurant or at a picnic.
14. When I can choose my own food, I choose food that is good for me as well as food that I like.
15. Whenever I go anywhere—whether on foot or by bike, car, bus, or train—I travel in a safe, lawful manner.

When you have answered all the questions, give yourself 3 points for each check in the *Almost Always* column, 1 point for each check in the *Sometimes* column, and no points for each check in the *Never* column.

If you scored 30 points or more, you are unusually responsible and adult for your age. If you scored 20 points or less, you probably need to take much more responsibility for yourself in order to be ready for the independence that lies ahead. If you scored between 20 and 30, you have developed some ability to take care of yourself, but you are still more dependent on others than you should be.

YOUR NEED FOR SELF-ESTEEM Even small children need self-esteem in order to be emotionally healthy. But the need for self-esteem, like the need for independence, grows as you grow. By the time you are adult, you need to respect yourself both for what you are (brave, just, kind, pleasant, and clever, for example) and for what you can do (useful work, artistic endeavors, skillful sports, perhaps). To maintain your self-esteem, you need to receive some attention, recognition, and respect from other people, too, for your achievements and your character (see Figure 17.4).

How are values established?

What do you value most in life? Each person answers this question a little differently. The same person may answer it differently at different periods in life. For example, a person who values independence more than anything else may take a job as a firewatcher, alone in a high tower in a national forest. In time, however, this same person may want more love and friendship in life, or more security (a real home and a better job). When a person is alone in a forest, self-esteem may suffer because other talents cannot be developed there, or because there is little praise and appreciation given for the job done. The firewatcher may return to the city with values somewhat changed by experience.

The following activity may help you become a little more aware of what you value most at present. There are no right and wrong choices. Any answer can be the right one for you:

YOUR PART

On your paper, arrange the three numbered items in each of the following groups in order, from most important (to you) to least important. For example, for group A you might write: A—2, 1, 3.

WHAT IS MOST IMPORTANT TO YOU?

A.
1. To have a steady, secure job.
2. To have work I like and to do it very well.
3. To be free of responsibilities that will tie me down.

B.
4. To develop my talents fully.
5. To be an important person.
6. To have a family of my own.

C.
7. To be well known for the work I do.
8. To have a satisfying marriage that will last.
9. To go into business for myself.

D.
10. To have a close-knit, happy family of my own.
11. To be known as an expert in my work or business.
12. To be free to travel, to see the world, and to live in many different places.

276   **Find Out About Yourself**

E. 13. To live an interesting, often exciting life.
   14. To make a lot of money.
   15. To have many loyal friends.

F. 16. To have important friends who can help me get ahead in the world.
   17. To have many amusing and interesting friends.
   18. To have friends I can count on.

G. 19. To be generous toward other people.
   20. To be my own boss.
   21. To have understanding friends.

H. 22. To be well liked.
   23. To be free from having to obey rules.
   24. To be in a position to tell others what to do.

I. 25. To do what I think is right.
   26. To go out of my way to help others.
   27. To have people willing to offer me a helping hand.

Items 5, 14, 16, and 24 show a high interest in financial security. If you put many of those items first, you probably are very interested, at present, in making money. Or job security (item 1) may be of first importance to you. Or emotional security (items 19 and 26 indicate a wish to help others; items 15, 18, 21, and 27 indicate a wish to depend on others; items 17, 21, and 22 show a wish for many friendships; items 6, 8, and 10 indicate a wish for a family of your own.) Perhaps you put independence first (items 3, 9, 12, 13, 20, and 23 show a wish for an independent, even adventurous, life). If self-esteem came first with you, you showed your wish to develop and use your talents (items 2, 4), to follow your own judgment (item 25), and to gain recognition from others (items 5, 7, and 11).

Chances are, your choices showed that you value love, security, independence, and self-esteem about equally. Fortunately, life is usually long enough to allow people to meet all of their emotional needs to some degree.

Let's Pause for Review

Who are you? Part of the answer is that you are a unique individual with at least four basic emotional needs—for love (and friendship), security, independence, and self-esteem. Your values in life are affected by the strength of these various needs. Like a race driver, for example, you may value self-esteem (which comes partly from achievement and recognition) more than safety.

Meeting Emotional Needs

No doubt you would like to arrange your life so that your basic emotional needs will be met. A good first step is to think about the plans you have already made for your future. You may say you have made no such plans, but you are sure to have some hopes, wishes, goals, and dreams floating around in your head. Do the following activity in private so that you can be honest about what you write:

YOUR PART

1. Write as fast as you can for at least 10 minutes. List *everything*, great and small, serious and silly, that you want to do or be or have in the future. The future includes tomorrow, next year, 20 years from now—all of it. Include goals of every kind—friendships, good health, attractiveness, vacations, jobs, courses in school, weddings, plus things you want to own, learn, see, or experience.
2. Now read your list over and circle the items you care most about. From the circled items, select the five or ten that are most important to you. At present, these are your future goals.
3. Look at your list of future goals. If you reach these goals in the future, will your needs for love, security, independence, and self-esteem then be met? Are your goals well suited to your interests and your talents?
4. On a separate piece of paper, write down your answers and your overall opinion of your goals.

It pays to have your goals in mind, to keep them up to date, and to change them when necessary. Hang on to the goals list you have made. Keep it at home where you will see it from time to time. Every year or so, sit down and make new plans in the same way (first list every goal you can think of; then select the most important goals from your long list). Planning helps to keep you from drifting into a job, a way of life, or a marriage that is not what you really want and that will not meet your needs.

How can I control my emotions?

People rarely worry about controlling their joyful emotions. It's the emotions like anger and fear that can lead to trouble and that people feel they need to control. Why do anger and fear give us so much trouble? Part of the answer is that although we live in civilized society, our bodies are still equipped for living in the wilderness.

Find Out About Yourself

Figure 17.5. Admit it when you feel hurt or angry.

Remember the "fight or flight" hormone called adrenaline (refer again to page 81)? Whenever you are angry, excited, or afraid, your adrenal glands prepare your body to fight or to run away. Just when you need to be calm and clearheaded—in an emergency, for example, or when the principal has called you in for a little talk—your heart pounds, your breathing becomes rapid, your muscles tense, your hands sweat, and your mouth goes dry.

What can you do? The next time you feel yourself getting nervous just when you need to stay calm and relaxed, take a few deep breaths. Then ask yourself, "What's the worst thing that can happen?" When you realize that, at the worst, you may not get the summer job or the part in the play, you can often relax and stop worrying. After all, your body is preparing itself for danger. If you can convince yourself (and your body) that there is no real danger to your life and safety, you can sometimes avoid giving yourself the jitters. Even when you can't, it helps to remember that your nervousness is normal and that you know what causes it.

How can I learn to cope with emotional problems?

Everyone feels horror, delight, terror, fury, and joy at times. These emotions, or feelings, are not shameful or harmful in themselves. But sometimes emotions are expressed in words or actions that *do* harm others. Therefore, although it is important to control the *expression* of feelings, it is not necessary or healthful to control the feelings themselves. In other words, as most psychologists agree, when you are sad, hurt, or angry, you should admit it freely, at least to yourself (see Figure 17.5).

How can I get more privacy? My brother is a nuisance.

It is not always wise to express your feelings openly. But often, especially within the family, open expression of feeling is both possible and helpful. If you resent your brother's uninvited presence, for example, say to him, "It really makes me mad when you come into my room without knocking."

Note that you shouldn't express your feelings with fists or with words chosen to hurt your brother. Instead, choose words that describe how you feel about what he has done. So, for example, if your mother has hurt your feelings, instead of telling her she is mean, you might say, "It really hurts when you criticize the stories I write for school." After all, your mother can't consider your feelings if she doesn't know what they are.

How can I keep from yelling?

The more often you sincerely try to put your feelings into words, the more calmly and matter-of-factly you will be able to speak. You may not even feel like yelling so often. Psychologists agree that it is not the feelings you express in words that cause the most trouble. Instead, the most harm is done by bottled-up feelings that burst out suddenly in an uncontrolled explosion of yelling, hitting, or worse.

I have a ten-year-old sister, and I get blamed for what she does.

Suppose that you are getting blamed for your sister's deeds, or that your brother wants to use the car more often, or that your parents need your help to complete some family project. All of these problems need to be discussed in order to be solved. And since problems like this keep coming up, many families find regular family discussions very useful.

REGULAR FAMILY DISCUSSIONS Even if problems are not solved, free and frank discussions about them seem to improve family relationships. The young people in a family appreciate being taken into their parents' confidence on money matters and other adult problems. Parents are often relieved to hear how sensibly their youngsters talk. If each person has a chance to talk about plans, wishes, and problems, family members get to know and understand one another better.

Let's Pause for Review

Feelings can sometimes be a nuisance. For example, little worries can sometimes cause our bodies to prepare for "fight or flight" just when we want to be cool and calm. But everyone has feelings, and it is healthful to admit and express them. On the other hand, we must express our feelings in ways that do not harm others. Within our families, we can often express feelings openly. Regular family discussions give family members a chance to tell how they feel, to solve problems together, and to get to know one another better.

Find Out About Yourself

Figure 17.6. An example of displacement of anger.

Defense Mechanisms

People use many methods to handle their feelings and adjust to life's problems. Psychologists call some of them **defense mechanisms** because (1) they are mental processes used to defend oneself (from painful feelings and difficult problems) and (2) they are used the way a mechanical device works (unconsciously and automatically). In other words, people often use defense mechanisms without even knowing it.

Are defense mechanisms harmful? Not when used in moderation, as we shall see. But when used too often, defense mechanisms can keep people from taking responsibility, from facing problems, and from being honest with themselves. Let us examine some of these situations.

DISPLACEMENT   Displacement, or "taking it out" on the wrong person, is a defense mechanism that family members use often. For example, your big brother borrows some of your records without asking. You feel like yelling at him, but since it is safer, you yell at your little brother, instead. Adults who are really angry with each other yell at their children or slam doors.

Everyone displaces anger at times. But sometimes displacement is overdone, as when family members continue to pick on the same person; then, displacement can be cruel and destructive. Besides, it is more healthful to admit who it is who has really made you angry and, when possible, to express your feelings openly (see Figure 17.6). As you may

You're Growing Up Emotionally

Figure 17.7. An example of projection.

remember from Chapter 13, pages 189–190, daily exercise helps, too, by releasing the tension caused by feelings that are not expressed.

REPRESSION

Some days I'm depressed and irritable. Why?

Sometimes people *repress*, or force themselves to forget, certain painful feelings or experiences. **Repression** can be a useful and necessary defense mechanism. After a war, for example, survivors often need to forget some of their experiences in order to regain peace of mind. But ordinary, everyday feelings should be admitted, and, if possible, expressed. Many psychologists believe that repressed anger, for example, helps to cause that sad, discouraged, hopeless feeling about oneself and one's life that is called **depression.** Repressed feelings make people irritable, too. Of course, both depression and irritability may have causes other than repressed feelings.

PROJECTION

Why am I so ugly? Why do people not like me?

Projection is another commonly used defense mechanism. As a movie projector casts a picture upon a screen, people project their own feelings onto others. For example, on a day when you feel rather worthless and

Find Out About Yourself

unlovable, you may think to yourself, "Nobody likes me." But the feelings of dislike are actually your own. See Figure 17.7 for another example of projection.

How do you overcome embarrassment?

Feelings of self-consciousness and embarrassment are often projected, too. You may feel that others are staring at you when, in a way, you are staring at yourself. You are more self-conscious than you were in childhood. You are more aware of your own growth. You are far more conscious of how you look to others and of how they look to you. All of this self-directed thought may cause you to be easily embarrassed at times, but it also helps you to grow up. Increased self-awareness helps you to see more clearly both yourself and the adult part you soon will play.

RATIONALIZATION *Rational* means reasonable, and a **rationalization** is a reasonable-sounding, but untrue, explanation for something (see Figure 17.8). Just as we make untrue excuses to fool other people, we make rationalizations to fool ourselves. If we fool ourselves too often, we don't know the truth about our abilities or the true reasons for our successes and failures.

VACILLATION *Decisiveness* is the ability to make decisions—an important part of maturity. Some people hate to take responsibility for their decisions. They are afraid their choices may turn out to be the wrong ones. So they *vacillate*, or waver back and forth between two choices (see Figure

Figure 17.8. Rationalization on "Report Card Day."

17.9). People who vacillate too long force other people to make all of the difficult decisions. **Vacillation** is sometimes mistaken for politeness.

WITHDRAWAL   Another way of avoiding problems is to withdraw, or keep away from, people or situations you don't want to face. Some emotional **withdrawal** is healthful, for everyone needs to be alone at times. But anyone who withdraws from other people whenever he or she can do so is withdrawing to an unhealthy degree. And it is usually just as bad to withdraw from responsibilities you would rather not face (see Figure 17.10).

FANTASY   Fantasy, the substitution of imagination for reality, is another defense mechanism that can be either helpful or harmful, depending on how it is used. When people *fantasize,* or daydream, so much that they have little time left to do anything else, they are obviously overdoing their daydreaming. People who choose to daydream that their problems are solved will never learn to face those problems realistically.

But it is healthful and normal to let one's imagination roam at times. Fantasy can be a form of rehearsal, helping you to picture in your mind what you will do and say in a situation you may have to face someday. Daydreaming about your future—as a writer, a dancer, a teacher, an engineer—may help you work harder to achieve your goal (see Figure 17.11).

COMPENSATION   A small-sized football player can still be a valuable team member by being especially quick, aggressive, and good at running. People who use the defense mechanism called **compensation** do the same

Figure 17.9. Who is vacillating? Who makes the decision?

Figure 17.10. Could this be an example of withdrawal?

Figure 17.11. Fantasies on graduation day.

You're Growing Up Emotionally

thing. They compensate, or make up for, a real or imagined inferiority by making an extra effort to excel in the same or in a different field.

Long ago, Demosthenes overcame a speech defect to become not just a normal speaker, but the greatest of the Greek public orators. There are notable examples of compensation in our own century, too. Glen Cunningham, crippled by severe burns at the age of 8, went on to become a great Olympic miler. Former Supreme Court Justice William O. Douglas, a childhood victim of polio, became not only a great jurist, but a famous hiker and outdoorsman, as well. And Wilma Rudolph, who at age 4 lost the use of her left leg as a result of double pneumonia and scarlet fever, became, in 1960, the first American woman to win three Olympic gold medals for running.

The entertainment world is full of performers who overcame speech defects, partial paralysis, crippling, and—most common of all—overwhelming feelings of inferiority and unattractiveness. Compensation is not rare. People use it all the time, usually in ways that make them proud.

What does it take to make a mature adult?

Many people grow up physically without maturing in other ways. Even mature adults are not mature all of the time. However, most mature adults try to:

1. Think well of themselves and others, most of the time.
2. Be honest with themselves and others about their feelings and ideas, without relying heavily on defense mechanisms.
3. Look ahead and make plans that will help meet their needs for self-esteem, independence, security, love, and friendship.
4. Take responsibility for their own health, safety, appearance, promptness, etc., and willingly take on other responsibilities at home and at work.
5. Make decisions without too much vacillation.
6. Handle problems as they come up.
7. Do things in moderation:

    a. They don't sacrifice health to success.
    b. They don't do everything for others and nothing for themselves.
    c. They don't do everything for themselves and nothing for others.
    d. They don't take on so much responsibility that there's no time for recreation.
    e. They balance the time spent with others and the time spent alone.

Perhaps you do all of these things to some extent already. No one is responsible, decisive, honest, and kindly toward himself or herself and others all of the time. But most people keep trying. If you manage to behave maturely most of the time, you should be happy with your achievement.

Find Out About Yourself

How can I achieve happiness?

Those who expect too much of life are sure to be disappointed. Happiness depends in part on realistic expectations. Expect that each day will bring its share of small irritations and that each year will bring new responsibilities. Expect to have conflicts with others and within yourself. Expect to have problems to solve. Expect to work hard for worthwhile achievements. If you expect these things, you probably won't be disappointed.

When it comes to happiness, it helps to keep your sense of humor about the human situation. Here you are, trying to live a civilized life with the "fight or flight" instincts of a coyote. You daydream of fame, yet you turn red when someone looks at you. You hope soon to be an adult, but your room looks worse than a nursery, and you still watch the Saturday morning cartoons. You feel that life makes sense, but you can't prove it. You note that people can change for the better but hate to do so.

The main thing you're counting on is that life can't be as tough as older people say it is. If it were, how could all the ordinary people all over the world live through it the way they do?

Looking Back

Who are you? You are a unique individual. But like other people, you need love and friendship, security, independence, and self-esteem in order to be emotionally healthy. If you hope to know yourself well, you must be honest with yourself and others about what you think and feel (without too much repression, rationalization, withdrawal, displacement, or projection).

Feelings can be a nuisance. They can make you nervous when you want to be calm. They can make you feel like exploding. Admit your feelings, but control the way you express them. You have a right to your feelings but no right to harm others.

Feelings bring happiness, too. You feel affection for friends, for example, and pride in the way you are growing up. Growing up should bring with it a kindly feeling toward oneself and others. A mature person should show moderation in all things (including the use of defense mechanisms like repression, displacement, projection, rationalization, vacillation, withdrawal, and fantasy). A mature person should be willing and able to plan ahead, to be independent, to take responsibility, to make decisions, and to handle problems as they arise.

MODIFIED TRUE-FALSE QUESTIONS

1. At maturity, emotional growth _stops._
2. All human beings have _the same_ emotional needs.
3. When they grow up, babies who do not receive tender, loving care are _more_ confident and happy than babies who do.
4. During adolescence, it is _easy_ to go to extremes about friendship.
5. Wars make people _less_ secure.
6. Feelings of security depend on your _beliefs_ about life and the world.
7. In the business world, as elsewhere, people who show evidence of responsibility are given _less_ freedom than those who do not.
8. People need _less_ self-esteem as they grow older.
9. People show _little_ concern about controlling joyful emotions.
10. The "fight or flight" hormone is _insulin._
11. Bottled-up feelings _often_ cause uncontrolled fits of anger.
12. Defense mechanisms represent _an abnormal_ body response to an unpleasant situation.
13. Your opinion of yourself _helps_ fulfill an important emotional need.
14. In general, people have _the same_ values about life.
15. Once your mind is made up about your future goals, you should be _unwilling_ to change it as you learn more about yourself.

MATCHING QUESTIONS

Column A	Column B
1. fantasy	a. unable to make choices
2. vacillation	b. having a "chip" on your shoulder
3. projection	c. avoiding people or situations
4. displacement	d. yelling at the wrong person
5. withdrawal	e. attributing the reason for one's own feeling to others
	f. daydreaming

COMPLETION QUESTIONS

1. You need to give love as well as to _____ it.
2. Much of our behavior is _____ from others.
3. A mature person has more freedom than one who is immature and also takes on more _____.
4. Four basic needs are love, security, independence, and _____.
5. In unknown situations, it is _____ to be nervous.

Find Out About Yourself

6. Family discussions are (usually/never) _____ helpful in solving adolescent problems.
7. Mental processes used to defend oneself are automatic and _____.
8. Forgetting painful experiences is a defense mechanism called _____.
9. "Taking it out" on the wrong person is a defense mechanism referred to as _____.
10. A reasonable-sounding but untrue explanation of behavior is called _____.

MULTIPLE-CHOICE QUESTIONS

1. John just failed the final examination in health. He paid little attention all semester and rarely studied for tests. After being informed he would not pass the course, he told his friends, "I would have passed if the teacher didn't hate me." What defense mechanism was he using?
   a. displacement   b. rationalization   c. projection   d. depression
2. Linda and Susan walked by Ronnie and David. As they passed by, Ronnie said, "All they think about is boys." David thought, "All you think about is girls." What defense mechanism is being used?
   a. displacement   b. rationalization   c. projection   d. depression
3. Every time an important examination is scheduled, Allen becomes ill and stays home from school that day. What defense mechanism is he using?
   a. withdrawal   b. vacillation   c. projection   d. compensation
4. An older brother angrily asks his younger brother if he has used his stereo. The younger brother answers, "Are you mad at your girlfriend again?" What defense mechanism is the older brother using?
   a. displacement   b. rationalization   c. projection   d. depression
5. Your need for independence is *least* likely to cause conflict with
   a. parents   b. friends   c. yourself   d. teachers
6. The *least* positive way of preventing family arguments is to
   a. put your feelings into words   c. write down your feelings
   b. speak the truth   d. yell and scream
7. Of the following, which do babies need the most?
   a. freedom   c. self-esteem
   b. love and safety   d. independence
8. Attaining happiness depends most often on
   a. money   c. realistic expectations
   b. how you dress   d. a drive to succeed
9. Of the following, which is *not* a part of financial security?
   a. forming lasting friendships   c. ability to save
   b. ability to earn a living   d. ability to use money wisely
10. In any family conflict, you should be ready to accept blame
   a. always   c. some of the time
   b. never   d. when you feel like it

THOUGHT QUESTIONS

1. We all have at least four basic emotional needs. List them, explain what each means, and give an example of how they can be fulfilled for a young, growing individual.
2. Answer the following question and explain your answer: Suppose that you are someone else; would you like to be friends with your present self?
3. Why is it unlikely that we can ever satisfy our emotional needs completely?
4. When should you seek professional help in solving an emotional problem?

Looking Ahead

In Chapter 18, you will read about the social self, or personality, you are still building. You will learn ways of improving your relationships with others as you explore the subjects of love and friendship.

Find Out About Yourself

Chapter 18: You're Growing Up Socially

Social growth refers to your relationships with other people—your family and friends. Like emotional growth, social growth is an ever-continuing process, influenced by your state of health, your educational level, your job, and your surroundings. How well you adapt socially very often has direct bearing on whether you will be happy or unhappy in what you do throughout life.

Social Maturity

Learning to get along with others and yourself is a natural part of growing up, or maturing. But the word *mature* means fully developed. And in that sense, no one is ever completely mature. People can continue to learn and develop for as long as they live. However, most people try, as early as they can, to develop such qualities of emotional maturity as moderation, responsibility, independence, decisiveness, and honesty, as well as kindness toward and liking for themselves and others. A person who is socially mature tries to put all of these qualities into practice in her or his dealings with others.

Social maturity rests first upon the ability to think of others. As a baby you were totally self-centered, and as a young child you were only a little less so. You were interested in what others could do for you. You found it hard to be thoughtful of them (see Figure 18.1*a*, page 292).

I want to know about other people.

An interest in others is the basic requirement for social maturity (see Figure 18.1*b*). Now that you are in your teens, you find it easier than in childhood to consider the feelings of others. You are curious about them and want to understand them, at least some of the time.

Figure 18.1. Which situation shows interest in others?

Why do people judge others on superficial things, following fads, etc.?

Many people, including adults, are immature in some ways. They may judge others on the basis of superficial things such as material possessions, accents, or clothing styles. Or they may use their own *prejudices* (biased opinions) to condemn individuals or groups. A few examples would be disliking all police officers, gun owners, or recent immigrants from other countries. Normally, however, as judgment matures, people learn to evaluate others as individuals rather than as members of some group or by surface appearances.

JUDGING FOR YOURSELF   As you mature, you should learn to trust your own ideas about people and things, rather than judge on the basis of what your friends and family think. To overcome prejudice, learn to be slow to judge, making up your mind about others only when you really know them.

Mature judgment also tends to be kinder and more *positive* (accepting, approving) than the self-centered, often *negative* (disliking, disapproving) judgment of childhood. A young person who is socially mature is likely to be more generous with compliments, for example, than a less mature young person. So, as you mature, even though you note the shortcomings of others, you look for their good qualities, too.

Find Out About Yourself

I understand myself and am satisfied.

The preceding statement comes from a young person who sees him- or herself in a kind, fair-minded way. Just as maturity brings a more positive attitude toward others, it should bring a more positive attitude toward yourself, as well.

Being immature and self-centered, children can often be cruel to one another. As a result, most children are occasionally the targets of a certain amount of unfriendliness, dislike, and downright meanness. In childhood, any unusual name or physical feature is pointed out and made fun of. Consequently, children often begin to grow up feeling unattractive and unintelligent. Such negative feelings, stemming from childhood judgments, are usually mistaken. If you have any lingering doubts about yourself, now is the time to correct them in your mind. Judge for yourself what you are like.

If you're a dud like me, how can you become graceful?

If you don't like everything about yourself, don't be discouraged. Remember those people who compensated so magnificently for things they didn't like or couldn't help about themselves (see pages 284–286)? You, too, are flexible and can change. If you need to be more graceful, for example, you can take dance or exercise at the Y. Use the list you made of things you liked and didn't like about yourself (see page 271) to do the following activity:

YOUR PART

1. Reread and think about your list. Revise it, if you wish.
2. Choose one or two items from your list that you really want to do something about. (You may have a talent you want to develop, or a habit you want to change.) Write down some steps you could take, now or in the future, to achieve your aim.

Do you want to study music, improve your posture, become smoother socially, learn to play tennis, or stop chewing your nails? Achieving any of these aims would help you mature socially by improving your personality, because your personality *is* your social self. You can go a long way toward achieving your aims by attending classes in instrumental music, gymnastics, dance, speech, tennis, art, or other activities that help build your social self.

I would like to understand my personality.

Your personality is everything about you that shows up in your relationships with others. Your interest in others, your judgment, your appearance, your ways of moving and speaking, your manners, and your skills are all part of your personality. In addition, your character (your ideas of right and wrong and the way you put them into practice) shows in your behavior and, therefore, forms part of your personality.

The word **personality** comes from an old word meaning mask. At times, as you doubtless realize, you use your social skills not to express your real feelings and ideas, but to mask them. This act of masking is called *tact*, which means touch and, by extension, a sensitive social touch. A tactful person can imagine how others feel and, therefore, in difficult situations says and does whatever maintains good relations and avoids giving offense to others (see Figure 18.2). Can one be both tactful and honest? Think about that question as you do the following activity:

YOUR PART

1. Write down the words you might use to (a) get off the phone, (b) leave a party, (c) end a conversation, and (d) thank a thoughtful person for a gift you dislike—all without either lying or hurting anyone's feelings.
2. Rate as either mature or immature the following ways of behaving:

   a. A nephew, who always insists on telling the truth, tells his aunt that he hates the birthday gift she has given him.

Figure 18.2. Would you be as tactful?

b. Without asking, Joe's next-door neighbor "borrows" Joe's bike, and when the neighbor later returns the bike, Joe says nothing.

c. A girl who is proud of her frankness tells a school friend in a new outfit that she looks awful.

In excusing yourself (step 1), did you say something like, "I'm really sorry. I wish I didn't have to leave (or hang up or end our conversation). I've enjoyed myself (or our talk) so much. But I really do have to leave (or hang up or get going)." You may also have added a reason for having to excuse yourself. And perhaps you expressed thanks for the gift by saying, "I can't thank you enough for your gift. It's really unusual. I've never seen one like it. And I appreciate your thoughtfulness so much."

In step 2, perhaps you decided that the truthful nephew and the frank girl were immature and unkind, and that both needed to be more tactful. Individuality and inner honesty are vital, but you don't have to show them off on every occasion. Joe, on the other hand, seemed more timid than tactful. You may have agreed that he should have spoken up honestly and told his neighbor to get permission before using the bike again.

I like to feel grown up, but adults say, "You're only 12." Why do they do this? It hurts a lot.

Hurt feelings, angry feelings, sorry feelings—everybody has them often enough. They are as much a part of social life as laughter, joy, and pride. People say things that hurt you. You say things you are sorry for. In short, people of every age make social mistakes, no matter how mature, in general, they have become.

When things go wrong socially, learn what you can from the situation (don't discuss politics with Maria, for example, and never criticize Sam's mother). Think about why you are upset, so that you know your own feelings in the matter. Express your feelings if it seems wise and helpful to do so (see pages 279–280). Then forget about the upset, and go on to the next thing in your life. A mature, healthy person doesn't keep thinking about old hurts and angers. You may even go to the next picnic with a little more courage and confidence than you had before, because of what you learned about Sam and Maria at the last one.

Who am I?

During your teens, you may grow and change so quickly that you have trouble keeping track of what your character and personality are really like.

For example, you may have been a shy child, but now you find yourself growing bolder by the minute. You may like things you once hated. Formerly unattractive members of the opposite sex may have begun to look better (see Figure 18.3). So, although a good part of your personality was formed in childhood by heredity and environment, the work is far from finished. In fact, as long as you live you will go on developing.

Does acting mature at 12, 13, or 14 hurt your personality?

"Acting mature at 12, 13, or 14" may be your rehearsal for the adult role you soon will play. You are still building your character and personality, still trying out new ways of "being adult" to see if they suit you. And you are building far more consciously than in childhood. You are aware now that you can, to some extent, choose the kind of person you want to be. You can choose, for example, to develop your cooking skills, your muscles, your singing voice, or your social skills.

How can you overcome shyness?

People often feel shy because they don't quite know what to do in a social situation. So, improving your social skills is a good way to overcome shyness. Social skill is part of maturity, too. You needn't learn a great many complicated rules. Just remember to show interest in and consideration for others. Be courteous.

Learn to introduce yourself and others, pronouncing each name clearly and, if possible, giving people who are strangers some clue about each other's identity ("Mrs. Jackson, this is Lettie, my cousin from Boston. Mrs. Jackson is our principal, Lettie.").

Learn to start a conversation in a pleasant, positive way ("Swell party. I like the music."). If you form the habit of looking for the nice things about people, you can often begin by complimenting the person's talent ("Your tuba solo was terrific."), or school ("I saw your team play—they were great."), or town ("I like the zoo.").

Asking questions of people you have just met is always a good way of breaking the social ice. It also helps you draw an easy response from the other person, who may be even shier than you in a new social situation.

Have in mind several things you can talk about when the conversation doesn't flow easily. The field of entertainment, for example, interests almost everybody. The latest news (about sports, fashion, your school, community, country, the world, outer space) interests many people, too. You can talk about the things you may have in common (classes, teachers, leisure activities). Or try finding your conversational partner's special field of interest (motorcycles, music, scouting, poetry, electronics). Or make a common topic interesting by telling intriguing, or curiosity-arousing, stories ("It's cold today, but I remember once walking home during an ice

Find Out About Yourself

Figure 18.3. Your changing viewpoints may surprise you.

storm—" or "The best summer I ever had—"). Or ask an imaginative question ("We've lived in this town all our lives, but if you could live anywhere in the world, where would you live?").

In short, try to interest both your conversational partner and yourself. Chances are, if you are bored, the other person will be bored, as well. Chances are, too, that if you are really interested in getting to know the other person, your interest will show and be *reciprocated* (returned in kind), no matter what you find to talk about.

What is right and what is wrong?

When in doubt about what is right socially, try treating the other person as you would like to be treated in the same situation. You like others to be friendly to you at school, for example, so you should do your best to be friendly to others, whether or not they are popular, stylish, or attractive. If you don't like to be pushed around, don't push others around, either. Your behavior is mature when you treat others with the same kindness, fairness, and respect that you yourself wish to receive.

YOUR PART

1. List three ways of showing consideration for others when you telephone.

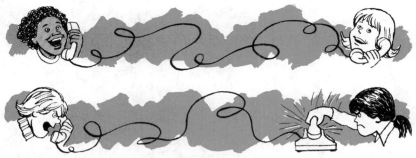

Figure 18.4. A friendly manner is catching — and so is rudeness.

2. Write down steps you could take to make a newly arrived visitor feel at ease in your home.
3. Write down the way in which you might introduce yourself to a stranger at a party. (Good manners call for you to greet and chat briefly with everyone at a small gathering.)
4. List ten conversational topics that interest you and would probably interest others your age.

In step 1, you probably said that when telephoning you identify yourself, ask if you are calling at a convenient time, try to be a cheerful conversationalist (see Figure 18.4), and end your conversation before too much time has passed. In step 2, you may have said that you welcome a visitor, ask her or him to sit down, and offer refreshment. Some people like to play music or show guests around the apartment or house and garden. As for introducing yourself (step 3), you may have said that you would smile, pronounce your name clearly, say something nice if you honestly could, show your interest in the other people by paying attention to what they say, and (step 4) be ready to talk about several topics that interest most people (entertainment, sports, the latest news, current fashions, famous or admired people in the news, a coming holiday, mutual friends, pets, food, and vacation plans).

Let's Pause for Review

If you are a socially mature person, you have real interest in and consideration for others. Your aim is to treat others with the same kindness, fairness, and respect that you wish to receive yourself. You are slow to judge others. You make up your own mind about yourself and others in a positive, fair-minded way.

You have, or are working toward, a well-balanced, well-developed personality, or social self. Your social skills are well developed. You can usually make other people feel comfortable. You have enough conversational skill to enjoy talking to many

Find Out About Yourself

kinds of people. You can discuss such subjects as show business and the news, which seem to interest almost everybody. But you can also discover interests you share with another, as well as special interests another person may have and love to talk about. You can make the usual topics unusual by asking imaginative questions or by telling good stories and drawing them out from others.

Making and Keeping Friends

Is there any knack to picking friends well?

Often, people are so eager to have friends that, in the words of the old saying, they "take what God sends." In general, however, your close friends—especially those who turn out to be lifelong friends—are much like you in one or more important ways. Usually, your *fundamental* (deep, basic) beliefs about life, people, right and wrong, and politics are similar to those of your close friends.

In addition, you and your close friends may be alike in ability or in *temperament* (disposition). You may share deep and lasting interests. For this reason, one good way of finding friends of either sex is to go where your interests lead you. If you like writing stories, for instance, you may find mutual interests with the other writers on the school newspaper.

Emotional and social maturity are important to friendship, too. A friendship with a person who is inconsiderate or untrustworthy is likely to be stormy. The following activity will lead you into a frank discussion of friendship:

YOUR PART

1. List qualities you like your friends of either sex to have. (Include manners, interests, abilities—whatever is important to you.)
2. Turn your paper over. This time make two lists. Head one column *Like* and the other column *Dislike*. Now list those qualities you like or dislike in members of the opposite sex. When finished, hand your paper in without writing your name on it.
3. As your teacher reads the lists or asks students to copy them on the board, discuss the lists together as a class. Are the lists much the same or very different? Do some qualities appear on many lists? What qualities do most members of the class seek in their friends? Common interests? Thoughtfulness? Mature behavior? An attractive appearance?

The discussion should have helped you think about some of the qualities that bring friends together. Friendships with both sexes grow out of respect and liking, plus shared interests. But in boy-girl relationships there is usually a sexual attraction, as well. Friendships based on sexual attraction alone, however, are not likely to be completely satisfying or long-lasting.

What is love, the kind that sustains a marriage for 40 or 50 years?

Long-lasting "love" is part love and part friendship, and it depends upon the maturity of both people. Sexual attraction and physical love can be very strong, but they are not strong enough to sustain a marriage between a man and woman who are not also friends. A young couple considering marriage should ask themselves whether or not they would be good friends if they were of the same sex. They should also ask themselves how mature (responsible, independent, decisive, moderate, kind, cooperative, considerate, honest with each other) they are.

It is an excellent idea to take a hard look at the realities of marriage, as did some students in a Midwestern high school. These students wondered how much it might cost a young married couple to live. Two students looked for an apartment, reporting later to the class on prices, problems, and finds. Other students shopped for groceries, furniture, clothing, baby furnishings, and the like. All of the students were surprised by how much it cost to live. One student noted that decision making was very hard when two people's wishes always had to be considered.

As a result of their investigations, all of the students in the class decided against early marriage for themselves. They all wanted to be better off financially and more mature emotionally than they thought they could be in their teens.

It is hard to concentrate on schoolwork and get good grades when you're really concentrating on boys. What's the answer?

Why can't I get anything done because of thinking of girls?

What does "going steady" mean?

Is it wrong to go out with a boy a year or two older?

Find Out About Yourself

Figure 18.5. School dances are a lot of fun — for almost everyone.

At what age should you date?

I am not planning to marry. Should I date?

These questions express normal, natural interests. The young people who asked these questions probably realized that there are no set answers. Of course, each young person has the responsibility for first considering the wishes of parents and the need to do schoolwork and other chores. Once you have taken care of those obligations, you must answer such questions for yourself. For one thing, young people mature at different rates (with girls usually maturing physically, emotionally, and socially ahead of boys). For another thing, customs and opportunities differ from place to place.

Group dating often comes first. Most young people enjoy church, temple, or school parties long before they think of dating in couples (see Figure 18.5). Get-togethers like parties and picnics, organized either by individuals or by groups, give young people a chance to have fun together, to practice their social skills, and to learn about characteristics in others that they respond to positively.

Next, some young people double-date for a movie, a picnic, or a hike. Double dating provides a more personal atmosphere, shared by only four people—an atmosphere in which your own social skills and preferences will play a more important part than they did before. Later still, some people date as couples. There is no set age for any kind of dating to begin.

Whether or not you plan to marry, you will have friendships and working relationships with members of both sexes all of your life. Your happiness and success depend in large measure on how well you get along with others. Therefore, it is wise to take advantage of some of the opportunities for group dating offered by your school and your community. The following activity may help you to consider your ideas about dating. Write down your answers:

YOUR PART

1. At what age do you think you may be interested in group dating? Double dating? Single dating?
2. At what age do you think the average boy is mature enough to date? The average girl?
3. Should young people date people a few years older than they are? Why or why not?
4. Should people date if they are not planning to marry? Why or why not?
5. By what time do you think young teenagers should be home on week nights? On weekend nights?
6. Do you think parents have a responsibility for knowing where their children are, who they are with, and when they will be home?
7. In your opinion, what part should parents play in dating? Should they "lay down the law"? Should teenagers and their parents discuss dating and decide on rules together?
8. Write a one-sentence definition of "going steady." List two advantages and two disadvantages.
9. Who do you think is more likely to marry wisely, a person who has known and dated many persons of the opposite sex or one who has known and dated only a few?
10. At what age do you think the average young woman is mature enough to marry? The average young man? Why do you think so many marriages between teenagers fail?
11. In small groups or as a class, compare and discuss your answers.

No doubt, you and your classmates disagreed on many points. You may have agreed with the students in the Midwestern high school that many young marriages fail because marriage requires both more maturity and more money than most teenagers have. And you may have thought of another reason—the fact that adolescents are still changing and developing rapidly and will continue, for a time, to do so. Two young people with only school life in common may develop in different directions as soon as they leave school. Their interests and goals in life may change a great deal in a few years' time.

I hope some day we will have a real liking for one another; that we'll understand people of different races, colors, creeds.

No one ever achieves complete maturity. But socially mature people keep trying to be considerate, responsible, and fair towards others—all others, no matter what their age, sex, religion, race, or whatever. A mature person votes, for example, and does his or her fair share of work on community problems. In other words, a mature person's interest in others extends beyond family and friends to include the community, the nation, and the world (see Figure 18.6). If you have worked on recycling or some other school or community problem, you have shown the kind of responsibility that maturity should bring.

Looking Back

A socially mature person has real interest in and consideration for others. Your aim should be to treat others with the same kindness, fairness, and respect that you wish to receive. Be slow to judge others. Make up your own mind about yourself and others in a positive, fair-minded way. You should have, or be working toward, a well-balanced, well-developed personality, or social self. Develop your social skills, especially in conversation. And remember, no one's social skills are ever perfect. You will mature socially by learning from your own and others' mistakes. And don't keep thinking about old hurts and angers. Instead, forgive, forget, and go on to the next thing in life.

Friendship grows out of respect and liking, plus shared

Figure 18.6. International understanding grows through student exchange programs.

interests, abilities, and beliefs. Sexual attraction also plays a part in friendships between the sexes. Friendship, love, and marriage are usually less stormy and more satisfying when the people involved are fairly mature, both emotionally and socially.

MODIFIED TRUE-FALSE QUESTIONS

1. Social maturity rests upon your ability to consider *yourself.*
2. Judging a person on the basis of a foreign accent is a mark of *maturity.*
3. People who are prejudiced are generally *immature.*
4. Young children often make judgments that are generally *negative,* that is, they are likely to dislike strange foods and people.
5. Your social self is best described as your *personality.*
6. Tact is an important part of your *health.*
7. It is often possible to be *honest* and tactful at the same time.
8. When you reach maturity, your character and personality *stop* growing.
9. Improving your *social* skills may help overcome shyness.
10. *Quickness* in judging others is a sign of growing up.
11. You and your close friends are often *alike* in many respects.
12. Friendships based on sexual attraction alone are *likely* to be lasting.
13. Some teenage marriages fail because the couple lacks *money.*
14. Forgiving and forgetting past mistakes are signs of *weakness* in people.
15. During the teen years, a person's character and personality generally change *slowly.*

COMPLETION QUESTIONS

1. Social growth refers to your _____ with other people.
2. The word *mature* means _____.
3. *Biased opinion* means _____.
4. Your total social self is referred to as your _____.
5. A long-lasting marriage depends upon the love and _____ of the couple.

THOUGHT QUESTIONS

1. Using the letters *M* for *mature* and *I* for *immature,* indicate on a separate sheet of paper whether the individuals in each of the following situations are mature or immature. Defend your choice in each case:

   a. Tom cheated on the math test because he needed to pass math to continue to play football.

Find Out About Yourself

b. Mary decided to date Jack because she did not want to hurt his feelings.
c. Miguel returned to his teacher the purse he found in the school auditorium.
d. Leo agreed to remain in school until graduation just to please his parents.
e. Larry admitted it was his fault when his car struck Jim's bike in the parking lot.
f. Linda "knew" that Harry was the only boy for her when he won his varsity letter in track.

2. You have just met a new classmate. How would you decide if it is a good idea to try to develop a friendship with him or her?

3. You find that you are "blowing your top" too often. What might you do to lessen this immature behavior?

4. Referring to Figure 18.1, page 292, explain the differences in behavior between the self-centeredness of the toddlers and the sociability of the teenagers.

5. You are a teenager and would like to get married. List the arguments you would use to convince both sets of parents. If you were the parents in this case, what arguments would you use to convince the young couple that they ought to wait a few years?

Looking Ahead

In Chapter 19, you will learn how to make some important decisions concerning tobacco use. You will probably find answers to many of the questions you have about smoking, as well.

Unit Seven: DECIDE ABOUT DRUGS

Some drugs, like the anesthetics that make modern surgery possible, are very helpful and seem to be completely safe. Actually, however, every drug can be a poison if too large a dose is taken. Some painkilling drugs can also cause addiction. And the calming drugs that are so useful in treating mental illness can cause death when mixed with alcohol. In other words, like almost everything else in the world, drugs can be either helpful or harmful, depending on the way in which human beings use them.

Before deciding about drug use, you have to know what the word *drug* means. In a general sense, a drug is a substance that helps cure sickness or ease pain. Think of what you can buy in a drugstore—from flavored cough drops to the many medicines available only with a doctor's prescription.

In a wider sense, drugs can mean any nonfood substance that changes either the internal structure of the body or the way the body or mind works. Certainly, curative medicines would also be included in this category. But, in addition, we would have to list some often misused substances that can affect your body or mind for the worse—tobacco, alcohol, and *mind-altering chemicals*.

Finally, there is the third, well-known sense of the word, which refers *solely* to the usually addictive, mind-altering chemicals by which people seek utter relaxation, deep sleep, unfamiliar experiences of the mind, or escape from pain or problems. The illegal use of such drugs has grown alarmingly during the last several decades.

The next three chapters will suggest answers to questions that many students have about drugs:

Does smoking stop tension?

Are they sure you can get cancer from smoking cigarettes?

What substance in tobacco causes cancer?

Does smoking affect the heart?

Can you give me any other reasons besides disease for not smoking?

I smoke. How do I go about stopping?

What are the effects of alcohol on the body and brain?

What emotional and physical reactions are caused by drinking?

Why do adults drink?

Why do young people drink?

What causes alcohol to make a person drunk?

Why do people become alcoholics?

Who is an alcoholic?

Why do people use marijuana?

Does marijuana addict?

Young people also say, "Don't try to scare us. Just give us the facts about drugs and let us make up our own minds."

It is easy to give the facts about tobacco, because people have used it for a long time, and its effects are fairly well known. The facts about the drug called alcohol are fairly well understood, too. But many of the facts about what we have come to call the mind-altering drugs have not yet come to light.

Many questions about marijuana and LSD, for example, cannot be answered because these drugs have not yet been scientifically investigated to a sufficient degree. So, as young people read about the mind-altering drugs, they must take into account the fact that much about these substances is still unknown. As honestly as possible, the coming chapters give what is known at present about drugs in the news today.

Chapter 19: Tobacco and Health

What is your opinion of smoking? How much do you already know about smoking and health? To find out, try the quick true-false quiz on page 310, using a separate piece of paper for your answers.

You will find the answers and scoring instructions for the quiz at the end of this chapter, page 328. For an explanation of the answers and for more information on the subject of tobacco and health, read on.

An Old Habit

Tobacco use is not new (Figure 19.1, pages 310–311). The Persians had an old saying: "Coffee without tobacco is meat without salt." Long before Columbus sailed to the New World, American Indians used tobacco in religious and political ceremonies. The Indians smoked tobacco in pipes or in cigars made by wrapping the tobacco in its own leaves. When Columbus returned to Spain, he took some tobacco seeds back with him.

From Spain, tobacco use spread quickly throughout the rest of Europe. In the 16th century, Jean Nicot, the French ambassador to Lisbon, sent some tobacco seeds to his queen. Nicot, from whose name we get the word *nicotine*, thought tobacco was a valuable medicine and recommended its use as such. In the same century, Sir Francis Drake—the noted explorer—took tobacco seeds, leaves, and pipes back to England from America and gave them to his friend Sir Walter Raleigh. Raleigh introduced tobacco use to the English.

The word *tobacco* came from San Domingo, where smokers used a Y-shaped instrument called a *tabaco* to inhale the fumes of the burning leaves. These Caribbean Indians put one end of the tabaco into the smoke, and the other two ends into their nostrils, and thus inhaled the smoke. In this way, several smokers could simultaneously use the same tobacco.

From the first, many individuals and governments bitterly opposed tobacco use. A tsar of Russia once banned smoking and imposed terrible penalties; smokers who got caught had their noses slit or cut off and were

Figure 19.1. Things associated with older forms of tobacco use: (a) American Indian pipe; (b) Sir Walter Raleigh's clay pipe; (c) hookah (waterpipe); (d) snuff and snuffbox; (e) spittoon.

Cigarette Quiz

		True	False
1.	Lung cancer is the only serious disease associated with smoking.	____	____
2.	Cigarettes don't hurt teenagers.	____	____
3.	Smoking is not a health hazard for women.	____	____
4.	Whether or not you've smoked a long time, your risks go down when you quit.	____	____
5.	Filters make cigarettes safe.	____	____
6.	The longer (more years) you smoke, the greater the risk.	____	____
7.	Most doctors don't smoke cigarettes.	____	____
8.	Some people gain weight when they quit smoking.	____	____
9.	Some people can smoke a few cigarettes without getting the habit.	____	____
10.	The more cigarettes you smoke, the greater the risk.	____	____
11.	Young smokers aren't necessarily "hooked" by the cigarette habit.	____	____
12.	The report of the Surgeon General of the United States Public Health Service, *Smoking and Health*, left some doubts that smoking really is harmful.	____	____

Adapted from the American Heart Association *Cigarette Quiz* © 1967.

Decide About Drugs

(d)

(c)   *(e)*

then sent to Siberia. At one time, anyone convicted of smoking in Turkey was put to death. Anyone using or selling tobacco in Germany used to be heavily fined.

In spite of fines and penalties, people have continued to smoke. The following activity should help you think about the reasons why. Write down your answers:

YOUR PART

1. Why do you think people first start to smoke?
2. Why do you think many people continue to smoke in spite of health warnings?
3. Do you believe that smoking is dangerous to health?
4. Why does a health warning now appear on every pack of cigarettes (see Figure 19.2, page 312)?
5. Why do you think so many adults smoke?
6. As a class or in small groups, compare and discuss your answers.

Perhaps you agreed that people first smoke out of curiosity or just to be one of the gang. Did you mention how important group pressure can be for teenagers trying to make up their minds to act one way or another? Did you have any ideas about how to resist such pressure? You and your friends probably already know many of the unpleasant facts about smoking; if you do, you should *want* to resist any pressure from

Tobacco and Health

smokers in your group. And it's much easier to resist the temptation to start smoking than to try to give it up later on.

Because many adults smoke, young people feel grown up when they do, too. At the same time, some young people use smoking as a way of defying adults and the law. Many adults have probably warned you against smoking. Lighting up may be a way of showing them that you can do as you please.

Does smoking stop tension?

It's not too surprising that young people are willing to try something that may make them feel sophisticated, daring, independent, and adult (see Figure 19.3). But why do people continue to smoke? Does smoking ease tension and help people relax? In a way, the answer is yes.

Psychological Dependence

Let's say you are at a party that has just begun. Everyone is nervous. The guests are sitting in a circle, trying—and failing—to start an interesting conversation. The nonsmokers feel a little awkward, but not the smokers. They are too busy to feel awkward—taking out a pack, shaking loose a cigarette, lighting it, puffing it, flicking ashes from its burning end, and finally grinding it out. A smoker soon learns to "relax" by lighting up whenever she or he feels nervous (and the smoker soon feels nervous when "in need of a smoke").

In the same way, other smoking habits gradually form. After a time, a smoker has learned to reach for a smoke to finish each meal, to take a break from work, and to fight tension, fatigue, boredom, or the blues. The important thing to remember is that all of these smoking habits can be changed in exactly the same way that they were formed in the first place. People who have taught themselves to be smokers can teach themselves to be nonsmokers.

Figure 19.2. Modern tobacco use and warning.

How? A good first step is to learn to relax without cigarettes or other forms of tobacco. Here are four quick relaxers to use at school or work:

Decide About Drugs

Figure 19.3. Is this a good reason for smoking?

1. Take three deep breaths.
2. Relax your mouth and chin by letting your mouth droop open.
3. Relax your shoulders by twice hunching them up to your ears and twice rotating them forward and backward.
4. Relax your neck and back with neck rolls; gently drop your head forward, then backward, then to each side, three times each. Next, move your head gently around to "draw" a circle, three times in one direction, three times in the other.

Another valuable relaxer is regular exercise, such as running and stretching, cycling, and gymnastics (see Figure 19.4, pages 314–315). People who know how to relax can more easily break the smoking habit.

Physical Dependence

But smoking is more than a habit. Sooner or later, the bodies of smokers become *physically dependent* on a harmful, habit-forming substance in tobacco called **nicotine** (NIK-uh-teen). This means that their body cells gradually change the way that they work in order to adapt to the presence of nicotine. In the same way, body cells adapt to the habitual intake of caffeine, alcohol, and other drugs.

WITHDRAWAL SYMPTOMS   When a longtime smoker gives up smoking, he or she is jumpy and irritable at first because body cells lack a substance they have learned to live with. The discomfort, jumpiness, and irritability are symptoms of the physical **withdrawal** (removal) of nicotine. (Note the difference in the meaning of withdrawal in the physical sense from withdrawal in the emotional sense, as defined on page 284.) Gradually, however, the body cells return to normal, and the ex-smoker's disposition returns to normal, too. You can see why a young smoker, not yet physically dependent on nicotine, has an easier time giving up tobacco than a longtime smoker does.

Tobacco and Health

Are they sure you can get cancer from smoking cigarettes?

The answer to this question is yes. The statistics linking smoking and lung cancer were so conclusive that, in January 1964, the Surgeon General of the United States issued a report called *Smoking and Health* to warn of the danger. And in every year since, more evidence has come in that has been made available periodically in report form.

Recent statistics like these also indicate that, at every age from 35 on, illness and death rates among both men and women are higher for smokers than for nonsmokers. Among men between 45 and 54, the death rate for smokers is *three times* that for nonsmokers.

In its 1975 booklet *Cancer Facts and Figures*, the American Cancer Society said of lung cancer: "This is largely a preventable disease, since most lung cancer is caused by cigarette smoking. Unfortunately, it is difficult to diagnose in time for cure. Only about 10 percent of all cases are being saved."

What Is Cancer?

Cancer is not one disease but many diseases that affect different parts of the body. Irritation by such things as chemicals and excessive radiation of some

314   **Decide About Drugs**

Figure 19.4. Exercise releases tensions and leads to greater control over mind and body.

types is one cause of cancer. Cancer is wild, uncontrolled cell growth. Like weeds in a garden, cancerous cells crowd out normal cells by robbing them of food and space. Unless they are kept from spreading, cancer cells end by crowding out so many normal cells that the body can no longer carry on its work.

What substance in tobacco causes cancer?

Tobacco smoke is a mixture of many different substances. To date, nearly 300 of them have been identified. About 60 percent of these substances are *gases*. The solids, or tiny particles, found in tobacco smoke are called *tars*, which have been identified as **carcinogens** (KAHR-sin-oh-jenz), or cancer starters. When applied to the skin of laboratory animals, tars cause cancerous growth to begin.

However, certain of the gases in tobacco smoke, though not cancer starters, are cancer promoters. These gases slow up and later entirely stop the cleansing action of tiny broomlike projections in the air passages, called **cilia** (SIL-ee-uh). Normally, **mucus** (MYOO-kus), a moist secretion covering the surfaces of the air passages, traps pollen, dust, and other inhaled particles. Healthy cilia beat continuously, moving mucus upward

Tobacco and Health

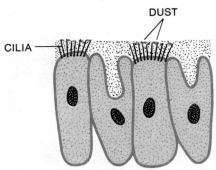

Figure 19.5. Healthy cilia help to keep air passages free from dust and other foreign matter.

and into the back of the throat and mouth (see Figure 19.5). In this way, the air passages of the lungs are constantly and automatically cleaned.

But in a smoker's air passages, the cilia are paralyzed or destroyed, and the inhaled cancer-causing tars stay in the lungs, where they coat and irritate the linings of the air passages. Why do longtime smokers cough? Because they have no other way of trying to remove mucus and foreign particles from the air passages.

YOUR PART

1. Find an adult smoker who is willing to help with the following homework assignment.
2. Have the smoker take a puff from a lighted cigarette and then hold all of the smoke in the mouth rather than drawing it down into the lungs. As quickly as possible, place a clean tissue, stretched as firmly as possible, over the smoker's mouth. Have the smoker blow out through the tissue. Examine the tissue for stains. (These stains come from the tars.)
3. Have the smoker inhale once more, this time allowing the smoke to go into the lungs. Again, place a clean tissue over the mouth while the smoker exhales. Examine the second stain.

How much tar is left in a smoker's lungs each time he or she inhales tobacco? The difference between the two stains in this experiment should give you a rough idea.

Let's Pause for Review

Smoking is an old habit. People have continued to use tobacco in spite of fines, penalties, and (as now shown conclusively), the

Decide About Drugs

likelihood of early death or disability. Why? Because smokers become physically dependent on the nicotine in tobacco, and because they form strong habits of psychological dependence on tobacco use at many moments in their daily lives (to relax, to socialize, to fight fatigue and boredom, and to end a meal, for example). But such habits can be gradually unlearned just as they were gradually learned in the first place. Learning to relax can help smokers become ex-smokers. A program of daily exercise helps, too. Daily exercise provides not only a sure release of tension, but also real control over mind and body.

Chemicals and other irritants cause some forms of cancer. Since most lung cancer is caused by cigarette smoking, this disease is largely preventable. The tars (or tiny solid particles in tobacco smoke) irritate the bronchial linings and can, in time, cause lung cancer. Normally, the cilia lining the body's air passages constantly and automatically cleanse the lungs. But some of the gases in tobacco smoke slow and then stop this vital cleaning. After this stage, even more tars are left behind to irritate the lungs whenever tobacco smoke is inhaled.

Does smoking affect the heart?

Somewhat surprisingly, statistics now show that tobacco smoking may contribute to as many deaths from heart disease as from lung cancer. First of all, heart disease kills more Americans than any other disease. Since smoking puts an added strain on the heart, it follows that smoking plays a major part in many of the 750,000 heart disease fatalities each year. By way of comparison, lung cancer kills about 80,000 yearly, and another lung disease called **emphysema** (em-fuh-SEE-muh or em-fuh-ZEE-muh) (see page 319) kills about 20,000 more. In addition, a smoker is five times as likely to have a **stroke** (a cerebral, or brain, hemorrhage often resulting in paralysis) as a nonsmoker is.

Nicotine and the Heart

The best-known ingredient of tobacco smoke is nicotine. Since it is poisonous even in fairly small amounts, nicotine is used in many *insecticides* (chemical insect-killers). If the nicotine in one cigar or in two cigarettes were injected into your bloodstream, it would kill you. Luckily for smokers, however, only about 15 percent of this nicotine is still in the smoke by the time it reaches the mouth. And a still smaller amount finally enters the bloodstream.

The inhalation of nicotine often causes dizziness and digestive upsets at first, but in time these effects disappear. More lasting are nicotine's effects on the appetite and the circulatory system. Nicotine continues to reduce the appetite. More seriously, nicotine speeds up the pulse, increases the blood pressure, and *constricts* (squeezes, reduces the diameter of) certain blood vessels. Smokers' hearts often become irritated (excessively sensitive) and their heartbeats more irregular. These circulatory changes make the heart work harder. Over the years, such unnecessary strain helps account for the fact that two to three times as many smokers as nonsmokers under 60 years of age die of heart disease.

Carbon Monoxide and the Heart

Another poison present in small amounts in tobacco smoke is the gas **carbon monoxide.** Carbon monoxide is also the deadly ingredient in automobile exhaust fumes. At times, smokers seem to absorb enough carbon monoxide to reduce the oxygen-carrying capacity of the blood. This effect may well increase the strain that smoking puts on the heart.

The following activity will help you to see how tobacco affects the heart. Once again, you will need to find an adult smoker who doesn't mind helping you with a homework experiment:

YOUR PART

1. Take a smoker's pulse for a full minute before he or she smokes a cigarette. Record the result.
2. Have the smoker light a cigarette and inhale four times. Again take the pulse and record the result.
3. When the smoker finishes the cigarette, take and record the smoker's pulse rate every 15 minutes until it returns to normal.

This demonstration showed you one way in which smoking makes the heart work harder. Unfortunately, you could not see either the smoker's increased blood pressure or the greater irritation to and irregular beat of the smoker's heart.

Bronchitis

As previously mentioned, lung cancer is not the only respiratory disease that is caused or made worse by smoking. The common ailment **bronchitis** (brahn-KY-tis), or inflammation of the bronchial tubes, is caused by continuous irritation of the bronchial lining. The well-known "smoker's cough" is a familiar symptom of bronchitis. And according to the 1964 report of the Surgeon General of the United States, "Cigarette smoking is the most important of the causes of bronchitis, and it increases the risks of dying from chronic bronchitis."

318   **Decide About Drugs**

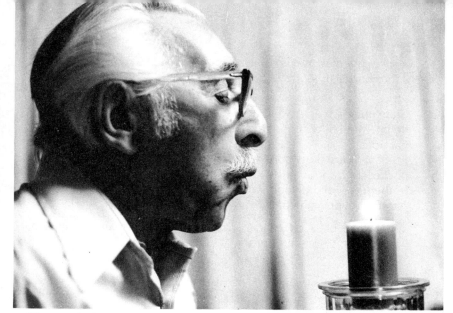

Figure 19.6. Emphysema can make a simple action like blowing out a candle very difficult.

Emphysema

The word *emphysema* comes from the Greek word for inflation (filled with gas). A person with this disease has trouble inflating the lungs because, as emphysema develops, the lungs lose their elasticity. The walls of the lungs' tiny air sacs are stretched and sometimes destroyed. Dead-air pockets form, and the lungs enlarge.

Emphysema may be a late effect of chronic infection or irritation of the bronchial tubes. To help keep yourself free of emphysema, therefore, keep fit, take care of colds and other respiratory infections, and don't smoke.

A person with emphysema can't take in enough oxygen to provide fuel for normal activity. He or she is weak and out of breath after walking up a short flight of stairs or bending over to pick up something. The emphysema sufferer may not even be able to blow out a match or candle (see Figure 19.6). The following activity should help you see why:

YOUR PART

MATERIALS
- Three balloons of the same size and elasticity
- A bell jar
- A one-hole rubber stopper
- A Y tube

Tobacco and Health

- A rubber sheet or membrane
- Rubber bands or string

PROCEDURE

1. Blow up one balloon and let it stay inflated for a day or two. Then deflate the balloon and compare its size to that of the other two balloons.
2. Insert an unused balloon into the used one and note the space or air pocket surrounding the unused balloon. (Air pockets also develop in the lungs of a person with emphysema.)
3. Assemble your materials as follows:

    a. With rubber bands or string, attach the remaining unused balloon to one end of the Y tube (see Figure 19.7).

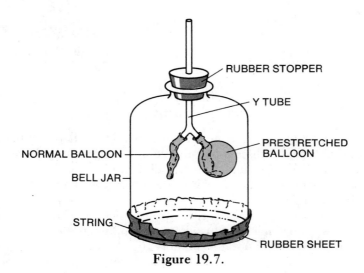

Figure 19.7.

    b. Attach the double balloon (unused balloon inside the prestretched balloon) to the other end of the Y tube. (The balloons represent air sacs in the lungs.)
    c. Insert the remaining end of the glass tubing into the hole of the stopper.
    d. Set the stopper into the neck of the bell jar.
    e. Stretch the rubber sheet (representing the diaphragm) across the bottom of the bell jar and tie it in place. (See page 66 for a reminder of how your diaphragm works as you breathe.)

4. Now, to make the air-sac balloons "breathe," pull down on the center of the stretched rubber membrane. Write down what hap-

Decide About Drugs

pens to the balloons. Release the rubber membrane and push it a short way into the jar. Write down what happens to the balloons. Why does the double balloon work differently from the single balloon? Write down your answer.

In emphysema, the walls of the lung's tiny air sacs are stretched like the balloon in this demonstration. Similar dead-air pockets form. You can see why a person with emphysema becomes less and less able to inhale and exhale normally.

What does all of this have to do with smoking? Like lung cancer, emphysema has shown a dramatic increase in recent years. One study of emphysema in California has revealed a 300-percent increase over a period of eight years. For this reason, cigarette smoking is strongly suspected to be one cause of emphysema. And scientists already know that smoking makes emphysema worse. In addition, deaths from emphysema are less frequent among nonsmokers.

Other Tobacco-Related Diseases

Smokers are also more likely to develop stomach ulcers than nonsmokers are. Smoking mothers are more likely to give birth to smaller babies, and low birth weight is often linked to slow or poor physical and emotional development. Even young smokers have less breath capacity for athletics and often suffer from hacking coughs.

Most of the adults smoking today knew nothing of all these dangers when they first began to smoke. In 1964, when the case against tobacco was proved, many people stopped smoking. Many more switched to pipes and cigars because, since pipe and cigar smokers rarely inhale smoke, the death rates for them are almost as low as for nonsmokers. (Cancers of the lip, mouth, esophagus, and larynx, however, are more frequent among pipe and cigar smokers than among nonsmokers.)

Many nonsmokers are sensitive to the tars and nicotine in tobacco smoke and become uncomfortable or ill when they are in the same room with someone who is smoking. This is the reason for new laws banning smoking in public places such as elevators, stores, and no-smoking sections of airplanes.

Why Doctors Quit

One interesting fact is that more doctors and other medical personnel have stopped smoking than people in any other group. Many smokers simply avoided the new evidence. But for professional reasons, medical people

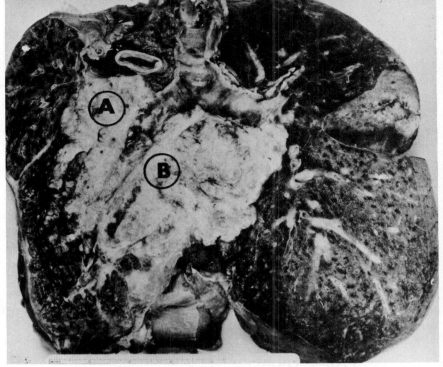

Figure 19.8. Cross section of the lung of a heavy smoker who died of lung cancer (cancerous tissue is shown in areas A and B).

had to examine the telling statistics and photographs (see Figure 19.8). In the days before the facts were known, 51 percent of doctors smoked; today less than 30 percent of them do.

Cigarette Advertising and Manufacture

Although the smoking rate is lower now than when the facts first became known, there has been an upturn in smoking in recent years. The American Cancer Society blames this rise in large part on advertising. After cigarette advertising was banned on radio and TV, the networks chose not to run many antismoking spots either, especially in prime time. The American Cancer Society is now working for a ban on all cigarette advertising in this country. In addition, the American Cancer Society wants not only a listing of tar and nicotine content but also a stronger health warning on all packs of cigarettes.

The American Cancer Society is also working for the reduction of tars in cigarettes and improvement of filters. At present, manufacturers have agreed not to improve the flavor of their tobacco products by increasing tar content and reducing filter effectiveness without letting the public know, but this agreement is not legally binding. The following activity will help you learn more about cigarette filters:

322 **Decide About Drugs**

MATERIALS
- A clean, clear, squeezable plastic container (such as a liquid soap container)
- Rubber or plastic tubing, the same size in diameter as a cigarette, or slightly larger
- Clay
- Absorbent cotton
- A filter cigarette
- A nonfilter cigarette

PROCEDURE

1. Make an opening in the cap of the container, and fit the tubing into the opening (see Figure 19.9).
2. Seal in the tube tightly with clay, if necessary.
3. Insert loosely packed cotton into the tubing.
4. Insert a filter cigarette into the open end of the tubing.
5. Press firmly on the plastic container to force the air out. Now light the cigarette. Release the pressure on the container. Proceed with a slow and regular pumping action until the cigarette burns down. Put the cigarette out.
6. Take the cotton out of the tube. Write down what you see on the cotton.
7. See if you can detect any odor in the container.
8. Repeat the entire procedure, this time using clean cotton and a nonfilter cigarette. Again write down what you see on the cotton. Which piece of cotton is more discolored, the first or second one? Why?
9. Open the filter. Is it stained? If so, and if it was meant to filter out tar, why is the cotton also stained? Write your answers down.

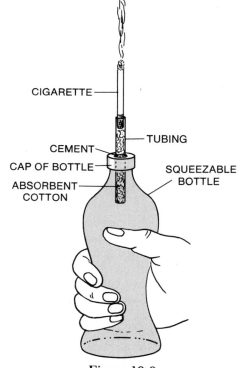

CIGARETTE

CEMENT

CAP OF BOTTLE

ABSORBENT COTTON

TUBING

SQUEEZABLE BOTTLE

Figure 19.9.

The American Cancer Society believes that filters can be made to be much more effective. But at present, as this demonstration shows, a smoker can't depend on filters to protect the lungs.

Can you give me any other reasons besides disease for not smoking?

Of course, cigarettes themselves cost a great deal of money over a lifetime. But the financial cost of smoking doesn't stop there. Because nonsmokers have fewer auto accidents and fewer home fires than smokers, they may be able to get cheaper auto and home insurance. (Cigarette smokers cause an estimated 90,000 fires each year.) Nonsmokers have lower medical bills and miss fewer paychecks because they aren't sick as often or for as long a time as smokers are.

The cost of smoking goes beyond money, as many a puffing athlete-smoker could tell you. Good athletic skills and smoking just don't go together.

I smoke. How do I go about stopping?

Chances are that many of you already know some helpful tips for giving up smoking. For more helpful information on quitting, you should call or write the American Heart Association and the American Cancer Society.

Dr. Donald Fredrickson, whose TV programs on the subject helped many New Yorkers to give up smoking, says you need to do three things to give up cigarettes:

1. *Find a motive or reason for stopping* (television and magazine warnings about health hazards, the expense, your athletic ambitions, stains on your fingers or teeth, a dulled sense of taste).
2. *Change your behavior.* Some people quit gradually, giving up the most enjoyed cigarettes first. Others give up the least enjoyed cigarettes first. Still others find it easier to quit all at once. Many people give up smoking several times before they are able to give it up for good. So don't be afraid of failing. Just keep on working at changing your habits from those of a smoker to those of a nonsmoker.
3. *Change your attitude.* In Doctor Fredrickson's words: "A positive attitude—a feeling that you are giving yourself a gift—will be most helpful." You can further reward yourself by using the money you save by not smoking for something you want very much.

The Effects of Stopping Smoking

Let us say you are a smoker and you stop. What happens? You soon find you can be more active without getting out of breath. Stains no longer accumulate on your teeth and fingers. The clothes in your closet and the rooms in your house smell fresher. Your breath is sweeter. Food often tastes better, too. Most important of all, damaged tissue in your lungs begins a gradual return to normalcy. This gradual improvement begins within three or four weeks after you stop smoking.

Unless the cilia have been destroyed by prolonged smoking, they gradually return to their work of sweeping the bronchial passages clean. Your heart, freed from unnecessary strain and irritation, becomes more resistant to disease. After ten years without smoking, the death rates of ex-smokers come close to being the same as those of nonsmokers. In fact, if most people in our country gave up smoking, lung cancer would again become a rare disease. And much early death and disability from respiratory and circulatory disease could be avoided.

Looking Back

Lung cancer is largely a preventable disease since most cases are caused by cigarette smoking. Tars are the carcinogens in tobacco smoke. But certain gases in the smoke promote cancer by gradually paralyzing the cilia, which would otherwise continue to sweep the bronchial passages clean.

Cigarette smoking is hard on the heart, too. When a person smokes, blood pressure rises, certain blood vessels constrict, and the heart becomes more irritated and beats faster and possibly more irregularly. A smoker is more than twice as likely to die of heart disease before age 60 as a nonsmoker. A smoker is five times more likely to have a stroke than a nonsmoker.

In addition, cigarette smoking is not only the most important cause of bronchitis, it also increases the risk of death from bronchitis. Deaths from emphysema, too, are more frequent among smokers. All in all, smokers pay a heavy price for their habit. First, the cost of smoking is great. Second, smokers go through life feeling less well than they otherwise would. Third, they are likely to die younger than necessary.

However, smokers can give themselves the gift of better health and longer life by gradually changing their habits back to those of a nonsmoker. When smokers give up cigarettes, their bodies respond by gradually returning to normal. The heart becomes more resistant to disease. The cilia recover and go back to their work of sweeping the air passages clean. After ten years' time, in fact, the death rates for ex-smokers differ little from those for nonsmokers.

MODIFIED TRUE-FALSE QUESTIONS

1. _All_ drugs can be poisonous, if improperly used.
2. The fewer cigarettes one smokes, the _smaller_ is the risk of emphysema.
3. When longtime smokers stop smoking, they undergo _withdrawal_ symptoms.

Tobacco and Health

4. _Most_ lung cancer is caused by cigarette smoking.
5. Cancer cells grow in _a controlled_ fashion.
6. About _20_ percent of cigarette smoke consists of gases.
7. The _tars_ in tobacco smoke are cancer-producing.
8. The air passages are constantly cleaned by the action of the _cilia._
9. _Lung cancer_ kills more Americans than any other disease.
10. Nicotine _decreases_ the heartbeat.
11. Carbon _dioxide_ is the deadly ingredient of automobile exhaust.
12. Inflammation of the bronchial tubes is called _emphysema._
13. Stretched air pockets form in the lungs of people who suffer from _bronchitis._
14. Stomach ulcers are _more_ prevalent in smokers than in nonsmokers.
15. A smoker _can_ depend on filters to protect his lungs.

MATCHING QUESTIONS

Column A		_Column B_
1. carcinogen	a.	carbon monoxide in tobacco smoke
2. cilia	b.	wild growth of body cells
3. nicotine	c.	increases blood pressure
4. bronchitis	d.	gives rise to cancer
5. cancer	e.	smoker's cough
	f.	air-passage cleaners

COMPLETION QUESTIONS

1. Many young people consider smoking a sign of being _____.
2. After a time, the bodies of smokers become physically _____ on the nicotine in tobacco.
3. Disagreeable reactions from discontinuing the use of a drug are referred to as _____ symptoms.
4. Carcinogens are substances that cause _____.
5. A cerebral hemorrhage resulting in paralysis is called a (an) _____.
6. Nicotine _____ the appetite.
7. Generally, pipe smokers have death rates almost as low as nonsmokers unless they _____ the smoke.
8. In the last few years, smoking has increased because of continued clever _____.
9. Nonsmokers generally have _____ medical bills than smokers.
10. Smoking mothers are more likely to give birth to _____ babies than nonsmoking mothers are.

Decide About Drugs

MULTIPLE-CHOICE QUESTIONS

1. The substance in cigarette smoke that reduces the oxygen-carrying capacity of the blood, thus increasing the strain on the heart, is
   a. carbon dioxide   b. carbon monoxide   c. nicotine   d. tar
2. "Smoker's cough" is a well-known symptom of
   a. cancer   b. colds   c. bronchitis   d. tuberculosis
3. A person who feels tense can relax safely by means of
   a. exercise   c. tranquilizing pills
   b. cigarette smoking   d. alcoholic beverages
4. Withdrawal symptoms when cigarette smoking is given up include
   a. severe cramps   c. jumpiness and nervousness
   b. sweating   d. decrease of appetite
5. Generally, the chances that a smoker, as compared to a nonsmoker, will get a stroke are
   a. the same   b. greater   c. less   d. unpredictable
6. Which body system does emphysema, a disease that is aggravated by smoking, affect?
   a. circulatory   b. digestive   c. nervous   d. respiratory
7. The habit-forming substance in cigarettes is
   a. smoke   b. tar   c. nicotine   d. gas
8. Of the following diseases, smoking is *least* related to
   a. heart disease   c. emphysema
   b. lung cancer   d. beriberi
9. The cancer-producing substance in cigarette smoke is
   a. carbon dioxide   c. nicotine
   b. tar   d. carbon monoxide
10. Nicotine does *not* cause
    a. reduction in appetite
    b. speeding up of the circulatory system
    c. reduction in the diameter of surface blood vessels
    d. decrease in blood sugar

THOUGHT QUESTIONS

1. Some say smoking decreases appetite. Do you agree? Why or why not?
2. Most smokers offer a variety of excuses for smoking. State three such excuses people use. Suggest a different action that they could take in each case to help them stop smoking.
3. Answer the following questions on our current knowledge about the harmfulness of tobacco:

   a. When did the controversy start in the United States?
   b. What did the Surgeon General's report contain?
   c. Explain the American Cancer Society's role in fighting cigarette smoking.

Tobacco and Health   327

4. How do smoking-control centers operate? If possible, discuss these organizations with a friend or relative who has stopped smoking after taking part in such a program.
5. Suppose a law that made smoking illegal were enacted. Would this action solve the smoking problem? Defend your position.
6. Students in school have asked that special areas be designated for smokers. How do you feel about such a request?

Answers to True-False Quiz, Page 310

1.	false	4.	true	7.	true	10.	true
2.	false	5.	false	8.	true	11.	true
3.	false	6.	true	9.	true	12.	false

Scoring Instructions: Give yourself 1 point for each statement you checked correctly. A score of 12 is very good; 9 is not too bad; 6 is not good.

Looking Ahead

In Chapter 20, you will read about alcohol, the oldest and most widely misused drug.

Decide About Drugs

Chapter 20: Alcohol and Health

On Monday morning before school, the students in Teresa's first-period math class gathered to talk about their classmate.

"Did you hear what happened to Teresa?" Ruby said.

"I heard she was killed in a crash," said Mark.

"Nat was driving, ran a red light, and hit another car," Dot said.

"The police say Teresa and Nat had been drinking," Ruby added.

Have you heard stories like this before? Most young people do at some time during their school years. Such stories point up an important problem. Because we live in an age of automobiles and other complex machinery, alcohol use may be more dangerous than ever in the past. At least half of all fatal accidents involve drinking drivers, which means that alcohol helps cause 27,000 deaths and 500,000 major injuries each year.

Alcohol, Alcoholism, and Crime

Today, both alcohol use and the crime rate are at an all-time high. The two are not unconnected. In our country, a third of all crimes, a fourth of all suicides, and half of all murders involve the use of alcohol. However, the average person is more likely to be affected by another statistic: The National Institute on Alcoholic Abuse and Alcoholism says that about one drinker in ten is either an *alcoholic* (a person addicted to alcohol) or a problem drinker (a person who drinks enough to cause problems for him- or herself and for society). Should you use alcohol? The information contained in this chapter may help you make your decision.

Kinds of Alcohol

When people say "alcohol," they usually mean **ethyl** (ETH-ul) **alcohol,** or drinkable alcohol. But there are other kinds. Most of the other alcohols—compounds similar to, but not identical with, ethyl alcohol—cannot be safely drunk.

Table 20.1: Alcohols

Name	Chemical Formula	Used In
Ethyl alcohol	C_2H_5OH	Wines, liquors, manufacture of plastics and explosives
Methyl alcohol	CH_3OH	Antifreeze and cleaning solutions, manufacture of shellac
Isopropyl alcohol	C_3H_7OH	Rubbing alcohol, shaving lotions
Ethylene glycol	$C_2H_4(OH)_2$	Antifreeze solutions
Glycerol (glycerin)	$C_3H_5(OH)_3$	Hand lotions, manufacture of plastics and explosives

Study Table 20.1. *Methyl alcohol* (wood alcohol), for example, which is often used in antifreeze and cleaning fluid, is poisonous if taken *internally* (inside the body). *Isopropyl* (eye-suh-PROH-pul) *alcohol* (rubbing alcohol) evaporates quickly and is, therefore, useful in such products as aftershave lotion and perfume. By its rapid evaporation, rubbing alcohol, when applied *externally* (outside the body), also helps to lower the body temperature of a person with fever. But rubbing alcohol, too, is a poison if taken internally.

THE OLDEST DRUG   Ethyl alcohol is the oldest drug we know. Five thousand years ago, the people of Mesopotamia drank beer and recorded the fact on clay tablets—the oldest surviving written documents. The ancient Egyptians, too, brewed and drank beer. Wherever they went during the age of exploration, European explorers found the native peoples making alcoholic beverages. Only 17 years after their arrival on the *Mayflower,* the people of the Massachusetts Bay Colony built the nation's first brewery. And today, alcohol is probably used in every country in the world and by almost every agricultural people.

Fermentation   Most agricultural peoples use part of one of their food crops to make some alcoholic beverage. A natural process called **fermentation** turns fruit juice into wine and grain mixed with liquid into beer. What causes fermentation? The answer is microscopic organisms such as **yeasts** (YEESTS) and bacteria.

Wild yeasts are found in nature—floating in the air, for example—and on the skins of fruits and vegetables. When they act on the sugar in fruit juice, yeasts produce alcohol and carbon dioxide. When commercial yeast

Decide About Drugs

is used to bake bread, the bubbles of carbon dioxide make the bread rise, and the heat evaporates the alcohol. When yeast is used to make wine, on the other hand, the alcohol is not allowed to evaporate; it is kept in the processed liquid. The carbon dioxide, however, is allowed to escape. (In the case of champagne or other sparkling wines, however, some of the carbon dioxide bubbles are kept in the wine.)

To find out in more detail about alcohol's past and present uses, do the following activity:

YOUR PART

1. The accidental discovery of how fermentation works must have taken place many times in the history of the world. Write down one possible way in which this discovery could have been made.
2. Wine was pasteurized before milk. Choose several classmates to investigate and report to the class on Pasteur's work on the fermentation of wine and beer.
3. Choose several classmates to investigate why milk is pasteurized. (In addition, refer again to page 19.)
4. Choose several classmates to investigate and report on the medicinal uses of ethyl alcohol today and in the past.
5. At home, make a list of products in your household (other than beverages) that contain alcohol. Bring your list to school for comparison.
6. As a class, compare and discuss your answers to steps 1 and 5.

No doubt you agreed that wild yeasts have caused fermentation to begin in fruit juices and in moist grains over and over again in the history of the world.

In the past, people must have explained fermentation as an act of the gods. Their fruit juice changed as if by magic. They themselves changed almost miraculously when they drank the fermented juice.

Perhaps for these reasons, alcohol has been used in religious ceremonies from the earliest days to the present. A feeling of magic still clings to alcohol. Many people who don't usually drink nevertheless use alcohol to mark special occasions, to toast outstanding accomplishments, and to wish each other well (see Figure 20.1, page 332).

Preservative, Disinfectant, and Anesthetic   In addition to its religious uses, alcohol has long been used as a *preservative*. In past times, and even today in many places, alcoholic drinks have been used in place of unsafe drinking water, polluted by such things as garbage, sewage, and

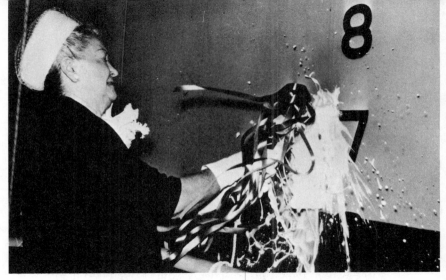

Figure 20.1. Traditionally, a bottle of champagne is used to celebrate the launching of a new ship.

dead animals. In the days before refrigeration, many foods spoiled quickly. But alcohol, like spices, helped both to preserve food and to disguise its "mature" flavor.

Alcohol is also a *disinfectant*, which means that it kills disease germs. So, people often dab a bit of alcohol on a break in the skin to help prevent infection.

Moreover, whiskey, which contains ethyl alcohol, was drunk to deaden pain during surgical operations before the development of modern *anesthetics* (an-us-THET-iks).

How Much Alcohol?

The various alcoholic beverages contain different amounts of alcohol. In beer making, for example, fermentation is stopped when the alcoholic content reaches about 4 percent. In wine making, on the other hand, fruit juice is allowed to ferment until most of its sugar has been changed into alcohol and carbon dioxide. At this point, because there is enough alcohol (12 to 14 percent) to kill the yeast, fermentation stops.

DISTILLED BEVERAGES Hard liquor (whiskey, gin, vodka, rum, brandy, liqueur) has an alcoholic content well beyond the 12 to 14 percent obtainable by natural fermentation. In making hard liquor, grains like rye, corn, and barley are fermented to produce alcoholic solutions. From these solutions, ethyl alcohol and desired flavors are extracted. Additional flavoring and aging are usually needed before the extract becomes the final product.

The Chinese are thought to have been the first to distill liquor,

Decide About Drugs

Table 20.2: Alcoholic Content of Some Beverages (Approximate)

Beverage	Proof	Percent	Calories per Usual Serving
Whiskey	80	40	75
Liqueur	60	30	100
Wine	24	12	80
Mixed drink	14	7	100
Hard cider	10	5	100
Beer	8	4	100

although the Arabs are given credit for first introducing it to the people of Europe. (Our word *alcohol* comes from the Arabic word *alkohol,* meaning spirit or essence.) You yourself know how **distillation** (dis-tuh-LAY-shun) works if you have ever boiled water and left it to cool in a covered pan. First, by boiling it, you changed some of the water from a liquid into a vapor (steam). Then, as you let the water cool, the steam collected inside the cover and condensed (changed back into liquid form). V*aporization* and *condensation* are the two main steps in distillation.

People often distill pure water from contaminated water by boiling the water and collecting the steam in a tube, which can then be cooled so that the steam condenses. Solids in the water are left behind in the boiling container. In liquor distilleries, the fermented liquid is kept below the boiling point of water: the alcohol, which becomes a vapor at a lower temperature, is boiled off, cooled, and condensed.

Distillation produces beverages that are 40 to 50 percent alcohol. The liquor industry uses the word *proof* to express alcoholic content. However, the proof figure is about double the alcohol percent figure. A bottle of 90 proof whiskey, for example, is approximately 45 percent alcohol (see Table 20.2). Most hard liquors are between 80 and 100 proof.

Let's Pause for Review

Ethyl (drinkable) alcohol is the most ancient drug. Alcohol is produced by fermentation, a natural process in which yeasts (either natural or commercial) and bacteria act on the sugar in fruit juice or on grain broth to produce alcohol and carbon dioxide. In beer making, fermentation is stopped when the level reaches about 4 percent. In wine making, fermentation continues until there is enough alcohol (12 to 14 percent) to kill the yeast, thus ending the fermentation. Hard liquors (which may contain as much as 40 to 50 percent alcohol) are produced by fermentation and distillation. In liquor distilleries, the fermented liquid is heated enough to allow the alcohol to be boiled off, cooled, and condensed, but not enough to boil off the water in the mixture.

Alcohol has long been used in religious ceremonies and to mark special occasions. From past to present, alcohol has been used in place of polluted drinking water. In addition, alcohol has a long history of use as a preservative, a disinfectant, and an anesthetic.

What are the effects of alcohol on the body and brain?

The brain is the organ that alcohol affects most noticeably. Many people believe that alcohol is a **stimulant.** Stimulants speed up bodily activity. But alcohol is really a **depressant,** which slows things down. Its slowing effects become obvious when the alcohol level in the blood reaches .10 percent, or $^1/_{10}$ of 1 percent (see Table 20.3). By that time, a drinker's walk, balance, coordination, speech, sight, hearing, and judgment are seriously affected. In fact, in many states a driver with a .10 percent blood alcohol level or more is considered legally "under the influence of alcohol" and, therefore, subject to arrest for drunken driving.

What emotions and physical reactions are caused by drinking?

It is true that a drinker's first few drinks may make him or her feel more stimulated than slowed down. Perhaps the first effect that a drinker feels is a relaxation of the self-control usually maintained by the brain. The drinker may well feel the impulse to speak freely, perhaps to dance, or to join friends in song. The part of the brain that usually guides social behavior is no longer working normally. With the first drink, a drinker becomes less self-conscious, less easily embarrassed, less careful, and less controlled.

The drinker may also feel a glow of warmth as surface blood vessels enlarge and more blood passes through them. But this warm glow is misleading. As you may remember, enlargement of surface capillaries cools the body, and constriction of surface capillaries conserves body warmth. Therefore, alcohol can cool a drinker's body in hot weather. But a chilly traveler who stops for a "warming" drink on a cold day is actually chilling his or her body further.

In addition, a drinker may feel more energetic with the first few drinks. There are two reasons for this. First, alcohol masks the awareness of fatigue. Second, alcoholic drinks contain a good many Calories (see Table 20.2, page 333). The liver changes alcohol into a substance that the cells can use to provide energy. In fact, alcohol often provides an alcoholic with half the Calories needed each day. For this reason, alcoholics usually suffer from malnutrition because, in spite of its Calorie count, alcohol contains no vitamins, minerals, or other necessary nutrients.

334   **Decide About Drugs**

Table 20.3: Effects of Increasing Amounts of Alcohol in the Blood

Alcohol Level in the Blood	Approximate Number of Drinks, Quickly Absorbed	Effects
.01%*		Drinker feels stimulated.
.03%	1 ounce of whiskey or 1 pint of beer†	Drinker feels warm, mentally relaxed.
.05%	2 ounces of whiskey or 2 pints of beer	Drinker's judgment, balance, coordination, and control are no longer normal.
.10%	4 ounces of whiskey or 4 pints of beer	Drinker's speech is slurred and loud; hearing is dulled; walking, balance, and coordination are noticeably affected. Drinker is legally "under the influence" in some states.
.15%	6 ounces of whiskey or 6 pints of beer	Drinker is legally "under the influence" in all states. Drinker's driving ability (hearing, vision, motor control, reaction time) is significantly worsened.
.20%		Drinker is staggering.
.30%		Drinker has trouble standing, staying awake, understanding what is going on nearby. Drinker vomits.
.40%		Drinker will be unconscious.
.50%		Drinker's life is in danger because of paralysis of parts of the nervous system that control breathing. This concentration of alcohol is usually fatal.

*.01% = 1/100 of 1%, or 1 part alcohol to 10,000 parts blood.
†1 ounce = 30 cubic centimeters; 1 pint (16 ounces) = 480 cubic centimeters, or almost a half-liter.

(a) (b)

Figure 20.2. An evening of "social" drinking: (a) that warm glow; (b) the energy kid; (c) stupor; (d) the party's over.

(c) (d)

Why do adults drink?

Some people drink only on religious occasions. Others drink only at special celebrations. To others the world over, wine is part of mealtime. Still others are called *social drinkers*, because they use alcohol moderately as a

Decide About Drugs

regular part of their social lives; they enjoy the effects of moderate alcohol use—relaxation of self-control, a warm glow, an energy pick-me-up. Unfortunately, there are also people who drink to get drunk, often to escape painful feelings about themselves and their lives. It is these drinkers who often become problem drinkers and alcoholics (see Figure 20.2).

Why do young people drink?

Young people who drink do so for all of the reasons mentioned and more. Like smoking, drinking may seem sophisticated and adult. When friends press them to try alcohol, young people may be easy to persuade because they may already be curious about its effects. What is the harm in all of this? Exactly where and when do the dangers of alcohol use begin? The following activity may help you to think about these questions. Write down all your answers:

YOUR PART

1. Do you think there is any harm in moderate drinking? Why or why not?
2. In your opinion, when does it become dangerous for a drinker to drive? After one drink? After two? After three? (See Table 20.3, page 335.)
3. A drinker with a .10 percent blood alcohol level has duller than normal hearing and is developing temporary tunnel vision:

    a. Tape two sheets of notebook paper together so as to make one piece measuring 8½ by 22 inches.
    b. Put the paper on your head so that it comes down on both sides and cuts off your side vision.
    c. Now turn to Chapter 8, page 95, and repeat the *Your Part* test for tunnel vision, once with the paper on your head and once without.
    d. Record the results.

4. Do you think there is any way of knowing beforehand which people will become alcoholics if they begin to drink?
5. As a class, compare and discuss your answers and the results of your vision tests.

No doubt your discussion pinpointed the two great dangers of alcohol use: (1) the danger of operating a car (or other machinery) when judgment and control are less than good, and (2) the danger of becoming an alcoholic. Let's examine these dangers in detail.

Alcohol and Health

Figure 20.3. How much of his brain has been affected?

Alcohol in the Bloodstream

The effects of alcohol vary with the size of the drinker, the strength of the drink, and the circumstances in which the drinking is done. Alcohol has no effect on behavior until it reaches the bloodstream. The alcohol in 1 ounce (30 cubic centimeters) of whiskey drunk quickly on an empty stomach, for example, will reach the bloodstream fairly quickly. Part of the alcohol is absorbed by blood vessels in the stomach walls. But most of the alcohol is absorbed by blood vessels in the small intestine.

Anything that slows the passage of alcohol from the stomach into the small intestine, therefore, slows the absorption of alcohol into the bloodstream. Because it is mixed with food, wine with dinner is absorbed more slowly than the same amount of wine drunk on an empty stomach. Naturally, sipping a drink makes for slower absorption than gulping.

Diluting a drink with water helps, too. (Diluting a drink with carbonated soda is not as helpful; the dissolved bubbles of carbon dioxide in soda and in champagne increase the rate of alcoholic absorption.) Oddly enough, the fluids in a drinker's body also dilute the alcohol that is taken in. So the larger the size of the drinker, the slower the absorption of alcohol into the bloodstream.

Decide About Drugs

Alcohol and the Liver

As soon as alcohol enters the bloodstream, the body begins to eliminate it. The liver, which begins the process of elimination, can process about a half ounce (15 cubic centimeters) of alcohol—the alcohol in a pint (480 cubic centimeters) of beer or in half an average mixed drink—in an hour. If more than a half ounce of pure alcohol—a little more than an ounce (30 cubic centimeters) of hard liquor—is drunk in an hour, the excess alcohol circulates in the bloodstream and produces the various effects of **intoxication** (in-TAHK-suh-KAY-shun), or drunkenness (see Table 20.3, page 335).

What causes alcohol to make a person drunk?

The excess alcohol circulating in the blood travels to the brain and slows down the centers that control judgment, speech, sight, hearing, and motion (see Figure 20.3). The habit of mixing drinks—changing from beer to wine, for example—though it may upset some stomachs, does nothing to increase intoxication. It is the amount of alcohol in the blood that counts, not its source. A person who knows how alcohol is absorbed and eliminated is better able to use good judgment about alcohol use. Try out your judgment on the following questions:

YOUR PART

1. In one hour, the body can eliminate about a half ounce (15 cubic centimeters) of pure alcohol—the amount in half an average mixed drink or in a pint (480 cubic centimeters) of beer. Therefore, how long should one wait to drive after one drink? One beer? Two drinks? Three drinks?
2. Of late, a number of states have lowered the legal drinking age. Do you think there are now more or fewer arrests for drunken driving in these states? Explain your answer.
3. In England and in some Scandinavian countries, drunken drivers lose their driver's licenses the first time they are caught. As a result, these countries have greatly reduced drunken driving. Do you think that our country should have drunken driving laws as strict as those in England? (In the United States, drunken drivers are often allowed to continue driving until the third offense.)
4. Invite a local police officer to class to discuss drunken driving and the tests given to detect it; or visit your local police department, ask to see the equipment used (see Figure 20.4, page 340), and report to the class on your visit.
5. Compare and discuss your answers and your findings.

Alcohol and Health

No doubt you agreed that it takes the body at least one hour to eliminate from the bloodstream the alcohol contained in an average mixed drink or in a pint (480 cubic centimeters) of beer. Your discussion may have turned up another fact: In those states that have lowered the drinking age, arrests for drunken driving are up more than 100 percent.

Why do people become alcoholics?

The sad truth is that nobody knows the answer to this question. Many health scientists believe that emotional problems help cause alcoholism. Some researchers think that differences in body chemistry help cause alcoholism. Group customs play a part in causing alcoholism, as does social change. For example, during the Westward Movement, a hard-drinking way of life developed on the American frontier. For another example, as the ways of life of some ethnic groups within larger societies have been destroyed or greatly changed, those groups, too, have had problems with alcoholism.

YOUR PART

1. Form groups to investigate and report on the following topics:
   a. The Temperance Movement.
   b. Alcohol use among various groups in our own and other countries.
   c. Prohibition in this country.

Figure 20.4. Testing the alcohol level in a person's body.

2. As a class, discuss the effects of Prohibition on our country.

No doubt you agreed that both the Temperance Movement and Prohibition failed to stop alcohol use or abuse. Perhaps you also agreed that America needs to replace the hard-drinking traditions of the past with new traditions of moderation and responsibility.

Who is an alcoholic?

An alcoholic is a person who needs, or is *addicted* to, alcohol. Prolonged misuse of alcohol can cause certain marked symptoms of alcoholism, the chief of which is **delirium tremens** (dih-LIR-ee-um TREE-munz). Tremens means trembling or shaking, and delirium is a state in which one **hallucinates** (huh-LOO-suh-nayts), or sees things that aren't there. People who suffer from delirium tremens also have disorganized speech and mind confusion.

But alcoholism is a complicated problem, and there is more to it than simple addiction. The Rutgers University Center of Alcohol Studies says that an alcoholic is one who is unable consistently to choose whether to drink or not; once under the influence of drink, the alcoholic is unable consistently to choose whether to stop or not. The Committee on Alcoholism and Drug Dependence of the American Medical Association defines alcoholism as an illness in which there is preoccupation with alcohol and loss of control over its use (see Figure 20.5, page 343).

A person who is becoming alcoholic usually gets drunk more and more often, frequently lapsing into drunken unconsciousness. Such a person usually starts drinking earlier in the day, often in secret, and drinks faster, too. It often becomes impossible to get through a single day without alcohol. Blackouts (periods of time for which the alcoholic has no memory) are common. So are arrests for drunkenness or drunken driving.

Because years of heavy drinking can permanently enlarge surface blood vessels, a drinker's face may become permanently rose-colored. Illnesses associated with alcoholism, such as **cirrhosis** (suh-ROH-sis) of the liver —the disease that kills most alcoholics—begin to develop. In cirrhosis, tough fibers develop within the liver, causing it to harden and contract until, in the end, the liver can no longer do its vital work. You have already read about the liver's work in eliminating alcohol from the body, so you are probably not surprised to learn that prolonged alcohol use can damage and finally destroy the liver.

The amazing thing is that most alcoholics continue with work and family life, though they generally have problems both at work and at home. Their marriages are seven times more likely to end in divorce or separation than those of other people, for example. But alcoholics often succeed in hiding their problem from outsiders, and they themselves often fail to recognize that they are alcoholics. Only about 5 percent of the alcoholics in this country are the so-called typical homeless, jobless "bums." The total number of alcoholics in the United States is much larger than most people realize (see Table 20.4).

As you decide for yourself about alcohol use, the following activity may help with some of your decisions:

YOUR PART

1. You may choose never to use alcohol, or to drink only on religious or other special occasions. You may choose to be a responsible social drinker who never drives with alcohol in the bloodstream. But it is quite unlikely that you want to become an alcoholic. As a class or in small groups, discuss what standards young people might set to guide them if they decide to use alcohol.
2. Discuss ways by which young people can avoid becoming heavy drinkers, problem drinkers, or alcoholics.

Perhaps you decided that one should never drink to get drunk and that one should never drink alone. Perhaps your discussion stressed moderation. Or perhaps you agreed that while alcohol might be part of a meal, a special occasion, or an evening shared with friends, alcohol should never be the main part.

Curing Alcoholism

Curing alcoholism is not easy, but workers in the field insist that two-thirds or more of all alcoholics could be cured (in the sense that they could be helped to give up drinking entirely). Today, there are many more groups working against alcoholism than in the past. In most of these groups, alcoholics help one another to get well; they help one another resist the temptation to drink. And by sharing their feelings and experiences, they help one another to regain their faith in life and in themselves.

ALCOHOLICS ANONYMOUS, AL-ANON AND ALATEEN In Alcoholics Anonymous, or AA—the oldest and most successful of the groups at work to fight alcoholism—alcoholics help one another without professional help. (In addition, Al-Anon works to help the other adults in an alcoholic's family, and Alateen works to help the young people in an alcoholic's family.) In groups other than AA, professionals and patients work together to overcome the drinker's addiction to alcohol.

Former alcoholics like actress Mercedes McCambridge and Senator Harold Hughes of Iowa often work long and hard to help those still addicted

342   **Decide About Drugs**

Table 20.4:   Alcoholism in the United States

Age Groups	Estimated Number of Alcoholics
0–19	12,000
20–29	55,000
30–39	440,000
40–49	1,200,000
50–59	1,810,000
60–69	1,500,000
70–79	785,000
80 and over	200,000
	6,002,000 total

Figure 20.5. Alcoholics are found in most normal settings — home, factory, and office.

to alcohol. Having beaten their own addiction, they want to help others do the same. Workers in the field make two points: (1) in order to succeed, the alcoholic must really want to stop drinking, and (2) if the alcoholic keeps trying, he or she will find a cure that works.

AVERSION THERAPY AND INDUSTRIAL PROBLEMS If AA or some other group doesn't help an individual, perhaps hospitalization or **aversion therapy** will. In aversion therapy, drugs or other means are used to make drinking a painful or sickening experience. However, because of the drastic nature of the proposed cure, many experts regard aversion therapy with suspicion.

In a recent promising development, about 200 American companies have set up programs to help cure the alcoholics who work for them. Among those workers who have agreed to undergo treatment, two out of three have been cured.

Looking Back

Ethyl alcohol is the oldest and the most widely used drug. Alcohol is produced by fermentation, a natural process in which a yeast acts on the sugar in fruit juice or on grain broth and produces both alcohol and carbon dioxide. Beer is about 4 percent alcohol, wine about 12 percent, and hard liquor (produced by fermentation plus distillation) about 40 to 50 percent.

Alcohol has a long history of use as a preservative, a disinfectant, and an anesthetic. From past to present, alcohol has been used in place of polluted water and as a food preservative. In addition, alcohol has long been used in religious ceremonies and to mark other special occasions.

To many people the world over, an alcoholic beverage is part of mealtime. To social drinkers, moderate alcohol use is an enjoyable part of many social occasions. Problem drinkers, however, drink enough to cause trouble for themselves and for society. And alcoholics are unable to lead normal lives because of their addiction to alcohol.

No one knows for certain what causes alcoholism. But workers in the field insist that two-thirds of all alcoholics can be helped to give up drinking if they really want to, and if they keep trying until they find a cure that works for them.

Alcohol is a depressant that acts mainly on the brain. Alcohol reaches the brain by way of the bloodstream. The speed with which alcohol enters the bloodstream depends on the size of the drinker, the strength of the drink, and the presence or absence of food in the stomach. Once in the bloodstream, alcohol is changed by the liver—at the rate of ½ ounce (15 cubic centimeters) per hour—into a substance that the cells can burn for energy.

Any excess alcohol (over ½ ounce per hour) circulates in the blood and produces the effects of intoxication. By the time a drinker's blood alcohol level reaches .10 percent—4 ounces (120 cubic centimeters) of whiskey or 4 pints (nearly 2 liters) of beer can produce this level if absorbed quickly—the drinker's hearing, vision, reaction time, balance, and coordination are so badly affected that some states consider him or her legally "under the influence of alcohol" and, if driving, subject to arrest. However, even one drink masks a person's self-awareness that driving skills are becoming disorganized. So, a responsible social drinker does not drive when he or she has been drinking.

MODIFIED TRUE-FALSE QUESTIONS

1. _Methyl_ alcohol is drinkable alcohol.
2. _Isopropyl_ alcohol is used in rubbing alcohol.
3. Alcohol is _a new_ drug.
4. Fruit juice is turned into wine by _fermentation._
5. Yeasts act on sugar to produce alcohol and _oxygen._
6. _Disinfectants_ kill disease germs.
7. The alcoholic content of beer is about _10_ percent.
8. _Champagne_ is an example of hard liquor.
9. A bottle of 90 proof whiskey is about _30_ percent alcohol.
10. Alcohol, taken in large quantities, is _a stimulant._
11. In many states, if a driver's blood contains _one-tenth_ of 1 percent of alcohol, the driver is considered to be legally drunk.
12. When drunk outdoors, alcohol can be more harmful to the body on _a cold_ day than on a hot day.
13. Because alcohol contains no vitamins, its excessive use can contribute to _malnutrition._
14. Alcohol is absorbed largely by the blood vessels in the _stomach._
15. The process of eliminating alcohol from the body is begun in the _liver._
16. Alcoholism is _unrelated_ to a person's emotional health.
17. The sight and hearing centers of the brain are _stimulated_ by alcohol.

Alcohol and Health

18. Heavy drinking usually *enlarges* surface blood vessels.
19. Alcohol evaporates *slowly.*
20. Making the drinking of alcohol *painful* is one kind of therapy used in the treatment of alcoholism.

MATCHING QUESTIONS

Column A	Column B
1. delirium tremens	a. liver disease
2. cirrhosis	b. loss of memory
3. blackout	c. addicted to alcohol
4. alcoholic	d. painkiller
5. anesthetic	e. stomach disorder
	f. shaking and hallucinations

COMPLETION QUESTIONS

1. One drinker out of every _____ may become an alcoholic or problem drinker.
2. About _____ percent of fatal auto accidents involve drinking drivers.
3. Hard liquor is made by the process of fermentation followed by_____.
4. Alcoholic drinks contain _____ (few, many) Calories.
5. The larger the size of the drinker, the_____ is the absorption of alcohol.

MULTIPLE-CHOICE QUESTIONS

1. The oldest recorded form of drinkable alcohol is
   a. wine   b. beer   c. whiskey   d. rum
2. Which of the following is *not* a factor in becoming drunk?
   a. body size
   b. drinking on an empty stomach
   c. amount consumed
   d. time of day
3. Alcohol use and the crime rate are
   a. often related   c. unrelated
   b. always related   d. at an all-time low
4. When yeast is used to make wine, the alcohol formed is
   a. allowed to escape   c. methyl alcohol
   b. kept   d. fermented
5. Alcohol is generally not used as a
   a. preservative   b. disinfectant   c. anesthetic   d. flavoring

Decide About Drugs

THOUGHT QUESTIONS

1. At a party you are attending, your friends insist that you drink some whiskey. How can you go about refusing the drink and not risk being ridiculed?

2. List the reasons that adults give for drinking. List the reasons that young people give for drinking. Compare both lists for similarities and differences.

3. The Eighteenth Amendment to the Constitution outlawed the manufacture and sale of alcoholic beverages. Why was this amendment adopted in the first place, and why was it later repealed?

4. Using the library if necessary, find out how Alcoholics Anonymous works. Be concerned especially with these questions:

   a. How does an alcoholic get help?
   b. What is a typical program to fight alcoholism?
   c. Is the treatment lasting?

5. Why is alcoholism considered a disease?

Looking Ahead

In Chapter 21, we will take a look at other drugs and discuss some problems related to them. Once again, information will be provided to enable you to make some important decisions, if the question of drug usage arises.

Alcohol and Health

Chapter 21: Mind-Altering Drugs and Health

Each day, surgery saves lives that would once have been lost. And modern anesthetic drugs make modern surgery possible. In the years since World War II, modern "wonder drugs" like penicillin have saved thousands of lives. And we are confident that one day science will develop even more effective drugs to fight cancer and other diseases. In the last 20 years, drugs called **tranquilizers** (TRANG-kwuh-ly-zurz) have helped more mentally ill persons than ever before to return to normal life. The bright side of drug use is very bright indeed.

The dark side of drug use has, at times, seemed almost equally dark. During the fifties and sixties, illegal drug use (see Figure 21.1) spread like a plague through American cities, ruining thousands of young lives. As drug addicts turned to crime to support their habits, American homes and streets became less safe. As Americans now know, drugs can both save life and destroy it.

What Is a Mind-Altering Drug?

A **mind-altering drug** is a chemical that can change either the structure of cells—especially those of the brain—or the way in which they work, with a resultant change in mental perceptions. For example, **caffeine** (kaf-EEN), a substance in coffee, tea, and cola beverages, speeds up the work of cells in the brain and central nervous system; alcohol, on the other hand, slows it down. Drugs can not only powerfully affect cells, they can also poison them. When taken in excessive amounts, all drugs become poisons. Even an overdose of aspirin can be fatal.

DEPENDENCE AND ADDICTION   The use of a drug may lead to **drug dependence,** or **addiction.** A person may become psychologically dependent on a tranquilizer to provide relief from painful stress, for

348

Figure 21.1. A young life ruined by drugs.

example. As you may remember, a longtime smoker becomes physically dependent on nicotine; that is, the body cells gradually change the way they work in order to adjust to the presence of nicotine in the body. When a drug that produces physical dependence is withdrawn, moderate to severe withdrawal symptoms result. Addicts are so dependent, psychologically, physically, or both upon some substance that they are no longer able to lead normal lives.

DRUGS FIGHT ILLNESS AND CHANGE FEELINGS Primitive people, testing to see which plants could safely be used for food, must have found that certain plants could be used to fight illness and that certain other plants changed human feelings. Drugs made from plants and other sources are still used in the same ways. That is, some drugs are used as medicines. Among these are penicillin, which is prescribed as an infection fighter; aspirin, as a pain reliever; procaine, as an anesthetic; and ascorbic acid (vitamin C), as a substance the body needs.

Still other drugs, which act on the central nervous system (CNS), are used to change human feelings and behavior. Among these are chlorpromazine (thorazine), which is prescribed as a tranquilizer; amitriptyline (Elavil), as a mood elevator; and amphetamine, as a stimulant. Now as in the past, some people use CNS drugs to provide a brief escape from everyday reality.

Mind-Altering Drugs and Health   349

Drug Use in the Past

Do you remember the 5000-year-old clay tablets that mentioned beer (see page 330)? Some of those ancient tablets recommended that certain drugs be dissolved in beer and taken as medicine. As long ago as 400 B.C.—the time of Hippocrates, the founder of medicine—"the juice of the white poppy," or **opium** (OH-pee-um), was used to relieve pain (see Figure 21.2). Even today, **morphine** (MAWR-feen), which is made from opium, is the drug most widely used to relieve great pain.

YOUR PART

1. Choose several classmates to investigate and report to the class on the use of opium in Asian countries in the past.
2. Choose several classmates to investigate and report on which areas of the world grow and export opium today.

Are there similarities in the problems of opium production and use today and in the past? What? How has opium figured in the economic and political development of some of the countries investigated?

Figure 21.2. The white, or opium, poppy. Opium is made from juice oozing from cuts made in unripe seed capsules.

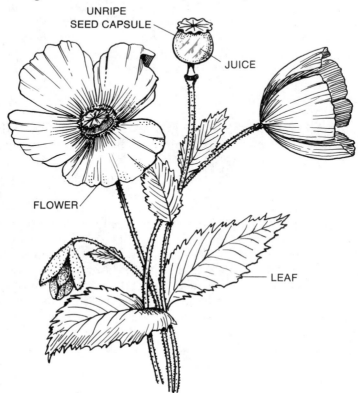

UNRIPE
SEED CAPSULE

JUICE

FLOWER

LEAF

IF YOU WANT YOUR CHILDREN TO BE HEALTHY & STRONG

GIVE THEM IRON BITTERS

Figure 21.3. Advertisement for an old-time patent medicine; the secret ingredient was a mind-altering drug.

As you may have learned from the activity reports, drug use has plagued many eras and many countries. In our own country, morphine and opium addiction were not uncommon a century ago. Scientists learned how to make morphine from opium in 1805. (Morphine is more powerful than opium.) In 1843, other scientists perfected the hypodermic needle. As a result, it became possible to relieve great pain by means of drug injections. Unfortunately, these developments also led to widespread morphine addiction.

THE SOLDIER'S DISEASE   During our Civil War (1860–1865), soldiers wounded in battle or suffering from the painful diarrhea of **dysentery** (DIS-un-ter-ee) were given injections of morphine. Quite innocently, many soldiers became drug addicts. In fact, morphine addiction came to be known as "the soldier's disease."

PATENT MEDICINES   During the same period, many ordinary citizens used opium regularly. **Laudanum** (LAWD-un-um), a preparation containing opium, was freely available. In addition, a number of **patent medicines** (see Figure 21.3) secretly contained laudanum or alcohol or both. (Patent medicines, also called proprietary drugs or over-the-counter drugs, are those that can be bought without a doctor's prescription.)

THE FIRST PROTECTIVE LAWS   Doctors and journalists campaigned against the secret ingredients in patent medicines. Finally, in 1906, Congress passed the first Pure Food and Drug Act, which required that ingredients like opium and alcohol must be listed on the labels of medicines containing them. In 1909, Congress made it illegal to import opium for other than medical purposes. And in 1914, Congress passed the Harrison Narcotic Act.

The Harrison Act regulates the importation, manufacture, distribution, and sale of **narcotic** (nahr-KAHT-ik), or sense-dulling, drugs like opium and **cocaine** (koh-KAYN) in any form. Since that time, all who buy or sell these drugs have been required by law to register, have a license, and keep records of all sales. And only doctors have since been allowed to prescribe preparations containing narcotics. Better laws and better education helped reduce drug addiction in the United States until the 1950's, when drug use again began to rise.

YOUR PART

1. With your parents' permission, list in two columns all of the medicines in your home. In one column, list all the prescription drugs along with the dates on which they were prescribed. In the other column, list the over-the-counter drugs. Review your list with your parents. Together, you may decide to throw away some of the outdated medicines you found (refer again to rule 4, page 201).
2. During one evening, watch for over-the-counter drug ads on TV. List some of the promises the manufacturers make. Compare these modern promises with those made for the patent medicine in Figure 21.3. Write down your explanation for the differences between the old and new ads.

The old patent medicines were usually advertised as cure-alls. Modern drug ads promise less. Did you explain this difference by saying that modern "truth-in-advertising" laws require modern ads to be somewhat more honest and detailed than ads in the past?

Chemical Analysis

Ancient peoples didn't know just which ingredients in plants cured them, soothed them, or put them to sleep. In fact, nobody knew until about 100 years ago. Then, chemists learned how to *analyze*, or break down, plant and animal substances so as to discover what ingredients they contained. As a result, today's chemists can make both *natural drugs* (from plant and animal sources) and *synthetic* (sin-THET-ik) *drugs* (by combining chemicals in the laboratory). That is why so many drugs are available today that were unknown a century ago.

Decide About Drugs

Table 21.1: The Most Commonly Abused Drugs

Drug	Slang Name	How Taken	Effects
Marijuana	Pot, grass, weed, hay, Mary Jane	By mouth or smoking	Slow reactions, hallucinations, change in moods, poor judgment
Hashish	Hash	By mouth or smoking	Same as for marijuana but more powerful
Lysergic acid diethylamide (LSD)	Acid, sugar, cubes, 25	By mouth	Possible chromosome damage, anxiety, hallucinations, possible insanity
Amphetamines	Uppers, ups, pep pills	By mouth	Decrease in appetite, irritability, high blood pressure, stimulation
Methedrine	Speed, crystal	By mouth or injection	Same as for amphetamines
Cocaine	Coke, C, snow	By mouth, sniffing, or injection	Stimulation, cessation of pain, decrease in appetite, sleeplessness, irritability
Barbiturates	Downers, downs, barbs, goofballs	By mouth	Sleepiness, depression, poor speech
Opium	Op, pen yan, tar, black stuff	By mouth or smoking	Decrease in appetite, sleepiness, cessation of pain
Morphine	M, Miss Emma, hard stuff, white stuff	By mouth or injection	Same as for opium, but more powerful
Heroin	H, horse, Harry, smack, junk	By mouth, sniffing, or injection	Same as for opium and morphine, but more powerful
Phencyclidine (PCP)	Angel dust, peace	By mouth, smoking, or sniffing	Slow reactions, poor speech, loss of memory, hallucinations, nausea, unconsciousness, possible brain damage and insanity

The Most Commonly Abused Drugs

Table 21.1 shows the drugs most commonly *abused* (used illegally or in a way that endangers health) today. Scientists divide these drugs (by their effects on the central nervous system, or CNS) into four groups: **hallucinogens** (huh-LOO-suh-nuh-junz), **stimulants, depressants,** and **narcotics.** Hallucinogens are also called **psychedelic** (sy-kuh-DEL-ik) drugs.

LEGAL CLASSIFICATIONS   Legal classifications are sometimes different from scientific classifications. For example, drug control laws often classify marijuana as a narcotic. Scientifically speaking, however, marijuana is a mild hallucinogen. Since drug law classifications vary, the following discussion will use scientific drug classifications.

FOUR KINDS OF CNS DRUGS   Hallucinogens produce hallucinations. That is, hallucinogens like LSD and marijuana can make people see, hear, smell, or taste things that are not really there. Even when no hallucinations are produced, people's senses are affected so that the world looks strange and different. Time and space seem to stretch or shrink. And people themselves feel different from their everyday selves.

A stimulant like caffeine, as you may remember, speeds up the workings of the brain and other parts of the central nervous system.

A depressant like alcohol, on the other hand, slows down the workings of the brain and central nervous system. Tranquilizers, which help calm and relax people, are usually depressants. So are **sedatives** (SED-uh-tivz), which help people to relax and sleep.

Narcotics in moderate doses relieve great pain and produce deep sleep. Morphine and **codeine** (KOH-deen), for example, are widely used for these purposes. In poisonous doses, narcotics produce stupor (numbness, unawareness of what is going on around one), coma (deep unconsciousness), convulsions, and death. At present, **heroin** (HER-uh-win) is the most commonly abused narcotic.

Let's Pause for Review

Drugs are chemicals that can change cell structure or function, as well as mental perceptions. Drugs make lifesaving surgery possible, fight infection, and supply needed substances.

Some people may use drugs that affect the central nervous system (CNS drugs) to change their feelings and the way their senses work. CNS drugs are of four types: hallucinogens produce hallucinations; stimulants speed up the workings of the CNS; depressants slow down the workings of the CNS; and narcotics relieve pain and produce deep sleep or stupor.

Figure 21.4. The Indian
hemp plant, source of
marijuana and hashish.

The Most Commonly Used Hallucinogen

Millions of Moslems and East Indians use drugs derived from the Indian
hemp plant. These drugs are **marijuana** (mar-uh-WAHN-uh) and **hashish**
(HASH-eesh). Like alcohol, the hemp drugs cause more problems in some
societies than in others. In North Africa, for example, where hashish is
heavily used, it causes problems like those we have with alcoholism in the
United States.

The scientific name for the Indian hemp plant is **Cannabis** (KAN-uh-
bis) (see Figure 21.4). Its active ingredient is **tetrahydrocannabinol** (tet-
ruh-HY-druh-kuh-NAB-uh-nawl), or THC, which is found in the flowering tops and leaves of the female plant. In marijuana (the Mexican name
for both the plant and the drug), which is made by drying the flowering tops
and leaves, the THC is less concentrated than in hashish, which is made by
drying the saplike resin of the plant. Because it is stronger than marijuana,
hashish is the more dangerous and troublesome of the two hemp drugs.

Why do people use marijuana?

Most people who use marijuana do so, in part, because it is the drug some
of their friends use. The drug affects different people in different ways. But,
like alcohol, marijuana can change the way people see, hear, and otherwise experience reality. Again like alcohol, marijuana provides a brief
escape from everyday reality. Unfortunately, as with alcohol, some users
seek more than a brief escape.

Mind-Altering Drugs and Health   355

Does marijuana addict?

When a substance addicts, it causes dependence so great that its users can no longer lead normal lives. And when a substance addicts, its users feel such a strong need for more of the addicting substance that they can no longer control its use. Does marijuana use ever result in this kind of dependence? Researchers have not yet answered this question with certainty. At present, however, researchers believe that marijuana can cause psychological dependence, but not physical dependence. You may be able to read some recent research for yourself as you work on the following activity:

YOUR PART

1. Investigate and report to the class on the results of longtime marijuana use. Ask the librarian for help in finding information. Use the *Reader's Guide* to find newsmagazine reports of recent studies.
2. Investigate and report to the class on the penalties for marijuana possession and sale in your state and in other states.
3. As a class, discuss the findings reported on.

Your reports and discussions probably turned up two important facts. First, in some states marijuana sale or possession is still a crime as serious as the sale or possession of narcotics. Yet marijuana does not relieve great pain and produce deep sleep or stupor, as narcotics do. And marijuana probably does not cause physical dependence.

Second, a great deal remains to be learned about the results of marijuana use. Experts disagree, findings conflict, and a great many questions have never been investigated at all.

If they are honest with themselves, marijuana users must face two facts:

1. In states where users are subject to criminal arrest, they may acquire a criminal record that will dog them for life.
2. Marijuana use may have harmful effects that are as yet unknown (see Figure 21.5).

The Most Powerful Hallucinogen

Discovered by accident in 1938, **LSD,** or **lysergic** (lye-SUR-jik) **acid diethylamide** (dye-eth-uh-LAM-eyd), comes from **ergot** (ER-gut), a fun-

Figure 21.5. Does this effect seem harmful to you?

gus that grows on rye. LSD is a hundred times more powerful than marijuana. An ounce (about 30 grams) of LSD would be enough to produce hallucinations in 300,000 people.

At first, LSD had many defenders. It was used to fight alcoholism and drug addiction. It was praised as a medicine. Like morphine and heroin, LSD was originally thought to be both harmless and medically helpful. LSD seemed to enrich experience, allowing people to see themselves and the world in what they thought was a truer, deeper, and more vivid way.

LSD hallucinations can be unusually pleasant—for example, when music seems to have vivid color. But they can be full of horror, too. On "bad trips," many people panic. Some even kill themselves. Others end up in the psychiatric wards of hospitals (see Figure 21.6, page 358). LSD has come to be recognized as a harmful drug.

An LSD user can go on a "repeat trip," or flashback, up to two years after last taking the drug, so LSD's effects can be long-lasting. Therefore, the mental illness produced in some people by LSD may be more or less permanent. What is more, the children of LSD users show evidence of more birth defects than do the children born to people who have not used the drug.

DMT

DMT, or **dimethyltryptamine** (dy-meth-ul-TRIP-tuh-meen), is a hallucinogen found in the seeds of various West Indian and South American plants. Like LSD and other hallucinogens, DMT produces physical dis-

Mind-Altering Drugs and Health

Figure 21.6. A young
girl, hospitalized
after a bad LSD trip.

comfort (dizziness, weakness, upset stomach) as well as hallucinations. DMT's effects usually last for about three hours. By contrast, LSD's effects may last as long as ten hours.

Mescaline and Psilocybin

Mescaline (MES-kuh-lun *or* MES-kuh-leen) comes from the buttons of the **peyote** (pay-OH-tee) **cactus.** This hallucinogen is used in religious ceremonies by some American Indians. Such use is legal. In Mexico, too, a plant hallucinogen—the drug **psilocybin** (sy-luh-SY-bun), found in certain mushrooms—is used in religious ceremonies. Like LSD, these strong plant hallucinogens make most users feel ill, besides providing them with long-lasting hallucinations (from 6 to 12 hours).

STP (DOM)

STP (Serenity, Tranquility, Peace) is a dangerous hallucinogen closely related to mescaline. Like LSD, STP sometimes kills its users. This is because STP, which begins by making it hard for the user to see, swallow, or breathe, may end by paralyzing the breathing mechanism completely. (The drug STP and the motor oil additive STP are two different things.) The chemical abbreviation for STP is **DOM**.

Decide About Drugs

PCP

PCP or **phencyclidine** (fen-SYK-luh-deen) is another drug that causes dangerous, often prolonged hallucinogenic effects in humans. Technically, however, PCP is a tranquilizer, often used by veterinarians to anesthetize large animals, such as gorillas.

PCP is very strong and unpredictable stuff. Even in moderate doses, it can produce hours of spaced-out feelings, visual distortions, and strange or frightening thoughts. The effects of larger doses can last for days, weeks, or months, and permanent brain damage and insanity are possible consequences. A recent official estimate cited PCP as the drug responsible for one-third of the yearly deaths from drug overdose in a large city on the West Coast.

PCP use is increasing dramatically, even though many of its users do not know what they are taking. Since PCP is a very inexpensive chemical to make, drug dealers often blend it with more expensive hallucinogens to increase their profits. Even when sold under its own name, PCP's relative cheapness makes it a tempting choice for addicted drug users.

Bad Stuff

During prohibition, illegally obtained liquor blinded and killed many people. Because there was no governmental regulation of the undercover liquor business, customers had no way of knowing what they were getting to drink. A similar problem with mind-altering drugs exists today. Every year, people die because they get hold of some "bad stuff." Only chemists can check on the purity and strength of LSD, DMT, or mescaline, for example.

Let's Pause for Review

Hallucinogens change the way people sense reality (see, hear, feel, taste, smell), and they usually produce hallucinations, as well. The hemp drugs (marijuana and hashish) are the world's most commonly used hallucinogens. Social customs affect their use.

It is believed that people become psychologically rather than physically dependent upon marijuana. Whether or not they become addicted depends on the answers to two questions: (1) Does the desire for marijuana ever become so strong that the user loses control over its use? (2) Does marijuana use ever keep its user from leading a normal life? If the answers are no in every case, then marijuana does not addict. But the answers in some cases may be yes. Science as yet knows little about the hemp drugs. Users must face the fact that marijuana may be harmful in ways not yet known. Moreover, at present, users in some states are subject to arrest.

LSD, the most powerful hallucinogen, is now known to have very harmful effects. LSD may cause birth defects, and its use leads in some cases to death or permanent mental illness.

Like LSD, other hallucinogens such as DMT, mescaline, psilocybin and PCP, make most users dizzy, weak, and sick to their stomachs, as well as providing them with hallucinations. STP is one hallucinogen that sometimes kills its user by respiratory paralysis.

Stimulants

What is the world's most widely used stimulant? If you answered caffeine—in coffee, tea, and cola drinks—you were right. Since they speed the workings of the brain and other parts of the central nervous system, stimulants in small to moderate amounts make people feel more alert and wide awake. They may be used medically to ward off fatigue and mental depression.

AMPHETAMINES　　The most commonly abused stimulants are the **amphetamines** (am-FET-uh-meenz). Because, at first, they make a person feel alert and self-confident, amphetamines are called "uppers" and pep pills. Additional effects are rapid, unclear speech, a rapid pulse, trembling hands, nervousness, restlessness, excitability, and sleeplessness. Large doses can even produce hallucinations.

Some athletes, entertainers, and long-distance truck drivers may take amphetamines to get themselves "up" to do their work. Complete exhaustion often results, because with amphetamines masking fatigue, people can easily push themselves to the point of collapse.

Tolerance and Overdose
Amphetamines are dangerous on two counts. First of all, amphetamine users often develop not only physical dependence on, but also tolerance for, the drug. *Tolerance* means that the human body adapts so well to the presence of a drug that larger and larger doses must be taken to produce the original effects. Such large doses are poisonous, and they damage the central nervous system.

The second danger results from the use of **Methedrine** (METH-uh-dreen), also called **methamphetamine** (meth-am-FET-uh-meen), *speed*, and *crystal*. Methedrine is the most powerful and dangerous of the amphetamines. As with STP, an overdose of methedrine sometimes kills the people who take it.

COCAINE　　**Cocaine** comes from the leaves of the South American *coca bush*. The dried leaves are chewed by the native people. Drug users sniff purified cocaine crystals so that the drug is absorbed through the mucous membranes of the nose.

Persons taking cocaine first experience a burst of energy and good feeling. Soon, however, they are likely to feel shaky, restless, excited, and irritable. Large doses can produce intoxication like that received from hemp drugs. These feelings sometimes lead to violent behavior on the part of the users of cocaine and other stimulants.

In this connection, a distinction about violent behavior should be made. The violent behavior of some stimulant users is a direct result of the properties of the drug itself. Narcotics addicts, on the other hand, may commit violent crimes in order to pay for their drugs, but such violence is not a direct result of the action of narcotics on their bodies (see page 362).

Depressants

Sedatives and tranquilizers are the two main types of depressants. Both promote relaxation, but doctors prescribe tranquilizers mainly to calm and relax people during their waking hours. Sedatives, on the other hand, are more often prescribed to bring on sleep.

Alcohol is the most commonly abused depressant, but **barbiturates** (bahr-BIT-chur-its) are the most commonly abused of the sedative-type depressants. Most barbiturate preparations have names ending in al (Nembutal, Seconal, Amytal). As you may remember (see Table 21.1, page 353), barbiturates artificially induce sleepiness, with resultant depression and poor speech. So barbiturate use should be temporary, except for conditions like epilepsy (see page 428).

Barbiturates can produce psychological and physical dependence, plus tolerance. Therefore, barbiturates should always be used under medical supervision. Otherwise, addiction can develop. Furthermore, because the body learns to tolerate barbiturates, more and more pills must be taken to achieve the original effect. Addicts have been known to take as many as 50 sleeping pills a day.

A person taking large doses of barbiturates may seem intoxicated. Speech, walk, coordination, judgment, and memory are usually affected. Instead of becoming calmer, the user may well become restless, excited, disoriented, aggressive, and delirious. Often, the barbiturate user may begin to take amphetamines, as well, to counteract each morning's barbiturate hangover.

BARBITURATE DEATHS   Barbiturates kill more people than heroin does. Each year, some 3000 people commit suicide by swallowing barbiturates. Others kill themselves accidentally because they can't remember how many pills they have already taken. Still others die accidentally when they take barbiturates after drinking a good deal of alcohol. In addition, withdrawal from barbiturates and other depressants is much more danger-

Figure 21.7. Without tranquilizers, this group of mental patients might not be able to discuss their problems with the doctor (with papers on her lap).

ous than withdrawal from narcotics, and should not be attempted without medical supervision.

TRANQUILIZERS Tranquilizers, so useful in the treatment of mental illness (see Figure 21.7), can be abused like any other drug. Many people fail to realize that they can teach themselves to relax and that, normally, daily exercise is the most healthful tranquilizer. Such people may easily become psychologically dependent on tranquilizers—afraid to face any tense situation without first taking a pill.

Unfortunately, physical dependence and tolerance can develop when tranquilizers are abused. Large doses can produce drowsiness, confusion, double vision, and memory loss. As with alcohol, drivers under the influence of tranquilizers cause accidents. What is more, the combination of tranquilizers and alcohol can be fatal.

Narcotics

Narcotics relieve great pain and produce deep sleep and, in large doses, stupor. The major narcotics are opium, morphine, and heroin. Morphine and heroin are **opiates** (OH-pee-uts *or* OH-pee-ayts), which means that they are made from opium.

As you have read, opium itself has been used for more than 20 centuries. Charles Dickens and other writers have described opium addicts in their works. Opium is still responsible for widespread addiction in Asia (see Figure 21.8). Morphine, which is ten times more powerful than opium, is extracted from raw opium. Heroin, which is three times more powerful than morphine, is made from morphine by a complicated chemical process.

Since they are more powerful than opium, morphine and heroin are more addicting, too. Yet, when originally developed, both of these opiates

362   **Decide About Drugs**

were believed to be safe, nonaddicting drugs that could be used to fight addiction to other drugs. Actually, morphine and heroin can produce physical dependence and addiction in a period of a few weeks.

What is more, tolerance for opiates develops to a greater degree than for any other drugs. An addict can generally tolerate a dose that would be fatal to a nonuser—up to an amount 50 times greater than a normally fatal dose. Thus, many addicts, in their ever-increasing need for drugs, are forced to turn to crime.

Needing at least $30 a day, or $11,000 a year, to buy drugs, an addict must steal about $50,000 in merchandise yearly (see Figure 21.9, page 364). An addict knows that withdrawal will cause extreme sickness for two or three days; nevertheless, the addict sometimes volunteers to go through withdrawal in order to reduce the body's tolerance and get the habit back to a size he or she can afford.

Many heroin addicts die young. But even when they don't, their existence is a kind of living death in which nothing matters but obtaining and using drugs. The danger of overdose is always present. Dealers mix heroin with other substances, such as lactose (milk sugar), so that a user never knows the drug's strength. In addition, dirty needles used to inject heroin often cause infection, tetanus, and *hepatitis* (hep-uh-TY-tis), a sometimes fatal inflammation of the liver.

KINDS OF TREATMENT **Methadone** (METH-uh-dohn) is a synthetic, or artificially made, narcotic sometimes given to addicts in place of heroin. Supporters of methadone drug treatment centers say that addicts can thus avoid the dangers of infection and overdose, hold jobs, and otherwise live normal lives. But since methadone also addicts, critics of methadone treatment say that it merely substitutes one addicting drug for another.

Other drug treatment centers like Synanon (SIN-uh-nahn) use group discussion and support, as Alcoholics Anonymous does. At Synanon, ex-addicts live and work together in a group without using drugs of any kind. In addition, many hospitals offer supervision and treatment during withdrawal periods.

Figure 21.8. An opium den in the Philippines.

As we learned, there is some disagreement among experts about the best course of treatment for heroin and other forms of drug addiction. You may want to think more about the problem yourself and develop your own point of view. The following activity will help:

YOUR PART

1. One or more students in your class should investigate and report on methadone treatment for heroin addiction.
2. Now that you have heard the above report, what do you think of methadone treatment? As a class, compare and discuss your opinions.
3. Why do you think people risk their lives by using a "hard drug" like heroin? How do you think heroin use could be limited? Prevented? What about dangerous drugs like amphetamines and barbiturates? Why do people use these drugs? Can you think of any ways to reduce their use? As a class, compare and discuss your answers.
4. Have one class member record any recommendations made by the class for the treatment of addicts and the prevention of drug misuse.

Did you agree on any steps that might be taken? It's quite likely that you agreed that young people can be relied on to make intelligent decisions when they know the facts. Indeed, various studies and reports show that American young people have already turned away from dangerous drugs like LSD, STP, and the amphetamines, the dangers of which have been demonstrated. Saddened by the drug-related deaths of favorite recording, TV, movie, and stage performers, these young people seem less willing to experiment with unknown drugs that may endanger their own lives.

Figure 21.9. The high rate of theft for the sake of drugs has made it necessary for many people to live with barred windows like these.

Volatile Chemicals

A **volatile chemical,** such as airplane glue, paint thinner, gasoline, lighter fluid, or aerosol spray, changes readily into a gas, or vapor. When inhaled, the gas fumes from some of these chemicals produce intoxication. Unfortunately, such fumes can also damage the body in various ways. Airplane-glue sniffing, for example, can damage the brain, kidneys, liver, and bone marrow, and such damage may result in death.

Looking Back

Drugs can both save life and destroy it. Medically, drugs are used to fight infection, to relieve pain, to supply needed substances, and, as anesthetics, to make modern surgery possible.

People also use four types of drugs to change their feelings and the way their senses work. Hallucinogens produce hallucinations and alter the senses of sight, hearing, touch, taste, and smell. Stimulants speed up, whereas depressants slow down, the workings of the brain and other parts of the central nervous system. Narcotics relieve great pain, produce deep sleep or stupor, and, when used without medical supervision, can addict in days.

Drugs vary in their effects. Little is known, scientifically, about marijuana's long-term effects, a fact its users should face squarely. However, a number of drugs are known to be harmful. LSD can cause mental illness and death, as well as some birth defects. STP and PCP sometimes kill their users directly, as does the stimulant methamphetamine, or Methedrine (speed). The depressant barbiturates kill more people each year than do opiates.

People can become psychologically dependent on almost any drug. Users of amphetamines, barbiturates, and narcotics can also develop physical dependency (addiction) and tolerance, as well. When there is physical dependence or addiction, withdrawal is difficult and sometimes deadly. Withdrawal from barbiturate addiction, especially, should be undertaken only under medical supervision. Narcotic addiction dies hard. But some addicts have been helped by hospitalization, methadone treatment, or group treatment in places like Synanon.

MODIFIED TRUE-FALSE QUESTIONS

1. *Penicillin* is an example of a "wonder drug."
2. Alcohol *slows down* the activity of brain cells.

3. A drug prescribed by physicians to relieve great pain is _heroin._
4. Laudanum is a preparation containing _opium._
5. The first Pure Food and Drug Act was passed by Congress in _1945._
6. Drugs that come from plant and animal sources are called _synthetic._
7. Hallucinogenic drugs are also called _psychedelic_ drugs.
8. The two common hemp drugs are marijuana and _cocaine._
9. _All_ of marijuana's harmful effects are known.
10. In certain cases, some _narcotic_ drugs may be obtained legally on physicians' prescriptions.
11. Examples of hallucinogenic drugs are PCP and _marijuana._
12. Drugs that speed up body processes are referred to as _depressants._
13. Tolerance results in the _increasing_ use of a drug.
14. The most commonly abused sedative drugs are _barbiturates._
15. Drugs used in the treatment of mental illness are called _depressants._
16. Morphine is extracted from _heroin._
17. A drug used in the treatment of heroin addiction is _Seconal._
18. Sniffing airplane glue is a _harmless_ practice.
19. _Amphetamines_ are examples of pep pills.
20. The most widely used stimulant is _caffeine._

MATCHING QUESTIONS, GROUP 1

Column A	Column B
1. Indian hemp plant	a. mescaline
2. ergot	b. psilocybin
3. peyote cactus	c. cocaine
4. mushrooms	d. Nembutal
5. coca bush	e. LSD
	f. hashish

MATCHING QUESTIONS, GROUP 2

Column A	Column B
1. narcotic	a. needed by healthy people
2. stimulant	b. calms and relaxes people during waking hours
3. depressant	
4. hallucinogen	c. speeds up the work of the central nervous system
5. tranquilizer	
	d. slows down the work of the central nervous system
	e. distorts perception and judgment
	f. produces deep sleep periods and relieves pain

Decide About Drugs

COMPLETION QUESTIONS

1. Addiction means _____ on drugs.
2. CNS refers to the _____ .
3. The founder of modern medicine is the Greek physician _____ .
4. A proprietary drug is also called a (an) _____ .
5. The _____ Act regulates the importation, manufacture, distribution, and sale of narcotic drugs.
6. Scientifically, marijuana is classified as a (an) _____ drug.
7. Drugs that help a person to relax and sleep are called _____ .
8. An unawareness of one's surroundings brought on by large doses of narcotics is referred to as _____ .
9. The active ingredient in the Indian hemp plant is _____ .
10. Marijuana may cause _____ dependence.

MULTIPLE-CHOICE QUESTIONS

1. Distortion of time, space, and distance is most closely associated with the use of
   a. hallucinogens
   b. stimulants
   c. depressants
   d. narcotics
2. Diminished response to a drug and the need to increase its dose is called
   a. tolerance
   b. habit
   c. abuse
   d. addiction
3. One of the meanings of drug abuse is
   a. buying a patent medicine without a doctor's advice
   b. not buying a drug prescribed by a doctor
   c. selling a drug illegally
   d. taking a drug illegally
4. Marijuana generally does *not*
   a. cause hallucinations
   b. affect judgment
   c. release inhibitions
   d. produce sleep
5. Among the common groups of hallucinogenic drugs are
   a. morphine, codeine, heroin
   b. mescaline, LSD, DMT
   c. Seconal, Nembutal, Amytal
   d. cocaine, opium, Methedrine
6. LSD is
   a. a weak hallucinogenic drug
   b. no different in action from other hallucinogenic drugs
   c. stronger than other hallucinogenic drugs
   d. a narcotic
7. Barbiturates are commonly known as
   a. sleeping pills
   b. uppers
   c. stimulants
   d. hallucinogens

8. Addicts
   a. can learn how to use drugs without harming themselves
   b. must continue drug taking to prevent withdrawal symptoms
   c. can get off drugs any time they wish without any difficulty
   d. take drugs only on rare occasions
9. Which of the following phrases most closely describes drug addicts?
   a. very concerned with others
   b. generally have healthy appetites
   c. will go to great lengths to obtain needed drugs
   d. care about their physical condition
10. Which of the following terms is *not* associated with drug abuse?
    a. psychological dependence   c. addiction
    b. physical dependence   d. adequate nutrition

THOUGHT QUESTIONS

1. What purposes do drugs serve when prescribed by physicians?
2. List five ways in which you might tell if someone is under the influence of drugs. Name the drug in each case.
3. Describe at least four risks involved in the misuse of drugs.
4. In what type of situation would a doctor prescribe *(a)* narcotics? *(b)* depressants? *(c)* stimulants?
5. Suppose, near your school, you are approached by a stranger who offers to get you all the drugs you want. The stranger also mentions the names of several of your friends as good customers.

   a. What should be your answer to this individual?
   b. What should you tell your friends?
   c. Should you notify school authorities?

   In every case, defend your answer.
6. Why are drug problems worldwide rather than restricted to the United States?

Looking Ahead

In Chapters 22, 23, and 24, you will read about the age-old fight against diseases other than those brought on by drug abuse. You will study the causes of these diseases, as well as prevention and cure. And because regular medical examinations play a part in the fight against disease, you will be taken step by step through the medical examination of a young person about your age.

Decide About Drugs

Unit Eight: PROTECT YOURSELF AGAINST DISEASE

The age-old fight against disease has been most successful in the last 100 years. In 1900, diseases that could be transmitted (passed from person to person), such as diphtheria, smallpox, typhoid fever, and cholera (KAHL-uh-ruh), were the leading cause of death. Only 30 years ago, polio epidemics forced young people to stay away from movies, swimming pools, and dances. Only 15 years ago, measles continued to deafen, cripple, or kill some of its victims.

But today in the United States and in other developed countries, all of these diseases, and more, seem to have been conquered. The next three chapters trace this modern progress against disease. Other coming chapters will also help you understand the part you and your community have to play in maintaining this progress. For example, although venereal diseases like syphilis (SIF-uh-lis) and gonorrhea (gahn-uh-REE-uh) can be cured, these diseases are still widespread because they often go untreated.

In addition, diseases like heart disease and cancer kill and disable more people than in past years. Are there steps you can take to protect yourself from these and similar diseases? In some cases the answer is yes. The coming chapters will discuss how individuals and communities may be able to prevent, cure, or reduce suffering from the diseases we still have with us.

Chapter 22: Fighting Communicable Diseases

"What does the word *disease* mean to you?" Ms. Bailey asked, as Maria's health class began its study of disease.

"A fever is a disease," said Godfrey. "So is a headache."

"No they aren't," Maria said. "Headache and fever are signs, or symptoms, that something is wrong with your health. Diseases are things like measles and mumps."

"That's right," Ms. Bailey said. "Can you think of some more examples?"

As class members named more diseases, Ms. Bailey listed them on the board:

measles	tuberculosis	epilepsy
mumps	the common cold	gonorrhea
pellagra	diabetes	lung cancer
appendicitis	syphilis	smallpox
chicken pox	beriberi	polio
arthritis	heart disease	alcoholism

"Those aren't all diseases, are they?" Maria asked.

"Yes, they are," Godfrey said. "They just aren't all the same kind."

YOUR PART

1. The list that the class made contains two main kinds of disease. Can you figure out what they are? When you figure them out, make two lists on your paper from the one list that the class made. Label your two lists.
2. As a class, compare lists.

Table 22.1: Familiar Communicable and Noncommunicable Diseases

Disease	Cause
Communicable	
African sleeping sickness	Protozoan
Amebic dysentery	Protozoan
Athlete's foot	Fungus
Cold	Virus
Diphtheria	Bacterium
German measles	Virus
Gonorrhea	Bacterium
Hepatitis	Virus
Hookworm	Roundworm
Infectious mononucleosis	Virus
Influenza	Virus
Malaria	Protozoan
Measles	Virus
Mumps	Virus
Pneumonia	Bacterium or virus
Poliomyelitis	Virus
Rabies	Virus
Ringworm	Fungus
Rocky Mountain spotted fever	Rickettsia
Scarlet fever	Bacterium
Smallpox	Virus
Syphilis	Bacterium
Tapeworm	Flatworm
Tetanus	Bacterium

As you probably noted, people can catch measles, mumps, chicken pox, tuberculosis, the common cold, syphilis, gonorrhea, smallpox, and polio from one another. Such "catching" diseases, or diseases that can be transmitted, are also called **communicable, contagious** (kun-TAY-jus), and **infectious** (in-FEK-shus). On the other hand, diseases such as pellagra, appendicitis, arthritis, diabetes, beriberi, heart disease, epilepsy, lung cancer, and alcoholism are not passed from person to person. Such diseases are called **noncommunicable, noncontagious,** and **noninfectious** (see Table 22.1).

Some noncommunicable diseases, such as pellagra and diabetes, are also known as **deficiency diseases,** which are caused by the lack of some necessary substance. The other noncommunicable diseases shown in Table 22.1 are also called **chronic** (KRAHN-ik) **diseases,** which means that they can continue for a long time.

Protect Yourself Against Disease

Table 22.1 (concluded)

Disease	Cause
Communicable (continued)	
Trichinosis	Roundworm
Tuberculosis	Bacterium
Typhoid fever	Bacterium
Typhus fever	Rickettsia
Venereal herpes	Virus
Noncommunicable	
Allergies	Pollen or other protein substances
Cancer	Chemicals, radiation, possible other causes
Cerebral palsy	Nervous system damage very early in life
Diabetes	Undersecretion of insulin
Epilepsy	Inflammation or injury of brain
Heart disease	Damage by some infection, advancing age, excess cholesterol, possible other causes
Hemophilia	Heredity
Multiple sclerosis	Unknown
Pellagra	Lack of niacin and protein
Sickle-cell anemia	Heredity

Why Some Diseases Are Communicable

In communicable diseases, tiny living creatures called **microorganisms** invade the body. There they multiply and attack cells of various types, making us sick. Some give off poisonous wastes, or **toxins** (TAHK-sinz), as they multiply, and these poisons make us sick. Such disease-producing microorganisms, commonly called **germs**, are passed from person to person. Noncommunicable diseases, on the other hand, have a wide variety of causes not involving microorganisms.

Many microorganisms are helpful rather than harmful. Micro-organisms of every kind live all around us in great numbers—in the air, in water, in the soil, in our own bodies, and in the bodies of other living things. The following activities will help you learn how numerous and widespread these microorganisms are:

1. Ask your health teacher or librarian for help in listing some of the many helpful jobs that microorganisms do.
2. Yeast is a plantlike microorganism that is helpful in a number of ways. To see why yeast is used in making bread, do the following:

MATERIALS

Yeast (fresh or active), sugar, warm water, a teaspoon, a cup or other container.

PROCEDURE

a. Put 1 teaspoonful of sugar in a cup of warm water and stir until it is dissolved.
b. Add the yeast and stir until mixed.
c. Put the yeast mixture in a warm place for a half-hour.
d. At the end of a half-hour, look for the presence of bubbles.
e. Write down the answers to the following questions:

- Was some yeast left at the bottom of the container? If so, how can you account for this?
- Why did the yeast start to bubble (refer again to page 330)?
- Why does bread dough rise when yeast is added?
- Why is yeast used to make bread?

3. Microorganisms reproduce by dividing. Some germs divide every half-hour. At first, a single germ divides into two. Those two germs divide a half-hour later and become four. At this rate, how many germs will be present at the end of 12 hours?
4. As a class, compare your answers to steps 1, 2, and 3.

As you probably found, microorganisms living inside the large intestine help us manufacture at least one vitamin. Other helpful microorganisms enrich the soil, dispose of wastes, and help produce foods like bread and cheese.

You also observed that yeast, like other microorganisms, grows and multiplies when supplied with moisture, food, and water.

When you calculated, you found that a single germ could produce more than 16 million germs in a 12-hour period. You can easily see why the world is plentifully supplied with microorganisms.

Figure 22.1. Three shapes of bacteria.

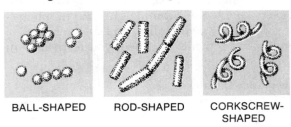

BALL-SHAPED   ROD-SHAPED   CORKSCREW-SHAPED

Figure 22.2. Drawing of an influenza virus.

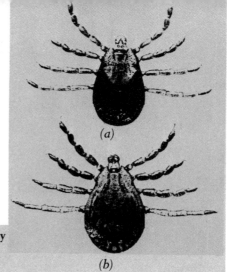

Figure 22.3. Ticks that carry Rocky Mountain spotted fever: (*a*) female; (*b*) male.

Six Kinds of Microorganisms

Bacteria (the singular is *bacterium*) are one-celled plantlike, nongreen microorganisms found everywhere in nature. Bacteria have three main shapes: they are ball-shaped, rod-shaped, or spiral (corkscrew)-shaped. Though most bacteria are harmless, some ball-shaped forms cause strep throat and pneumonia, among other things. Some rod-shaped bacteria cause tuberculosis and typhoid fever, whereas a spiral-shaped bacterium causes syphilis (see Figure 22.1).

Viruses are the smallest disease agents known today. Bacteria can be seen only with a microscope. But viruses are so tiny that they can be seen only with the much more powerful electron microscope, which was not developed until 1932 (refer to Figure 22.6, page 377). Since that time, scientists have found ways of preventing both measles and polio, two virus-caused diseases. However, hundreds of other viruses continue to cause influenza, colds, and intestinal upsets the world over (see Figure 22.2).

Rickettsias (rih-KET-see-uz) are smaller than bacteria but larger than viruses. They cause diseases carried and spread by certain insects. Body lice, for instance, carry the rickettsias that cause typhus fever (not to be confused with typhoid fever, caused by bacteria), and ticks carry rickettsias that cause Rocky Mountain spotted fever (see Figure 22.3).

Fungi (FUN-jy) or **funguses** (FUNG-guh-sez), like bacteria, are plantlike organisms. Some fungi, like those that cause athlete's foot and ringworm of the scalp, can be harmful. Other fungi, like mushrooms, yeasts, and molds, are useful to human beings.

Protozoa (proh-tuh-ZOH-uh) are one-celled animallike organisms. Of the estimated 20,000 different kinds of protozoa, only a few are known to cause disease. Malaria and amebic (uh-MEE-bik) dysentery are two of these (see Figure 22.4, page 376).

Fighting Communicable Diseases

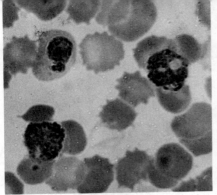

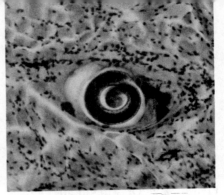

Figure 22.4. The protozoa that cause malaria are seen among the blood cells.

Figure 22.5. The roundworm that causes trichinosis.

Worms are many-celled animals. Some are microscopic, some larger. Worms such as tapeworms, hookworms, and roundworms are *parasites* (PAR-uh-syts). Parasites live on or in the bodies of other living things, using their food and destroying their tissues. For example, worms that live in the bodies of pigs cause the sometimes fatal disease trichinosis (trik-uh-NOH-sis) (see Figure 22.5). Thorough cooking destroys these worms, but people who eat meat from pigs (especially uncured pork) without cooking it thoroughly may take in live worms and later develop trichinosis.

YOUR PART

1. Choose several classmates to find out for the class what cooking temperature bacon, ham, and pork must reach in order to destroy the worm parasites they may contain.
2. Investigate and report to the class on the symptoms of trichinosis.

Because trichinosis is rarer nowadays than in the past, you may have been surprised to hear how severe its symptoms can be. Although you may not remember the exact temperature you need to use in cooking pork, you can easily remember to check the temperature recommended in a good cookbook whenever you cook pork.

Let's Pause for Review

The two main kinds of disease are communicable and noncommunicable. Communicable diseases are caused by invading microorganisms that are passed from person to person. Bacteria and viruses cause many communicable diseases. Viruses, for example, cause the many kinds of colds and influenza. Certain rickettsias, fungi, protozoa, and worms also cause communicable diseases.

Protect Yourself Against Disease

From Leeuwenhoek to Pasteur

Suppose you had lived in George Washington's time. Even if you had been a doctor, you would not have known the real cause of communicable disease. Why? In part, because microorganisms are too small to be seen without a microscope. But the microscope had been invented by Washington's time (see Figure 22.6). In 1676, Anton van Leeuwenhoek (LAY-vun-huhk), the famous naturalist (see Figure 22.7, page 378), had used his microscope to look at the "tiny animals" (protozoa) no one had ever seen before. And in 1683, he discovered bacteria. However, the connection between bacteria and disease was not established until 150 years later when the great Pasteur first guessed, then proved, that certain microorganisms cause disease (Figure 22.7). For a brief look at the history of communicable disease, do the following investigations:

YOUR PART

1. Divide your class into several discussion groups that will investigate and report on:

   a. The careers of Anton van Leeuwenhoek, Edward Jenner, Louis Pasteur, Joseph Lister, and Robert Koch.
   b. Bubonic plague (the Black Death), cholera epidemics, and typhus epidemics (see page 15).

2. Select one of your classmates to read to the class descriptive excerpts from Daniel Defoe's *Journal of the Plague Year* and Albert Camus's *The Plague*.

Figure 22.6. Microscopes: *(left)* **new;** *(right)* **old.**

Figure 22.7. Two important men in the fight against disease; *(below)* Anton van Leeuwenhoek; *(right)* Louis Pasteur.

As you heard in the reports of your classmates, the Black Death killed at least a fourth of Europe's people during the 14th century. Because microorganisms were unknown, people in ages past fought diseases in hundreds of useless ways. They used witchcraft against disease, wore charms to ward off evil spirits, and closed their windows against the "dangerous" night air.

Weapons Against Disease

But in the past two centuries, health scientists have made great progress in the fight against communicable disease. Many **epidemics** (outbreaks of disease affecting many people at once) and **pandemics** (worldwide outbreaks of disease) have been checked (see pages 18–19). This great progress was made possible by a growing knowledge of the real causes of communicable disease.

VACCINATION   Dr. Jenner's work with smallpox (see Table 22.3, page 382) illustrates one method of fighting communicable disease. During Dr. Jenner's time, dairymaids and other farm workers often caught a mild disease called **cowpox** from the animals in their care. These farm workers never developed smallpox, the serious, often fatal, form of the disease that most people caught.

So Dr. Jenner made a vaccine (from *vacca*, the Latin word for cow) with material taken from the sores of infected cows. He used his vaccine to give people cowpox. Like people today, the boy who got the first smallpox shot developed a sore arm, nothing more (see Figure 22.8, page 380). Later, when injected with smallpox microorganisms, the boy stayed well. The vaccine made from a milder form of the same disease had kept him safe from, or immune (im-YUHN) to, smallpox.

How Vaccinations Work   Unlike smallpox, most diseases don't have a milder form like cowpox from which an immunizing vaccine can be made. However, scientists have been able to make vaccines from weakened or killed disease germs (see Table 22.2). Scientists have also been able to weaken the toxins given off by germs and to use these weakened toxins, called **toxoids** (TAHK-soydz), to make immunizing substances. How do weakened germs or toxins make people immune? They do so by stimulating the human organism to produce **antibodies**.

Antibodies   Antibodies are proteins that circulate in the blood for months, for years, or for life. Like white blood cells, antibodies destroy invading disease germs. As long as they are present in the blood, antibodies provide protection against the specific germ that caused them to develop.

Polio antibodies, for example, protect you only against polio, not against influenza or smallpox. In addition, polio antibodies—developed in

Table 22.2:   Types of Vaccines

Disease	Vaccine
Bubonic plague	Dead plague bacteria
Cholera	Dead cholera bacteria
Diphtheria	Toxoid (weakened toxin of diphtheria bacteria)
German measles	Live German measles viruses
Influenza	Dead influenza viruses
Measles	Weakened, live measles viruses
Mumps	Weakened, live mumps viruses
Polio	Weakened, live polio viruses or dead viruses
Rabies	Weakened, live rabies viruses
Smallpox	Live cowpox viruses
Tetanus	Toxoid (weakened toxin of tetanus bacteria)
Typhoid fever	Dead typhoid bacteria
Typhus fever	Dead typhus rickettsias
Whooping cough	Dead whooping cough bacteria
Yellow fever	Weakened, live yellow fever viruses*

*This vaccine is now considered unreliable. At present, the best means of combating yellow fever is mosquito control.

Fighting Communicable Diseases

response to the Salk and Sabin polio vaccines (see Table 22.3, page 382)—last a lifetime, once a child has received the original vaccine series and an additional booster on entering school. Tetanus antibodies, on the other hand, don't last as long. In such cases, booster shots must be given from time to time in order to stimulate the body's production of more antibodies.

YOUR PART

1. Make a list of the immunizations (also called vaccinations, inoculations, and shots) you think you have received.
2. Now list those communicable diseases (like chicken pox) that you have actually had. (You are probably still immune to most of them.)
3. Do you think you have any natural immunities? If so, list them, too.
4. At home this evening, go over all three lists with a parent or guardian to make sure you have left nothing out. (Save your lists to use again as you read Chapter 23.)

IMMUNITY Did you find that you are immune to a long list of diseases? Immunity may be **acquired** (by having shots or by having the disease) or **inherited** (natural). If you are a hiker, you may have seen natural immunity at work. A group of your friends may have hiked through a wood without most of them being affected by the poison oak, ivy, or

Figure 22.8. Dr. Jenner giving the first smallpox vaccination.

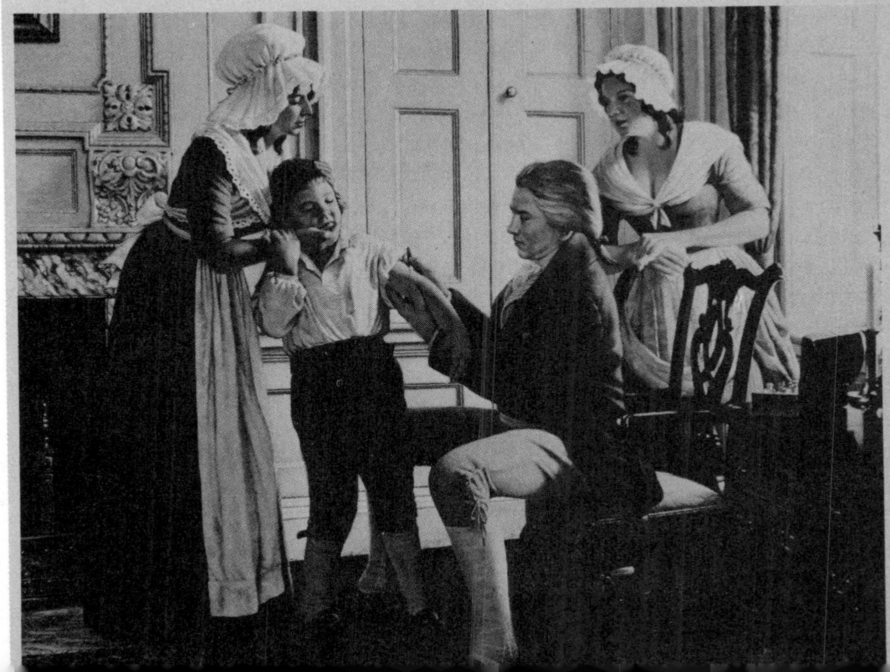

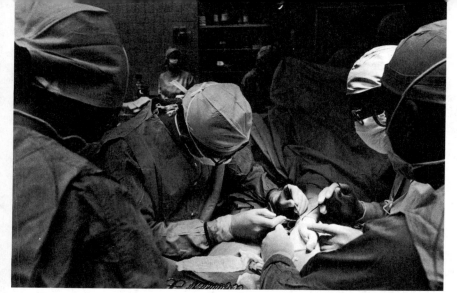

Figure 22.9. Cleanliness, sterilized instruments, and chemicals in the operating room keep the patient safe from infection.

sumac they may have touched. Why? Because many people, especially in youth, have a natural immunity to these poisons.

Remember, too, that immunity may or may not be permanent. If you think you may need one or more booster shots, check with your doctor to see whether you need additional immunizations. Local public health departments often provide low-cost immunizations.

HEAT AND ANTISEPTICS   Pasteur, you will remember, used vaccination against anthrax (refer again to page 9). He also killed germs with heat (pasteurization). And little more than a hundred years ago, the English surgeon Joseph Lister (see Table 22.3, page 382) discovered a third weapon against germs. He was the first to use a chemical germ killer, or antiseptic, against microorganisms.

Before Lister's time, infected wounds killed more soldiers in wartime than any other cause. All too often, surgical patients also died of infection. As he thought about Pasteur's work, Lister decided that germs might cause these fatal infections. So he tried using *carbolic acid*, a strong chemical, as an antiseptic. He cleaned a wound with carbolic acid and the expected infection never developed. Lister went on to make surgery safer through the use of antiseptics in the operating room (see Figure 22.9).

CHEMOTHERAPY   Paul Ehrlich, a German health scientist born 25 years after Lister, is often called the father of **chemotherapy** (kee-moh-THER-uh-pee), a word which means the treatment and control of disease by chemical means. Like Lister, Ehrlich wanted to find a chemical that would kill germs. But Ehrlich wanted a chemical that would work inter-

Fighting Communicable Diseases   381

Table 22.3: Pioneers in Fighting Disease

Name	Date	Country	Discovery
Behring, Emil von	1854–1917	Germany	Antitoxin for treating diphtheria.
Dick, George	1881–1967	U.S.A.	Test to determine immunity to scarlet fever.
Duggar, Benjamin	1872–1956	U.S.A.	Antibiotic: Aureomycin.
Ehrlich, Paul	1854–1915	Germany	Salvarsan 606 treatment for syphilis.
Enders, John	1897–	U.S.A.	Measles vaccine.
Fleming, Alexander	1881–1955	Scotland	Penicillin.
Jenner, Edward	1749–1823	England	Smallpox vaccine.
Koch, Robert	1843–1910	Germany	Identified the germ of tuberculosis. Proved that specific germs cause specific diseases. Developed method of growing and staining disease germs for laboratory identification.
Leeuwenhoek, Anton van	1632–1723	The Netherlands	Bacteria.
Lister, Joseph	1827–1912	England	Antiseptics.
Pasteur, Louis	1822–1895	France	Germ theory of disease. Proved that vaccination could provide immunity for certain diseases. Pasteurization.
Reed, Walter	1851–1902	U.S.A.	Mosquito-carried virus that causes yellow fever.
Sabin, Albert	1906–	U.S.A.	Polio vaccine (oral).
Salk, Jonas	1914–	U.S.A.	Polio vaccine (injection).
Schick, Béla	1877–1967	Hungary, U.S.A.	Test to determine immunity to diphtheria.
Waksman, Selman	1888–1973	U.S.A.	Antibiotic: streptomycin.

nally, not externally, in wounds. He was looking for what he called a "magic bullet," which would kill the germs that cause syphilis without harming the person who had the disease. To find out more about Ehrlich's work and about the history of chemotherapy, consult Table 22.3 and do the following investigations:

1. Choose several students to investigate and report on the development of the sulfa drugs.
2. Choose a classmate to report to the class on the meaning of the word **antibiotic** (an-tih-by-AHT-ik).
3. Choose student teams to investigate and report to the class on the work of:

   a. Paul Ehrlich
   b. Alexander Fleming
   c. Selman Waksman
   d. Benjamin Duggar
   e. Jonas Salk
   f. Albert Sabin

4. The green molds that grow on lemons, grapefruits, and cantaloupes are similar to the mold from which penicillin was taken. Experiment with growing molds by following these steps:

   a. Slice a cantaloupe.
   b. Put one slice in a closed and one in an open container.
   c. Put both containers in the refrigerator.
   d. On a separate piece of paper, make a chart like the one shown. (*Note:* Make your day-by-day entry columns big enough for complete answers to the questions in step *f.*)

Mold Growth Experiment

	First Day	Second Day	Third Day	Fourth Day	Fifth Day	Sixth Day	Seventh Day
Cantaloupe in closed container							
Cantaloupe in open container							

   e. Examine the cantaloupe each day for a week. Use a magnifying glass to look for mold growing on either piece.

f. Record the results on your record chart. On the day a green mold begins to appear, answer the following questions:

- How long did it take for a mold to appear?
- Did molds appear at the same time on both slices? If the molds appeared at different times, how do you account for the differences?
- Describe the odor, color, and feel of the molds. On another piece of paper, draw a picture showing how the molds look under the magnifying lens. Are your molds the same as, or different from, the molds in Figure 22.10?
- Compare Alexander Fleming's discovery of penicillin and your experiment in growing a mold. What are the similarities? What are the differences?

As you learned from the reports, Dr. Ehrlich continued his experimentation patiently until, on the 606th try, he found his "magic bullet," Salvarsan 606, which would kill the syphilis germ.

In a way, antibiotics like penicillin, streptomycin (strep-tuh-MY-sin), Aureomycin (aw-ree-oh-MY-sin), and Terramycin (ter-uh-MY-sin) are "magic bullets," too, destroying disease germs without harming most patients. Antibiotics come from the world of living creatures. They are products of microorganisms that slow down or kill other microorganisms. Scientists all over the world are at work examining molds, soil samples, and other natural sources, hoping to find still more antibiotics.

CONTROLLING THE SPREAD OF DISEASE Another way to fight disease is to keep it from spreading. Certain diseases (yellow fever, malaria, bubonic plague, Rocky Mountain spotted fever) are spread by animal or insect carriers. Although drugs are useful against these diseases, carrier control is often more effective. For example, the health departments of developed nations fight bubonic plague by keeping rat populations under

Figure 22.10. Mold colonies: *(left)* **penicillin;** *(right)* **Terramycin.**

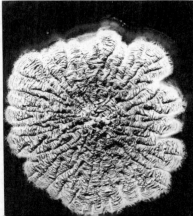

control. (Fleas transfer plague germs from rodents to people by biting.) And in the tropics, the destruction of mosquitos has almost done away with yellow fever—a disease that the mosquitos transferred from one person to another by biting.

Other diseases (cholera, typhoid fever, dysentery) are spread by means of water. Sewage in the water, for example, spreads cholera and typhoid fever. But developed nations treat sewage carefully and purify their water supplies with germ-killing chemicals.

Let's Pause for Review

Our knowledge that microorganisms cause disease is little more than 100 years old. But this knowledge has already made possible great progress in the fight against communicable disease. We can thank scientists like Leeuwenhoek, Jenner, Pasteur, Lister, Ehrlich, Reed, Fleming, Salk, and Sabin for this progress. Vaccines, which are made from weakened or killed germs, and immunizing substances, which are made with the aid of weakened germ toxins, are now available to protect people from bubonic plague, cholera, diphtheria, German measles, influenza, measles, mumps, polio, rabies, smallpox, tetanus, typhoid fever, typhus fever, whooping cough, and yellow fever.

The health departments of modern nations control diseases in various ways: they control the rat population to guard against bubonic plague; they prevent the spread of typhoid fever and cholera through careful treatment of water and sewage; they purify water supplies to prevent the spread of such diseases as amebic dysentery. In addition, antiseptics and antibiotics help fight infections of many kinds.

The Body's Defenses Against Disease

Germs do well in warm, moist, dark places like the inside of the human body. So it's a good thing that your body has so many natural defenses against germ invasions. Your body's first line of defense is the skin. Unless it is broken, this skin forms a barrier against most disease germs.

The saliva in your mouth contains a chemical that stops the action of some disease germs. The sticky mucous membrane lining your respiratory passages traps some of the germs that enter in the air you breathe. The cilia of these passages sweep out and remove some germs. At times, you remove germs by blowing your nose. Still other germs pass from the nose to the throat, where they are coughed up or swallowed. In your stomach, acids help to stop the action of disease germs.

Your eyes are constantly being bathed by a fluid that helps to remove and destroy some disease germs. More active cleansing takes place when you cry. And, as you remember, even when germs successfully invade the body, your white blood cells and antibodies destroy many of the invaders.

BUILDING RESISTANCE TO DISEASE   Can you do anything to help your body fight disease? If you think about it for a moment, you will probably answer yes. First of all, you can make sure your immunizations are up to date. Second, you can build your body's resistance, or ability to fight off disease (see Figure 22.11). Third, you can remember to see a doctor promptly for special problems and regularly for medical examinations (checkups or physicals). The following activity should help you think about your own resistance to disease:

YOUR PART

1. Write down the steps you can take to build your resistance to disease.
2. How often do you think you should see a doctor for a checkup?
3. Write down the signs, or symptoms, of ill health that you think should lead you to see your doctor early (before your regular medical examination is due).
4. As a class, compare your answers.

No doubt you wrote that you can build resistance by getting plenty of sleep, taking daily exercise, and eating healthful foods like raw and cooked vegetables and fruits, milk products, proteins, and whole grains.

When you compared your answers in step 3, you probably listed many symptoms, including: feeling of illness; a high, recurring, or long-lasting fever; unexplained headache; unexplained pain such as abdominal pain or pain during urination; unexplained bleeding; un-explained, long-lasting fatigue; a cough that doesn't clear up; unex-plained weight loss; an increased thirst that stays with you; increased frequency of urination.

The Medical Checkup

Because medical doctors (M.D.s, physicians) would rather prevent disease than treat it, they recommend regular examinations for everybody. How-ever, doctors are in short supply, and their examinations are expensive. Talk to your doctor to find out how often he or she feels it is necessary to see you.

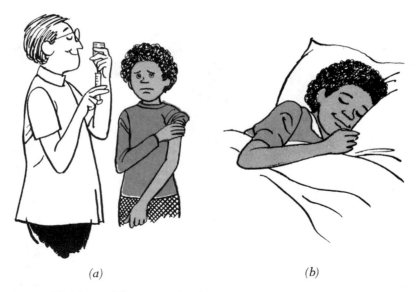

(a) (b)

Figure 22.11. Building your body's resistance to disease:
(a) immunization; (b) sleep; (c) food; (d) exercise.

(c) (d)

REASONS FOR A MEDICAL CHECKUP By means of a checkup, a physician can help you correct bad health habits before they do lasting harm. If you are overweight, for example, you can achieve the proper weight through diet and exercise, but it is always best to follow a doctor's advice in both matters. In addition, a checkup can uncover minor problems before they become serious.

Fighting Communicable Diseases 387

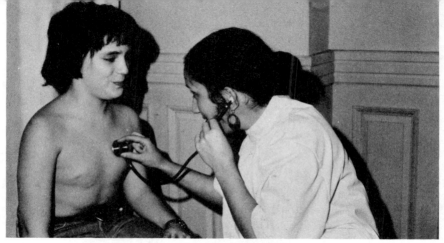

Figure 22.12. Using the stethoscope.

What is more, a checkup can uncover major problems before they become life-threatening. For example, if your examination should reveal that you have the disease diabetes, the doctor can put you on a diet to control the disease and also give you medication, if necessary. Diabetes used to kill many of its victims within a few years, but treatment under a doctor's care now helps nearly all diabetics to live a relatively normal life.

Although everyone knows that regular medical examinations are a good idea, people often put off seeing a doctor. In part, they may dislike going through an examination they don't quite understand. The words the doctor uses may be confusing, too. As one student said, "Half the time I can't remember what the doctor said when I get home."

The following section, which takes you step by step through a medical examination, may help you to feel more at home in a doctor's office. (And the next time you see a doctor, ask the doctor to explain anything you don't understand.) Now let's join Tony, a teenaged boy, as he visits his family doctor, Dr. Alice Martin, for a medical examination.

WHAT THE DOCTOR DOES AND WHY First, Dr. Martin measures Tony's height and weight. She asks him questions about how he is feeling during this important period of growth. She notes Tony's general development and determines that he is growing normally. (However, Dr. Martin notices a marked increase in Tony's weight—a common concern in adolescence. She advises him to watch his diet, paying particular attention to starches and sweets.) Since she has been his family doctor for many years, she knows how his present development compares with his past development. She adds the new figures to Tony's records.

MEDICAL HISTORY Had this been Tony's first visit to Dr. Martin, she would have started by taking his medical history. Tony's history is already in Dr. Martin's files, and she has checked it before starting to examine him. It includes:

Protect Yourself Against Disease

1. A record of the illnesses Tony has had throughout his life.
2. His immunization record.
3. Information on his eating, sleeping, exercise, and other habits of daily living.
4. A record of medicines prescribed for him and his reactions to them.
5. Previous laboratory test results.
6. A review of the health of close relatives (as a clue to diseases Tony may have inherited a tendency to develop).

During the examination, Dr. Martin will ask Tony questions to find out whether new information needs to be added to his records.

As the examination continues, Dr. Martin notes the condition of Tony's skin and observes his alertness, posture, and overall condition. She probes various soft-tissue areas of his body, checking for possible abnormalities such as a **tumor** (TOO-mur), which is an unnatural tissue growth or lump, or a **hernia,** which is the bulging of a tissue or organ through the muscular wall of a body cavity.

The Heart and Lungs   Then, Dr. Martin uses a **stethoscope** (STETH-uh-skohp) to listen to the sounds of Tony's heart and lungs (see Figure 22.12). When blood flows through the heart, the valves in the heart open and shut. This makes a sound the doctor can recognize. The sound tells her if the heart valves are in good working condition. Any abnormal sounds may indicate an illness. As part of the examination, Dr. Martin may send Tony for a chest X ray to see that the heart is of normal size and that the lungs are free from disease.

YOUR PART

You can make your own stethoscope to listen to heart sounds.

MATERIALS
- a small funnel
- one piece of rubber tubing 3 inches (8 centimeters) long and ½ inch (1.25 centimeters) wide
- a T or Y tube
- two pieces of rubber tubing to fit the T or Y tube, each 1 foot (30 centimeters) long

PROCEDURE
1. Slip one end of the short rubber tubing over the end of the funnel.
2. Insert the T or Y tube into the other end of the tubing.
3. Attach each of the longer tubings to the ends of the T or Y tube.
4. To use, have a friend hold the funnel over his or her heart while you put the ends of the long pieces of tubing to your ears and listen.

Fighting Communicable Diseases

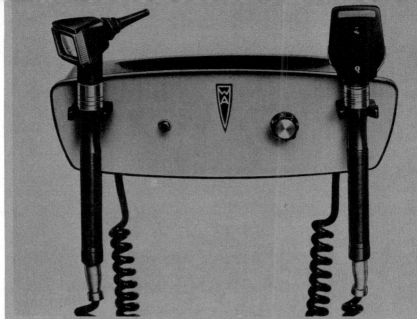

Figure 22.13. *(right)* The ophthalmoscope and *(left)* the otoscope, attached to the wall in the doctor's office.

The Eyes, Ears, Nose, and Throat   Using an **ophthalmoscope** (ahf-THAL-muh-skohp) like the one in Figure 22.13, Dr. Martin looks into Tony's eyes. This instrument lights up part of the inside of the eyeball so that Dr. Martin can examine the interior of the eye—the retina and blood vessels. Early signs of certain diseases may be seen in the condition of these structures.

Then, using an **otoscope** (OH-tuh-skohp) like the one in Figure 22.13, Dr. Martin examines Tony's ears. She looks for obstructions in the ear canals, such as accumulations of wax, and checks the eardrums.

Using a **tongue depressor,** a thin piece of wood that looks like a big ice-cream stick, the doctor checks the condition of Tony's teeth, tongue, mouth, and throat.

She examines his nose with the aid of a **nasal speculum** (NAY-zul SPEK-yuh-lum), a tubular instrument that, when inserted in the nose, makes inspection easier. She looks to see if there is any obstruction or defect. She also looks for signs of infection.

Blood Pressure   Next, Dr. Martin wraps a cuff containing an airtight bag tightly around Tony's upper arm and pumps air into it to make it even tighter. This is part of a **sphygmomanometer** (sfig-moh-muh-NAHM-uh-tur), an instrument used to measure blood pressure. You can see a picture of one in Figure 22.14. This instrument is used to measure the pressure in the arteries in Tony's arm. Two kinds of pressure are measured and recorded:

Protect Yourself Against Disease

1. The **systolic** (sis-TAHL-ik) **pressure**, read during the period when the heart contracts to pump blood throughout the body. The heart is working hardest during this step.
2. The **diastolic** (dy-uh-STAHL-ik) **pressure**, read during the period between contractions when the heart expands and fills with blood.

Dr. Martin records the blood pressure as a fraction:

$$\frac{120 \text{ (systolic)}}{80 \text{ (diastolic)}}$$

This blood pressure is considered to be normal for most people. A normal blood pressure reading is one indication of a healthy circulatory system.

Laboratory Tests   Finally, Dr. Martin takes samples of Tony's blood and urine to send to the laboratory for testing:

1. A *blood count* gives many clues to general health. If Tony's red blood cell count is low, it may indicate anemia (see page 54). A high white blood cell count may indicate an infection somewhere in Tony's body. The doctor can order a variety of other blood tests, but since all of her findings during the examination have been normal, she thinks that only one further test is necessary. Knowing that Tony's mother is a diabetic and that this disease may be hereditary, she orders a *blood sugar* (glucose) *test*.
2. A *urinalysis* (yuhr-uh-NAL-uh-sis) tells, among other things, how the kidneys are performing their job of helping to remove waste materials from the body and of regulating body fluids. These wastes are filtered from the body by the kidneys. They leave the body by way of the urine. If too many of these wastes were to build up in Tony's blood, he might become ill.

Figure 22.14. A sphygmomanometer.

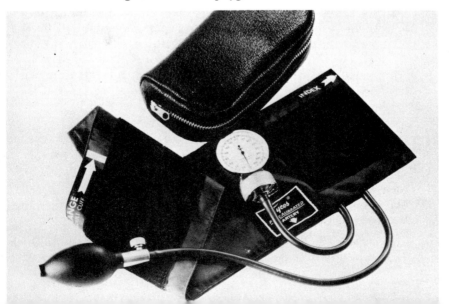

Immunization Tony's immunization record shows that his immunizations against communicable diseases like measles, diphtheria, tetanus, polio, and mumps are up to date. So Dr. Martin doesn't give him any *booster shots*.

Booster shots are given to improve the level of immunity; immunity against some diseases may decline with the passage of time. Thus, when entering school, a child should have boosters for diphtheria, tetanus, polio, and smallpox. Boosters for diphtheria and tetanus should also be given at age 12 and every five to ten years thereafter. At any age, any person who expects to be exposed to smallpox, tetanus, diphtheria, or whooping cough (by traveling or in the event of a new epidemic) should take boosters of these vaccines.

Looking Back

The two main kinds of disease are communicable (caused by invading microorganisms) and noncommunicable. A knowledge of microorganisms has made possible a successful fight against many communicable diseases. Vaccination can now prevent smallpox, measles, German measles, mumps, polio, diphtheria, tetanus, whooping cough, and other diseases. The health departments of developed nations also prevent the spread of diseases like cholera and typhoid fever (through modern water and sewage treatment) and bubonic plague (through rat control). In addition, antiseptics and antibiotics fight many kinds of infection.

Your own personal weapons against disease include up-to-date immunizations, good health habits, a healthy body well able to resist disease, and regular medical examinations. At a checkup, the doctor examines your heart and lungs with a stethoscope, your ears with an otoscope, your mouth and throat with a tongue depressor, your nose with a nasal speculum, your eyes with an ophthalmoscope, and your systolic and diastolic blood pressure with a sphygmomanometer. Blood is examined by blood count and chemical tests, and kidney function by urinalysis.

MODIFIED TRUE-FALSE QUESTIONS

1. Measles was brought under control about _50_ years ago.
2. The venereal disease _syphilis_ can be cured but is still widespread because it is often untreated.

3. ''Catching'' diseases are also called <u>contagious</u> diseases.
4. <u>Antitoxins</u> are poisonous wastes given off by microorganisms.
5. Yeast is <u>a harmful</u> microorganism.
6. An example of a virus-caused disease is <u>influenza</u>.
7. A rod-shaped bacterium causes <u>syphilis</u>.
8. Fungi are <u>animallike</u> organisms.
9. <u>Most</u> protozoa cause disease.
10. Thorough cooking of pork destroys the worms that cause <u>trichinosis</u>.
11. Bacteria were discovered by <u>Leeuwenhoek</u>.
12. <u>Cowpox</u> was also known as the Black Death.
13. <u>Pasteur</u> proved that microorganisms cause disease.
14. Invading disease germs are destroyed by <u>antibodies</u>.
15. When you have certain diseases and recover from them, you develop <u>an acquired</u> immunity to the disease.
16. An example of an antiseptic chemical used by Lister is <u>carbolic acid</u>.
17. The term ''magic bullet'' was first applied to a chemical developed by <u>Jonas Salk</u>.
18. A disease spread by an animal carrier is <u>bubonic plague</u>.
19. The presence of sewage in water is responsible for the spread of <u>typhoid fever</u>.
20. The body's first line of defense against disease is the <u>stomach</u>.

MATCHING QUESTIONS, GROUP 1

Column A	Column B
1. bacteria	a. plantlike microorganisms, having three main shapes
2. viruses	
3. a fungus	b. cause of athlete's foot
4. a protozoan	c. cause of malaria
5. rickettsias	d. carried by lice and ticks
	e. many-celled animals
	f. smallest disease agents known

MATCHING QUESTIONS, GROUP 2

Column A	Column B
1. Jenner	a. streptomycin
2. Ehrlich	b. penicillin
3. Sabin	c. polio
4. Fleming	d. smallpox
5. Waksman	e. syphilis
	f. diabetes

Fighting Communicable Diseases

COMPLETION QUESTIONS

1. A urinalysis shows how well the _____ are removing waste materials from the blood.
2. A _____ (high, low) red blood cell count is frequently associated with anemia.
3. To improve the level of a person's immunity to a communicable disease, the doctor uses a (an) _____.
4. An instrument used to measure blood pressure is a (an) _____.
5. Ears are examined with the aid of an instrument called a (an) _____.
6. Doctors use a (an) _____ to examine the eyes.
7. The sounds of the heart and lungs are heard with the help of a (an) _____.
8. A tissue or organ that bulges through the body wall is referred to as a (an) _____.
9. Germs multiply quickly in places that are warm, moist, and _____.
10. Your respiratory passages are lined with _____, which sweep out germs.

MULTIPLE-CHOICE QUESTIONS

1. An infectious disease is caused by
   a. a lowering of the blood pressure rate
   b. an increase in body temperature
   c. a specific living agent or its toxin
   d. an increased antibody level
2. Which of the following is not a defense of the human body against germs?
   a. skin   b. white blood cells   c. toxins   d. cilia
3. Scientific progress, including immunization, has helped shift our health problems from
   a. childhood to adolescent diseases
   b. communicable to chronic diseases
   c. chronic to communicable diseases
   d. female to male disorders
4. We now have available many kinds of "shots" to protect us from many specific diseases. For which one of the following do we not have such injections?
   a. common cold   b. German measles   c. polio   d. smallpox
5. The best source of information about immunization needs would probably be
   a. an advertisement in a magazine
   b. a pharmacy clerk
   c. a pamphlet published by your health department
   d. a friend or neighbor

Protect Yourself Against Disease

6. Of the following, which probably does *not* build body resistance to disease?
   a. sleep   *b.* exercise   *c.* food   *d.* smoking
7. The procedure that helps control diabetes is
   a. regular exercise and sleep   *c.* proper medication and diet
   b. sufficient rest and activity   *d.* more relaxing activities
8. A normal blood pressure reading is indicated by the fraction
   a. $\dfrac{80}{120}$ *b.* $\dfrac{120}{80}$ *c.* $\dfrac{40}{60}$ *d.* $\dfrac{60}{40}$
9. Modern water and sewage treatment helps prevent the spread of diseases like
   a. measles   *c.* typhoid fever
   b. smallpox   *d.* Rocky Mountain spotted fever
10. Vaccination cannot now prevent
   a. tetanus   *b.* cholera   *c.* bubonic plague   *d.* cancer

THOUGHT QUESTIONS

1. Tony has the symptoms of a cold. He doesn't want to stay home, so he goes to school. Which, if any, of the following results can you predict? Give reasons for your choices.

   a. He has only a cold, so there is nothing to worry about.
   b. His presence will have no effect on the other children.
   c. The teacher will insist that he see the school nurse, who probably will send him home.
   d. His cold symptoms may be an early sign of a more serious communicable disease, and Tony's condition may be highly contagious.

2. List four microorganisms responsible for the spread of communicable disease. Describe each, and give at least one example of a disease that the specific microorganism may cause.
3. Explain how our bodies defend us against communicable diseases.
4. Not all microorganisms are harmful. Describe how microorganisms can be beneficial.
5. Some people claim that it will be possible to wipe out all diseases some day. What can you, as an intelligent adolescent, do to help attain this goal?

Looking Ahead

Now that you know something of the history of communicable disease, you are ready to read about those communicable diseases that still trouble people today. As you read Chapter 23, you will also learn about ways of protecting yourself from some of these diseases.

Fighting Communicable Diseases

Chapter 23: Communicable Diseases Today

Kiki lay in bed with a fever of 101 degrees Fahrenheit (38.3 degrees Celsius), fatigue, a sore throat, and swollen lymph glands at the sides of her neck. Two weeks earlier, she had been sick with the same symptoms but felt better and went back to school. As soon as she tried to be active, she only felt sick again.

Yesterday, Kiki's father had taken her to the doctor, and now Kiki was back in bed. The doctor had ordered a blood test, which indicated that Kiki was suffering from **infectious mononucleosis** (in-FEK-shus mahn-oh-nyoo-klee-OH-sis). It was bad enough to be sick, Kiki thought, but it was even worse to have "mono, the kissing disease." All the kids at school would tease her. And she might miss so much school that she would not pass at the end of the semester and move on in school with her friends.

Infectious Mononucleosis

In spite of the great progress of the last century, many communicable diseases have not been conquered yet (see Table 23.1). Kiki's disease, infectious mononucleosis, is just one example. Because it affects so many young people (from junior high through college), mononucleosis is often called the student's disease or, as Kiki thought of it, the "kissing disease."

Doctors know that a virus causes mononucleosis. It is spread by direct and intimate contact with an infected person. Although doctors suspect that kissing often spreads it, they believe that mononucleosis can be spread in other ways as well.

A preventive vaccine has been developed, which may prove useful in the future. But at present, treatment consists largely of resting in bed and eating nourishing food. Fortunately, although fatigue may last for months, mononucleosis usually clears up without leaving any aftereffects.

Although a person with mononucleosis may miss weeks or months of work or school, there is another virus disease that results in more absences

Table 23.1: Some Unconquered Communicable Diseases

Disease	How Spread	Incubation Period
Cold	Direct contact, droplets	1–2 days
Gonorrhea	Direct contact	2–8 days
Hepatitis (infectious)	Contaminated food, water, soil	2–6 weeks
Hepatitis (serum)	Contaminated needles	4–23 weeks
Herpes (venereal)	Direct contact	(?)
Influenza	Direct contact, droplets	1–3 days
Mononucleosis (infectious)	Direct contact	4–7 weeks (?)
Pneumonia (bacterial)	Direct contact, droplets	1–3 days
Pneumonia (viral)	Direct contact, droplets	7–21 days
Syphilis	Direct contact	10–90 days
Tuberculosis	Direct contact, droplets	variable

from work or school than any other disease. Do you know what that disease is? If you said the common cold, you were right. Colds are so contagious that most people can count on catching a cold at least once or twice a year.

YOUR PART

1. Find out how many people in your health class have had colds since school began. Find out how many absences these colds have caused. Now total all absences due to other causes. As a class, make a chart showing your findings.
2. Try to get the information to prepare a chart similar to the one in step 1 for your whole school. Perhaps each student in your health class could survey a different class.
3. It may interest you to repeat your survey each month or during those months when you think people catch the most colds.
4. Appoint one member of your health class to talk to the person in charge of attendance at your school. Find out when most absences occur—which day(s), which month(s), and which season(s). Have the person report findings to the class.

The Common Cold

If your school is like most others, absences due to colds outnumber absences due to all other causes combined. Both now and in the past, all

Figure 23.1. Droplets expelled by a sneeze.

kinds of cold remedies have been tried. But the cold is still with us and will probably be so for some time to come. One reason is the number of viruses (perhaps as many as 100) that are thought to cause colds. Only a few of these viruses have been identified. A vaccine made from the few identified viruses would do nothing to protect you from infection by the other cold viruses.

DROPLET INFECTION   When you have a cold, cold viruses are present in great numbers in your nose and throat. When you talk, sneeze, or cough, you send out a fine spray of moisture, as Figure 23.1 shows. Each droplet of moisture contains cold viruses that can make another person sick. Table 23.1 includes other examples of diseases spread by such droplets.

INCUBATION PERIOD   With colds, the **incubation** (ing-kyoo-BAY-shun) **period** can be as short as several hours or as long as three days. The incubation period is the time between contact (with the source of infection) and the outbreak of symptoms (see Table 23.1). During this time, the invading microorganisms multiply until there are enough of them present in your body to make you feel sick. Unfortunately, during the incubation period people who don't yet feel ill can sometimes pass germs on to other people. The following activity gives you a chance to explore what you yourself have observed about colds:

1. Have you noticed any conditions (outside or inside your body) that seem to make you less resistant to colds? Write them down.
2. How can you keep from passing your colds on to other people? Write your answers down.
3. Write down how you can prevent the germs around you from entering your body.
4. Write down why it is important to take care of colds.

Perhaps you wrote that you seem to get more colds in wet, cold, and windy weather, or when you miss sleep, become overtired, eat improperly, or get chilled. It is important to observe the conditions that increase your chances of catching cold. It is also important to build up your resistance against chills by keeping indoor temperatures between 68 and 70 degrees Fahrenheit (20 and 21 degrees Celsius) and by keeping active when you are outdoors in cold weather.

PROTECTING OTHERS FROM YOUR COLDS You can sometimes keep from passing colds on to others by covering your coughs and sneezes. It also helps to stay at home in bed for the first day or two of your cold, when you are sneezing most often. In addition, it is wise to use disposable tissues, which can be either thrown away or put in a closed paper bag at your bedside.

SECONDARY INFECTIONS It is important to take care of a cold in order to prevent secondary infections, such as the following:

- Ear infections.
- Bronchitis.
- **Sinusitis** (sy-nuh-SYT-is), an infection causing inflammation of the sinuses, or skull cavities connected with the nostrils.
- **Pneumonia** (nyoo-MOH-nyuh), which will be discussed further (see page 400).

The bacteria that cause such infections are present most of the time in people's noses and throats. Normally, such bacteria have trouble getting a foothold in healthy tissue. However, after cold viruses have weakened the tissues of the nose and throat, bacteria often find it easier to cause infections.

If your cold has begun to improve but suddenly worsens again, you should call your doctor, because you may have developed a secondary infection. Antibiotics, which are useless against cold viruses, are successful in treating certain secondary bacterial infections.

Communicable Diseases Today   399

Influenza

Like the common cold, **influenza** (also called flu and grippe) is caused by a number of different viruses. Vaccines have been made from those flu viruses that have been identified, but such vaccines are not effective against other flu viruses. Furthermore, the viruses that cause flu may change slightly from year to year, so that last year's vaccine may not be effective against this year's virus. Your doctor or the public health agency in your area can tell you whether or not you should be immunized against influenza.

Flu viruses attack the respiratory, nervous, and digestive systems. Although flu viruses are present all year long, flu usually occurs in epidemics that affect many people at once. In 1918, a worldwide flu pandemic killed between 20 and 30 million people, half a million of them in the United States. In the winter of 1975, a few cases of swine influenza occurred in humans. The virus of this disease is believed to be related to the one responsible for the 1918 pandemic. In order to prevent another pandemic, the federal government set up a plan to vaccinate everyone in the United States before the 1976 flu season.

However, flu is not usually so serious. As with the common cold, flu's chief danger is that it lowers resistance to other serious infections, particularly pneumonia.

FLU SYMPTOMS   At first, the flu feels a little like a cold. Usually, though, there are more muscle aches and pains with flu and a greater feeling of weakness. People often have headaches, chills, fever, and, in some cases, delirium (mental confusion and hallucinations). The best treatment for flu is bed rest until strength returns. Antibiotics are useless against the virus. But doctors sometimes prescribe antibiotics for any secondary infections that may develop.

Pneumonia

Before the discovery of antibiotics, pneumonia was a great killer. At one time, 1 out of 3 pneumonia victims died, but today 19 out of 20 get well. This striking change has come about because antibiotics usually work well against pneumonia caused by bacteria.

BACTERIAL PNEUMONIA   Pneumonia usually develops as a result of a carelessly treated cold or flu that has lowered the body's resistance to infection. As the bacteria invade the lungs, the body pours fluids into the air spaces of the lungs. These body fluids in the lungs make breathing painful and difficult. Fortunately, when bacterial pneumonia is promptly treated, antibiotics can usually bring about a return to normal breathing in a day or two.

400   **Protect Yourself Against Disease**

What are the symptoms of pneumonia? Usually they include chills and shivering, rapid breathing, rapid pulse, high fever, painful cough, and sharp pains in the chest, side, or shoulders when one tries to breathe deeply. A person with these symptoms needs prompt medical attention.

VIRAL PNEUMONIA   Some kinds of pneumonia are caused by viruses rather than by bacteria. As with viral colds and flu, viral pneumonia is not counteracted by today's antibiotics. Fortunately, however, viral pneumonia is usually less severe than bacterial pneumonia. Although you may think you have only a bad cold or the flu, it is important to see your doctor if the following pneumonia symptoms appear: fever, cough, chest pains, and general weakness.

Let's Pause for Review

Some communicable diseases remain unconquered, particularly those caused by viruses. One such disease is mononucleosis, characterized by sore throat, swollen neck glands, and extreme fatigue. It is spread by direct and intimate contact, may take many months to clear up, but usually has no lasting aftereffects.

Other virus-caused communicable diseases are the common cold and flu (influenza). In each case, only some of the viruses have been identified. Certain flu viruses have been used successfully to make antiflu vaccines, but other strains of flu are still difficult to treat.

Cold and flu weaken the body's resistance to secondary infections, such as ear infections, bronchitis, sinusitis, and pneumonia. Pneumonia, in particular, is a very dangerous secondary infection of the respiratory system.

There are two kinds of pneumonia—bacterial and viral. Bacterial pneumonia is the more dangerous and was once a great killer. Now, however, it can usually be treated by antibiotics. Viral pneumonia has no cure at present but is fortunately a less severe disease.

Tuberculosis

Tuberculosis (tyoo-BUR-kyuh-LOH-sis), also called TB and consumption, is caused by a rod-shaped bacterium, or *bacillus* (buh-SIL-us). A person becomes infected with TB by inhaling or swallowing the germs. It was once the leading cause of death in the United States. But in our century, the TB death rate has dropped by more than 90 percent. A number of preventive measures have helped to bring about this change. Several drugs have proven to be useful in treating the disease. Better

Communicable Diseases Today

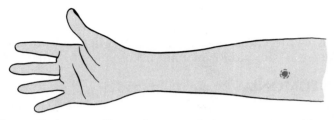

Figure 23.2. A swollen red spot indicates a positive TB test.

methods of detecting TB have helped, too. In fact, if everyone were regularly tested for TB, the disease could probably be completely conquered.

TESTS FOR TB Do you remember taking a TB skin test as a child? A positive reaction to this test meant that at some time TB germs had invaded your body. If you had a positive reaction (see Figure 23.2), the next step was a chest X ray to show whether the TB germs had done any damage to your lungs. However, most chest X rays show that the primary infection has healed and the lungs are clear (see Figure 23.3).

How does your body fight TB germs? It does so by killing them or by imprisoning them inside a hard, scarlike case to form a *tubercle* (TYOObur-kul). But the germs inside the tubercle are still alive. If bodily resistance is lowered at a later time, the germs can break out and attack the lungs again.

TB SYMPTOMS No symptoms are likely to appear in the early stages of TB when the disease can be most easily cured. Later, symptoms may include extreme tiredness, poor appetite, loss of weight, night sweating, low fever, coughing, and spitting up of blood. By the time these symptoms appear, control of TB is much harder.

TREATMENT TODAY In the past, little could be done to help a person with TB. Today, however, in addition to rest and good food, specific drugs are given to TB patients. The drugs slow down the multiplication of the germs, giving the body a better chance to fight off the disease. Sometimes, surgery is performed to remove the diseased part of a lung or to collapse a lung for a short period during which it can rest.

PROTECTING YOURSELF FROM TB If you have good health habits and if you get plenty of good food, exercise, and rest, your chances of developing TB are small. Even so, your lungs should be checked regularly. Your regular medical examinations should include either a TB skin test or a chest X ray. These regular tests are particularly important to you if you live in a community where there is overcrowding or where poor health is common.

402   **Protect Yourself Against Disease**

Hepatitis

Hepatitis (hep-uh-TY-tis) means inflammation of the liver. In **infectious hepatitis,** a virus infects the liver, causing inflammation. This strain of hepatitis virus is found in the **feces** (FEE-seez), or solid wastes, of infected persons or animals. The virus may be spread by contaminated, unwashed hands. Polluted food and water may spread the virus, too. One source of infection, for example, is shellfish from water that is polluted by sewage.

Serum hepatitis, caused by a different strain of virus, is spread by using contaminated equipment, such as hypodermic needles or by using infected blood (from hepatitis victims) for transfusions. Serum hepatitis is very common among drug addicts, who often use unsterilized needles. Unsterilized needles used for tattooing or ear piercing have also been known to spread serum hepatitis.

HEPATITIS SYMPTOMS A person with hepatitis is usually quite sick with fever, nausea, fatigue, stiffness of the joints, and pain in the upper right part of the abdomen. The urine becomes dark and the feces light. Hepatitis usually also causes **jaundice** (JAWN-dus), or yellowing of the skin and the whites of the eyes. Even when a hepatitis victim recovers, the damaged liver may not completely return to normal.

PROTECTING YOURSELF FROM HEPATITIS Cleanliness is the best protection against hepatitis. There is as yet no vaccine to prevent infectious hepatitis and no treatment to cure it, other than good general care and bed rest. (Doctors sometimes also prescribe special diets; a low-fat diet, for example, may ease the nausea caused by hepatitis.) However, when one family member gets hepatitis, it's possible to protect the other family members with injections of **gamma globulin** (GAM-uh-GLAHB-yuh-lun), an antibody chemical obtained from blood plasma.

Active and Passive Immunity As you remember, vaccination stimulates your body to produce antibodies that provide long-lasting or **active immunity.** However, when no vaccine is available, it is possible to borrow the antibodies from another person's blood by getting a shot of

Figure 23.3. Two chest X rays showing *(left)* tuberculosis of upper part of right lung and *(right)* lung cleared after treatment.

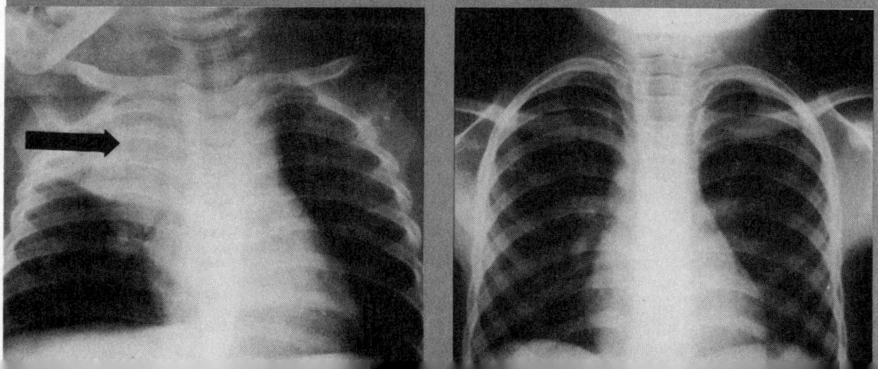

gamma globulin, the part of the blood that contains antibodies. This borrowed immunity is called **passive immunity.** It lasts only from two to six weeks. The armed forces in Vietnam used huge amounts of gamma globulin to fight hepatitis there.

Venereal Disease (V.D.)

Named for Venus, the goddess of love, **venereal** (vuh-NIR-ee-ul) diseases are spread by sexual contact. There are a number of venereal diseases, but in the United States the two most common are **syphilis** and **gonorrhea.** Both of these diseases can be cured if promptly treated. Free treatment is available at V.D. clinics maintained by public health departments throughout the United States.

Yet many health authorities believe there is a V.D. epidemic in the United States today. Over 750,000 cases of gonorrhea and over 25,000 cases of syphilis are reported each year. Over three-fourths of the cases are not reported. Thus, the number of cases of these diseases may be four times larger and still increasing, especially among young people.

How can there be an epidemic, when free, effective treatment is available? It's a difficult question to answer. But ignorance, irresponsibility, embarrassment, and fear all play a part in today's spreading V.D. epidemic.

Often, people don't know what the symptoms of V.D. are. Many people are unsure of how V.D. is detected and cured. Because symptoms appear on or near the reproductive organs, some people are embarrassed to go for treatment. Other people are careless about their health and the health of others. And young people are often afraid that if they go for treatment, their parents will find out about the infection.

V.D. CRIPPLES AND KILLS   Venereal diseases are too serious to neglect. Untreated syphilis lasts for life, and it may result in blindness, paralysis, insanity, and death. Untreated gonorrhea can cause blindness, arthritis, and heart disease, as well as painful infection of both the male and female reproductive organs. These infections often make both men and women **sterile** (STER-ul), or unable to have children.

SYPHILIS   Syphilis is caused by spiral-shaped bacteria (see Figure 22.1, page 374). The syphilis germ is so delicate that it dies in seconds when exposed to light and air. But inside the human body, the syphilis germ circulates rapidly in the bloodstream, multiplies with ease, and lives within every tissue of its human host. Within 10 to 90 days after the germ enters the body, the first symptoms of syphilis may appear.

First-Stage Symptoms   The syphilis germ usually enters the body of its new host through the mucous membranes of the reproductive organs.

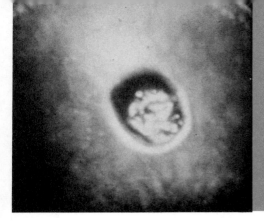

Figure 23.4. A chancre, or sore, that appears in the first stage of syphilis.

The first symptom, which usually appears in the same region, is a small, single, painless lesion (sore) called a **chancre** (SHANG-kur) (see Figure 23.4). Because it is painless and small, the chancre is often overlooked, especially in women.

But the chancre is very infectious. If there is sexual contact, syphilis germs pass easily from the chancre to another person. In a few weeks, the chancre disappears with or without treatment. This disappearance has led millions of people to believe that they are again well. Actually, however, by this time syphilis germs have traveled by way of the bloodstream to every part of the body.

Second-Stage Symptoms   One to six months after the chancre disappears, second-stage syphilis begins. This stage, like the first, is highly contagious. Second-stage syphilis has many symptoms. The victim usually feels unwell. Skin rashes and spotty, irregular, temporary baldness may develop (see Figure 23.5, page 406). Whitish sores may appear on mucous membranes of mouth and throat. Low fevers, headaches, swollen lymph glands, and pains in the bones and joints may add to the victim's discomfort.

Diagnosis and Treatment   In both its first and second stages, syphilis can be rather quickly cured. The first step is a blood test. If the test is positive (showing the presence of syphilis), a short course of treatment is begun. In the clinic or doctor's office, penicillin or other antibiotic shots are given. In many cases, two to five shots are enough to control the disease and produce a negative blood test.

In most states, a blood test for syphilis is required before a marriage license is issued. Such a test helps protect not only those about to marry but also any children that they may have. A pregnant woman with syphilis can pass the disease on to her unborn child. The unborn child may die or, if it lives, be born with syphilis. A syphilitic baby may be blind or deaf. Such a baby's teeth and bones may be malformed, and the baby may grow and develop poorly.

Communicable Diseases Today

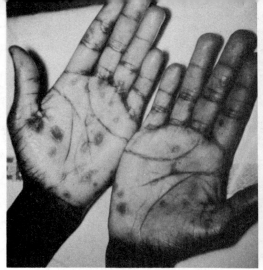

Figure 23.5. Symptoms of second-stage syphilis: *(left)* rash; *(right)* baldness.

The Latent Period   Untreated syphilis never really disappears. But in the latent (LAY-tunt) period that follows the second stage of syphilis, the disease *seems* to disappear. *Latent* means lying hidden, and during this period syphilis lies hidden in the tissues, gradually destroying the circulatory and nervous systems. There are no outward symptoms to be seen. Only a blood test can show the presence of syphilis at this time.

Late Syphilis   Five to thirty years after the first infection, late syphilis appears, attacking the heart and blood vessels, the brain and spinal cord, or the skin and bones. Running sores are common, as are blindness, deafness, paralysis, and insanity, followed by death. Late syphilis can sometimes be treated, but the damage already done cannot be undone.

Immunity   Syphilis and gonorrhea are two separate diseases, but a person can, and often does, catch both of them at the same time. Another thing to remember is that neither disease provides later immunity. That is, a person who has once been cured of syphilis (or gonorrhea) can be infected by the disease just as easily a second time. And there is no vaccine to prevent either disease. But prompt, proper treatment can usually cure both syphilis and gonorrhea.

GONORRHEA   Gonorrhea is caused by slightly bean-shaped, nearly round bacteria (see Figure 22.1, page 374). As with syphilis, the bacteria that cause gonorrhea are spread by sexual contact. Perhaps because it has a shorter incubation period (see Table 23.1, page 397), gonorrhea is more common than syphilis. Within two to eight days after exposure, gonorrhea's first symptoms appear.

How Symptoms Differ   In the infected male, there is almost always a discharge of pus from the penis and usually a painful, burning sensation when urinating. These symptoms usually cause a man to seek medical attention. Recently, however, doctors have learned that men may have gonorrhea without symptoms. If left untreated, the infection may spread to the coiled tubes inside the testicles, where it may cause sterility by blocking the passage of sperm.

In a way, gonorrhea may be more dangerous for a woman than for a man because, as in the case of syphilis, a woman may not notice the infection. She may have only a slight discharge and a mild burning when she urinates. (She may also have swollen glands in the reproductive area.) About 80 percent of women with gonorrhea have mild symptoms or none at all. With slight symptoms or none at all, a woman may feel she has no reason to see a doctor. By the time that abdominal pain warns her that something is wrong, the infection may already have spread to the internal sex organs and made her sterile.

Treatment   Before the days of penicillin, gonorrhea was called "the crippler" because it caused so much arthritis. The disease once caused much heart disease and blindness, too. If a pregnant woman had gonorrhea, the germs often got into the eyes of her baby during the process of birth. This infection blinded many babies. Nowadays, however, all states require that newborn babies be given eye drops to kill any gonorrhea germs that would otherwise cause blindness (Figure 23.6).

The arthritis, heart disease, and sterility caused by gonorrhea can usually be prevented, too. Prompt treatment at a doctor's office or free clinic can cure gonorrhea. As with syphilis, treatment with penicillin or other antibiotics is usually enough to cure the disease in its early stages.

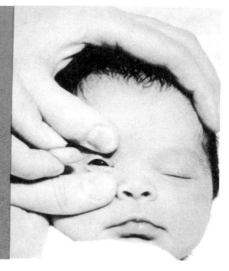

Figure 23.6. A newborn baby gets antigonorrhea eye drops by law.

VIRAL INFECTION   Syphilis and gonorrhea are both caused by bacteria. Another venereal disease is caused by a strain of virus called **herpes simplex** (HUR-peez SIM-pleks), **Type 2.** (There are, however, other strains of herpes virus that are nonvenereal in nature.) Like syphilis and gonorrhea, venereal herpes infections are epidemic in some parts of the United States today. The chief reason for concern is that the herpes virus can be transmitted from mother to baby during the process of birth, and for a baby such a herpes infection can be fatal.

In time, research may provide a means of preventing or curing this viral infection. At present, the only way to protect a baby whose mother has an active herpes infection is to deliver the baby by **Caesarean** (sih-ZAR-ee-un) **section,** an operation named for Julius Caesar, who was supposed to have been delivered in this way. A surgeon performing a Caesarean section makes an incision in the mother's abdominal and uterine walls and lifts the baby out through the surgical opening.

Looking Back

Your best defense against disease is a strong, resistant body. You also need to take good care of colds and cases of the flu in order to prevent secondary infections like ear infections, bronchitis, sinusitis, and pneumonia. Personal cleanliness and good public sanitation are your best protection against infectious hepatitis. Serum hepatitis, on the other hand, is caused by unclean needles (hypodermic and others that are meant to pierce the skin) and infected blood used for transfusions. In addition, you need regular testing to be sure you are free of tuberculosis.

If promptly and properly treated, syphilis and gonorrhea can usually be quickly cured with penicillin or other antibiotics. If left untreated, however, syphilis lasts a lifetime, gradually affecting the brain and spinal cord, the heart and blood vessels, or the skin and bones. In its late stage, syphilis often results in blindness, paralysis, insanity, and death.

Because gonorrhea can quickly cause sterility in both sexes, it should be promptly treated, also. Untreated, gonorrhea can result in arthritis and heart disease.

In addition to syphilis and gonorrhea, a third type of venereal disease—herpes simplex, Type 2—is also infecting large numbers of people in the United States today. A pregnant woman with herpes simplex risks the life of her unborn child, unless the presence of the disease is discovered and the child is delivered by Caesarean section surgery.

Protect Yourself Against Disease

MODIFIED TRUE-FALSE QUESTIONS

1. Mononucleosis is thought to be caused by _a bacterium._
2. The most common virus-caused disease is _the flu._
3. Antibiotics are effective in treating certain kinds of _pneumonia._
4. The syphilis germ is _a rod-shaped_ bacterium.
5. _A spiral-shaped_ bacterium causes gonorrhea.
6. Hepatitis means inflammation of the _liver._
7. The use of gamma globulin provides _active_ immunity to hepatitis.
8. An example of a viral venereal disease is _gonorrhea._
9. _Sinusitis_ is an example of a secondary infection.
10. An example of a disease that has been both epidemic and pandemic is _the common cold._
11. The best protection against hepatitis is _good diet._
12. Colds are caused by more than one _virus._
13. The tuberculosis germs inside a tubercle are _dead._
14. Bacteria that cause ear infections, bronchitis, and sinusitis are present most of the time in the _nose and throat._
15. _Venereal_ diseases are spread by sexual contact.

MATCHING QUESTIONS

Column A	Column B
1. mononucleosis	a. sometimes called the grippe
2. influenza	b. two types—viral and bacterial
3. pneumonia	c. disease that can destroy lung tissue
4. tuberculosis	d. also known as students' disease or "kissing disease"
5. serum hepatitis	e. a venereal disease
	f. spread by use of nonsterile hypodermic needles

COMPLETION QUESTIONS

1. The development time of a disease between contact and outbreak of symptoms is known as the _____ period.
2. Hepatitis usually causes _____, which is a yellowing of the skin and whites of the eyes.
3. Other infections that develop from a cold are known as _____ infections.
4. A painless sore, usually occurring during the primary (first) stage of syphilis, is a (an) _____.
5. Flu viruses attack the respiratory, nervous, and _____ systems.

Communicable Diseases Today

6. Your resistance to other serious infections _____ (increases, decreases) when you catch cold.
7. The less serious type of pneumonia is _____ pneumonia.
8. A viral disease that can be spread by eating shellfish from sewage-polluted water is _____ .
9. Venereal diseases include gonorrhea, syphilis, and _____ .
10. Newborn babies are given special eye drops to kill _____ germs.

MULTIPLE-CHOICE QUESTIONS

1. Which of the following is *not* true? A chancre
   a. is painless
   b. is highly contagious
   c. usually disappears by itself
   d. may be a symptom of tuberculosis
2. A symptom of gonorrhea in males is a
   a. painless sore
   b. body rash and low-grade fever
   c. burning sensation during urination, with a discharge of pus
   d. swelling of lymph glands and pain in joints
3. An infectious disease for which surgery is still sometimes required is
   a. influenza   b. tuberculosis   c. hepatitis   d. mononucleosis
4. Which of the following is *not* a symptom of syphilis?
   a. chancres   c. low fever
   b. swollen lymph glands   d. yellowish skin
5. Extreme tiredness, poor appetite, loss of weight, wheezing, night sweats, low fever, coughing, and spitting up of blood may be symptoms of
   a. influenza   b. tuberculosis   c. hepatitis   d. mononucleosis
6. Nausea, fatigue, stiffness of joints, pain in the upper right part of the abdomen, dark urine, and light feces may be symptoms of
   a. influenza   b. tuberculosis   c. hepatitis   d. mononucleosis
7. If you know you have mononucleosis, a doctor will tell you to
   a. exercise lightly
   b. get into bed when you are tired
   c. stay in bed
   d. get into bed when you come home from school
8. Which statement is *not* true for the common cold?
   a. it is a viral disease
   b. it is a bacterial disease
   c. it clears up with rest
   d. it has an incubation period
9. The chances of catching cold increase in all of the following situations, *except*
   a. during wet weather   c. when you are asleep
   b. when you are tired   d. during cold weather

410   **Protect Yourself Against Disease**

10. Antibiotics are useful in curing all the following diseases, *except*
   a.   the common cold   c.   gonorrhea
   b.   bacterial pneumonia   d.   syphilis

THOUGHT QUESTIONS

1.   Venereal disease is considered a social problem. Discuss the effect that V.D. can have upon *(a)* the infected person; *(b)* those with whom the infected person is in contact; *(c)* any offspring the infected person may have.

2.   Describe the differences between the symptoms of a cold, influenza, and pneumonia, and explain methods of preventing each disease.

3.   What is the difference between *(a)* viral and bacterial pneumonia? *(b)* serum and infectious hepatitis?

4.   Explain why most states require a blood test for syphilis before a marriage license is issued.

5.   Are communicable diseases increasing or decreasing in the United States? Defend your answer.

Looking Ahead

Now that you have completed your study of communicable diseases, you are ready for a study of the most common non-communicable diseases. Chapter 24 will also discuss ways of protecting yourself from some of these diseases.

Communicable Diseases Today

Chapter 24: Noncommunicable Diseases Today

As you remember, Pasteur found out that invading microorganisms cause communicable diseases. Such diseases had long been the leading cause of death the world over. But from Pasteur's time on, scientists found the real causes of many communicable diseases and were able at last to fight them effectively.

As Figure 24.1 shows, chronic (long-lasting) **noncommunicable diseases** like heart diseases and cancer now cause the greatest number of deaths. Some of these noncommunicable diseases will no doubt be conquered as scientists come to understand their causes better. Can you protect yourself from these diseases? To some extent you can, and the information in this chapter should help you.

Ease and Disease

The word *ease* means freedom from pain and discomfort. The word *disease* simply means lack of ease. The pain and discomfort of noncommunicable diseases can have many causes, some of which you already know about. The following activity will help you think about these causes:

YOUR PART

1. Working alone or in small groups, list as many noncommunicable diseases (diabetes, lung cancer, and arthritis, for example) as you can. For help, refer again to page 372 (text and Table 22.1).
2. Beside each disease, list its cause or causes, if you think you know what these causes are.
3. As a class, compare your answers.

No doubt you noted that noncommunicable diseases have all kinds of causes. For example, you know from your study of cigarette smoking

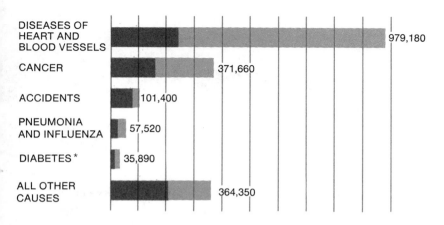

	NUMBER OF DEATHS	
DISEASES OF HEART AND BLOOD VESSELS		979,180
CANCER		371,660
ACCIDENTS		101,400
PNEUMONIA AND INFLUENZA		57,520
DIABETES*		35,890
ALL OTHER CAUSES		364,350

NUMBER OF DEATHS

▮ UNDER AGE 65

▮ AGE 65 AND OVER

*DEATHS FROM SUICIDE AND CIRRHOSIS OF THE LIVER
EXCEED THOSE FROM DIABETES FOR PERSONS UNDER
AGE 65.

**Figure 24.1. Leading causes of death, United States: 1975
estimates.**

that chemical irritation can cause lung cancer. However, you may also know that other kinds of cancers seem to have different causes. You also know that diet deficiencies can cause diseases like pellagra. And you probably also wrote down that disease can result when some part of the body is not working properly (as in diabetes).

Because you are young, you may not have thought of wear and tear as a cause of disease. But in the course of a long life, the human body, or parts of it, do wear out and grow weak. This wearing out and weakening may be one of the many causes of arthritis, a painful inflammation or swelling of a joint.

In addition, people's feelings sometimes seem to play a part in making them ill. And very often, illness seems to be caused by a combination of things. For example, you may have written that many causes working together (improper diet, irritation, stress, and lack of exercise, for example) might bring about an individual case of heart disease. You can compare all of the causes you listed with the causes of noncommunicable disease listed in Table 22.1, page 372.

Heart and Blood Vessel Disease

Heart disease, also called **coronary** (KAHR-uh-ner-ee) **disease,** often involves the blood vessels as well as the heart itself. In Figure 24.2 you can

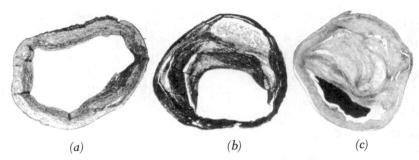

Figure 24.2. Progress of atherosclerosis: *(a)* **normal artery channel;** *(b)* **beginning of fatty deposits;** *(c)* **plugged artery channel.**

see the progress of disease in an artery. The pictured disease is called **atherosclerosis** (ATH-uh-roh-skluh-ROH-sis). In Figure 24.2*a*, you see a normal artery cut across. It has a wide blood channel. In Figure 24.2*b*, the deposit of fatty substances narrows the channel. In Figure 24.2*c*, the channel is so narrow and its lining so rough that a clot forms, resulting in a heart attack.

CAUSES OF ATHEROSCLEROSIS   In Chapter 12, page 170, you read how atherosclerosis can develop and cause a heart attack. Bit by bit, fatty deposits, such as **cholesterol** (kuh-LES-tuh-rawl), gather on the inner walls of arteries, narrowing the passageways through which the blood must travel. Although atherosclerosis usually doesn't show up until middle life, it may begin to develop in childhood or early youth as a result of some type of repeated injury to the inner walls of arteries. Fatty deposits have been found in the arteries of children, adolescents, and young adults.

So it's not too early for you to think about protecting yourself from atherosclerosis. How can you do this? As you read in Chapter 12, scientists don't yet know for sure what causes atherosclerosis, but they think that a diet high in saturated fats helps to cause the disease. Therefore, most doctors recommend a diet low in saturated fat. (See pages 170–171 for more diet information.)

HIGH BLOOD PRESSURE   **High blood pressure** is related to heart and blood vessel diseases. As you remember, blood pressure rises each time the heart contracts to pump blood through the blood vessels. And blood pressure falls each time the heart relaxes between the beats.

But sometimes, blood pressure goes up and remains above normal levels. This condition is called high blood pressure or *hypertension*. (The prefix *hyper* means over or above.) The increased pressure can damage blood vessels and make the heart work harder. In these and other ways, high blood pressure increases the risk of heart attack and stroke, which will be discussed shortly.

Causes of High Blood Pressure According to the American Heart Association, the causes of high blood pressure are unknown in more than 90 percent of all cases. Usually, though, the disease is easily detected by means of regular blood pressure tests. (On page 390 you can read how Dr. Martin took Tony's blood pressure as part of the physical examination.) Furthermore, once high blood pressure is detected, effective treatment is usually possible.

Treating High Blood Pressure High blood pressure can be treated with drugs that lower blood pressure. Special diets can be helpful, too. For example, a reducing diet may help to lower an overweight person's blood pressure. And a diet low in saturated fats and sodium (table salt, baking powder, and monosodium glutamate, or MSG, are high in sodium) also helps to lower blood pressure.

In addition, emotional stress seems to play a part in keeping some people's blood pressure high. Psychological counseling may help them. People with high blood pressure are also advised to stop smoking. The following activity will help you see why:

YOUR PART

MATERIALS
- Two large glass jars of equal size
- Two flexible siphon tubes 2 feet (60 centimeters) long, as follows: (1) a tube ¼ inch (6 millimeters) wide; (2) a tube ½ inch (12.5 millimeters) wide

PROCEDURES
1. Working at a sink, fill both jars to the same level with water (see Figure 24.3).
2. Have two student volunteers begin at the same time to siphon water from the two jars, each using a flexible tube of a different width.

Figure 24.3.

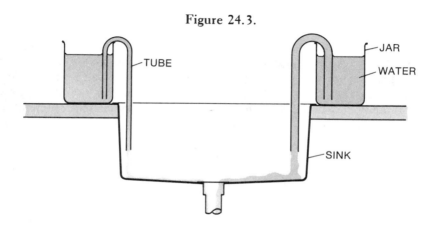

3. On a separate piece of paper, write down your answers to the following questions:
   a. Which tube empties a jar more quickly?
   b. Which tube, therefore, offers less resistance to the flow of water?
   c. Since smoking narrows, or constricts, blood vessels, how does smoking affect blood flow? What effect should this have on blood pressure?
   d. How does atherosclerosis, which also narrows blood vessels, affect blood pressure?
   e. Do you think that smoking increases the risk of heart attack and stroke?
   f. Do you think that high blood pressure increases the risk of heart attack and stroke?

No doubt you wrote that both smoking and atherosclerosis raise blood pressure and thereby increase the risk of heart attack and stroke. But you may not know how risky a combination of smoking, high blood pressure, and a high cholesterol level can be. Figure 24.4 illustrates these combined risks.

CAUSES OF A HEART ATTACK   A heart attack, also called a **coronary,** is caused by the blockage of an artery that supplies the heart with blood. Without oxygen and nutrients, the part of the heart that was formerly fed by the blocked artery begins to die. What blocks the artery? A blood clot does. Such clots are not likely to form in healthy arteries. But remember that the thick, rough deposits of cholesterol found in the arteries of people with atherosclerosis build up and jut out. Blood clots can then form around these deposits more easily. A narrowed artery is much more easily blocked than a healthy one.

Additional Circulatory Pathways   Luckily, when a clot blocks a blood vessel, nearby blood vessels gradually enlarge and open new branches in order to take over the work of the blocked blood vessel.

These new pathways for circulation can develop in a heart long before any blockage occurs.

When a person exercises regularly, the heart develops additional circulatory pathways through which the blood carries the extra oxygen and nutrients required by the body of the exerciser. This is one of the reasons why so many doctors advise a lifelong program of daily exercise, preferably begun in youth when health is most vigorous.

CAUSES OF A STROKE   A blood clot can block an artery at the spot where the clot forms. The clot can also break off and travel through the

Protect Yourself Against Disease

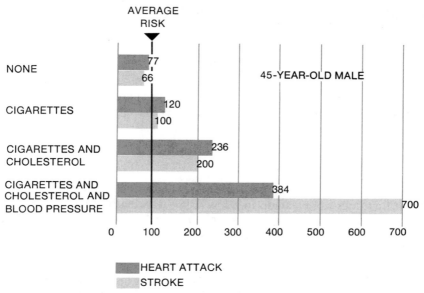

Figure 24.4. How danger of heart attack and stroke increases with a combination of risk factors. (As shown, the risk of stroke for a 45-year-old male who smokes cigarettes and has high cholesterol is two times greater than it would be if he didn't smoke and had a low cholesterol level. His risk of heart attack is even slightly higher. When high blood pressure is an added factor, his risk for stroke, in particular, increases dramatically.)

bloodstream until it comes to a passageway too narrow to let it pass. That blood vessel then becomes blocked. A blood clot blocking a blood vessel in the brain may cause a **stroke**.

A stroke may also result from the bursting of an artery in the brain. Such an artery may have been weakened or damaged by high blood pressure. The broken artery bleeds, and later a blood clot forms. Both the bleeding and the clot can block circulation to nerve cells in the brain that control mental and physical activity. As a result, a stroke victim's memory, speech, or movement may be slightly or severely affected, depending on where the blockage occurs.

REDUCING YOUR RISKS Prompt treatment is vital for victims of heart attack and stroke. And, fortunately, many such victims do recover. However, most people would rather prevent a heart attack than recover from one. The following activity will give you a chance to recall what you have learned in the last few pages about preventing heart attacks and strokes:

1. Write down the steps you can take now and in the future to reduce your risk of heart attack and stroke.
2. As a class, compare your answers.

Your list probably included such things as taking regular exercise, maintaining your ideal weight, cutting down on saturated fats, having regular checkups (including blood pressure tests), and not smoking.

There is another thing you can do. See your doctor if you have a sore throat that does not clear up in a few days—especially if you also have a fever. This is important because strep, short for **streptococcus** (strep-tuh-KAHK-us), infections of the throat can lead in many instances to rheumatic heart disease.

RHEUMATIC HEART DISEASE   Most heart disease develops slowly and shows up in middle age or later. But **rheumatic** (roo-MAT-ik) **heart disease** can begin in youth and continue to be troublesome from then on. In this disease, the heart valves (see pages 50–51) are damaged so that they no longer work properly. Surgery can sometimes partially repair the damaged valves. But prevention, which involves promptly treating strep infections with penicillin, is better than cure.

Penicillin for a Strep Throat   Many strep infections clear up without affecting the heart valves. But rheumatic heart disease never develops unless a strep infection (like strep throat) has occurred first. So a person with a very sore throat or with tonsillitis should have a throat culture test (see Figure 24.5). If a laboratory test shows that a strep infection is present, the doctor will prescribe penicillin to clear up the infection and prevent the development of rheumatic heart disease.

Figure 24.5. *(left)* **Taking a throat specimen to test for strep infection;** *(right)* **culturing the specimen.**

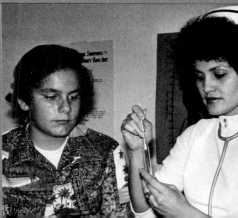

Let's Pause for Review

Noncommunicable diseases have many causes. For example, improper diet, stress, smoking, and inactivity may help to bring on heart disease, today's leading killer. When a blood clot blocks an artery that feeds the heart, a heart attack results. When a blood clot (or bleeding from a burst blood vessel) blocks an artery in the brain, a stroke results. Most doctors believe you can reduce the risk of heart attack and stroke by maintaining your ideal weight, cutting down on saturated fats, taking regular exercise, having regular checkups and blood pressure tests, and not smoking.

The best way to protect yourself against rheumatic fever is to see your doctor whenever you have a very sore throat or tonsillitis. If a strep infection is present, the doctor can treat it effectively with penicillin.

The Second Greatest Killer

Only heart disease kills more Americans than **cancer** does. Unfortunately, many people are so afraid of cancer that they delay doing the one thing they can do to protect themselves from the disease. They delay or even forget about seeing a doctor when they first notice some unusual symptom.

Yet cancer is mostly curable in its early stages. In fact, the American Cancer Society estimates that, at present, twice as many people could be saved from cancer if only treatment were begun earlier. (This means that in two thirds of all cases cancer can be cured.)

In addition, scientists are hopeful that they will soon be able to fight cancer even more effectively. For example, researchers who suspect that viruses cause some cancers hope to identify such viruses and to develop successful weapons against them. Already researchers have identified the cause of most lung cancers (cigarette smoking) and many mouth cancers (mouth irritations resulting from pipe smoking, for example).

HOW CANCER KILLS   As you learned in Chapter 19, "Tobacco and Health," cancer is not one disease, but rather many diseases affecting different parts of the body. Cancerous growth is abnormal, uncontrolled cell reproduction. Like weeds, cancerous cells crowd out normal cells by robbing them of food and space. In time, groups of cancerous cells break off and travel by means of the blood and the lymph to other parts of the body. In the end, cancerous cells crowd out so many normal cells that the body can no longer carry on its work (see Figure 24.6, page 420).

TREATMENT   The aim of cancer treatments is to find and destroy cancerous cells before they are able to spread. The most common and

Table 24.1:   Cancer's Seven Danger Signals

1. Unusual bleeding or discharge
2. A lump or thickening in the breast or elsewhere
3. A sore that does not heal
4. Change in bowel or bladder habits
5. Hoarseness or cough
6. Indigestion or difficulty in swallowing
7. Change in size or color of a wart or mole

effective cancer cure at present is complete removal of the cancerous growth by surgery. Another effective weapon against cancer is **radiation treatment.** X rays, *radium*, and substances such as *radioactive cobalt*, for example, all send out (or radiate) energy that can be used to destroy cancer cells.

In addition, drugs of many kinds have been used to slow cancerous growth. For example, surgery is useless against **leukemia** (loo-KEE-mee-uh), a form of cancer in which white blood cells crowd out red blood cells. But various drugs have been useful in slowing down the advance of leukemia.

PROTECTING YOURSELF AGAINST CANCER   How can you protect yourself against cancer? First, you can learn cancer's seven danger signals (see Table 24.1). And if any of these symptoms appear and persist for more than two weeks, you should see your doctor promptly. But remember, there is no need for panic. A great many abnormal growths, or tumors, are **benign** (buh-NYN) rather than **malignant** (muh-LIG-nunt). (Benign tumors will not spread to other parts of the body as malignant, or cancerous, tumors will.) And even malignant growths can be successfully removed, if they are discovered early.

Figure 24.6. Cancer growing alongside a blood vessel and entering the bloodstream.

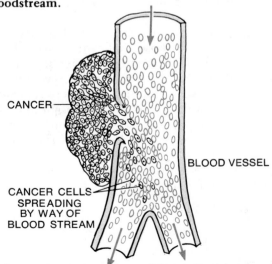

CANCER

BLOOD VESSEL

CANCER CELLS
SPREADING
BY WAY OF
BLOOD STREAM

Figure 24.7. Rheumatoid
arthritis of the hand.

Arthritis

Heart disease kills many people, and it disables (limits the activity of) many more. But next to heart disease, **arthritis** (ahr-THRY-tis) disables more people in the United States than does any other chronic condition. There are several kinds of arthritis. The two most common are *rheumatoid* (ROO-muh-toyd) arthritis and *degenerative* (dih-JEN-uh-ruh-tiv) arthritis.

Although researchers continue to work at discovering the cause or causes of rheumatoid arthritis, they have been unsuccessful to date. In this disease, the joints become inflamed and swollen. The inflammation may come on gradually or suddenly, accompanied by pain and fever. Repeated attacks may deform the joints (see Figure 24.7). Early medical treatment is

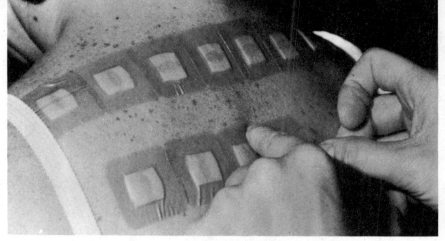

Figure 24.8. To test this person's sensitivity, the skin has been
scratched, and many different allergens have been applied.

important to lessen damage that this disease might cause to joints, to relieve pain, and to guide the patient in retraining affected joints.

Medical supervision is important with degenerative arthritis, too. Degenerative arthritis results from wear and tear on the joints. Overweight people, especially those who stand at their jobs for many years, develop this kind of arthritis more often than other people do.

Allergy

It isn't surprising to learn that about 3 million people in the United States must limit their activity because they have arthritis. It is a little more surprising to learn that almost half that number must limit their activity somewhat because they suffer from severe allergies.

Allergy is abnormal sensitivity to substances of vegetable and animal origin, including drugs. This sensitivity causes the body to produce a harmful substance called **histamine** (HIS-tuh-meen), which affects the skin, nose, bronchial tubes, and digestive system. Allergies can make some people uncomfortable and others quite sick. Allergies affect people of every age, race, and region. Heredity seems to play some part in the development of allergies. But nobody really knows why some people are allergic and others are not. Many allergy symptoms are treated with **antihistamines,** which are drugs that counteract histamine.

ASTHMA   Because **asthma** (AZ-muh) sometimes threatens life, it is the most serious of the symptoms of allergy. In asthma, the smaller bronchial tubes react allergically. The tube linings produce extra mucus. Spasms (involuntary contractions) of the muscular walls of the tubes squeeze the tubes together, reducing the size of the air passages. These changes make breathing extremely difficult.

Treatment   Severe asthma attacks can be treated with **adrenaline** (uh-DREN-uh-lin), which relaxes the muscle spasms. But longtime treatment begins with identification of the substance that causes the allergic reactions (see Figure 24.8). If this substance, called the **allergen** (AL-ur-jun), can be identified, the allergic person may be able to avoid it.

In addition, sensitivity can sometimes be lessened by a series of injections containing gradually increased amounts of the allergen. Such medical care is important, because some doctors believe that longtime asthma may make a person more likely to develop the lung disease emphysema. (Emphysema and bronchitis are discussed in Chapter 19, pages 318–321.)

Present-day researchers are hopeful about the future. Some researchers report success in coaching asthma sufferers to breathe normally during attacks. Other scientists are at work on drugs that they hope will block allergic reactions such as asthma.

Diabetes

Two people out of every hundred have **diabetes** (dy-uh-BEE-teez). But of those two people, only one knows that he or she has the disease. Like high blood pressure, diabetes may produce few noticeable symptoms. But, as with high blood pressure, a doctor can easily detect the presence of the disease and prescribe effective treatment to control it.

As you will probably remember from Chapter 7, page 82, the islets of Langerhans in the pancreas of a diabetic person produce too little insulin, or the person's body cells are unable to use the insulin present. Without sufficient insulin, the body cells can neither obtain nor store energy from glucose (a sugar) in a normal manner. As a result, the amount of sugar in the blood and in the urine rises.

Not long ago, diabetes was in every case a fatal disease. But in 1922, two Canadian scientists, Dr. Frederick Banting and Dr. Charles Best, succeeded in extracting insulin from the pancreas of sheep. This extract could then be injected into diabetics to supply the insulin their bodies lacked. And in 1957, a new preparation was developed that could be taken orally (by mouth). The kind of diabetes that appears in childhood must usually be treated with injections of insulin. But many adult diabetics can control the disease with the new oral medication.

WHO GETS DIABETES?   An overweight person over 40 years of age with a family history of diabetes is more likely to develop the disease than a slim person with no family history of diabetes. Also, women suffer from diabetes more often than men. You can't change your heredity, age, or sex. But by maintaining the weight that is right for you, you can help protect yourself from diabetes as well as from atherosclerosis, high blood pressure, and degenerative arthritis.

Noncommunicable Diseases Today   423

SYMPTOMS   At your regular physical examination, you may take a blood sugar test for diabetes if your doctor thinks it necessary. You should also be aware of the symptoms of diabetes. For one thing, a diabetic becomes unusually thirsty. And the extra water that is drunk produces frequent urination.

Because a diabetic's body can't make use of all the food eaten, a diabetic feels hungry and often increases the amount of food intake. In spite of the extra food, however, a diabetic often loses weight because the body can't make use of the carbohydrates in the diet. A diabetic may also have a low resistance to infections, itching, failing eyesight, and pain in fingers and toes.

Of course, you may have one or more of these symptoms without being a diabetic. But a person who has these symptoms for some period of time should see a doctor. Untreated diabetes can cause major health problems. And an estimated 2 million Americans have undetected, untreated diabetes. The following activity will give you a chance to observe one method of testing for this disease:

YOUR PART

The extra sugar in a diabetic's blood spills over into the urine, where its presence can be detected by chemical tests like the one you are now going to make. A water and corn syrup mixture will be used as a substitute for sugar-rich urine.

MATERIALS
- Clinitest reagent tablets (available from most druggists)
- Color chart for interpreting results (also available from most druggists)
- Liquid container holding 1 glass of water mixed with 1 tablespoon of corn syrup
- Liquid container holding untreated water (tap water)
- Two test tubes in a rack
- Two eye droppers
- Forceps (tweezers)

PROCEDURES
1. Using one of the eye droppers, draw up some of the water and corn syrup mixture and release five drops of the mixture into a test tube.
2. Place the test tube in the rack.
3. Using the other eye dropper, draw up some of the untreated water and release five drops into the second test tube.
4. Place the second test tube in the rack also.
5. Label each tube to show its contents.

Protect Yourself Against Disease

6. Using the eye dropper that has not been in contact with the water and corn syrup mixture, add ten drops of tap water to each test tube in the rack.
7. Shake the tubes gently and put them back in the rack.
8. Using the forceps to pick up the Clinitest tablets, carefully drop one tablet into each test tube without shaking or moving it in any way.
9. Observe each test tube carefully. (Caution: The tubes will become hot, so do not touch them for at least ten minutes.)
10. When the test tubes are again cool, remove them from the rack, shake them gently, and replace them in the rack.
11. What is the test for sugar?
12. Why were two test tubes used?

In the test tube containing the water and corn syrup mixture, you probably noted a series of color changes from green to brown after the Clinitest tablet was added. By matching these colors with the color guide on the chart, you can easily tell the percent of sugar in the tested sample. (The test tube containing untreated water was your control.)

In the same way that you used Clinitest tablets to detect the presence of sugar in a water and corn syrup mixture, diabetics use either such tablets or specially treated test papers to check for the presence of sugar in the urine. The test paper changes color if excess sugar is present. By regularly taking such tests, by following special diets, and by taking the necessary medication, most diabetics can lead normal lives.

Anemia

Anemia (uh-NEE-mee-uh), which means bloodlessness, can be a symptom of several diseases. Anemia sometimes refers to a simple shortage of blood—following an accident, for example, in which a good deal of blood has been lost. More often, however, anemia refers to a shortage of red blood cells or a shortage of the **hemoglobin** (HEE-muh-gloh-bun) that gives red blood cells their color.

A shortage of hemoglobin is most often due to too little iron in the diet. (Liver, lean meat, molasses, egg yolk, green vegetables, and nuts are all rich in iron.) **Pernicious** (pur-NISH-us) **anemia** (an increasing shortage in the number of red blood cells and an increase in their size) is a deficiency disease, too. It is more serious than common anemia. Extract of liver, vitamin B_{12}, and folic acid (another B vitamin) are used to treat pernicious anemia.

Usually, a well-balanced diet will prevent anemia. But, of course, you

NORMAL

SICKLE

Figure 24.9. A normal red blood cell compared with a sickled red blood cell.

should see your doctor if the symptoms of anemia appear. Anemia symptoms may include pale skin, loss of appetite, lack of energy, and weakness.

Sickle-Cell Anemia

Sickle-cell anemia is a hereditary disease that deforms the red blood cells (see Figure 24.9). When the oxygen supply is plentiful, the red blood cells are of normal shape. However, when the oxygen supply is poor, as in periods of exertion, the red blood cells become deformed and take on a sickle shape. In this shape, the red blood cells do not flow normally. Instead, they clog small blood vessels. For this reason, the body cells of a person with sickle-cell anemia do not receive as much oxygen as they need.

SYMPTOMS Like people who are deficient in iron, sickle-cell sufferers may lose their appetites and become pale, tired, and short of breath. In addition, sickle-cell victims may grow and develop more slowly than they should. They may have pains in their arms, legs, backs, and abdomens. (At times of attack, such pains may become extreme.) The whites of their eyes may take on a yellow color, and their joints may swell. What is more, they usually have a low resistance to infection.

TREATMENT As yet there is no complete cure for sickle-cell anemia, but recently scientists have discovered that a chemical called *cyanate* (SY-uh-nayt) tends to unsickle deformed red blood cells. There is hope that research will provide even more effective treatment in the future. However, doctors can now insure that their patients are made resistant to as many communicable diseases as possible. And doctors can help such patients maintain their general health at the highest possible level.

A HEREDITARY DISEASE   Far more black Americans have sickle-cell anemia than any other group in our country. Sickle-cell disease takes two forms. The milder form is called **sickle-cell trait** and is found in about one out of every ten black Americans. People with sickle-cell trait usually do not develop sickle-cell anemia, but they carry a gene for sickle-cell disease, which they can pass along to their children.

If a mother and a father both have sickle-cell trait, their child has one chance in four of being completely normal. The child has two chances in four of having sickle-cell trait like the parents. The child has one chance in four of being born with sickle-cell anemia, the serious form of the disease, which affects about one in every 400 black Americans.

Both sickle-cell trait and sickle-cell anemia can be detected by blood tests. Many cities have set up clinics to give such tests. These clinics make it easier for people to find out, before they marry, whether or not they are likely to pass sickle-cell disease on to their children.

Muscular Dystrophy

Muscular dystrophy is hereditary. It usually affects voluntary muscles but sometimes also affects heart muscle. Muscle in an affected person is replaced by connective tissue and fat. Strength is lost. This condition shows up when a child is beginning to walk. The child may waddle and fall frequently. There is no known treatment at present, except for encouraging the sufferer to keep active.

Let's Pause for Review

Cancer is abnormal, uncontrolled cell growth, which can spread throughout the body. Cancer is most easily cured in its early stages. You can help protect yourself from this disease by making regular visits to your doctor and by getting prompt medical attention if you notice any of the seven symptoms that may warn of cancer's presence. In addition, you can avoid smoking and overexposure to sunlight, X rays, and radium.

Prompt medical treatment is also important in the care of rheumatoid arthritis (a disease that affects the joints) and asthma (an allergy symptom that affects the bronchial tubes). Diabetes (a disease that results when the body's faulty production or use of insulin upsets normal oxidation of glucose in cells), anemia (a shortage of blood, red blood cells, or hemoglobin), and sickle-cell anemia (sickle-shaped red blood cells) must also be detected and treated by a doctor.

Muscular dystrophy is a hereditary disease that affects muscle tissue in small children. There is no known cure for this disease.

Diseases of the Nervous System

In Chapter 7, page 72, you studied the workings of the nervous system. A number of noncommunicable diseases affect this body system. **Epilepsy** (EP-uh-lep-see), **multiple sclerosis** (skluh-ROH-sis) and **cerebral** (suh-REE-brul) **palsy** are three such diseases of the nervous system.

EPILEPSY People with epilepsy have been the object of curious attention throughout human history. Epilepsy was long called the "divine sickness" because epileptics were believed to have special powers. In primitive societies an epileptic often became the tribe's healer.

Thirty years ago, it was impossible to attend a sizable school or to go about the streets of a large city without seeing an epileptic *seizure* (SEE-zhur), or fit, from time to time. But nowadays, thanks to modern drugs, epileptic seizures are much rarer. More than 50 percent of epileptics need no longer fear either their own seizures or the stares of the curious. In many other cases, the severity of seizures has been greatly reduced. Unfortunately, however, many old laws still reduce the rights and privileges of epileptics, as you may discover in doing the following activity:

YOUR PART

1. Have student volunteers phone or visit the local chapter of the Epilepsy Foundation of America and ask for information, in printed

Figure 24.10. Electrical impulses in the brain shown by an EEG (electroencephalogram).

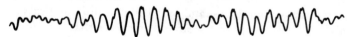

NORMAL BRAIN WAVES

EPILEPTIC BRAIN WAVES

form if possible, on the activities of the Foundation and its work in educating the government and the public about epilepsy.

2. Have the volunteer students display in class any materials they have obtained and report to the class on what they have learned about the Epilepsy Foundation of America.

No doubt you found that the Foundation was both helpful and informative. You may have learned that many jobs in your state are closed to epileptics. In some places, epileptics have been denied the privilege of driving and even the right to marry. Now try to answer the following questions:

1. Why have restrictive laws against epileptics been passed?
2. Is epilepsy inherited?
3. What do you now know about the types and the severity of epileptic seizures?

Epileptic seizures are of two kinds. In one kind, an epileptic falls to the ground unconscious. The body stiffens and goes into *convulsions* (a series of violent, involuntary muscular contractions). What causes the seizure? It is caused by a temporary disturbance of the electrical impulses in the brain (see Figure 24.10).

During the other kind of seizure, the epileptic loses consciousness for such a short period of time that the victim may not even be aware of the seizure. There may be a little twitching about the eyes and mouth, but the epileptic remains in the same position, seated or standing, without falling to the ground.

First Aid   With the help of modern drugs, many seizures have been brought under complete control. However, if you see an epileptic in a seizure, you can help by removing from the area any hard objects that the victim might otherwise bump into. Don't try to move or hold down an epileptic. Don't *force* any object into the mouth—you may break a tooth. But if the mouth is open and relaxed, you may place a soft object like a rolled handkerchief between the teeth to prevent the tongue from being bitten. And try to see that the position of the epileptic is such that the airway to the lungs is kept open.

Causes of Epilepsy   Epilepsy is not a single disease. Instead, epilepsy seems to be a symptom of several different diseases. For example, epilepsy can result from an injury to the brain before, during, or after birth. Other causes include poisoning, brain tumors, and inflammation of the brain or its coverings.

Injuries and inflammations are not inherited, of course. On the other

Noncommunicable Diseases Today   **429**

hand, some scientists believe that there may be a genetic (hereditary) factor in the development of some types of epilepsy. Epilepsy has no effect on intelligence or general health. Julius Caesar, famous Roman general, statesman, and writer, was an epileptic. Feodor Dostoevski, a great Russian writer and himself an epileptic, wrote about epilepsy in his novel *The Idiot*. And, except for the special laws affecting them, most epileptics today live normal, active lives.

MULTIPLE SCLEROSIS   Protective tissue surrounds nerve fibers. In some unknown way, multiple sclerosis (or MS) destroys some of this protective tissue. Where this happens, the protective tissue is replaced by scars. These scars interfere with nerve messages sent by the brain to the rest of the body. As a result, some of the nervous system's control over motion and speech is lost.

MS, which most often strikes people between the ages of 20 and 40, is disabling but rarely fatal. In fact, most MS sufferers lead long and useful lives. Medical supervision helps MS patients to maintain their general health. But MS sufferers look most hopefully to research (sponsored by the National Multiple Sclerosis Society) into possible causes of and cures for the disease.

CEREBRAL PALSY   A person with cerebral palsy also has imperfect muscular control as a result of damage to the nervous system. The damage may be caused by lack of oxygen or by an infection or brain injury before, during, or soon after birth. Thus, instead of being a single disease, cerebral palsy is a term for many disabilities, each of which may have a different cause. Some cerebral palsy patients, for example, lack voluntary muscular control. Others, known as **spastics** (SPAS-tiks), move jerkily because their muscular activity is poorly coordinated.

As with MS, research offers the best hope for cerebral palsy sufferers and their families. At present, there are no cures, and little is known about prevention. However, patient, longtime training can help cerebral palsy victims to move around as much as possible. Medical care and education are also important because disabilities in speech, hearing, sight, and learning are often part of cerebral palsy.

Looking Back

How can you protect yourself from noncommunicable disease? Most doctors believe that you can reduce the risk of heart attack and stroke by maintaining your ideal weight, cutting down on saturated fats, taking proper exercise, having regular checkups, and not smoking. The best protection against rheumatic heart

Protect Yourself Against Disease

disease is to have a medical checkup whenever you have a very sore throat or tonsillitis. A strep infection, if present, can be effectively treated with penicillin.

To protect yourself against cancer, you should avoid smoking, overexposure to the sun, and unnecessary exposure to X rays, radium, and similar radioactive substances. You should also make regular visits to your doctor, especially if you notice any of cancer's seven warning signals.

Regular visits to your doctor are also important for the detection and early treatment of rheumatoid arthritis, allergies (a severe symptom of which is asthma), diabetes, and anemia.

Muscular dystrophy and diseases of the nervous system also require prompt treatment or at least longtime supervision. In the case of epilepsy, seizures can often be completely controlled by medication. There are so far no cures for multiple sclerosis, cerebral palsy, or muscular dystrophy, but medical training and supervised exercise can help the victims of these diseases move about as much as possible and live fairly normal lives.

MODIFIED TRUE-FALSE QUESTIONS

1. The largest number of deaths in this country result from cancer and _tuberculosis._
2. Arthritis is a disease that may cause swelling of _joints._
3. Atherosclerosis often begins to develop in _childhood._
4. Diets _low_ in saturated fat produce deposits on the inner walls of blood vessels.
5. In most cases, the causes of high blood pressure are _unknown._
6. Diets _high_ in sodium help to control hypertension.
7. Blood clots form _more_ easily in arteries whose walls are lined with cholesterol.
8. Blood clots blocking blood vessels in the _heart_ produce strokes.
9. A strep throat requires medical attention because it may lead to _rheumatic_ heart disease.
10. Cancer is most curable in its _early_ stages.
11. Hypertension _increases_ the risk of stroke.
12. Common and effective cancer cures include surgical removal of the growth, radiation, and _use of drugs._
13. _Benign_ growths are cancerous.
14. Wear and tear on joints produces _rheumatoid_ arthritis.
15. During an allergy attack, the body produces a harmful substance called _adrenaline._

16. Spasms of the small bronchial tubes cause _asthma_.
17. Some doctors believe that longtime asthma may make the lungs more likely to develop _emphysema_.
18. Banting and Best extracted _insulin_ from the pancreas of sheep.
19. Women have diabetes _less_ often than men.
20. One kind of anemia that is hereditary is _pernicious_ anemia.

MATCHING QUESTIONS

Column A		Column B
1. diabetes	a.	deformed red blood cells
2. sickle-cell anemia	b.	red blood cells crowded out by white blood cells
3. leukemia		
4. hypertension	c.	high cholesterol level
5. asthma	d.	"divine sickness"
6. arthritis	e.	high glucose level
7. epilepsy	f.	disease of the joints
8. cerebral palsy	g.	vitamin deficiency
9. atherosclerosis	h.	spastics
10. lung cancer	i.	major cause is cigarette smoking
	j.	high blood pressure
	k.	allergenic disease

COMPLETION QUESTIONS

1. Pellagra is an example of a (an) _____ disease.
2. For those who suffer from atherosclerosis, doctors recommend a diet low in _____ fat.
3. The prefix _hyper_ means _____.
4. Hypertension can be treated with drugs that _____ (increase, decrease) blood pressure.
5. Emotional stress generally _____ (increases, decreases) blood pressure.
6. When a clot blocks a blood vessel, nearby blood vessels often open up new _____.
7. A common medication used to treat strep throat is _____.
8. Abnormal sensitivity to certain substances is called _____.
9. To counteract allergic reactions, doctors prescribe drugs that contain _____.
10. With too little insulin, the amount of sugar in the blood and urine _____.

Protect Yourself Against Disease

MULTIPLE-CHOICE QUESTIONS

1. The disease that ranks next to heart disease in disabling people is
   a. arthritis   b. diabetes   c. cancer   d. emphysema
2. Which of the following is *not* a chronic disease?
   a. hypertension   b. diabetes   c. cancer   d. influenza
3. The disease caused by some imbalance between production of insulin and the body's demand for it is
   a. arthritis   b. diabetes   c. cancer   d. emphysema
4. Atherosclerosis can be promoted by a
   a. diet high in saturated fats   c. fat-free diet
   b. diet low in saturated fats   d. high vitamin diet
5. Which of the following is *not* a treatment for hypertension?
   a. drugs   c. cyanate
   b. low sodium intake   d. reducing diet
6. In rheumatic heart disease, the parts of the heart that are damaged are the
   a. valves   b. muscles   c. auricles   d. ventricles
7. The second leading cause of death in the United States is
   a. heart disease   b. cancer   c. emphysema   d. diabetes
8. When the bronchial tubes produce excessive mucus, with spasms and difficulty in breathing, the person is suffering from
   a. asthma   b. bronchitis   c. emphysema   d. lung cancer
9. Of the following persons, the one *least* likely to develop diabetes is the one who
   a. is slim
   b. is overweight
   c. has a family history of diabetes
   d. is slim with *no* family history of diabetes
10. Which of the following is *not* true about multiple sclerosis?
    a. does not prevent sufferers from leading long and useful lives
    b. most often strikes between the ages of 20 and 40
    c. is rarely fatal
    d. is always fatal before age 20
11. Diabetes affects
    a. 2 people out of every 100
    b. 5 people out of every 100
    c. 10 people out of every 100
    d. 20 people out of every 100
12. Which of the following is *not* a symptom of diabetes?
    a. itchiness
    b. loss of appetite
    c. increase of appetite with weight loss
    d. excessive thirst
13. The most common cause of shortage of hemoglobin in the blood is lack of
    a. iron   b. calcium   c. iodine   d. vitamin C

Noncommunicable Diseases Today   433

14. All of the following are used in the treatment of pernicious anemia, *except*
    a. extract of liver   c. vitamin B_{12}
    b. high doses of vitamin C   d. folic acid
15. In first aid treatment of an individual suffering from an epileptic seizure, which of the following should you do?
    a. force objects into the mouth
    b. hold the person down
    c. remove hard objects that are near the victim
    d. move the individual

THOUGHT QUESTIONS

1. Most people can help protect themselves against heart disease. Keeping this in mind, answer the following questions:

    a. List the risk factors that make an individual more apt to develop heart disease.
    b. Which of the factors you listed involve habits that can be controlled by the individual?
    c. What advice can you give people to decrease the chances of a heart attack?

2. Sickle-cell anemia and sickle-cell trait are different conditions. Discuss the differences and similarities by answering the following questions:

    a. Who may get these conditions?
    b. Statistically, how many suffer from these conditions?
    c. What are the symptoms of each condition?
    d. How can these conditions be detected?

3. Refer again to Figure 24.4, page 417. What is the danger of a heart attack or a stroke if *(a)* a person smokes but has low cholesterol? *(b)* a person smokes and has high cholesterol? *(c)* a person smokes and has high cholesterol and high blood pressure?

4. Malignant tumors commonly occur in the breasts and in the digestive and reproductive systems of females. Using Table 24.1, page 420, list the danger signals that could be symptoms of cancerous growths in these areas.

5. People who are better educated generally suffer from fewer diseases. Take a position on this statement and defend your answer.

Looking Ahead

Now that you have studied ways of protecting yourself from disease, you are ready in Chapter 25 to consider ways of protecting both yourself and your community from pollution.

Unit Nine: LIVE AND WORK IN A HEALTHIER WORLD

Already you are adult in many ways. Soon you will be fully adult, with adult freedoms and concerns. This unit will discuss a few of those concerns. Some, like the choice of a career, are personal. Others, like consumer education and reduction of pollution, should be important to you in your role as a responsible member of the community.

Whatever the area of concern, a little forethought is usually helpful. For example, if you think well and imaginatively about yourself as a candidate for a wide variety of jobs, chances are you will make good career choices. And the more you learn about problems such as pollution and consumer protection, the more effective and useful you can be as a voter and community member.

Each past generation has made its own special changes in the world, and yours will, too. Your generation has already given clear signs that it will work hard to lessen pollution and help to preserve the natural beauty of the world.

Chapter 25: Pollution and Health

On a small, crowded spaceship, every inch of space is used and nothing is wasted. On a spaceship designed to leave the earth for a very long period of time, air and water would be *recycled* (used, purified, and used again). As we now are learning, our earth is like a spaceship, too.

Spaceship Earth speeds around the sun at the rate of about 18½ miles (30 kilometers) a second. And although our earth is roomy and well supplied with everything we need to live, our space and our natural resources are not limitless. If we waste many materials or dirty our air and water too much, we cannot survive any more than a careless, wasteful astronaut could survive in outer space.

Figure 25.1. Natural recycling of carbon dioxide, oxygen, and other natural materials.

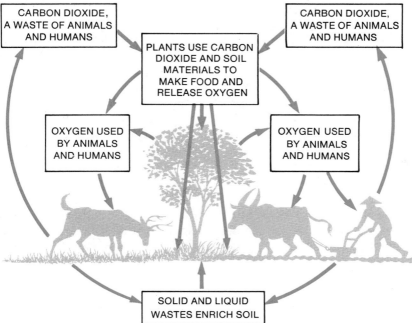

Figure 25.2. Industrial pollution.

Natural Recycling

For most of human history, recycling has occurred naturally. For example, oxygen, a plant by-product, helps support human and animal life. Plants feed animals. Plants and animals feed people. Human and animal solid and liquid wastes return to the earth and enrich the soil in which plants grow. Carbon dioxide, a waste gas given off by humans and animals, is taken in by plants, which need it to live. Plants then release oxygen, which helps support more human and animal life (see Figure 25.1). Until about 200 years ago, there were few wastes that could not be taken up and used by organisms and then returned and reused naturally.

Furthermore, natural processes tended to keep things tidy. As you know, insects, molds, and bacteria soon consume a peach that drops from a tree or a butterfly that dies and falls to the ground. In the past, natural processes also maintained a balance between population and food supply. If insects, animals, or people multiplied so fast that they outstripped their food supply, many of them soon died of starvation or disease.

Two Revolutions

These natural processes are still at work, of course, but they can no longer purify all waste materials. Moreover, many natural balances (like the one between population and food supply) have been upset. In the last 200 years, two great revolutions (so called because they have brought about rapid, fundamental change) have repeatedly upset the balance of nature

Live and Work in a Healthier World

and interfered with natural recycling. They are the Industrial Revolution and the Scientific Revolution.

THE INDUSTRIAL REVOLUTION The *Industrial Revolution* changed the way in which things were made. Before 1750, most of the things people owned and used were handmade. But from about that time on, a great many machines were invented. Before long, items made by machine were more common than items made by hand, at least in the industrialized countries.

Industrial Pollution Industrial **pollution** began at once. (Pollution is the addition of dirt or injurious substances to our air, water, or food.) Ever since, factories have been pouring smoke into the air and chemicals into the rivers (see Figure 25.2). Why couldn't natural processes take care of these industrial wastes? First of all, too much industrial waste was often produced for natural processes to purify it. And second, some industrial wastes and products are not **biodegradable** (by-oh-dih-GRAY-duh-bul), which means that natural processes cannot break them down (or degrade them) into simpler, usable forms (see Figure 25.3).

YOUR PART

1. As a class or in small groups, list any materials you know of that are not biodegradable.
2. Discuss what can be done with products that are not biodegradable. Should there be laws against their manufacture? How can such products be prevented from cluttering the environment?

You probably noted that certain synthetic detergents (soaplike materials) and certain kinds of plastic are not biodegradable. You may

Figure 25.3. Plastics are not broken down by natural processes.

have recommended that nonbiodegradable plastics be labeled as such so that they can be collected, recycled by their manufacturers, and reused. You may have agreed that some detergents should not be used in areas where drains and sewers empty into lakes and rivers.

But plastics and detergents are only two troublesome products. There are thousands more—thousands of products and thousands of industrial waste materials. The problem of recycling all of these materials is enormous. But it is a problem the industrial nations must solve if they are to remain healthy and continue to have attractive places in which to live (see Figure 25.4). It is also a problem that each family must deal with, as the following activity shows:

YOUR PART

1. Make two columns on a piece of paper. Head one column *Disposable Items*. Head the other column *Recycling*. Now go through your home, listing all of the items that are made to be thrown away. In the kitchen, for example, list disposable containers (bottles, packages, cans), as well as such disposable items as paper towels. Next, add to your list any appliances (like a refrigerator or TV set), furnishings (like a sofa or rug), or vehicles (like a car or bike) that are likely to need replacing within the next five years.
2. Do you think the items you have listed can be recycled? In the *Recycling* column, write your answer (*yes* or *no*) opposite each entry in the *Disposable Items* column. Take your list to class.
3. As a class, discuss your lists and your ideas about recycling.

THE SCIENTIFIC REVOLUTION In the last three chapters, you read about the scientific conquest of disease. You therefore know that hundreds of thousands of people who once would have died during infancy or childhood now reach middle or old age. Thus, a person born in 1910 could expect to live, on the average, about 47 years. But a person born in 1974 can expect to live, on the average, about 72 years. The Industrial Revolution has turned us into great polluters, and the *Scientific Revolution* has enabled us to live long enough to do more and more polluting.

Together, the two revolutions have created another problem. When there were fewer people, the earth and its resources seemed limitless. But as the world's population grew, improved industrial methods had to be developed to supply the needs of more and more people. Today, the

Live and Work in a Healthier World

Figure 25.4. Recycling in action: *(above)* community collection; *(below)* an aluminum recycling plant.

Figure 25.5. A methane recovery plant for converting wastes into energy.

industrial nations use huge amounts of raw materials, some of which are now in short supply. And because of population growth, in some places there is even a shortage of living space.

Changing Goals

Today, faced with overcrowding, shortages, and pollution, modern nations are changing their goals. In particular, four new goals have become important:

1. To return to a world in which materials are used, recycled, and used again.
2. To waste fewer raw materials.
3. To find sources of energy for home and industry that do not contribute to pollution.
4. To preserve the beauty of the natural world, preserving at the same time the forests, waterways, and wildlife on which our own lives depend.

A Job for Young People

In towns and cities all across the United States, young people have led the drive to recycle paper, bottles, and cans. Youth organizations have set up hundreds of recycling centers, and young people have volunteered to do the work. Convinced by the recycling successes of their young people, many cities and towns have gone on to set up broader recycling programs that reach many more people.

Trash and Garbage

Most of our ancestors owned little, wasted little, and threw little away. But today, we own, waste, and throw away a lot. For example, each year we throw away about 48 billion cans, 26 billion bottles and jars, 4 million tons (about 3½ million metric tons) of plastic, 7.6 million television sets, 7 million cars and trucks, and 30 million tons (about 27 million metric tons) of paper. If recycling ever becomes a nationwide practice, it will greatly reduce this mountain of trash.

Recycling probably will not be effective in taking care of the garbage resulting from cooking and serving food. In the past, Los Angeles and other cities have experimented with selling their garbage for pig feed, but such programs were not very successful, primarily because of the difficulties involved in sorting and collecting such garbage.

However, solid food wastes, if properly treated, can be used to generate heat and power, thereby recovering energy that is now wasted (see Figure 25.5).

At present, the disposal of trash and garbage is a big problem. Open dumps are still widely used, but they have many drawbacks. Disease-carrying rats and insects breed freely in open dumps. Liquids seep down through the trash and pollute the groundwater. Burning trash pollutes the air.

LANDFILLS AND INCINERATORS   Trash can be compacted and then buried under many layers of soil, where land is available for this purpose. When complete, such areas, called *sanitary landfills*, can be landscaped and used as parks (see Figure 25.6). Or trash can be burned in high-heat incinerators that leave little ash behind (the remaining ash can then be buried in landfills).

However, there are sound objections to both of these solutions. First, the space available for sanitary landfills is limited. Second, most in-

Figure 25.6. Sanitary landfill becomes a park.

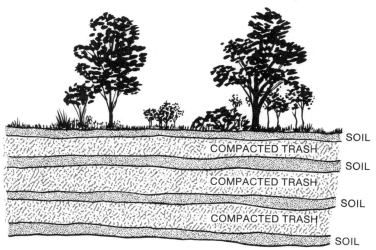

SOIL

COMPACTED TRASH

SOIL

COMPACTED TRASH

SOIL

COMPACTED TRASH

SOIL

Table 25.1: Causes of Air Pollution

Source	Percent
Transportation (cars, buses, trucks, etc.)	54.5
Burning fuel in furnaces and generators	16.9
Industrial processes	13.2
Burning trash and other wastes	4.2
Forest fires and other miscellaneous sources	11.2

cinerators pour out smoke that pollutes the air. So at present, our best hope lies in reducing the total amount of trash by wasting less and recycling more.

Air Pollution

Wherever air pollution occurs, one of the first steps taken against it is to ban the burning of trash. This makes sense, because the burning of various substances causes most of our air pollution. As you can see in Table 25.1, the burning of gasoline in our cars, trucks, and planes, plus the burning of fuel in our furnaces, power plants, and trash incinerators, produces about 75 percent of our air pollution. (Industrial sources account for about 13 percent more.)

If all of this fuel were completely burned, what remained would be mainly water and carbon dioxide, which is useful to plants. But because most fuel is incompletely burned, tiny particles of soot and ash are released into our skies, along with many kinds of poisonous gases. In the United States alone, over 280 million tons (about 254 million metric tons) of such wastes are released into the air each year.

AIR POLLUTION AND HEALTH   Other pollutants combine with oxygen in the presence of sunlight to form new and harmful substances. Some air pollutants, like carbon monoxide, are poisonous by themselves. The most dramatic recent example of air pollution by a poisonous substance occurred in July, 1976, in the nothern Italian region of Brianza. An explosion at a chemical plant there released into the surrounding atmosphere large amounts of a powerful poison called *dioxin* (dy-AHK-sin). As a result, large numbers of wildlife and domestic animals died immediately, and more than 500 people began to suffer from severe skin rashes and other complaints. The long-range effects of dioxin poisoning may also include damage to internal organs and the respiratory and nervous systems, and deformities in unborn children. It seems likely that what remains of this area after it is *decontaminated* (dee-kun-TAM-uh-nay-tud), or made harmless for human beings, will be largely desert.

Air pollutants are most dangerous when stagnant (nonmoving) weather

Figure 25.7. The spreading of city-produced air pollution to a popular beach.

conditions hold them in one place. For example, in 1948—in Donora, Pennsylvania—air pollution killed 20 people during a four-day period of stagnant weather. And in London, in 1952, 4,000 people died in one week as a result of long-lasting air pollution.

Who dies as a result of air pollution? Mostly people with respiratory illnesses, especially the very young, the very old, and those in poor health. But air pollution does long-term damage, too, by increasing the number of cases of emphysema, bronchitis, and asthma. And, like tobacco smoke, certain pollutants slow the action of the cilia and damage the air sacs in the lungs.

What is more, air pollutants can travel great distances, sometimes falling hundreds of miles from their source. From the cities, air pollution spreads easily over the countryside, damaging crops and other plants and spoiling formerly healthful recreation areas (see Figure 25.7). Thus, the problem, which once affected only a few large cities, is now worldwide.

CLEANING UP THE AIR   What can be done to clean up the air we breathe? The real solution lies in finding clean sources of energy. For example, half of all air pollution would disappear at once if all our cars and trucks could use a clean source of energy, such as electricity. Another 20 percent of our pollution would disappear if we had a clean fuel to use for heating and for power plants.

Nuclear (NYOO-klee-ur) **power** (energy obtained from the splitting of atoms) and **natural thermal power** (energy from heat inside the earth) will probably provide us with much additional electricity in the future. Cars

Pollution and Health   445

can be designed so that they use less fuel. Buildings, too, can be designed so that they are heated in part by **solar** (sun) **power** and cooled by breezes, thus using less fuel (see Figure 25.8). Public transportation can be improved so that fewer people drive fuel-consuming vehicles. But all of these developments take time. What can be done at present?

The federal government, through the Environmental Protection Agency, has established national air quality standards. All states and territories are now required by law to clean up their air to meet these standards. Other federal laws require auto manufacturers to design engines that burn fuel more completely. State and local governments, too, have clean air laws.

However, the problem of enforcing these laws quickly has been complicated by several factors. For one thing, a change in clean air standards means that we must develop new techniques of industrial production. Such efforts—always expensive—are particularly hard to finance in a time of ailing economy, such as the late 1970's. Then, too, there is a natural, if unfortunate, resistance to the inconveniences and expense of change on the part of both industry and the public at large.

What about the air you breathe? Is it clean? If not, what is your local government doing to improve air quality?

YOUR PART

Individually or in small groups, write your answers to the following questions:

1. How is trash disposed of where you live?
2. Is open burning allowed?

Figure 25.8. The panels on the roof gather heat from the sun and heat the house without causing any pollution.

3. Is your local government taking any steps to cut down on the use of private cars? List the steps.
4. List any steps that your local government is taking to improve public transportation.
5. Has industrial air pollution caused any problems where you live? List the problems. Find out what steps are being taken to solve these problems.
6. Are other types of air pollution a problem where you live? If so, is pollution heavy, medium, or light? Why? Is pollution frequent, occasional, or rare? Why?
7. As a class, compare your answers. If you and your classmates were members of the local government, what would you do to clean up the air you breathe?

Perhaps you live in a region where the air is clean. If not, it may help to remember that communities determined to clean up their air have succeeded. For example, although Los Angeles still has far too much **smog** (smoke and fog), the city has done away with most industrial air pollution. And air in London, England, is cleaner today than it was a century ago, because Londoners finally banned the coal that was causing most of the pollution.

Let's Pause for Review

On Spaceship Earth, our space and our supplies are limited. Like astronauts, we must use our living space wisely, avoid waste, and recycle materials we do use.

Before the Industrial Revolution, natural processes took care of all our recycling for us. Before the Scientific Revolution, population did not increase as quickly as it now does, and the individual's life expectancy was much shorter. But in supplying more and more people, who live longer, with the things they need, industrial nations now produce more waste materials than nature can recycle. Furthermore, some of these materials can never be broken down by natural processes.

Waste materials that pollute the air threaten our health. All of these environmental changes have helped to change our goals. We now hope that we can supply all people's needs and, at the same time, waste less, recycle more, keep our air, forests, and waterways clean, protect wildlife, and preserve natural beauty.

In order to achieve these goals, we need, for example, a nationwide recycling program, new cleaner fuels, and engines that burn present-day fuels more completely.

Pollution and Health   447

Figure 25.9. Wildlife destruction caused by an oil spill.

Water Pollution and Wastefulness

Over and over again throughout human history, people have polluted their water supplies with their own sewage. As you may remember (see page 385), sewage in water spreads cholera, typhoid, and dysentery. These diseases still sicken and kill people in many parts of the world. But most developed nations successfully purify their water by filtering it and adding the disinfectant *chlorine* (KLAW-reen).

However, we don't have enough modern sewage-treatment plants in the United States today. As a result, many communities pour their sewage without any treatment into waterways. Other communities use only primary treatment methods, which remove only 30 to 40 percent of the pollutants.

A complete, modern sewage-treatment plant, on the other hand, continues the breakdown of human wastes (by means of methods very much like those used in human digestion) and finally returns purified, usable water to the local water supply. Someday, especially if you live in a growing community, you may have to vote on whether or not to build a modern sewage-treatment plant.

Sewage is only one of many pollutants that dirty our water. Many industrial wastes are more poisonous than sewage. For example, in February, 1977, two spills within one week badly polluted tributary waterways of the Ohio River with *carbon tetrachloride* (tet-ruh-KLAW-ryd), a highly toxic liquid used in dry cleaning and fire fighting. At present, industrial wastes enter our waterways in larger amounts than do wastes from any other source.

Animal wastes from feedlots (where animals are fattened for market) seep down and pollute groundwater. **Pesticides** (chemicals such as DDT, which kill animal pests) and fertilizers enter the water by way of runoff from farms. And wherever small boats and large ships sail, they pollute by dumping sewage and spilling oil and gas.

The largest oil spills have come from offshore oil drilling or from today's huge ocean-going tankers. These large spills have done widespread

Live and Work in a Healthier World

damage to beaches and wildlife (see Figure 25.9). But little spills are important, too. Boat owners and industries spill thousands of barrels of oil each day into streams and lakes across the country.

Another kind of damage is brought about by **thermal** (heat) **pollution.** Water that is used to cool electric and nuclear power generators is put back into streams and oceans while it is still hot. This hot water upsets the pattern of life in the surrounding waters, destroying some living creatures and harming others.

BILLIONS OF GALLONS DOWN THE DRAIN Most Americans use water freely, even wastefully. We soak lawns, wash cars, and fill swimming pools. Our garbage disposal units, dishwashers, and washing machines guzzle more water. As a result, the average American uses around 170 gallons of water a day, for a daily grand total of 35 billion gallons. (A gallon is approximately equal to 4 liters.)

In addition, our factories use 160 billion gallons of fresh water daily. Our farms use at least 141 billion gallons every day. Add these numbers, and you will see the tremendous amount of water that we need (or think that we need). As population grows, the need for water will grow even more. Therefore, we must plan ahead if we are to meet this huge demand.

Preventing Water Shortages   We have no overall water shortage. But local water shortages occur all the time, often in areas where rainfall is usually plentiful. Such areas need more **reservoirs** (rez-uh-VWAHZ) in which to store rainwater for use in dry years. With good planning we can usually prevent water shortages by storing excess water during flood seasons and releasing it during dry seasons (see Figure 25.10).

Figure 25.10. Anderson Ranch Dam, Idaho, stores flood waters and releases them for irrigation and power.

Figure 25.11. These fish were killed by the pollution of their stream.

EFFECTS ON THE ECOLOGY We also need planning to clean up polluted lakes, rivers, and streams. Like other industrial nations, the United States has badly upset the **ecology** (ih-KAHL-uh-jee) of its waterways. (Ecology means the relationship of living things to their environment and to one another.) When people make great changes in the ecology of a region, they must expect, sooner or later, to be affected themselves by the changes they have made, because people are part of nature, too.

For example, when people pour industrial wastes into a lake or river, these wastes may at first kill only a few tiny plants. But plants release oxygen into the water. If such plant-killing pollution continues, so many plants may die that oxygen-using bacteria (which produce the carbon dioxide needed by plants) will die, too. In time, there may be so few oxygen-producing plants left that the fish will begin to die (see Figure 25.11). At this point, the odor will be so bad and the water so uninviting that people will stop swimming and fishing in the once-sparkling waters.

Most industrial wastes kill fish and birds indirectly (by first killing the tiny plants and animals they need). But some pesticides kill fish and birds directly. The pesticide DDT, for example, is fatal to fish. Because DDT takes a long time to break down, it also does indirect damage over a long period of time. During the time it takes to break down, DDT enters human

Live and Work in a Healthier World

tissues as well as the tissues of birds, fish, and other wildlife. The average American now carries an estimated 10 parts per million of DDT in the body's fatty tissues. Does this amount of DDT hurt us? No one yet knows for sure. But scientists think that DDT blocks the use of calcium in the tissues of birds. Because these birds lack calcium, many of their eggshells break before their chicks hatch. Such damage could cause some birds to become *extinct* (to die out).

Our DDT problem is a typical modern problem. Once praised as a very helpful pesticide, DDT has turned out to be harmful, as well. By means of water, much DDT enters the **food chain** (the chain that leads from plants to animals to people). Meaningful amounts of DDT have been found in mothers' milk. Indeed, any product we add to the environment may enter the food chain and end up in our own tissues. The following activity may help you to think about this very complicated problem of water pollution:

YOUR PART

1. As a class or in small groups, discuss how you would keep industrial wastes out of waterways. (Include discussion of how you would finance your cleanup program.)
2. As a class or in small groups, discuss water pollution in your own area. Are there problems? How might they be solved?
3. Individually or in small groups, volunteer to look up the following subjects and report on them to the class:

   a. *Mercury,* a poisonous metallic element and common industrial waste, is now present in the tissues of some fish widely used as human food. Is this mercury harmful to our health? What is the solution to this problem?
   b. *Lampreys,* eellike water animals, are now upsetting the ecology of the Great Lakes. How did the lampreys get into the lakes? What harm are they doing? How can the problem be solved?
   c. We depend on pesticides to keep farm production high. But because pesticides that enter the groundwater can be harmful, scientists are now working on other ways of fighting insect pests. What are these new methods and how do they work?

No doubt you agreed that water pollution is a very complicated problem. Furthermore, each part of the problem may require a different solution. In addition, new ways of doing things (such as controlling insects by interfering with their reproduction or by increasing their natural enemies in the environment) take time and money to develop. In spite of the difficulties, however, you probably decided that our waterways can, in time, be largely freed from pollution.

Noise Pollution

If you were a moviemaker in Hollywood today, you would have a hard time shooting many of your scenes out of doors. Why? Because modern cities—and even many rural areas—are so noisy. Before you completed even one scene, a neighbor might start up a power saw, a motorcycle might roar by, or a jet plane might fly overhead. Your sound recording would then be ruined.

In an industrial society, hundreds of thousands of engines roar day and night, and the result is called **noise pollution.** Of course, noise (unpleasant sound) isn't a pollutant in the sense that it dirties anything. But like other pollution, noise can change a region's ecology, or pattern of life. Noise can contribute to psychological stress, high blood pressure, chronic fatigue, and hearing loss (refer again to Chapter 9, pages 108–111).

People who live near modern airports realize that noise can threaten health. Most industrial workers realize it, too. In fact, everyone who lives in or near a large city is affected to some extent by noise.

The noise level has risen dramatically in the last 50 years. This level has risen and continues to rise at the rate of about 1 decibel per year. (For a review of decibels, see pages 108–111.) If this rate of increase continues, by the year 2000 sound levels will be more than 100 times greater than they are at present.

What can be done? Most airport communities have enacted ordinances to regulate airport noise. Many cities require mufflers on all motor vehicles. Some cities require outdoor machinery to be operated only within certain hours.

Is noise regulated where you live? Is more regulation needed? The following activity will give you and your classmates a chance to exchange opinions on the subject:

YOUR PART

As a class or in small groups, discuss the following questions. Then vote on each question to see what the majority opinion is:

1. Do you think all outdoor machinery should be operated only within certain hours? If so, what hours?
2. Do you think all motor vehicles should have mufflers?
3. Some vehicles (motorcycles and some trucks) are noisier than others. Should their use be limited? Should their manufacturers be required to make them quieter?
4. What about industrial noise? Should it be limited by zoning? By hours?
5. In your opinion, what other sounds should be regulated?

Live and Work in a Healthier World

You and your classmates may differ widely on the need to limit noise. But the problem of noise pollution reminds us that almost every important change we make has unforeseen effects. These effects may be helpful, harmful, or both.

Pollution: The Price of Progress?

What seems fairly harmless in small amounts (a bit of noise, a few industrial chemicals, a little sewage) is often very harmful in large amounts. Natural processes can take care of a little sewage, but a lot of sewage pollutes shellfish, and people who eat polluted shellfish may get hepatitis. Too much noise deafens. Too many cars pollute the air.

Often, too, helpful inventions turn out to be harmful under certain conditions. For example, it has been claimed that, under certain conditions, microwave ovens and color television sets can give off dangerous radiation. Indirectly, *phosphate* (FAHS-fayt) detergents remove dissolved oxygen from lakes. Nonbiodegradable plastics litter the countryside and oceans.

Of course, inventors of new industrial processes, new products, and new medicines expect their inventions to be helpful. But inventors, scientists, and the public must be on the lookout for possibly harmful effects, as well. Fortunately, young people today are alert to the dangers of pollution. Unlike earlier generations, they have some knowledge of ecology. Judging by the efforts they have put into recycling projects, they also have the energy and imagination needed to make our world a cleaner and more pleasant place to live in.

Looking Back

Industrial nations now produce more wastes than nature can recycle. Wastes in our water and air threaten our health and the health of other creatures who share the earth with us. Other waste products litter the earth's surface. Industrial nations are also running short of some important raw materials. Therefore, we must waste less. And we need to set up nationwide recycling programs.

Cleaner air will result from new and cleaner fuels, cleaner-burning engines, more public transportation, and buildings designed to make use of natural heating and cooling. Cleaner water can be achieved by the construction of more modern sewage-treatment plants. In addition, we need to control the dumping of industrial wastes, and we need to develop nonpolluting pesticides.

Pollution and Health

Noise pollution must be dealt with, too, and promptly. We already know that noise and other loud sounds can cause deafness, and the noise level in our cities, near our airports, and elsewhere is rising dramatically every year.

We are learning that new processes and products can cause unforeseen problems. Our best chance is to realize that we are part of natural ecology, too, and that, for our own survival, we must reverse the current pollution process.

MODIFIED TRUE-FALSE QUESTIONS

1. Space and natural resources on our planet are _unlimited._
2. _Carbon dioxide_ gas, a plant by-product, helps support life.
3. A waste gas produced by animals and humans is _oxygen._
4. In order for a community to survive, there must be a balance between population and _food supply._
5. As a result of the Industrial Revolution, items made by machine became _more_ common than handmade items.
6. Pollution _increases_ as more biodegradable materials are produced.
7. Hot water introduced into streams and oceans is an example of _sewage_ pollution.
8. The need for water continues to increase as population and industry _decrease._
9. The supply of metals and other raw materials is _decreasing._
10. Layers of compacted trash between layers of soil are an example of _trash pollution._
11. Unchecked industrial smoke and fog can produce _snow._
12. Carbon monoxide is _a nonpoisonous_ pollution.
13. A federal agency concerned with problems of _pollution_ is the Environmental Protection Agency.
14. Water supplies containing sewage may be purified by using _chlorine._
15. The chemical DDT is an example of _a fertilizer_ that is now polluting water supplies.
16. _Mercury,_ an industrial waste, is present in the tissues of certain fish that people eat.
17. Increasing the volume of your stereo or TV increases _air_ pollution.
18. Dissolved oxygen is indirectly removed from lakes by _phosphate_ detergents.
19. DDT may be stored in the _bones_ of people and food animals.
20. The relationship between living things and their environment is known as _ecology._

Live and Work in a Healthier World

MATCHING QUESTIONS

Column A	Column B
1. recycling	a. using chemicals to kill harmful germs
2. nonbiodegradable	b. cannot be broken down to simpler usable form
3. incineration	
4. disinfecting	c. burning
5. decibel rating	d. smog
	e. purifying and using again
	f. noise level

COMPLETION QUESTIONS

1. The Industrial Revolution began about _____.
2. Huge, ocean-going tankers pollute water by _____.
3. Solid wastes, if properly burned or otherwise treated, could become a source of _____.
4. High-heat incineration produces _____ (fewer, more) pollutants than incineration at lower temperatures.
5. The complete burning of gasoline produces carbon dioxide and _____.
6. Air pollution is especially harmful to people with _____ diseases.
7. Half of our air pollution would disappear if motor-driven vehicles used _____ instead of gasoline.
8. Household wastes and industrial wastes are major sources of _____ pollution.
9. The average American uses about _____ gallons of fresh water daily.
10. The process that leads from plants to animals to people is referred to as the _____ chain.

MULTIPLE-CHOICE QUESTIONS

1. Which of the following is *not* a process of natural recycling?
   a. plants feeding animals
   b. animals feeding people
   c. human and animal wastes returning to earth and enriching soil
   d. converting trash into landfill
2. Which of the following is *not* a form of industrial pollution?
   a. smoke poured into the sky
   b. animal waste returned to earth
   c. chemicals released into water
   d. nonbiodegradable plastics

3. Faced with overcrowding, shortages, and pollution, developed nations have changed their environmental goals. Which of the following is *not* such a goal?
   a. the use, recycling, and reuse of materials
   b. the use of more raw materials
   c. the discovery of clean sources of energy
   d. preservation of the beauty of the natural world
4. Which of the following sources of energy promises to be the least polluting?
   a. coal   b. nuclear power   c. solar power   d. electricity
5. Noise may cause all of the following, *except*
   a. loss of sight   c. chronic fatigue
   b. high blood pressure   d. loss of hearing

THOUGHT QUESTIONS

1. Name the federal agency responsible for setting air quality standards. Discuss other federal laws aimed at controlling air pollution.
2. Suppose you own a motorcycle. Discuss how this vehicle can contribute to noise, air, and other pollution problems. How can you control these problems?
3. In today's world, we must be ready to respond quickly to pollution warnings:

   a. What is meant by a smog alert?
   b. Suppose you are a camp counsellor and have nine children in your care. What should you do in the event of such an alert?

4. Pollution is a normal outgrowth of our ever-growing civilization. Do you agree with this statement? Defend your position.
5. In recent years, our capabilities for fast travel have advanced remarkably, particularly with the development of supersonic transports:

   a. What is a supersonic transport (SST)?
   b. Should supersonic transports be allowed to land in our airports—local, state, or national? Write a paragraph outlining your feelings in this matter.

Looking Ahead

You have been thinking about ways of making your community a cleaner, better place to live in. You are now ready to consider a closely related problem—how, as wise consumers, we should use the many products of modern industry.

Live and Work in a Healthier World

Chapter 26: Learning to Be a Wise Consumer

A **consumer** is a person who uses goods and services, so at one time or another we are all consumers. As a consumer, you decide on purchases of many kinds. As an adult consumer, you will spend thousands of dollars buying the things you need. Will you spend these dollars wisely? What about the money you are spending now? You, in company with other American teenagers, spend about 20 million dollars a year on health, grooming, and beauty aids alone. How much of this money is well spent? How much is wasted? Take a moment to think about what kind of consumer you are:

YOUR PART

1. What health and grooming products do you choose for yourself? Soap? Shampoo? Toothpaste? List these products. How did you decide on the brands you use? Did you follow someone's recommendation? Did you buy an advertised brand? Did you try several brands before you found one you liked? Write down how you usually make such consumer decisions.
2. As a class or in small groups, compare your answers. Which ways of deciding on products seem best?
3. Have one or two volunteers visit a drugstore and write down the prices of the various brands of aspirin for sale. Discuss the prices in class. Are the higher-priced brands of aspirin worth the extra money? Discuss how you might find out.
4. Have two or more volunteers investigate and report on the work of Consumers Union and Consumers' Research, Inc. (You can start by asking your librarian for a reference book called *Directory of Associations.*)
5. Other class members should be assigned to investigate and report on *one* product that is related to health, appearance, or the ecology.

Find the information you need in the publications of Consumers Union and Consumers' Research (both organizations put out a monthly magazine and a yearly handbook).

Perhaps you agreed that Consumers Union and Consumers' Research can help you guard your health and save your money in the years ahead.

Consumer organizations can be especially useful when the time comes for you to buy large, expensive items (refrigerators, washing machines, or cars, for example), which should be nonpolluting, thrifty in their use of energy, and manufactured to give good service for a number of years.

These organizations are not connected with any manufacturer, and they test many of the products you use each day. As a result, consumer organizations can help you judge the worth of advertising claims. Ads today don't promise as much as they once did, but they still bear watching.

The Federal Trade Commission (FTC)

The **Federal Trade Commission,** or **FTC,** keeps a continuous watch over all newspaper, magazine, radio, and television advertising. If it finds a case of false advertising, the FTC issues a formal complaint to the manufacturer. If necessary, the FTC can also issue a cease-and-desist order, which forces the advertiser to stop making false claims (see Figure 26.1). Another agency with even broader powers is the FDA.

The Food and Drug Administration (FDA)

In 1938, Congress passed the Food, Drug, and Cosmetic Act, a group of laws designed to protect consumers. A federal agency called the **Food and Drug Administration,** or **FDA,** was created to enforce these laws.

The FDA has many duties. For example, the FDA inspects factories that turn out foods, drugs, cosmetics, and medical devices. The FDA is responsible for the purity, safety, and wholesomeness of packaged foods. The FDA checks to see that foods are labeled properly and that their contents are listed on the label. It passes on the safety of food additives. It determines how much pesticide may be allowed to remain on food crops offered for sale. It also checks imported foods, drugs, and medical devices to make sure they comply with U.S. laws.

Recently, the FDA, in its role as watchdog of food purity, has acted on several occasions to protect consumers from possibly dangerous **chemical additives** in processed foods. Among the actions taken were bans against the following ingredients, which may be **carcinogenic** (KAHR-sin-oh-JEN-ik), or cancer-causing:

Live and Work in a Healthier World

- **Cyclamates** (SY-kluh-mayts), sugar substitutes formerly used in low-Calorie foods, especially beverages.
- **Red Dyes No. 2 and No. 40,** coloring agents formerly used to give a fresh color to such foods as meats, fruit juices, processed foods, and candy.

The FDA continues to investigate the possibly harmful side effects of food additives such as **antioxidants** (an-tee-AHKS-ih-dents), which slow up oxidation that often leads to spoilage; **hormones,** used to promote growth in cattle and fowl; and **saccharin** (SAK-uh-rin *or* SAK-rin), another sugar substitute.

In addition, the FDA requires manufacturers to prove the safety and effectiveness of new drugs before they can be sold to the public. The FDA also works to combat the illegal sale of prescription drugs. Another duty is to check medical devices for safety and for the truthfulness of labeling claims.

The U.S. Postal Service

Even the U.S. Postal Service plays a part in protecting consumers. There are federal laws against using the mails to *defraud*, or cheat, people. Therefore, the Postal Service investigates any complaints of fraudulent

Figure 26.1. How the Federal Trade Commission protects you. *Courtesy of CONSUMER REPORTS.*

False Claims Laid to Natural Salt Marketer

Biochemic Research Foundation, a Salt Lake City marketer of natural flake salt, signed a Federal Trade Commission consent order barring it from making false claims about its product. Natural flake salt contains no additives and consists of larger crystals than commercially processed salt, which contains iodine and anticaking additives.

The FTC said Biochemic falsely advertised that persons on low-salt or salt-free diets could safely ingest natural flake salt and that it would prevent, cure, or relieve arthritis, calcification, muscular inflammation, hardening of the arteries, and high blood pressure.

Besides banning such misrepresentations, the FTC consent order requires Biochemic to place a warning on all packages cautioning that natural flake salt does not differ from commercially processed salt in its effects on persons with physical conditions requiring a low-salt diet.

459

Figure 26.2. Esther Peterson, special assistant to the president for consumer affairs.

mail. If the complaints are well founded, the accused person must answer the charges and may even be subsequently tried and convicted for breaking the law.

The New Consumer Agencies

In recent years, a number of new consumer agencies have been added to local, state, and federal governments. In Washington, D.C., for example, the Office of Consumer Affairs and special members of the White House staff advise the president on ways of protecting the consumer (see Figure 26.2). The following activity will help you learn more about consumer-agency activities in your area and elsewhere:

YOUR PART

1. Does your city, county, or state government have a consumer agency? Choose several classmates to investigate and report on any such agencies, giving their names and the work they do.
2. Choose a classmate to investigate and report on the work of your local Better Business Bureau.
3. The American Medical Association, the American Dental Association, and the American College of Surgeons have set up special

Live and Work in a Healthier World

branches to protect the consumer. Find out if these branches are represented in your area. If so, investigate and report on their work.

4. Consumer education is a major concern of the voluntary health organizations. Choose several classmates to investigate and report on the consumer education work of the American Cancer Society and the Arthritis Foundation.

5. Choose a classmate to investigate and report on Dr. Harvey W. Wiley's battle against the sometimes spoiled, diseased, and unclean packaged food of his day.

6. Choose a classmate to investigate and report on journalist Samuel Hopkins Adams's campaign (through a series of articles in the old *Collier's* magazine) against laudanum and alcohol in patent medicines.

7. Choose a classmate to report on the work of Ralph Nader (see Figure 26.3). Include information about his early battle with General Motors and his work with the group called Public Citizen, Inc.

No doubt you discovered that today's consumer movement is a healthy one. You probably agreed that the American consumer owes much to people like Ralph Nader, Samuel Adams, and Dr. Wiley, who have fought for better products and more protective laws.

Consumer Education

How important is the consumer education work that is done by voluntary health organizations such as the American Heart Association? Quite important, it would seem. After increasing for many years, the rate of heart attack (and heart attack death) has begun to go down. Health authorities believe two things are responsible for this decline. One is better emergency care, and the other is consumer education on medical care, diet, and exercise.

Figure 26.3. President Jimmy Carter consults with consumer crusader Ralph Nader.

MEDICAL QUACKERY Consumer education is important for another reason. An educated consumer is better able to spot a *quack*—an ignorant or dishonest person who pretends to have medical training or knowledge. The old-fashioned quacks who hauled their medicine shows from town to town by wagon are gone (see Figure 26.4), but numerous modern quacks have taken their place.

Most of those who offer for sale worthless medicines and medical treatments do so to make money. But some of them sincerely believe themselves to be healers, and they can be dangerous, too, when their treatments delay regular medical care. As you have read, early treatment is an important measure against many illnesses, and against cancer it is vital. The following is an example of how harmful well-intentioned quackery can be.

Some years ago, a girl checked into a California hospital. She was awaiting surgery for a type of eye cancer. A man who was not a medical doctor convinced her parents that he could cure her cancer without surgery. The parents canceled the surgery that might have prolonged their daughter's life, took her out of the hospital, and allowed this man to treat her illness. When she died, the man, who had promised to cure her, was brought to trial and found guilty of second-degree murder.

In spite of some arrests and convictions, however, cancer quacks continue to do business. Like frontier medicine peddlers, many quacks sell medicines of their own making. One such "cancer cure" was found, upon analysis, to contain only distilled water.

Other quack cures have been more imaginative. But they are still medically unacceptable drugs because they have not been scientifically tested before being offered for sale. A regular drug company, on the other hand, puts each new drug through a long period of animal and human testing. Before such a new drug can go on sale, the FDA must be satisfied that the drug is both safe and useful. For example, the FDA has not approved the sale of *laetrile* (LAY-uh-tril), which is made from apricot pits and is claimed by some to be a cancer cure. At present, no scientific evidence exists that laetrile is either effective or that its long-term use might be harmless.

MECHANICAL QUACKERY The Food, Drug, and Cosmetic Act of 1938 brought medical machinery as well as drugs under federal control, and the FDA has the authority to regulate the manufacture and sale of all machines used in medical treatment. The many machines your doctor uses have been approved by the FDA. Unfortunately, the FDA has neither the employees nor the money to keep up with all of the worthless and fraudulent new medical machinery that continues to appear.

Fraudulent mechanical equipment may be very simple, like the *uranium* (yoo-RAY-nee-um) *mitt* containing radioactive ore and sold to cure arthritic hands. (Quacks have also been known to charge arthritics ten

462

Figure 26.4. A medical quack of frontier days.

dollars a day for the privilege of sitting inside an abandoned uranium mine.) Or the fraudulent equipment may be an impressive-looking machine complete with flashing lights, a fancy control panel, and clicking or buzzing sounds to show that the machine is "working" (see Figure 26.5, page 464).

Such equipment may be either for rent or for sale, and the price is often very steep. For example, the "magic spike," or Vrillium Tube, which was worth less than a penny, sold for $306.00. Its promoters claimed that it cured cancer, diabetes, and arthritis. They were jailed after a young diabetic bought one, stopped taking insulin, and died.

Fraudulent equipment makers often claim that their machines are powered by cosmic waves, atomic energy, or some form of radioactivity. They also claim that their machines can either **diagnose** (DY-ig-nohs *or* DY-ig-nohz) (which means identify) or cure the most serious illnesses. To back up such claims, these quacks tell their customers a few stories of individual "cures." On the other hand, a medically accepted machine, like a medically accepted drug, has been used experimentally on thousands of animals and humans before being accepted by the FDA for regular use.

It is also worth remembering that even reputable manufacturers make a great deal of money from equipment that is, in many cases, quite worthless. For example, vibrating mattresses, pillows, and pads are sold by the thousands to people with arthritis or with ailing necks and backs. For such conditions, this equipment is likely to do nothing beneficial. However, the manufacturers are not guilty of legal fraud. They have promised only that the electrical vibrations will help to relax the user.

Learning to Be a Wise Consumer

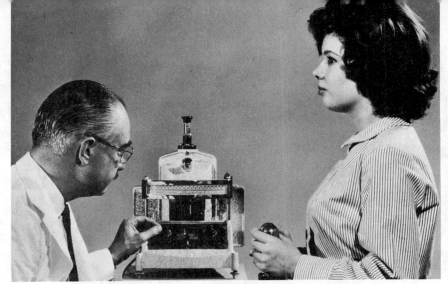

Figure 26.5. Can you tell that this impressive machine has no medical value? (It was priced at $875 and advertised to diagnose and treat almost all diseases; in fact, it could only detect perspiration on the patient's skin.)

RECOGNIZING HEALTH QUACKS Unsolved health problems, such as cancer and arthritis, attract quacks. And so do desperate people. So anyone desperate for a cure, a slender figure, a youthful appearance, or a full head of hair is a likely target. Quacks know that such people spend millions of dollars every year on worthless cures, reducing aids, skin beautifiers, and baldness preventives (see Figure 26.6).

In fact, it is estimated that Americans spend more than two billion dollars a year on quack cures. More important even than the wasted money is the fact that lives are lost that might have been saved by prompt medical care.

How can you recognize a health quack? The American Medical Association warns that quacks are likely to do many or all of the following:

1. Claim that their "secret" machines or formulas can cure disease.
2. Promise quick or easy cures. When questioned about their cures, they ask for a chance to prove their claims. But given the chance, they always have ready excuses for not following through with real proof.
3. Advertise by citing (referring to) individual case histories or testimonials as proof, rather than extensive scientific testing.
4. Give their businesses misleading names, such as *Foundation* or *Clinic*. In addition, they may use such respected labels as *Christian* or *Scientific*. Thus, a quack organization called the Union of Churches Foundation for Internal Medicine might be neither a foundation (a permanently funded institution) nor a branch of any organized Church.

5. Ask loudly and often for medical investigation and recognition.
6. Claim to be persecuted by medical authorities wary of competition.
7. Assure you that their methods of treatment are better than surgery, X rays, or recognized drugs.

YOUR PART

1. Find an ad in a magazine or newspaper that has some of the characteristics mentioned in the American Medical Association's warning about health quacks. Bring the ad or ads to class.
2. As a class, compare and discuss the ads you found, noting the use of misleading names, case histories, testimonials, and the promise of quick, easy results. Also note whether the promises are direct ("Guaranteed to restore a full head of hair.") or indirect ("Why not try this easy method of weight reduction that has worked for so many others?"). Tally the ads you found according to the promises made. (Do they promise clear skin, youthful skin, a slender figure, well-developed muscles, or what?)

No doubt you and your classmates found a great many misleading ads. Most, perhaps all, of these ads probably concerned bodily attractiveness and vitality.

As your health studies should have convinced you by now, your body needs no miracle lotions, stimulants, cleansers, or reducers. Your body,

Figure 26.6. What other advice does this dieter need?

Figure 26.7. Consult a medical directory to learn about a doctor's qualifications.

unbelievably complicated though it is, is admirably well fitted, or suited, to its work. It deserves your admiration and respect. In exchange for simple daily care, your body will quite naturally display the health and good looks you desire.

Finding a Doctor

You may feel that you now know how to avoid a quack, but how should you choose a good doctor? Chances are, when you grow up you will need to find a new doctor. How will you go about it? Will you ask for recommendations? To which recommendations will you give the most weight?

YOUR PART

1. List the qualities you would look for in a doctor.
2. List the steps you would take to find a doctor with those qualities.
3. Perhaps your teacher or a student can borrow a copy of the American Medical Association Directory (or a state or county medical association directory) and bring it to class. (If not, perhaps you can look into a copy at the library.) Discuss the information it contains. How might this information help you in finding a doctor?

Live and Work in a Healthier World

4. Would you rather have a doctor who practices alone or one who practices group medicine? (A group practice is one in which several specialists work together in the same building, sharing opinions, expenses, and diagnostic equipment like X-ray machines, and treating one another's patients in emergencies and during vacation periods.)
5. As a class, discuss your answers to these questions.

You may have disagreed in many of your answers. But you probably agreed on at least one thing—to look for evidence of medical training and experience. A doctor usually hangs his or her framed M.D. degree in a prominent place in the office or waiting room, along with a license to practice and any additional certificates, fellowships, or honors earned.

As you may have discovered, the American Medical Directory contains the same information that is visible in the doctor's office, and usually more. If the directory tells you that your new doctor is a member of one or more medical societies, is board-certified, is associated with a hospital where he or she teaches other doctors, or is a fellow (member) of some specialized medical society, you have very likely found a hard-working and well-qualified professional (see Figure 26.7).

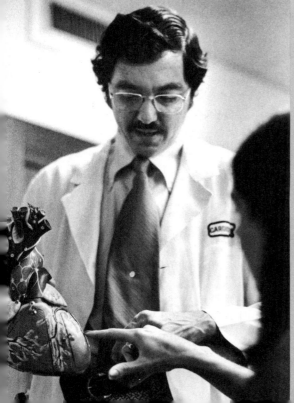

Figure 26.8. This doctor is prepared to answer patients' questions in a clear and helpful way.

Like Dr. Martin in Chapter 22 (see page 388), a good doctor keeps good records and takes down a health history of each new patient. And a good doctor usually chooses capable assistants to work in the office. So you should also look for signs of good recordkeeping and a well-run office.

You should also recognize that some of the most valuable recommendations for doctors can come from nurses and other medically trained people. If you know such people, their opinions will be worth listening to. If you're on your own in choosing a prospective doctor, you should look for a proper attitude toward patients and their health—an emphasis on health maintenance and prevention rather than on cure. Finally, look for personal qualities like intelligence, willingness to answer questions, and the ability to explain things about your bodily condition clearly (see Figure 26.8).

Looking Back

Consumers Union and Consumers' Research, two organizations unconnected with any manufacturer, test and report on most of the products you use each day. Their monthly and yearly reports can help you to be an intelligent and thrifty consumer. In addition, many governmental agencies—like the FTC, the FDA, the Postal Service, the Consumer Advisory Council, and the Office of Consumer Affairs—and many private agencies—like voluntary health organizations, professional organizations, and Ralph Nader's Public Citizen, Inc.—work to protect and educate the consumer. Educated consumers are better able to obtain good medical care, avoid poor care, and protect themselves against health quackery.

MODIFIED TRUE-FALSE QUESTIONS

1. Advertisements today that recommend goods and services are *more* honest than in the past.
2. Factories that turn out foods and drugs are inspected by the *Federal Trade Commission.*
3. If you receive a mail advertisement claiming to offer a health device to cure cancer, you can complain to the *Food and Drug Administration.*
4. The *Environmental Protection Agency* combats the illegal sale of prescription drugs.
5. A new federal consumer agency is the *Office of Economic Opportunity.*
6. Ralph Nader is an important leader in the *automobile industry.*
7. Consumer education has helped to *decrease* the rate of heart attacks.

8. Medical treatment by means of a mail-order "health device" is _a poor_ health practice.
9. The American Heart Association is _a government_ health organization.
10. The possessor of an M.D. degree who is listed, with association memberships and accomplishments, in the American Medical Directory is usually _a qualified_ doctor.

COMPLETION QUESTIONS

1. Consumers Union and _____ are organizations that can guard your health and save you money.
2. American teenagers spend about _____ million dollars a year on health, grooming, and beauty aids.
3. Better emergency care _____ (increases, decreases) the chances of heart attack deaths.
4. A (An) _____ is an individual who practices medicine without a license.
5. Reputable doctors _____ (do, do not) claim quick and easy cures for disease.
6. Both the FTC and the FDA are agencies of the _____ government.
7. To defraud means to _____ people.
8. Medical care involving several specialists working together is called _____ medical practice.
9. Red Dye No. 2 may be an example of a (an) _____ .
10. Before the _____ releases a new drug for physicians to prescribe, the drug is carefully tested.

MULTIPLE-CHOICE QUESTIONS

1. Which of the following activities is _not_ a function of the FTC (Federal Trade Commission)?
   a. to watch newspaper, magazine, radio, and TV advertising
   b. to test products to see if they meet standards
   c. to issue formal complaints in cases of false advertisement
   d. to issue cease-and-desist orders
2. The federal agency responsible for protecting the consumer from fraudulent use of the mails is the
   a. Food and Drug Administration   c. U.S. Postal Service
   b. Federal Trade Commission   d. Office of Consumer Affairs
3. Which of the following is the best statement about vibrating mattresses, pillows, and pads? They
   a. will cure arthritis
   b. will cure backaches
   c. have no value and should not be sold
   d. may help the user relax

4. Which of the following statements does *not* describe medical quackery?
   a. it claims support from recognized medical organizations
   b. it advertises, using testimonials instead of scientific data
   c. it claims treatment superior to all others
   d. it promises quick cures
5. A good way to select a well-qualified doctor is to consult
   a. a pharmacist   c. the yellow pages
   b. a friend   d. the local medical directory

THOUGHT QUESTIONS

1. You have just moved to a new city and want to choose a doctor:

   a. List the various groups or organizations that can be of assistance in your choice.
   b. Indicate what you would look for in a doctor's training and experience during your first visit to the doctor's office.

2. It has been claimed by some people that quacks serve a purpose, because they provide hope and promise to people suffering from incurable diseases. Take a position on this issue and defend your choice.

3. How can you, as a teenage consumer, contribute to programs of consumer education? Suggest some specific ways of doing this.

Looking Ahead

Already, you are a consumer of many goods and services. And before long, you will probably be a jobholder, producing or selling goods or performing a service. The following and final chapter, which explores careers in the field of health, may help you decide. At present, there are few vocational fields offering more career opportunities than health. And the opportunities can only increase in the years ahead.

Live and Work in a Healthier World

Chapter 27: Careers in Health

Joan and Tim stared at the list of speakers posted on the bulletin board. It was Career Day at their school, and they were trying to pick from the list a speaker they wanted to hear.

"Let's go to the lecture on jobs in health," Tim said.

"That's not for me," Joan said. "I don't want to be a doctor or a nurse."

"Neither do I," said Tim. "But look at this list of health jobs. It's longer than any of the others. And it says that the field is still growing."

When Joan looked at the list, she saw more than 40 different job categories. Among them was a job for a photographer—a medical photographer on a hospital staff (see Figure 27.1). The pay was good, and photography was Joan's hobby.

"Okay, Tim," Joan said. "Let's go to the talk on health jobs."

Figure 27.1. A medical photographer at work.

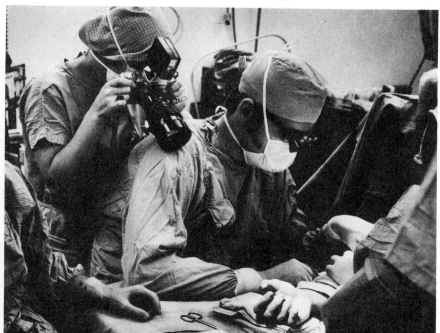

Table 27.1: Career Opportunities in Health Fields

Career	Educational Level
Dental assistant	1–2 years of training after high school or on the job
Dental hygienist	2–4 years of college
Electrocardiogram technician	High school and on-the-job training
Medical assistant	High school or junior college and on-the-job training
Medical technologist	4 years of college
X-ray technician	2–4 years of college
Registered nurse (R.N.)	2–5 years of college
Licensed practical nurse (L.P.N.) or licensed vocational nurse (L.V.N.)	1 year of college
Occupational therapist	2–4 years of college
Physical therapist assistant	2 years of college
Physical therapist aide	High school
Dietitian	4 years of college
Hospital administrator	4–6 years of college
Pharmacist	5 years of college
Sanitarian	4 years of college

Before long you will have to earn your own way in the world. Earning a living can be very satisfying in itself, but you are probably hoping for more specific satisfaction. You probably want a job that interests and pleases you because it fits your skills and abilities, your character and personality. In this chapter, we will explore job opportunities in health—a field so varied, there may very well be a job in it for you (Table 27.1 shows only a sampling). But first, take a moment to think about your own wishes, abilities, personal qualities, and experience:

YOUR PART

1. What jobs have you already thought you might like to do?
2. List your special interests.
3. List your special abilities.
4. List those skills you would like to develop.
5. Write down how many more years of schooling you would like to have: High school? College? Graduate work?
6. What salary do you want when you begin? In five years? In ten years?

7. What have you learned from part-time jobs, home chores, and so on, about the kind of work you might like to do permanently?

Make a list of the letters a through m. Then make three columns on your paper next to the list. Head the first column *Very Much* or *Very,* the second column *Yes,* and the third column *No.* Now put a check mark (√) in the proper column for your answers to each of the following questions:

a. Do science courses interest you?
b. Are you comfortable, quick, and skilled at working with your hands?
c. Do you like working with people?
d. Do you like working alone?
e. Do you like to organize and carry out large projects that involve many people, many stages, and much equipment?
f. Do you like to feel that you are helping others?
g. Do you like solving problems?
h. Do you get along with most people?
i. Are you responsible and dependable?
j. Are you willing to work hard at the right job?
k. Do people's health problems concern and interest you?
l. Are you a good student?
m. Are you a good science student?

Save your list and answers for later use. You may find that your interests and abilities fit a job that will be discussed in this chapter. For example, most people who work in the health field need to be highly responsible. In addition, a dentist needs to be a fine student, good at delicate handwork, and eager to work with and help people. A research scientist should have an excellent record as a science student and enjoy working alone to solve problems.

Figure 27.2. This well-paid medical clerk helps admit and discharge patients.

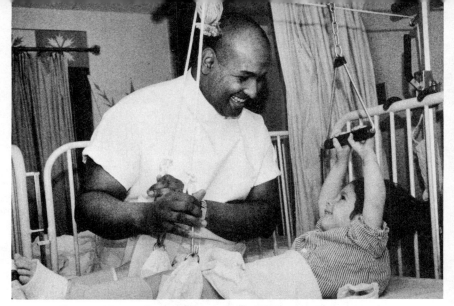

Figure 27.3. Physical therapist helping a patient exercise.

But what if science is not your favorite subject and school is not your favorite place? Is the health field closed to you? By no means. To give just one example, let us say that you are responsible and hard-working and want to be your own boss. If you are willing to learn all of the skills of office maintenance (cleaning, polishing, painting, and electrical and plumbing repair), you can build your own service business in the health field. Doctors and dentists who own their own offices often need the services of a reliable maintenance firm.

Hospital Employment

Since people actually live in hospitals, hospitals are like small communities. The patients must be supplied not only with medical care, but also with food, fresh clothing and bedding, and clean, well-maintained surroundings. **Dietitians** (dy-uh-TISH-unz) plan both regular and special diets. Cooks and helpers prepare and serve the food. Laundry workers supply fresh linen for all. Engineers keep elevators, maintenance equipment, and medical machines running. And cleaning crews work round the clock.

In addition, clerks, assisted by typists and filers, keep medical records, and accountants handle financial records and calculations, often with the aid of computers. So, computer specialists often work in hospitals, too. Some two-year colleges now train medical clerks, familiarizing them with medical terms and procedures so that they can be especially useful in admitting hospital patients and keeping medical records (see Figure 27.2).

Specially trained people do a variety of other jobs for hospitals. A large

Live and Work in a Healthier World

hospital may have a number of **social workers** to help patients with nonmedical problems. One librarian is probably in charge of the hospital's medical books; another supervises the library for patient use. A **pharmacist** (FAHR-muh-sist) stocks and supplies necessary medicines. **Physical therapists** (THER-uh-pists) treat various patients' conditions by means of heat, light, water, massage, exercise, supervised activity, and rest (see Figure 27.3). **Inhalation therapists** give patients oxygen and otherwise help them to breathe normally, especially after surgery.

HOSPITAL TECHNICIANS   A large hospital employs skilled technicians of many kinds. Laboratory technicians may work at any one of 12 different specialties, examining such things as blood, urine, tissue samples, and cultures of bacteria and viruses. X-ray and other technicians operate the hospital's many medical machines (see Figure 27.4).

THE NURSING STAFF   A hospital's nursing staff provides most of the direct care given to patients. **Registered nurses** (R.N.s) have from two to five years of college training and have passed licensing examinations. They give complete nursing care, involving a high degree of experience and skill. R.N.s can, with additional training, become specialists in critical care; emergency care; surgical nursing; labor, delivery, and pediatric nursing (see Figure 27.5, page 476); and care during recovery from surgery.

Licensed **practical nurses** (L.P.N.s), also called **licensed vocational nurses** (L.V.N.s), must have a year of college training. With some restrictions, their work is much like that of the R.N. **Nurse's aides,** who may be trained at special occupational centers, bathe patients, change their bedding, and help them to exercise, among other things. An *orderly* is a male nurse's aide and does similar work.

Figure 27.4. An X-ray technician at work.

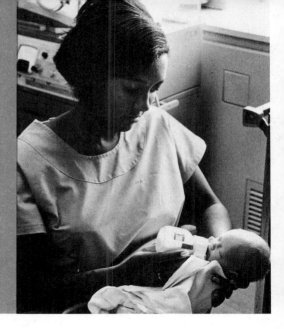

Figure 27.5. A registered nurse with specialized training in pediatrics.

THE HOSPITAL'S DOCTORS A person who wants to become a doctor usually studies for four years at a regular college and receives a B.A. degree. When accepted by a medical school, she or he studies for four more years, earning an M.D. degree. At this point, the future doctor must serve as an **intern,** or advanced student, putting in a year's work in a hospital to gain practical experience before being licensed to practice medicine.

If, at this point, the licensed M.D. decides to become a specialist rather than a general practitioner, he or she must become a **resident physician**—one who works in a hospital to gain experience in a specialty. Interns and residents do much of a hospital's medical work. But hospitals also have staff physicians, who have received special training.

Two common hospital specialties are **obstetrics** (ahb-STET-riks), which deals with childbirth, and surgery (see Figure 27.6). Many staff physicians are obstetricians or surgeons, and their training often takes a long time. To take just one example, a *plastic surgeon*, who reshapes surface tissues on the body and repairs them when damaged, may put in five years as a resident before being board-certified by other specialists in the field. Such a board-certified surgeon is sure to find a place on the staff of a fine hospital. Along with their hospital work, most staff physicians maintain their own practices outside the hospital.

THE HOSPITAL ADMINISTRATOR A hospital administrator runs the hospital. That is, the administrator oversees all hospital programs, trying to make sure that all departments get what they need, that the hospital's bills are paid, and that its payroll is met. A hospital administrator

Live and Work in a Healthier World

is usually college-trained, with a degree in business or hospital administration. He or she is a person who likes to organize and carry out large projects involving many people and things.

Let's Pause for Review

The health field is a large and growing one. It gives employment to many kinds of people. A large hospital, for example, employs dietitians, cooks, laundry workers, cleaning crews, clerks, typists, accountants, computer specialists, engineers, social workers, librarians, pharmacists, various kinds of therapists, dozens of kinds of technicians, interns, residents, staff physicians with many specialties, many kinds of nurses, and a hospital administrator. These jobs call for hard-working, responsible people who like helping others. Many, but by no means all, of these jobs also call for quick, skilled hands and an interest in science.

Figure 27.6. A surgical team at work in a hospital operating room.

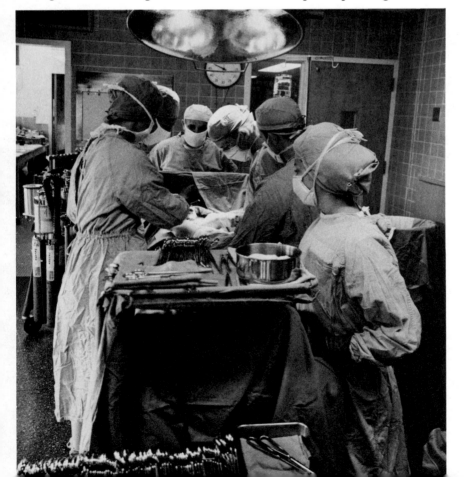

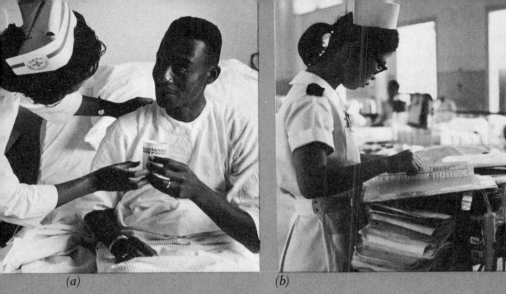

Figure 27.7. Varied experience within the nursing field: *(a)* patient care; *(b)* ward supervision; *(c)* rehabilitation assistance; *(d)* school nursing.

The Health Field Offers Great Variety

Educational requirements in the health field vary widely (see Table 27.1, page 472). Hospital laundry workers may learn how to do their job in a few weeks, whereas some surgeons may take fifteen years to master their specialties. As a result, salaries vary widely, too.

Working environments also vary widely. For example, nurses work not only in hospitals, but also in doctors' offices, schools, clinics, private homes, and industrial plants (see Figure 27.7). They may also work for local, state, federal, and even world health agencies. Many health specialists do all of their work outside hospitals. The following activity will give you a chance to investigate at first hand some of the many jobs in the field of health:

YOUR PART

1. Invite your school nurse to speak to your class on the many opportunities in the field of school nursing. Be sure to ask questions about many other health specialties, as well.
2. Invite your school's (or your school district's) speech therapist to tell the class about his or her career.
3. Do you know any other workers in the field of health? If so, invite them to speak to the class, after arranging for the visit with your health teacher.

478   **Live and Work in a Healthier World**

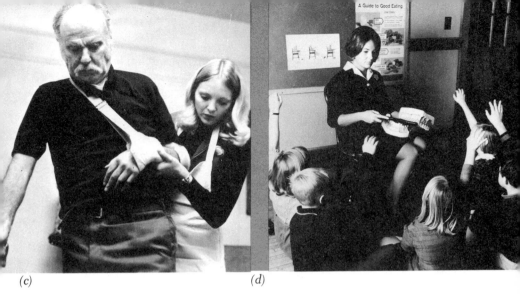

(c)   (d)

4. If you have not invited a speaker, make one of the following reports:

   a. If there is a pharmaceutical company in your area, telephone or write for permission to visit it. You may be able to observe research work or the manufacture of drugs. Report to the class on your visit.

   b. Visit a voluntary health organization like the American Red Cross or the American Heart Association. Find out how many volunteers and how many paid workers they use. Ask about research programs that they finance. Find out whether or not they pay writers and printers to turn out their consumer education materials. Report to the class on your visit.

   c. In some places, certain fire department members are trained **paramedics,** or medical assistants. Among other things, paramedics learn how to **resuscitate** (ree-SUS-uh-tayt), or revive, people in emergencies. If your locality has such squads—they are often called resuscitator or respirator squads—telephone and ask if you may visit one of them. Report to the class on the squad's training and equipment and on the kinds of emergencies it handles.

   d. Find the *Occupational Handbook* (put out by the Government Printing Office) in your school or local library. It contains thousands of job descriptions, among other things. Report to the class on health-related occupations it describes.

   e. If you are due for a dental checkup, use the opportunity to ask how your dentist decided on his or her career. Ask the dental receptionist, too, and the dental hygienist, if there is one in the office. Report to the class on your visit.

   f. If there is a veterans' hospital near you, write or telephone for permission to visit. Observe and report to the class on any of the hospital's facilities for physical therapy, rehabilitation, or vocational training.

g. If there is a school for the blind, the deaf, the physically handicapped, or the mentally retarded in your area, phone or write to arrange a visit. Then, observe the work of teachers and others there, and report your findings to the class.

h. Similarly, handicapped adults may receive vocational training somewhere in your area. If so, try to visit and report on these facilities.

i. If you know a pharmacist, ask if you may visit to observe this line of work. Report your observations to the class.

j. Visit your nearest nursing school. Find out what is involved in an R.N.'s training. Find out if the school trains people for any other medical specialties. If possible, visit classes, laboratories, and other facilities. Report to the class on your visit.

k. If you know a medical receptionist, set up an interview to ask about the work done and the skills required.

l. If you know a veterinarian, arrange a visit and observe the work. (For those interested in animal care and treatment, zoos also offer many rewarding career opportunities, which you might investigate.) Report on your visit to the class.

m. If several of you can get permission to visit the facilities of a hospital, assign individuals to inspect the hospital laboratory, the switchboard operator at work, the work of X-ray and other technicians, the pharmacy, the work of the clerical staff, and the physical therapy department. A visit to a teaching hospital (one connected with a college or university that trains doctors) will be of special interest. Report your observations to the class.

5. Local, state, and federal agencies employ many workers in the field of health. Write or telephone for permission to visit and report on the following facilities:

a. A water-treatment plant.

b. A sewage-treatment plant.

c. A public health clinic that provides immunizations and prenatal care.

d. The Bureau of Vital Statistics, which keeps local birth, death, and population records and employs statisticians and computer specialists.

e. The governmental department that inspects and licenses restaurants, markets, and drugstores.

f. The governmental department that inspects and passes on the safety of public beaches, rivers, swimming pools, and the like.

g. The governmental department responsible for the safety inspection of factories.

Live and Work in a Healthier World

h. The governmental department responsible for the inspection of meat and milk.
i. The governmental department responsible for insect and rodent control.
j. The governmental department responsible for the control of communicable disease.
k. The Department of Recreation and Parks. This department often employs many teachers of classes in swimming, exercise, and dance—activities that help maintain and improve health.
l. A county health agency.
m. A state health agency.
n. A federal health agency.
o. A branch of a world health agency.

You may want to investigate some health career not mentioned in this activity. After discussing your ideas with your health teacher, make your visits and report on them to the class.

The health field makes use of a great many abilities and skills. You may have been surprised to find out how many. Perhaps, on your visits, some of you learned about jobs that interested you and working environments that pleased you. If not, a job you like may open up in the future. Roughly one-third of the people working today hold jobs that did not exist when they were youngsters.

LOCAL HEALTH DEPARTMENTS   As you discovered, local health departments (town, city, or county) provide more services than do state and federal health departments. As a result, local departments hire many people to work as recordkeepers, public-information program developers, clinic personnel, visiting nurses, communicable disease investigators, sanitation experts, and inspectors of many kinds. Such people often work in large hospitals maintained by local governments.

STATE HEALTH DEPARTMENTS   State health departments also provide a fair number of jobs. Like local health departments, state departments are concerned with communicable disease control, sanitation, public information, and vital statistics. In these areas, state departments help local departments by providing leadership, advice, and money (from state or federal sources).

But state health departments have other responsibilities, too. For example, rehabilitation programs are often state programs. And mental hospitals are usually state-run. Many of the inspections you learned about earlier are carried out by the state (see Figure 27.8, page 482). And health

Careers in Health   481

Figure 27.8. A meat inspector paid by the state.

professionals like doctors, nurses, dentists, and pharmacists are tested and licensed by the state they work in.

FEDERAL HEALTH AGENCIES   The United States Public Health Service (PHS) is the chief public health agency of the federal government. The Surgeon General, whose reports on smoking you read about on page 314, is the director of the PHS. In cooperation with governments of other countries, the PHS works to improve the health of the world's people. But its chief responsibility is to protect and improve the health of our own people.

Through its stations at entry points along the borders of the United States, the PHS works to keep communicable diseases from entering the country. Through its information services, the PHS helps to spread new knowledge about the prevention and control of disease. The PHS also gives advice about and support to community health efforts, particularly those aimed at increasing the supply of well-trained health professionals.

The National Institutes of Health   The PHS also supports and carries out a great deal of research (see Figure 27.9). One of its subdivisions, the National Institutes of Health, located in Bethesda, Maryland, studies ways to prevent, diagnose, treat, and cure disease. These institutes include:

- The National Heart and Lung Institute
- The National Cancer Institute
- The National Institute of Allergy and Infectious Diseases
- The National Institute of Arthritis and Metabolic Diseases
- The National Institute of Dental Research

Live and Work in a Healthier World

- The National Institute of Child Health and Human Development
- The National Institute of Neurological (related to the nervous system) Diseases and Stroke
- The National Institute of General Medical Sciences
- The National Institute of Environmental Health Sciences
- The National Library of Medicine, which contains the world's largest collection of medical literature

As you can see, the PHS alone offers an enormous range of jobs. What is more, a public health worker can work not only for city, state, and federal agencies, but also for world health organizations.

THE WORLD HEALTH ORGANIZATION   After World War II, 51 nations agreed to form the United Nations. One of their first concerns was the improvement of world health. By 1948, the World Health Organization (WHO) of the United Nations was at work.

Although its headquarters are in Geneva, Switzerland, WHO has six regional offices that advise and aid governments that ask for help in solving health problems (see Figure 27.10, page 484). Member nations contribute money to WHO, receiving aid and services in return. Members also meet each year to plan tasks for the following year.

UNICEF AND FAO   Two other international health agencies, the United Nations Children's Fund (UNICEF) and the Food and Agriculture Organization (FAO), work to improve world health. Together, WHO, UNICEF, and FAO have improved nutrition in many parts of the world. These agencies have developed and distributed new high-protein foods in areas where protein deficiency has sickened and killed many children. These agencies also assign health experts to countries in need of them, train local health workers, and provide medicines and educational materials where needed.

Figure 27.9. A laboratory worker at the National Institutes of Health, located in Bethesda, Maryland.

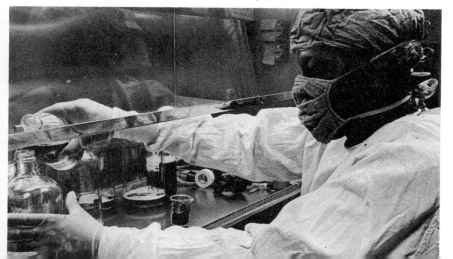

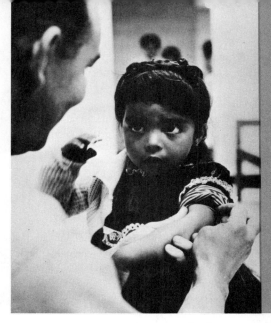

Figure 27.10. WHO
vaccination programs
against smallpox:
(left) in Mexico;
(right) in India.

You and the Health Field

Think over the reports you and your classmates have given as well as the material contained in this chapter. Look again at the answers you gave to the questions on pages 472 and 473. Perhaps you can now match your wishes, abilities, and skills with some specific job or jobs. Write down your answers to the following questions:

YOUR PART

1. List three or more jobs in the health field for which you could qualify (with further training, if necessary).
2. List any health jobs about which you would like to know more.
3. List any health jobs you think you might especially like.
4. Investigate one of the jobs you just listed. Find out about salary, job requirements, and places where you can receive any necessary training.

Of course, you may not ever work in a field related to health. Even so, your investigations into this field may have shown you how many kinds of people are needed to do the world's work. One way or another, it makes good sense, as you think about jobs, to consider the field of health, a field that is already one of the largest employers of people in the United States—and still growing!

Live and Work in a Healthier World

Looking Back

The health field is a large and growing one. It employs many kinds of people, whose training may take anywhere from a few weeks to a dozen years or more. Health workers do their jobs in many different settings—hospitals, doctors' and dentists' offices, clinics, libraries, research laboratories, factories, parks, and all kinds of government facilities at local, state, and national levels. Some health workers even work for world health agencies connected with the United Nations.

MODIFIED TRUE-FALSE QUESTIONS

1. Your choice of a career should be guided by your interests and _abilities._

2. A career in _a health_-allied field does not require that science be your favorite subject in school.

3. A hospital dietitian _cooks_ food for regular and special diets.

4. Hospital patients who are worried about their family's care during their absence can seek help from the hospital's _social worker._

5. Hospital patients who require oxygen or other aid in breathing are helped by _physical_ therapists.

6. To be a practical nurse, you need _more_ training than a registered nurse does.

7. Next to a physician, dentist, or hospital administrator, _a registered nurse_ is one of the most highly trained health workers.

Careers in Health 485

8. The business of running a hospital is in the hands of the *hospital administrator.*
9. The American Heart Association is *a profit-making* health organization.
10. The chief public health agency of the federal government is the *Public Health Service.*

COMPLETION QUESTIONS

1. The director of the Public Health Service is the ———.
2. The hospital employee responsible for running equipment, such as electrocardiograms, is the ———.
3. The individual who fills doctors' prescriptions and supplies necessary medicines is known as a (an) ———.
4. The exercise program for hospital patients is the chief function of the ———.
5. After completing medical school, doctors gain the necessary experience required for a license to practice by serving as a (an) ———.

MULTIPLE-CHOICE QUESTIONS

1. After high school, training for dental assistants usually takes about
   a. two years or less   c. four years
   b. three years   d. five years
2. The most direct patient care is given by a
   a. social worker   b. librarian   c. therapist   d. nurse
3. Local health departments do all the following, *except*
   a. operate clinics
   b. inspect hospitals
   c. maintain a visiting nurse service
   d. keep communicable diseases from crossing the borders of the country
4. The chief responsibility of the United States Public Health Service is to
   a. cooperate with other governments
   b. control communicable diseases
   c. improve and protect the health of its people
   d. keep vital statistics
5. The National Institutes of Health are supported by
   a. the United States Public Health Service
   b. local public health departments
   c. private donations
   d. state public health departments
6. The chief function of the National Institutes of Health is to
   a. conduct research about disease
   b. treat disease
   c. disseminate health information
   d. protect the health of government officials

7. Advice and aid to governments with health problems are obtained from the United Nations through the
   a. World Health Organization
   b. International Red Cross
   c. United Nations Children's Fund
   d. Food and Agriculture Organization
8. Nutrition in many parts of the world has been improved by all of the following agencies, *except*
   a. WHO   b. UNICEF   c. FAO   d. PHS
9. A medical specialty that deals with childbirth is
   a. pediatrics   b. obstetrics   c. gynecology   d. urology
10. All of the following are aims of a health course, *except*
    a. to provide important health concepts
    b. to present health situations that require specific treatment
    c. to develop proper attitudes toward good health
    d. to discourage health students from making their own decisions about health practices

THOUGHT QUESTIONS

1. List five specialized hospital careers (requiring considerable training) and five nonspecialized hospital careers (requiring minimal training). For each, indicate *(a)* the nature of the job, *(b)* the requirements of the job, and *(c)* present-day job opportunities.
2. Why is health care of the people one of the most important functions of the federal government?
3. Throughout this course, we have referred to the ability to make decisions:
   a. What is meant by decision making?
   b. Why is decision making an important educational goal?
   c. Why is decision making an especially important objective of a course in health?
4. Will a set of rules for good health insure the health of an individual? Defend your answer.
5. Why must health be an international concern rather than merely the concern of one country or its parts?

A Look Into the Future

Although you may now have completed your study of health, no doubt your interest in achieving and maintaining the best possible health will last for a lifetime. Let's hope that this course has given you some of the information you will need to achieve physical, emotional, and social well-being.

Let's hope, too, that this course has helped provide you

with a positive attitude toward your own health and that of others. As your studies may have convinced you, simple daily care of the wonderful machine that is your body will quite naturally reward you with the health and good appearance you want. And with good health, you can more fully enjoy your life—at work, at home, and as part of your community.

As you play a larger part in community life in the years ahead, you will make many decisions that affect your health and the health of others. The attitudes and understandings provided by your health course should help you in making some of these decisions. Your generation will have much to say, for example, about the control of pollution and the worldwide battle against hunger and disease. The wisdom of your generation's decisions will help determine your future and the future of the world.

Glossary

abrasion   surface wound in which some skin has been scraped off

abscess   painful collection of pus within the body that does not develop a channel of discharge to the outside

acne   infection of skin oil glands that produces pimples and, often, scars

addiction   psychological and physical dependence on a drug

adenoids   lymph glands located at the back of the nasal passages and above the throat

adrenal gland   ductless gland situated on each kidney; secretes the hormones adrenaline and cortisone

adrenaline   hormone secreted by the adrenal glands when an individual becomes excited or frightened

allergy   abnormal sensitivity to substances of plant and animal origin; results in a release of histamine in the body

alveoli (*sing.* **alveolus**)   tiny air sacs at the ends of bronchioles in the lungs

amino acids   compounds composed mainly of carbon, oxygen, hydrogen, and nitrogen; end product of protein digestion; chemical units from which the body builds its own proteins

amnion   fluid-filled sac, or bag, that cushions an unborn baby; the "bag of waters"

amphetamine   stimulant drug that is dangerous when abused; promotes alertness but causes rapid pulse, nervousness, sleeplessness, and other effects; "uppers"; "pep pills"

anemia   condition in which there is a shortage of either blood, hemoglobin, or red blood cells

antibiotic   drug, usually produced by some living thing, that kills certain germs or slows their growth

antibodies   protein compounds formed in the body and circulated in the blood; can destroy germs or make their poisons harmless

antidote   preparation that counteracts the effect of a poison

antihistamine   drug that counteracts histamine released in the body during allergic reactions

antiseptic   chemical applied to wounds to destroy germs or prevent their growth

antivenin   substance that counteracts the venom, or poison, produced by certain snakes, spiders, and insects

anus   body opening through which solid wastes (feces) are passed

anvil   middle bone of the three small bones that stretch across the middle ear in a chain and transmit vibrations to the inner ear

appendix   short wormlike tube extending out from the large intestine near its beginning; has no digestive function

arterial blood   blood in arteries, which is usually bright red and has a high oxygen content

artery   blood vessel that carries blood away from the heart to capillaries elsewhere in the body

arthritis   often painful joint inflammation

489

artificial respiration first aid procedure in which air is forced into and out of the lungs of a person who has stopped breathing

asthma breathing difficulty caused by allergic or emotional reactions that decrease the size of the air passages in the smaller bronchial tubes

astigmatism blurred vision caused by uneven curvature of the cornea or lens of the eye

atherosclerosis narrowing of blood vessels; interferes with blood circulation; caused by fatty deposits in walls of arteries

atrium (*pl.* **atriums** *or* **atria**) one of two upper chambers of the heart; receives blood from veins; auricle

auditory canal short tube of outer ear between the funnel-shaped ear flap and the eardrum; hearing canal

auditory nerve nerve carrying impulses from the cochlea of the inner ear to the brain; hearing nerve

auricle *See* atrium

autonomic nervous system part of nervous system that controls automatic internal activities of body; connected to medulla oblongata and spinal cord by special nerves

axon branch of a neuron that carries nerve messages away from the cell body toward another neuron or a muscle or a gland

bacteria (*sing.* **bacterium**) one-celled, plantlike, nongreen microorganisms; some types (germs) cause disease

barbiturate depressant drug that is dangerous when abused; promotes sleepiness; in large doses, interferes with coordination, judgment, and other activities; can become addicting; "downer"; "goofball"

benign tumor abnormal growth in the body that is noncancerous and will not spread to other parts of the body

beriberi disease caused by a deficiency of vitamin B_1; characterized by exhaustion, paralysis, and heart disease

bicuspid tooth having two raised parts, or points; aids in tearing and grinding food

bile juice secreted by the liver; helps digest fats

bladder, urinary thin-walled elastic bag that stores urine in the body; *see also* gallbladder

blood cell one of two types of cells (red and white) carried by the plasma; blood corpuscle

boil painful collection of pus in the skin; eventually develops a channel to the outside through which pus is discharged

brain computerlike mass of nerve cells located in the head; controls and coordinates body activities; processes nerve impulses into sensation and thought

brain stem portion of the brain composed of the midbrain, pons, and medulla oblongata; passageway for nerve impulses between brain parts; regulates many reflex actions

brain waves tiny electric currents produced in the brain when nerve impulses travel between parts of brain and to and from it; recorded by electroencephalograph machine

bronchial tube one of two wide tubes branching off from the trachea into the lungs

bronchiole one of many narrow tubes in the lungs that branch off from wider bronchial tubes

bronchitis inflammation of the bronchial lining caused by continuous irritation resulting from infection or inhalation of foreign particles such as cigarette smoke

Caesarean section surgical operation for delivering a baby, by which the surgeon cuts through the mother's body wall and uterus and lifts out the baby

caffeine stimulant drug present in coffee, tea, cola, and chocolate; speeds up activities of the nervous system

Calorie amount of heat that raises the temperature of 1 liter of water by 1 degree Celsius

cancer malignant tumor; abnormal body growth in which cells divide in uncontrolled fashion and often break away and spread to other parts of the body

canine tooth having one raised part, or point; aids in tearing food; cuspid; "eye tooth"

capillaries microscopic blood vessels having very thin walls; connect with small arteries and small veins

carbohydrate quick-energy food compound, such as sugar and starch, composed of carbon, hydrogen, and oxygen

carbon monoxide colorless, odorless, very poisonous gas; released whenever a substance containing carbon does not burn completely; present in cigarette smoke and auto exhausts

carbuncle large, deep boil that forms in the skin and underlying tissue

carcinogen substance that can cause cancer

cartilage springy, slippery, tough supporting tissue present in joints, outer ears, nose, and some ribs

cataract cloudy condition of eye lens; a leading cause of blindness; can be treated surgically

cavity hole or hollow area in enamel or underlying layers of a tooth, resulting from the action of acid-producing bacteria

cell body part of nerve cell containing the cell nucleus and cytoplasm and surrounded by the cell membrane; joins dendrites at one end with axon at opposite end

cell membrane very thin, soft sheet surrounding a cell; controls the passage of materials into and out of the cell

cementum bonelike material covering the root of a tooth

central nervous system part of the nervous system composed of the brain and spinal cord

cerebellum part of the brain located beneath the cerebrum and between the cerebrum and medulla oblongata; controls balance and coordination

cerebral palsy condition in which afflicted person has imperfect muscular control as a result of brain damage before, during, or after birth

cerebrum top portion and largest part of the brain; center for thinking and control of voluntary activities

cervix lower, narrow part, or neck, of the uterus

chancre small, single, painless sore that is an early symptom of syphilis

chemotherapy treatment and control of disease by chemical means

cholesterol fatty substance normally present in the body; in many people, it collects in the walls of arteries, causing atherosclerosis

chromosomes threadlike bodies inside a cell nucleus; composed mainly of DNA; location of genes; *see also* X chromosome; Y chromosome

chronic disease disease that continues for a long time

cilia tiny, constantly moving hairs projecting from the surface of certain cells, such as the cells lining the air passages

circulatory system blood system, which carries to cells oxygen and other needed substances and carries away from cells carbon dioxide and other cell wastes

circumcision surgical removal of foreskin of the penis

cirrhosis disease in which the liver becomes scarred, hard, and shrunken; associated with alcoholism

cocaine sense-dulling stimulant drug that is often abused; large doses can lead to intoxication and violent behavior

cochlea coiled tube of inner ear; contains endings of auditory nerve

codeine narcotic drug derived from opium; used to relieve pain and coughing and to promote sleep

cold sore mild infection caused by a virus; associated with a cold or fever; fever blister

communicable disease "catching," infectious, or contagious disease

cone specialized nerve cell of the retina that is affected by bright light and colors

control part of an experiment that acts as a standard of comparison

convulsion series of violent, involuntary muscular contractions, such as those occurring in a type of epilepsy; seizure; fit

cornea curved transparent tissue of the eye in front of the pupil, iris, and lens

Glossary 491

coronary disease   disease of the heart involving the blood vessels of the heart muscle

cortisone   hormone secreted by the outer layer of the adrenal glands; regulates salts and water balance of body; used as a drug to relieve inflammations

crown (of tooth)   part of a tooth projecting above the gum line

cuspid   *See* canine

cuticle   hardened margin of skin around a nail

cytoplasm   living material located in a cell between the nucleus and the outer layer of cell membrane

decibel   unit used for expressing the relative loudness of sound

defense mechanism   mental process by which some people unconsciously and automatically protect themselves from painful feelings and difficult problems

deficiency disease   unhealthy condition resulting from a lack or shortage of a substance necessary for health

delirium tremens   condition in which a person hallucinates, shakes, and exhibits mind confusion; associated with alcoholism

dendrites   branching fibers that carry nerve messages into a neuron and toward the cell body

dental caries   condition caused by destruction of tooth enamel through the action of lactic acid produced by certain bacteria; tooth decay

dental pulp   soft material in center of tooth; contains nerves, blood, lymph vessels

dentine   bonelike tooth material, softer than enamel, located under the enamel

deoxyribonucleic acid   chemical compound that is the chief component of chromosomes and is the storage place for hereditary information; DNA

depilatory   liquid or cream that can remove unwanted hair

depressant   substance, usually a drug, that slows body activities

depression   mental state of hopelessness, sadness, and discouragement about oneself and one's life

dermis   layer of skin under the epidermis; contains sweat glands, sebaceous glands, hair erector muscles, nerves, capillaries, and papillae

diabetes   condition of raised level of blood glucose (sugar); results from release of too little insulin by the islets of Langerhans in the pancreas or from the inability of body cells to use the insulin present

diaphragm   large, flat muscle that separates the chest cavity from the lower body cavity and is used in breathing

diastolic blood pressure   pressure in the arteries when the heart is relaxing and filling with blood between contractions

digestive system   organs that change food into a form that body cells can use

dislocation   injury in which a bone is displaced from the joint where it is normally connected to another bone

distillation   process involving (1) evaporation of a liquid from a solution and (2) condensation of the vapor produced; used to remove alcohol from fermented grains in the manufacture of alcoholic beverages

DNA   *See* deoxyribonucleic acid

dominant trait   trait that overshadows a recessive trait, when the genes for both traits are inherited together

duct   body tube through which a fluid flows from one region to another

eardrum   membrane located between the inner end of the auditory canal and the middle ear; passes sound vibrations from the auditory canal to the bones of the middle ear; tympanic membrane

ecology   relationship of living things to their environment and to one another

EEG   *See* electroencephalogram

egg cell   female sex cell produced by ovaries

electroencephalogram   tracings of brain waves recorded by an electroencephalograph machine; EEG

electrolysis   process that destroys hair roots electrically

embryo   unborn individual formed by the cell divisions of a fertilized egg

emetic   preparation that causes vomiting

emphysema   disease in which air sacs of lungs become stretched and inelastic, making breathing difficult

enamel   shiny material, harder than bone, that covers the crown of a tooth

endocrine system   ductless glands and hormones that, together with nervous system, regulate, coordinate, and control bodily activity

environment   biological, social, and physical conditions that surround and affect a living thing

enzymes   body-produced chemicals that enable chemical reactions, such as the digestion of food, to take place rapidly at body temperature

epidemic   outbreak of a disease affecting many people in a community or more widespread area at the same time

epidermis   outer layer of skin; consists of several layers of dead cells and a single layer, the Malpighian layer, of living cells

epiglottis   flap of tissue at base of throat; keeps swallowed food from entering trachea

epilepsy   symptom of several noncommunicable diseases of the nerous system; characterized by recurring seizures (convulsions) of greater or lesser intensity and, sometimes, loss of consciousness

epithelial tissue   tissue composed of cells that fit closely together, covering the body and lining the internal organs

erector muscles   tiny muscles in dermis of the skin, attached to the base of hairs; upon contraction, they generate some heat, pull on hairs, and make the hairs stand erect (causing "goose bumps")

esophagus   part of the food tube connecting the throat with the stomach

Eustachian tube   channel extending from the middle ear to the throat; equalizes air pressure inside the middle ear with air pressure outside

Fallopian tubes   part of female reproductive system consisting of funnellike openings, which receive egg cells from the ovaries, and ducts, through which eggs reach the uterus

fats   long-lasting, energy-food compounds, such as butter and lard, composed of carbon, hydrogen, and oxygen

fatty acids   compounds composed of carbon, hydrogen, and oxygen; end product of fat digestion; chemical units making up fats

feces   solid body wastes composed of unusable and undigested substances, bacteria, and dead body cells

fermentation   process by which microscopic organisms, such as yeasts, feed upon carbohydrates and release alcohol and carbon dioxide

fetus   unborn baby from about two months of development, at which time its major body features appear and it begins to look human, until birth

fever blister   *See* cold sore

first-degree burn   burn that reddens the skin but does not blister or break it

fluoridation   addition of chemical compound containing fluorine (fluoride) to drinking water to promote formation of decay-resistant teeth in children

follicle   tiny pocket from which a hair grows and into which a sebaceous gland secretes oil

food chain   the obtaining of food energy by one organism from another in the environment; begins with green plants, which use sun's energy to make food, and continues with other living things, which either feed on green plants or on organisms that feed on green plants

foreskin   loose skin that covers the tip of the penis

fracture   break in a bone

fraternal twins   two children born of the same mother at the same time, formed from the union of two different eggs with separate sperms; can be of opposite sexes

frostbite   freezing or partial freezing of some part of the body; treated by quickly warming the affected part in warm water

fungus (*pl.* **fungi** *or* **funguses**)   nongreen plantlike organism related to bacteria; some kinds cause diseases such as ringworm; others, such as some mushrooms and yeasts, are useful

gallbladder   sac, or pocket, in which bile from the liver is stored temporarily

gamma globulin   antibody chemical in blood plasma

gangrene   tissue death and decay caused by disease or cutoff of the tissue's blood supply

genes   parts of the DNA molecules of chromosomes; determiners of heredity

germs   microorganisms that invade the body and cause disease

gingivitis   inflammation of the gums, caused by irritation from dental plaque and tartar

gland   organ that produces a fluid useful to the body

glaucoma   eye disorder in which increased fluid pressure inside the eyeball damages it; second greatest cause of blindness

glucose   simple sugar composed of carbon, hydrogen, and oxygen; end product of digestion of starches and complex sugars

glycerin   end product, along with fatty acids, of fat digestion; glycerol

goiter   enlarged thyroid gland, often caused by lack of iodine in the diet

gonorrhea   communicable venereal disease, caused by a certain bacterium

hallucination   sight or hearing of something that does not really exist

hallucinogen   drug that causes hallucinations; psychedelic drug

hammer   first or outermost bone of the three small bones that stretch across the middle ear in a chain and transmit vibrations to the inner ear

hashish   drug extracted from Indian hemp plant; like marijuana but more powerful

Heimlich Maneuver   first aid procedure for treating severe choking; done by encircling victim's abdomen and quickly thrusting upward in the soft region above the navel and below the ribs

hemoglobin   iron-containing pigment that carries oxygen to body cells and carries away some carbon dioxide; gives red blood cells their color; a shortage in the blood results in one kind of anemia

hepatitis   inflammation of the liver

hernia   bulging of tissue or organ through the wall that normally holds it in place

heroin   strongly addictive narcotic drug derived from opium; its use is normally prohibited

herpes simplex, Type 2   communicable venereal disease caused by a strain of herpes virus

high blood pressure   dangerous condition in which pressure of the blood in arteries is higher than normal as a result of emotional stress, smoking, or other causes

histamine   substance that is harmful when released by the body during allergic reactions

hormones   compounds secreted directly into the blood by endocrine (ductless) glands; "chemical messengers" that help control body activities

hyperopia   farsightedness, often occurring when eyeball is too short from front to back to permit the focusing of nearby objects into a sharp image on the retina

immunization   protection from a disease, resulting from injection or oral intake of a vaccine that makes the body disease-resistant

impacted tooth   tooth wedged between the jaw and another tooth so that it cannot push out through the gum in a normal manner

incision   single, clean cut in the skin and deeper tissues, such as one made by a surgeon

incisor   one of the eight front teeth that cut food

incubation period   time between contact with a source of infection and outbreak of disease symptoms

infectious mononucleosis disease characterized by fever, fatigue, sore throat, and swollen lymph glands; caused by a virus; spread mainly by direct contact; "kissing disease"

influenza disease of the respiratory, nervous, and digestive systems; caused by a virus, spread by contact and droplets; flu

insomnia prolonged inability to sleep

insulin hormone released by islets of Langerhans in the pancreas; regulates the body's use of sugar

intoxication drunkenness or a condition that resembles it

involuntary muscles muscles, such as those of the stomach, that, under ordinary circumstances, cannot be controlled at will

iris colored part of the eye; regulates the amount of light entering the eye

islets of Langerhans scattered groups of cells within the pancreas that secrete the hormone insulin

jaundice yellow condition of skin and whites of the eyes, associated with a damaged or diseased liver

joint region where a bone is connected to another bone

kidney one of the two bean-shaped organs, located along the back near waist level, that remove from the blood dissolved wastes produced by body cells

kwashiorkor protein-deficiency disease

laceration wound in which there is a jagged, irregular tearing of tissues

lactic acid acid that causes tooth decay, produced by the action of bacteria in plaque on sugars in food; also, a waste product of muscle activity that causes fatigue when muscles have no chance to rest

large intestine part of the food tube after the small intestine; removes water from waste material, forming solid wastes, and stores wastes temporarily until they pass out of the body

larynx organ in which the vocal cords are located; voice box

lens transparent material shaped so that it can bend light rays to a focus

leukemia form of cancer in which white blood cells crowd out red blood cells

ligaments bands of tough tissue that hold bones together at joints

liver digestive gland that secretes bile, which helps digest fats

LSD dangerous hallucinogenic drug extracted from the fungus ergot; much more powerful than hashish or marijuana; lysergic acid diethylamide

lymph clear fluid that surrounds every body cell and fills all spaces between tissues; medium for the exchange of substances between the blood and the cells

lymph glands (nodes) masses of special tissue through which lymph flows in its course through lymph vessels; filter lymph and produce some types of white blood cells, especially those that destroy germs and their products

malignant tumor *See* cancer

malocclusion condition in which upper and lower teeth do not meet properly

Malpighian layer single layer of living cells at the base of the epidermis

marijuana drug extracted from the Indian hemp plant

marrow soft tissue in center of long, hollow bones; substance in which red blood cells and some white blood cells are formed

medulla oblongata part of the brain connected to the spinal cord; helps regulate the automatic actions of vital organs, such as the heart and breathing muscles

menopause time of life in females when ovulation and menstruation stop; change of life

menstruation monthly discharge of unused lining of the uterus

methadone synthetic narcotic drug given in place of heroin to treat heroin addicts

methamphetamine strong, addicting stimulant drug; Methedrine; "speed"; "crystal"

microorganism living thing so small that it can be seen only with a microscope

midbrain middle part of the brain; controls automatic reactions to sound and light

mind-altering drug chemical that can change the structure or functioning of cells, especially those of the brain, and produce abnormal mental changes

minerals natural compounds containing elements such as calcium and iron; needed by the body in small quantities to help in processes such as bone building and carrying of oxygen to cells

mitosis process by which a cell nucleus divides and, as new cells are formed, distributes equally an original and a copied set of chromosomes to the new cells

molar broad-crowned, grinding tooth

mole raised, often pigmented skin blemish that a person is born with

morphine narcotic drug derived from, but stronger than, opium; often prescribed by physicians for patients in great pain

mouth-to-mouth resuscitation first aid procedure for treating breathing stoppage; done by mouth-to-mouth blowing of air into victim's lungs

mucus moist secretion covering the lining of air passages and other internal organs

multiple sclerosis nervous system disease in which protective tissue around nerve fibers is destroyed and scarred, resulting in loss of control over motion and speech

muscular dystrophy hereditary disease in which normal muscle tissue is replaced by connective tissue and fat, with a resulting loss in strength and control of the arms and legs

muscular system all the voluntary and involuntary muscles that cause bones and other body structures to move

myopia nearsightedness, often occurring when eyeball is too long from front to back to permit the focusing of distant objects into a sharp image on the retina

narcotic sense-dulling drug used to relieve great pain and produce deep sleep

nerve bundle of tiny sensitive nerve fibers

nerve impulse signal, or message, that moves along nerves

neuron nerve cell, composed of dendrites, cell body, and axon

nicotine habit-forming harmful substance present in tobacco leaves

noncommunicable disease noncontagious disease resulting from heredity, dietary deficiency, or causes other than germs

nucleus (of cell) tiny body within a cell; contains genes, which control cell activities such as growth and division

nutrients nourishing substances in food that are required by body cells; through digestion, they become available for use in the small intestine

obstetrics medical specialty dealing with childbirth

olfactory nerve nerve of smell connecting the nose to the brain

opiate narcotic drug made from opium, such as morphine and heroin

opium drug made from juice of seed capsule of the white poppy; used to relieve pain

optic nerve nerve of vision connecting the retina with the brain

organ body part, composed of several tissues, that performs a special function

otosclerosis abnormal bone growth in inner ear that interferes with movement of the stirrup bone (of the middle ear) and the oval window; results in deafness

ova (*sing.* **ovum**) female reproductive cells, or egg cells, produced in ovaries

oval window opening between middle ear and inner ear; covered by a membrane on which stirrup bone rests

ovary female sex gland which produces egg cells and female sex hormones

ovulation body process by which an egg cell is released from an ovary

oxidation energy-releasing union of oxygen with another substance

pancreas digestive gland that produces a juice that aids in breaking down carbohydrates, proteins, and fats; *see also* islets of Langerhans

pandemic outbreak of a disease affecting many people in the world at the same time

papillae (*sing.* **papilla**) ridges, or raised projections, from the dermis of the skin into the epidermis; lie under the ridges that make up fingerprints

paralysis loss of ability to move

paramedic medical assistant trained to give first aid and resuscitation to unconscious victims of accidents and other emergencies

parasite living thing that lives on or in the body of another living thing (host) and uses the host's food; may destroy host's tissues

parathyroid glands tiny ductless glands embedded in back of the thyroid gland; produce a hormone necessary for use of calcium by the body

pasteurization process by which heat greatly decreases the number of bacteria in milk or other liquids

patent medicine drug that can be bought over the counter without a doctor's prescription

PCP very strong, unpredictable hallucinogenic drug; can cause brain damage and insanity; "angel dust"; phencyclidine

pellagra disease caused by a deficiency of vitamin P-P (niacin); characterized by skin irritation, tongue inflammation, and digestive and nervous disturbances

penis organ used by male in transferring sperm cells to female and in urinating

periodontal membrane tissue covering root of a tooth and wall of its socket; helps hold tooth in socket and acts as a shock absorber during chewing

periodontitis severe gum inflammation caused by dental plaque bacteria; can result in drawing away of gums from teeth, pus pockets, abscesses, and loss of teeth; pyorrhea

peristalsis automatic wavelike movements of muscular walls of the food tube; mixes food with digestive juices and moves food along the food tube

perspiration the part of the body's liquid wastes given off by the sweat glands; sweat

pigment material, or agent, that provides color, such as melanin and carotene in skin

pineal gland small ductless gland located in the center of the brain; its function in humans is unknown

pinkeye contagious inflammation of the lining of the eyelids and the covering of the front of the eyeball; conjunctivitis

pituitary gland small ductless gland located at base of the brain; secretes several hormones that control activities of other ductless glands; the "master gland"

placenta structure in a pregnant female that connects an unborn child to the mother and through which food, oxygen, and wastes are exchanged between the unborn child and mother

plaque sticky, colorless material that forms constantly on teeth; contains bacteria that produce the acid responsible for tooth decay

plasma liquid part of blood; carries blood cells and dissolved substances

platelets tiny blood particles that aid in clotting when blood vessels are injured

pneumonia disease of lungs caused by either bacteria or viruses; characterized by painful, difficult breathing and fever

pollution addition of dirt or injurious substances to the air, bodies of water, or food

pons part of the brain that acts as a bridge, or passageway, for nerve impulses to and from other parts of the brain

pores tiny openings in the skin through which perspiration from sweat glands leaves the body

pressure point place in the body where a major blood vessel lies close to bone; at such a place, severe bleeding can be controlled by pressing a blood vessel against a bone

protein cell-building food compound, such as egg white, composed of carbon, hydrogen, oxygen, nitrogen, and a few other elements

protoplasm jellylike living material in a cell; includes the nucleus, cytoplasm, and cell membrane

protozoa (*sing.* **protozoan**) one-celled animallike organisms, a few of which cause diseases such as malaria and amebic dysentery

puberty time of life when the sex glands become active and produce either sperm (in males) or egg cells (in females)

pubic region triangular body section that is the lowest part of the abdomen

puncture wound hole in the skin and deeper tissues made by a pointed object

pupil (of eye) circular opening in front part of eye through which light passes on its way to the lens and retina; size is controlled by the iris

pus thick yellowish fluid produced by infection; consists of germs, dead cells, and body fluid

rabies virus-caused disease of the nervous system, transmitted by bites of some animals

radiation treatment destruction of cancerous cells by means of high-energy rays such as those produced by X-ray machines, radium, and radioactive cobalt

rapid eye movements back-and-forth eye movements under closed lids occurring during dreaming; takes place shortly after the onset of sleep; REM

receptors sense organs, such as the skin and eyes, that receive impressions from the outside or from inside the body

recessive trait trait that is overshadowed by a dominant trait when the genes for both traits are inherited together; usually shows up only when two recessive genes are inherited together

rectum lower end of large intestine; stores feces until they are eliminated from body

red blood cell hemoglobin-containing cell in blood that carries oxygen to body cells and carries away some carbon dioxide from them

reflex speedy, automatic reaction of the body, such as the reaction to pain, controlled by the spinal cord or medulla oblongata

respiratory system the organs that provide the body with oxygen and get rid of the waste carbon dioxide

retina sheet of light-sensitive nerve cells lining the eyeball; light passing through the lens is focused on it, forming an image and stimulating the nerve cells to transmit image signals to the optic nerve

rheumatic heart disease disease of heart valves caused by a streptococcus infection

rickets disease caused by a deficiency of vitamin D; characterized by bone deformities such as bowlegs, knock-knees, swollen joints, and badly formed teeth

rickettsias germs that are smaller than bacteria but larger than viruses; cause diseases such as typhus fever and Rocky Mountain spotted fever

ringworm fungus infection of scalp, skin of foot (athlete's foot), or other body areas

rod specialized nerve cell of the retina that is affected by dim light

root canal narrow channel in the root of a tooth; contains a nerve and blood and lymph vessels

root (of tooth) part of tooth below the gum; anchors the tooth in the jawbone

saliva watery juice secreted into the mouth by the salivary glands; moistens food and makes it slippery; contains an enzyme that begins the digestion of starches

saturated fat fat associated with the deposit of cholesterol in blood vessels; usually hard at room temperature

scrotum protective pouch in which the testes lie

scurvy disease caused by a deficiency of vitamin C; characterized by soft bleeding gums, loose teeth, swollen joints, and bleeding under the skin

sebaceous glands skin glands that secrete oil into hair follicles; become overactive shortly after puberty

sebum oil produced by sebaceous glands

second-degree burn burn that blisters the skin and may break it

secretion useful juice produced in the body by one of its glands

sedative depressant drug that helps people relax and sleep

semen thick white liquid carrying sperm cells produced by male reproductive glands

semicircular canals three bony canals within the inner ear, containing a liquid and nerve endings; sense organs that help us keep our balance

shock overall body reaction to injury, characterized by a pale, cold, and clammy skin; a fast, weak pulse; dull, vacant-looking eyes; irregular breathing; listlessness; mental dullness; vomiting

sickle-cell anemia hereditary disease in which red blood cells collapse into crescent shapes when the oxygen supply is low

Silvester Method first aid procedure for treating breathing stoppage; done by placing the victim face up, tilting victim's head back, applying pressure to victim's chest, and stretching and lifting victim's arms

skeletal system the skeleton, cartilage, ligaments, and tendons that, together, support the body and protect internal organs; provides attachment points for muscles, thus making body movements possible

small intestine part of the food tube connecting stomach and large intestine, where most digestion occurs and where digested materials are picked up for distribution to cells by the bloodstream

spastic cerebral palsy victim; moves jerkily because of poor muscular coordination

sperm cell male reproductive cell produced by the testes

sperm ducts tubes through which sperm cells pass in leaving the testes

spinal cord part of the nervous system that connects the brain with many nerves located in the lower part of the body; controls many reflexes

splint stiff material used to keep a broken bone and the nearest joints from moving while victim is moved

sprain injury to a joint's soft tissues, such as ligaments

sterile (*reproduction*) unable to have children; (*medicine*) free of bacteria and germs

sternum flat bone in center of the chest to which front ends of most ribs are attached; breastbone

stimulant drug or druglike substance that speeds up bodily activity

stirrup third or innermost bone of the three small bones that stretch across the middle ear in a chain and transmit vibrations to the inner ear

strain injury to the muscles associated with a joint

streptococcus type of bacterium associated with some kinds of throat infections

stroke brain damage resulting from a clot or bursting blood vessel; often produces paralysis

sweat gland skin gland that opens to the skin surface through a pore and gives off perspiration composed of water and cell wastes

synapse gap region where the ends of an axon of one neuron lie close to the dendrites of another neuron

syphilis communicable venereal disease caused by a certain bacterium

systolic blood pressure pressure in the arteries when the heart is contracting and forcing blood out to the rest of the body

tartar hard substance formed from minerals in saliva and deposited in dental plaque around teeth

taste buds sense organs of taste located in the surface of the tongue

tendons bands of tough tissue that connect muscles to bones

testis (*pl.* **testes**) one of the two male sex glands which produce sperm cells and male sex hormones; testicle

tetanus disease caused by certain germs that enter a wound and multiply there in the absence of oxygen; lockjaw

third-degree burn burn that destroys and often chars the skin and underlying tissues

thymus gland ductless gland located behind the breastbone in early life, at which time the gland releases a hormone and certain cells that aid in fighting future infections; disappears by adulthood

thyroid gland   ductless gland located at the base of the neck in front of the trachea; produces the hormone thyroxin

thyroxin   hormone of the thyroid gland; regulates the speed of energy production in cells

tissue   group of similar cells that work together

tonsils   lymph nodes located at the back of the throat

tourniquet   flat bandage with a small pad on the inside surface; placed on a pressure point and tightened by a strong stick or rod in order to stop severe bleeding

toxin   poison produced by organisms such as bacteria

toxoid   weakened toxin injected into the body to help produce immunity to a disease

trachea   part of the respiratory system from which the bronchial tubes branch; windpipe

tranquilizer   depressant drug that relieves tension and helps people to relax

tubercle   hard sac, or case, enclosing a mass of tuberculosis germs; formed by the body as it fights tuberculosis

tuberculosis   contagious lung disease caused by a certain germ; TB; consumption

tumor   unnatural tissue growth or lump

tunnel vision   seeing defect that allows a person to see only what is directly ahead

umbilical cord   structure containing blood vessels that carry blood between an unborn baby and the placenta of its mother

universal antidote   preparation that counteracts the effects of several kinds of poison

ureter   tube leading from a kidney to the urinary bladder

urethra   tube leading from the urinary bladder to the outside of the body

urinary system   the organs that dispose of cell wastes dissolved in water

urine   dissolved cell wastes and excess water removed from the blood by the kidneys and expelled from the body through the urethra

uterus   hollow muscular organ of female reproductive system, in which an unborn baby develops; located between the Fallopian tubes and vagina

vagina   channel from the uterus to the outside of the female body

valves   flaps that allow fluids, such as blood, to flow in one direction only, as from auricles to ventricles of the heart

veins   blood vessels that lead blood from capillaries all over the body back to the heart

venereal disease   any contagious disease spread by sexual contact; V.D.

venom   poison injected by bites or stings of certain snakes, spiders, and insects

venous blood   blood in veins, which is usually dark red and has a low oxygen content

ventricles   one of two lower chambers of the heart that receive blood from auricles and force it into arteries

virus   smallest disease agent, visible only by means of the electron microscope

vitamins   nutrients, naturally present in various foods, needed in very small quantities for proper functioning of the body

volatile chemical   substance that changes readily into a gas, or vapor; when inhaled, certain of such vapors can damage the brain, liver, or other organs

voluntary muscles   muscles, such as those attached to bones, that are controlled at will and work when desired to

wart   hard outgrowth of the skin, produced by virus infection

white blood cell   colorless cell in blood that fights infection

wisdom teeth   third molars that break through gums, usually between ages 18 and 21

X chromosome   sex chromosome present in all egg cells but in only half the number of sperm cells; two X chromosomes (XX) in a fertilized egg determine femaleness

Y chromosome   sex chromosome present in half the number of sperm cells; one X and one Y chromosome (XY) in a fertilized egg determine maleness

Index

Blood (*continued*)
clotting of, 81, 159, 163
diseases of, 420, 425–427
in heart, 51
manufacture of, 41, 56
and skin color, 123
vitamins needed to form, 162
waste removal from, 68, 121–122
See also Bleeding, Circulatory system,
Red blood cells, White blood cells
Blood cell count, 54–55, 391
Blood cells, 54
See also Red blood cells, White blood
cells
Blood corpuscles, 54
See also Red blood cells, White blood
cells
Blood plasma, 54, 403
Blood pressure, 51, 390–391
high, 414–416, 423, 452
and nicotine, 318
in shock, 214
during sleep, 180
Blood sugar (glucose), 60, 156, 423
hormones regulating, 81, 82
testing level of, 391, 424–425
Blood tests, 405, 427
Blood vessels, 53–54, 62
in bone membrane, 41
constricted by nicotine, 318
diseased, 413–414, 415–417
enlarged by alcohol, 341
in penis, 253
in skin, 121, 123
voluntary control of, 45
Blushing, 123
Boating safety, 204
Body temperature, 121, 171, 181, 330, 334
Boils, 128
Bone conduction hearing aid, 112–113
Bone marrow, 41, 365
Bones, 41–43
broken, 237–238, 239
conduction of sound by, 112–113
dislocated, 239
in ear, 106, 112
minerals in, 159
moved by muscles, 44–45
vitamin D for, 163
Booster shots, 380, 381, 392
Braces, dental, 149
Brain, 73–74, 75–77
alcohol and, 334, 339
damage to, 359, 365, 416–417, 429
during sleep, 180–181
Brain stem, 77
Brain waves, 182, 186
Bread and cereal group, 168
Breakfast, 168
Breastbone, 41

Breasts, 82, 260
Breathing, 64–66, 78
and adrenaline, 81
first aid for, 213, 221–226
and paralysis of nervous system, 335, 358
during sleep, 180, 183
See also Lungs, Respiratory system
Broken bones, 41, 237–238, 239
Bronchial tubes, 66, 318, 422
Bronchioles, 66
Bronchitis, 318, 399, 445
Brown recluse spider, 232
Brushing of teeth, 142–145
Bubonic plague, 16, 18, 378, 379, 385
Burns, 124, 236–237

Caesarean section, 408
Caffeine, 169, 348, 354, 360
Calciferol, 163
Calcium, 41, 80–81, 145, 155, 159
Calories, 170–175, 334
Camera, compared to eye, 89–90
Cancer, 373, 419–421
and food additives, 458–459
and hair dyes, 131
and overexposure to sun, 124
quack cures for, 462
and smoking, 314–316, 321, 325
Canine teeth, 139
Cannabis, 355
Capillaries, 53, 66, 121, 125
Carbohydrates, 60, 62, 127, 156–157
Carbolic acid, 381
Carbon, 155, 156, 157
Carbon dioxide, 51, 54, 55, 64
and absorption of alcohol, 338
and fatigue, 187
and fermentation, 330–331
Carbon monoxide, 318, 444
Carbon tetrachloride, 448
Carbuncles, 128
Carcinogens, 315, 458–459
Cardiologist, 6
Careers in health, 6–7, 471–484
Caries, 141–142
Carotene, 123
Cartilage, 41–42
Cataract, of eye, 100
Cavities, dental, 141, 142, 146–147
Cell body, 74
Cell membrane, 29–30
Cells, 29–30, 49, 53
blood, 41, 54–55
bone, 41
cancerous, 315, 419
division of, 34–36
drugs affecting, 313, 348, 349
energy production in, 64, 80, 159
fat, 157
grouped into tissues, 37